The Cycle of Leadership

ALSO BY NOEL M. TICHY

The Leadership Engine (with Eli Cohen).
New York: HarperCollins, 1997.

Control Your Destiny or Someone Else Will
(with Stratford Sherman). New York: Doubleday/Currency, 1993.

*Managing Strategic Change: Technical, Political and Cultural
Dynamics.* New York: John Wiley and Sons, Inc., 1983.

*Organizing Design for Primary Health Care:
The Case of the Dr. Martin Luther King, Jr. Health Center.*
New York: Praeger, 1977.

Global Citizenship (with Andrew R. McGill and Lynda St. Clair).
San Francisco: Jossey-Bass, October 1997.

Every Business Is A Growth Business (with Ram Charan).
New York: Three Rivers Press, 1998.

The Transformational Leader (with Mary Anne Devanna).
New York: Wiley, 1986.

The Cycle of Leadership

How Great Leaders Teach Their Companies to Win

Noel M. Tichy
with Nancy Cardwell

HarperBusiness

An Imprint of HarperCollins*Publishers*

HarperCollins books may be purchased for educational, business, or sales promotional use. For information please write: Special Markets Department, HarperCollins Publishers, Inc., 10 East 53rd Street, New York, NY 10022.

FIRST EDITION

Designed by Joy O'Meara

Library of Congress Cataloging-in-Publication Data

ISBN 0066620562

03   04   05   06   10   9   8   7   6   5   4

Virtuous Teaching Cycle:
Knowledge Creation

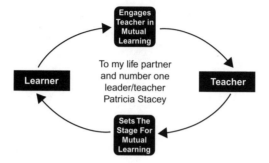

Contents

Acknowledgments

This book exists because I have participated in many Virtuous Teaching Cycles as a professor, consultant, community member, father and husband. The world is a great classroom, and I try to practice what I preach in this book, namely to teach and learn interactively in all kinds of settings around the globe.

The most important Virtuous Teaching Cycle for this book was the one that Nancy Cardwell and I created on our journey as we researched and wrote it. We started out to do a "new economy" e-Leadership book. As we conducted our research in Silicon Valley, Austin, Denver and other high-tech hot spots, we were reminded of the truth: the fundamentals of great leadership have nothing to do with "bubbles." Nancy is both an avid learner and a tough-minded teacher. As I taught her the things I was learning out in the field through my practice and interviews, she would come back with her questions and insights, based both on her extensive knowledge of the business world and her experiences as a leader in her career as a journalist. She helped me develop a new Teachable Point of View and to bring it to life through this book. Not only did she do a great deal of writing and editing, but she contributed substantially to the ideas.

I am thankful for the intellectual and academic learnings from Warner Burke, Charles Kadushin, Harvey Hornstein, Karl Weick, Kim Cameron, Ram Charan, Warren Bennis, and Larry Selden. Michael Brimm, Carole Barnett, Andy McGill and Suzy Wetlaufer deserve special thanks for being there throughout the process: from initial concept through research, to rethinking, revisions and final product. Both David Murphy and Charlie Tharp provided invaluable encouragement and practical insights.

Jack Welch continues to be one of my great teachers along with Dick Stonesifer, both of whom taught me how to create Virtuous Teaching Cycles on a large scale through their work at GE. Larry Bossidy not only taught me at GE but also through his experiences at Allied and Honeywell.

My collaborator on THE LEADERSHIP ENGINE book, Eli Cohen, continues to teach me. Chris DeRose has been there in the trenches with me as we field-tested the concepts. He deserves the lion's share of the credit for the HANDBOOK.

Every one of the leaders and their colleagues in the book were more than generous in teaching me what world-class leader/teachers are all about. I thank the teams at Accenture, Cisco, Dell, EDS, GE, Genentech, Focus: HOPE, Limited Brands, 3M, Home Depot, Nokia, Royal Dutch/Shell, Southwest Airlines, the United States' Special Operations Forces, Trilogy, and Yum!Brands.

Having spent the last thirty years as a professor, first at Columbia University and then at the University of Michigan, I have taught over 5,000 MBA and Ph.D. students. They have taught me more than I have taught them. Many have gone on to not only use some of what I tried to teach, but have taken the time to stay in touch and teach me what they are learning as they progress in their leadership careers. The same is true for the thousands of executives I have worked with globally.

The one institution that is my greatest role model for a Teaching Organization and where I continue to learn the most about leadership and human development is Focus: HOPE. Eleanor Josaitis and her team of colleagues are always teaching me new lessons about courage and learning. I also want to give a special thanks to Jac Nasser for giving so much to Focus: HOPE and the community, and for being a world-class leader/teacher who has taught me a lot about compassion and courage in tough situations.

The team at HarperCollins made all this happen. Adrian Zackheim and Dave Conti were great editors, with Knox Houston there to support the effort down the stretch. Lisa Berkowitz deserves a special thanks. Always believing in this book, she was an incredible source of support and energy. As always, thanks.

Finally, no book is ever produced—certainly, not ones by me—without a very strong support team. Ida Faye Webster, my administrator, played quarterback to this team and somehow managed to keep everyone energized and focused so that they always delivered. The team of Margie Heinzman, Melissa Donaldson and Nancy Tanner were terrific right down to the wire.

Ann Arbor, Michigan
June 2002

Foreword by Robert Knowling

The Cycle of Leadership

This book is a milestone in a journey I have been on with Noel Tichy for twelve years. His books and advice have been invaluable to me. As a senior executive at Ameritech and U.S. West, as CEO of Covad and now of Simbion Technologies, as a board member at Hewlett-Packard, Heidrick & Struggles and Ariba, and as a committed community leader, I have applied many of the practical lessons from Tichy's work.

There are two aspects of his work that I find invaluable. First, he is always ahead of his time and his lessons are of enduring value. Second, and more importantly from where I sit, Tichy lives it. He is out in organizations struggling side-by-side with business leaders, helping them apply his concepts.

This book introduces the concept of the Virtuous Teaching Cycle and places it in the core DNA of winning companies. I am certain that in the future, it will be how we develop leaders, how we generate knowledge, how we align people and how we drive results.

Because Tichy goes into the field not only as a theorist/observer—your typical academic—but also as a practicing clinician, his advice is extremely practical and realistic about what it takes to execute his frameworks. He has tested it all out many times over in his clinical practice. The Handbooks at the end of his books are really a clinician's field guides—based on his own experience—to applying his concepts. This is really important, because the good CEOs I know are all on a continuous mission to improve their organizations and do not have time for irrelevant chatter.

My Leadership Development Wake-Up Call

Earlier in my career, I used to think that being in a state of development or admitting that you were learning and growing on the job were signs of weakness, which led me to suppress any hint that I might be an incomplete product.

This attitude was in part a result of my growing up in the old Bell System, where a leader could never show vulnerability. Leaders were expected to know the answers and to be the "answer man." In fact, once you reached a certain level, you stopped attending management development training and, other than an obligatory summer "executive development" tour at some university, the idea of development didn't apply to you.

My orientation changed when I began to work with Noel Tichy. It's important to note here that I was a tough convert. I wasn't at all convinced about his methodology, so had it not been for the commitment of Bill Weiss (CEO of Ameritech) and later Dick Notebaert (successor to Weiss, currently CEO of Qwest) to change the Ameritech management system, I would probably not have come around. It was their embracing of the process and their willingness to make themselves vulnerable that made Tichy's process work and started me on a leadership learning journey that continues to this day.

Back in the early days, I didn't understand that my personal development and my work in the new role of leader/teacher was an evolving process that never ends. I'm almost certain that the greatest leader/teacher of our modern era, Jack Welch, would probably tell us from the retirement deck that he's still learning and developing.

When I look at the successful championship runs of great CEOs like Welch, Phil Condit at Boeing, John Chambers at Cisco, Dick Brown at EDS, etc., I see leaders who have made teaching, learning and development a cornerstone of their business models. I see these leaders making themselves vulnerable, and I see them embracing the fact that they are growing and developing just like everyone else in the organization.

Herein lies the key to their success: they set a tone in the environment of the company that it's okay that we don't have all the answers, and it's okay that we don't have it all figured out. It's even okay if we make mistakes sometimes. So, while these very direct, high-energy and hard-driving CEOs command the complete attention of their organizations and have delivered stellar business results, they are real-life player/coaches that employees can feel and touch.

The Bell System wasn't like this. It was a highly political environment that valued continuous learning on the technical side but largely ignored the possibility that any of its executives might need help with their leadership skills. The companies were very hierarchal and the emperor was never seen without clothes. So, it comes as no surprise when I say that I was highly skeptical when the senior leaders at Ameritech took off their jackets, rolled up their sleeves and started working with Coach Tichy on building up their leadership strength.

I can recall my efforts to thwart the Tichy program. He had been working very closely with the top 120 leaders of the company to help us reinvent the business. The process was long, painful and time consuming, and we all still had our regular day jobs to do. The group of 120 had gotten together for four days with the senior leaders to assess progress and map out the next legs of the journey.

One night after a grueling day of debate and planning, I took the initiative in the bar to convince three of the four senior leaders to put a halt to a process we were going to be put through by Tichy and the senior leaders. Tichy was going to have us rank one another on how we were doing as team players, how much progress we were making getting the transformational work done in the business, how well we assisted and helped others, and how much we were growing as a leader.

This process frightened me. I felt that the rankings would expose my weaknesses. I would be naked as a leader and, even worse, the exposure would come at the hands of my peers—the same peers I had competed against for years to get ahead in the game. I had been in plenty of close games before in my athletic career, and I'm the type of guy who wants the last shot, or the last at bat, or to be the guy with the ball in my hands when the game is on the line. This Tichy-devised process took the control completely away from me. I would clearly be exposed.

The next morning, after I did my insurrection and thought I had won, I remember Dick Notebaert saying to me, "I think you're one of the most terrific people we've got in this business. You know how I feel about you. But there's a fundamental difference between you and me. I have navigated my career a lot like you have, all bent on my individual achievement, all about me, etc., but I've been exposed to some new things here and I've got a different perspective. The difference between you and me is that I'm willing to try this new stuff, I'm willing to make myself vulnerable, and you're not. But if somehow, Bob, you can trust this process and make yourself vulnerable and just be willing to try it, I think you might come out of this thing with a different perspective. My hope for you is that you don't bullshit the process and that you engage in it and do some analysis." It hit me, if Dick is willing to try this, what do I have to lose? His participation and vulnerability really got me in the gut.

It also marked an important inflection point in my career and in my journey. The forced rankings were the most emotional yet fulfilling development intervention in my entire career. The things that I feared would come out about my "Lone Ranger" style indeed did come out. The feedback was not filtered or sanitized, so it felt like 2 x 4s across the head. On the other hand, I also got some wonderfully rewarding feedback on things I did exceptionally well that I had taken for granted.

But, most importantly, this process allowed us senior executives to experience real-time the power of an emotionally shared experience. For us, it was the first encounter with open and candid feedback. It was so new to us that we even had a forum to talk about what had just happened to us.

Imagine the tension in the air as people were confronting one another with feedback. Every emotion was in the room: tears, anger, elation and shock played out real-time. The process was not designed to create an emotional flood, but it did because we were all so used to being buttoned up.

Confronting and getting through these emotions was an important watershed and a transformational experience for many of us. It broke us out of the old bureaucratic silos we lived in. This was not your normal management consultant workshop. We were playing with real bullets or, to put it another way, we were doing total engine replacement while flying the aircraft. Tichy gave us the important transformational experience and building blocks to become leader/teachers.

The Need for Great Leadership Is Greater than Ever

We can certainly expect to be flooded over the next few years with books on corporate governance and business ethics. This will be one result of the the rash of business scandals and failures in the past few months. When you factor in the capital markets correction and the end of the high-tech growth period, attention to business performance and business discipline has never been higher.

I believe that the challenges we see in 2002 are not new issues. The current environment is merely exposing poor leadership. When the economy was booming, a lot of inept leaders were able to ride the tide that lifted all boats. In our current environment, where market value has decreased some 40% to 90% in countless firms, the spotlight shines on the operating business plan, the ability to execute, the ability to retain your top talent and the ability to lead in difficult times.

The successful companies and leaders will be those who understand that the greatest resource we have in the enterprise is people and that the human capital we are entrusted with has to be developed and turned into a more valuable resource. Understanding the potential capacity of an employee and the role that you play in the development of that person is a competitive advantage. So, a highly engaged leader who truly embraces the leader/teacher model has a better chance of winning than someone who doesn't.

Difficult times require great leadership. People look to the leader when things are not going well. The absence of a Teachable Point of View will not give employees and shareholders confidence. During my tenure on the board at Heidrick & Struggles, I've seen the level of attention to leadership traits and qualities heighten as market conditions erode. Every CEO search keeps demonstrating that there is a shortage of great leaders. The supply of jobs at the top is there even in a down economy. The challenge is that there is a scarcity of leader/teachers.

What Is the Cycle of Leadership?

My basketball career has been over for some time now, but I can recall an interesting transformation that occurred between my junior and senior years in high school. I had played for a great coach in Indiana, Ben Bowles. He worked tirelessly with me year-round to make me the complete basketball player. I had set all sorts of scoring records my junior year and arguably was the finest basketball player in my area and one of the top ball players in the state. He had great plans for me and it looked like we were going to make a run at the conference and state championship since there were numerous returning lettermen coming back.

But then Coach Bowles left and was replaced by another Indiana high school legend. I did not bond with the new coach. I regarded him with a great deal of skepticism, and it was clear that he had a style that he wanted us to embrace that stressed ball movement, getting all five players in the mix and strong defense. A big preseason article came out on the team and the new coach had this to say about me: "Bobby is perhaps the finest individual player that I have ever seen or coached, but he is going to have to make his teammates better and stay in a team game in order for us to be successful."

I didn't understand the comment and at seventeen years of age, I didn't have the maturity to ask him about it. We proceeded to go out and lose our first five games! We were highly ranked, I was highly decorated, and we started my senior year campaign 0–5!

Coach Dick Haslem finally sat me down and taught me my first lesson in leadership. I was scoring at will during those five losses, but there was no team. In fact, my teammates looked to me, deferred to me and stood around watching me score. When the game was on the line, I didn't look for them and I surely didn't trust them to take a last shot. I had to change and I had to change quickly.

I ended up scoring only 18.0 points per game for the season, which was way off from the previous years, but we won the rest of the conference games and were champs. I led the team in assists and two of my teammates received post-season awards for their play. It was the most gratifying athletic experience in my life and I took some valuable lessons away.

You can see this process played out in sports today from time to time. Larry Bird and Michael Jordan are two prime examples. Both were head and shoulders above everyone else in terms of their individual ability, but both brought out the best in their teammates. They were able to lift the games of everyone around them because they invested in their teammates and made it their priority to help and teach people to reach their potential.

The concept of a Virtuous Teaching Cycle is just that. Continuing your personal development and growth at the same time that you are helping others reach their potential with you as the role model teacher/coach. Michael and Larry did not just demand greatness of others, they led by example. It's common knowledge that Larry and Michael were fanatical about leadership and worked harder than anyone on their teams. They were first to practice and last to leave. Great CEOs do the same thing.

Jack Welch didn't just make cameo appearances at GE's Crotonville leadership institute. He spent a significant amount of time there in the "pit," teaching, learning, growing, developing others and setting the example. I've had numerous sessions with former GE Appliances CEO Dick Stonesifer, who would tell me stories about his business reviews with Welch and that he always took something away from these sessions in terms of his own development. Dick would turn around and model the same behavior with his direct reports, and they with theirs. I got a sense of how the GE system replicated the Virtuous Teaching Cycle over and over.

Likewise, my work with Dick Notebaert at Ameritech gave me a sound framework for leadership development. I had the fortunate opportunity to work for both Dick Brown (CEO of EDS) and Notebaert (CEO of Qwest) while there, and in both cases, coaching was the common ground for everything we did. The feedback loop was very much a part of how we operated in the senior ranks. There were numerous occasions where I was able to give Notebaert honest and candid feedback and hard-nosed coaching—he expected me to do it. In fact, he once told me that I was not doing my job by letting him slide on things. I took these models of leadership and organizational development to my next three assignments at U.S. West, Covad Communications and now at Simbion Technologies.

The essence of Tichy's model is that leaders must teach and do it in an interactive way so that everyone gets smarter and more aligned. It starts with me: I require my leaders to teach. When I run a workshop with my leaders, I challenge them by telling them to embrace and engage in this process with me, because the requirement going forward is for them to emulate the experience we have been through with their teams. They, too, have to be the teachers. These are not workshops where consultants or staff are up front teaching; the leaders themselves are up front.

It is scary but rewarding when they go off and share their Teachable Points of View and take their people off-site for a three-day workshop. It works: The leader/teacher concept is practical and delivers both short-term performance and long-term leadership development.

The Hardest Part—Longevity

I have been fortunate in my career to have had repeated opportunities to move on to bigger leadership positions. First, I moved from Ameritech to a position with wider responsibilities at U.S. West, and from there, I went on to become CEO of Covad, and now I am CEO of Simbion Technologies. This movement has had a downside, however. It is that I did not stay long enough to change the DNA of these organizations, to ensure the perpetuation of the leadership cycle.

The most painful thing that I've ever gone through as a leader is leaving an organization and seeing the good work, the results of a lot of hard effort on my part and on the part of the brave and dedicated team members who worked with me, get erased because we didn't get the needed mind-sets and values encoded deeply enough in the DNA of the organization.

At Ameritech, the leaders developing leaders model that Tichy helped us establish was incredibly powerful at both transforming the business and developing leaders. Note the number of current CEOs developed as a result of that process: Dick Notebaert at Qwest, Dick Brown at EDS, Gregg Brown at MicroMuse, Gary Drook at Affina, and John Edwards at CDW. However, during that time, Ameritech became so successful that SBC offered to buy it at a price shareholders couldn't refuse. SBC had a different management model and, as a result, the many great changes we had put in place at Ameritech slipped away because they hadn't had time to become sufficiently embedded.

When I became CEO of Covad, one of the first things I did was start a leaders developing leaders process. This allowed the business to get the right kind of framework so that we could grow in a disciplined way in the the hypergrowth DSL world. But again, when I left, it hadn't taken root with the rank and file, and there wasn't a cadre of leaders who could then carry it on.

I now understand that the reason for that is that I didn't stay long enough. I don't care how good the group of immediate reports behind a CEO are, long-term sustained leadership development will only happen when there is a CEO who is totally committed and focused on it. So, if the CEO leaves before the process has reached throughout the organization and before the teaching and learning has become ingrained in the culture, it won't last.

One of the keys to Welch's success in changing the DNA of GE is his longevity. Welch spent twenty years building a whole new generation of leaders, who not only carry on Virtuous Teaching Cycles at GE but, as Tichy shows in this book, build them in other companies when they leave. It's what Bob Nardelli is doing at Home Depot, and Jim McNerney at 3M, and Tom Tiller at Polaris.

Another world-class leader/teacher I admire is Phil Condit, CEO of Boeing. I have had the good fortune to work side-by-side with him on the HP board of directors. Condit typifies the impactful, important leaders spotlighted in all of Tichy's books. His commitment to developing leaders is legendary, and it isn't just folklore.

I have heard stories from Boeing employees about Condit and his leadership institute that send chills down my spine. And, I have seen him in action. This man lives and breathes the importance of teaching. Once when we were trying to set a quick date for a special board meeting, we ran into the traditional issues of "I'm out of the country" or on-vacation conflicts, yet the only time Phil posted an objection was when one of the potential dates conflicted with a commitment at the Boeing leaderhsip institute. It struck me that one of the busiest executives in the world, who more than likely had the tightest calendar in the board room, was able to make other trade-offs on his time to make the board meetings. But when it came to his commitment to leadership development, this was sacred. I am not sure that an invitation from the president of the United States could get Condit to miss a commitment to the leadership institute. When he retires, I have no doubt that his legacy of leadership development will survive.

This book, *The Cycle of Leadership,* is an important milestone for leaders who want to create a legacy of developing other leaders. But, more importantly, it really synthesizes much of Tichy's earlier work. He began with *The Transformational Leader,* written in 1986 with Mary Anne DeVanna, which laid out a three-act drama for creatively destroying and remaking an organization that I still use. *Control Your Destiny or Someone Else Will,* written with Stratford Sherman in 1994 along with the *Handbook for Revolutionaries,* showed how Jack Welch successfully transformed GE and gave guidelines for other leaders to follow suit. It has provided many tools for me, as well. *The Leadership Engine* introduced the notion of leaders as teachers and the powerful concept of a leader needing to have a Teachable Point of View in order to develop other leaders. This is something I've been working on continually for more than a decade.

The Cycle of Leadership builds on Tichy's previous work, but it is also a huge breakthrough on how winning leaders will have to behave in order to win in the twenty-first century. Those leaders will have to build organizations with knowledge creation embedded in their DNA, where people teach and learn interactively and instinctively. The concept of a Virtuous Teaching Cycle cracks the code on how to institutionalize the process. This book then provides great benchmarks of how to scale this process to hundreds of thousands of people as well as how to build Virtuous Teaching Cycles into operating systems and the day-to-day running of a big organization.

Finally, the book implores—indeed, inspires—us all to remember that we operate in communities and that we have a global citizenship responsibility to create Virtuous Teaching Cycles in the community. I have been involved with Focus: HOPE in Detroit for more than a decade. So has Tichy. Focus: HOPE is the epitome of a Teaching Organization, led by the most inspiring leader I have ever met, Eleanor Josaitis, who every day lives the mission of Focus: HOPE, "intelligent and practical solutions to racism and poverty." With her 600 colleagues on the forty-acre campus, she transforms people—through programs that provide food, machinist training, bachelors' degrees in engineering, child care and operate for-profit businesses—into leader/teachers. Together, they show all of us what is possible with a Teachable Point of View that aims to build a better world. In this book, Tichy opens doors to corporate board rooms and takes us into inner-city streets, to spotlight for us Josaitis and many other cutting-edge leaders.

Tichy has done it again! He is ten years ahead of everybody else in the field. Read this book to find out what you will need to be doing to win over the next ten years.

Robert Knowling
Chairman and CEO of Simbion Technologies
June 24, 2002

Introduction

World Demands Great Leadership More than Ever

In the preface to our 1986 book *The Transformational Leader,* co-author Mary Anne DeVanna and I stated: "This book is about corporate leadership, America's scarcest natural resource." My subsequent works, including the 1997 book *The Leadership Engine,* have been built on the theme that there are not enough good leaders in the world.

When I started this book I did so with that same theme in mind. My idea was that we were entering an era when the scarcity of leadership talent was going to become more acute. I was right about that. However, the environment in which I foresaw that scarcity was 180 degrees off of the one in which we were living by the time we finished the book.

I started out writing about how to get enough good leaders to fuel the hypergrowth Internet bubble. In 1998, it appeared that the big scarcity was going to be how to develop enough leaders at all levels to be able to scale Cisco, Oracle, Dell, Sun Micro, Yahoo, Webvan, Trilogy and the plethora of hot digital companies facing hypergrowth. Several years into the project, as recently as January 2000, I would have predicted that by 2002 we would be facing a post–cold war world of free enterprise growth coupled with technological breakthroughs launching the digital and biotech century.

My view would have been yes, we would face some discontinuities, but we would be on an upward spiral of global opportunity building the knowledge economy. Therefore, we would need leaders to grow all these exciting new enterprises.

Events since then have tempered my optimism about the future, as they have intensified my belief that the world desperately needs more and better leaders.

The reality we have is a world fraught with uncertainty, symbolically and literally changed by 9/11, the ensuing battles in Afghanistan, the escalating violence in the Mideast, and the stand-off between India and Pakistan, both nuclear powers. At the same time, we face a myriad of additional global problems, some new and some long-standing, such as the AIDS epidemic ravishing the African continent, the collapse of Argentina's economy and the Japanese malaise.

Around the world, the need for leaders has never been greater. We are traversing terrain that weak or sleazy self-aggrandizers cannot take us across safely. We need smart, gutsy leaders with vision and integrity to get us through the minefields. And, unfortunately, these leaders are in woefully short supply.

In the business arena, the picture is no better. The Enron debacle, the demise of Arthur Andersen, the questionable practices at Tyco, Sotheby's, Global Crossing, Qwest, WorldCom, Xerox and a seemingly endless list of others, have pushed public regard for business and business leaders to new lows. The pervasive problems signal systemic rather than individual failures. The resulting lack of trust and perception of greedy self-dealing among CEOs, on Wall Street and by accounting firms have driven investors out of the stock market in record numbers.

To sustain a healthy free-enterprise system, we must have transparency and trust in the system. Changes in the regulatory apparatus can diminish the likelihood that certain egregious behaviors will occur, but new rules and regulators are only a piece of the solution. The other part of rebuilding trust and confidence is the more important part: We must have world-class leaders with unyielding integrity who will transform their organizations and develop a new generation of leaders. Without such leadership, our free-enterprise society is undermined

The scandals here in the United States have diminished our role as a global benchmark. Sustainable development around the globe is dependent on the wealth-producing entities of the world—namely, businesses—delivering financial performance with integrity. We need great leaders across all sectors of society. This book is about how to develop those leaders.

Leadership Supply

The tank is low; we are not producing enough leaders at all levels, especially at the senior and CEO levels. Just consider the blue-chip companies that in the past decade have had to find outside candidates to replace their departing CEOs. The long list includes Merck, IBM, AT&T (twice), HP, 3M, Home Depot and Kodak. This is a terrible track record when you consider that perhaps the No. 1 responsibility of a CEO is to develop other leaders who can carry on the legacy of the organization. Our leadership pipelines are broken. And this is also true in politics, diplomacy and religious and social organizations as well as in business.

Even when organizations do select insiders to take over the top spot, they often have to settle for players who lack the needed leadership skills. These inadequate leaders are unable to drive needed transformations or develop others to be leaders. Thus, they suffer both performance problems in the short-term and continuing leadership crises in the long-term. This leaves our society and economy vulnerable.

The *Cycle of Leadership* is about how to replenish the supply of winning leaders.

My Leadership Journey

This book, as in my previous books, is a blend of academic research, clinical work with organizations, and a personal leadership journey to try to make a difference in the world. I studied to get a Ph.D. in social psychology at Columbia University in the late 1960s because I wanted to dedicate my career to using the behavioral sciences to help organizations of all types—civil rights, health care, educational and business—to improve the world. I became a student of change, writing my Ph.D. dissertation on all types of change agents, ranging from Ralph Nader's Raiders to civil rights leaders, to Black Panthers to Minutemen, to community organizers to McKinsey consultants and organizational psychologists.

I also dedicated my career to teaching leadership and organizational change as well as being a practitioner. This has led me down a number of paths, both in academia and out in the world. They have run from leading a health clinic in the 1970s to helping Jack Welch revamp GE's Crotonville Leadership Development Center in the 1980s.

In 1972, I started out as an assistant professor at the Graduate School of Business at Columbia where I headed up a Ph.D. program and taught MBA students. In order to deal with my ambivalence about joining the "establishment" in those days, I also worked with health care organizations in under-served inner city settings, such as the south Bronx of New York. And I actually took a year off to run the Hazard Family Health Services in Hazard, Kentucky.

In all this work, the goal was to use the behavioral sciences to make for healthier people and stronger communities. My personal journey has been about social change—health care for the under-served in the 1970s to corporate transformations in the 1980s, to global citizenship in the 1990s. Now that we are in the new millennium, my focus is on developing institutions throughout society with the capacity to develop leaders at all levels. To do this, I am working to help leader/teachers create Teaching Organizations with what this book calls Virtuous Teaching Cycles—dynamic, interactive processes in which everyone teaches, everyone learns and everyone gets smarter, every day.

On my journey, I have come to realize that leadership is the whole game. No institution—religious, military, educational, political or business—can be great unless it has a great leader at the top who develops leaders at all levels of the organization. The goal is leaders at all levels who all teach and develop other leaders.

Along the way, I have been disappointed many times—by national leaders, health care leaders and business leaders. The scale, it seems to me, is tipped in the direction of more failed leaders than great ones. However, there is hope. There are some wonderful role models who can help us all tip the scale the other way.

Societal change agents such as Martin Luther King, Jr. and Mother Teresa in India were among the best. They were inspirations to me even though I never met them. There are other world-class leaders whom I have had the privilege and honor to work with. They include the late Father Cunningham and his Focus: HOPE co-founder Eleanor Josaitis, GE's Jack Welch, PepsiCo's Roger Enrico, Nokia's Jorma Ollila, Yum! Brand's David Novak, Genentech's Myrtle Potter and Accenture's Mary Tolan. You will meet them and others in this book.

These are all leaders who lead with vision and courage, but more importantly, they are leader/teachers who embody the principles in this book. They are the ones who taught me what a Virtuous Teaching Cycle is. I learned it by trying to explain the phenomena that I observed with them: Namely, that they lead by teaching and they teach interactively, in a way that they and the "students" both learn. Creating this interactive teaching and learning interchange is the essence of the Virtuous Teaching Cycle.

The World of Teaching and Learning

One lesson that I hope leaders will take away from this book is that once they start to apply the concept of a Virtuous Teaching Cycle, they must wrestle with the issue of scale. Leaders of large organizations must create the conditions for thousands of people to engage in Virtuous Teaching Cycles. This book provides examples of how GE has built teaching infrastructures to engage 300,000+ people, and Yum! Brands is building one to keep 750,000 people teaching and learning.

The other impact I hope this book has on readers is to start them looking at the world through the lens of Virtuous Teaching Cycles. They are everywhere. Parents engage in them when they both teach and learn from their children. Good music and art teachers do the same. Likewise, in medicine, great clinical faculty learn from their residents. The U.S. military's Special Operations Forces operate this way, always teaching and learning from each other, regardless of rank.

Our goal in writing this book is to make a difference to leaders at all levels across a wide range of institutions. Therefore, the benchmarks are from places as diverse as Focus: HOPE, a civil-rights organization, the Navy SEALs and an array of businesses around the world.

Of all the great leaders in this book, I want to single out two who have been particularly inspiring to me. I am purposely highlighting them because they are not business leaders, yet they are both committed to creating the conditions for our free-enterprise system to succeed. They are:

• Wayne Downing, who transformed the Special Operations Forces (SOF) and made it a Teaching Organization. As the four-star general leading this organization, he spent the majority of his time in the field teaching and learning from his troops at all levels. He transformed the SOF from a singularly focused cold-war entity to a very multifaceted team of leaders with humanitarian aid skills in addition to their awesome combat abilities. After 9/11, President Bush named him his Special Assistant and the Deputy National Security Advisor for Combating Terrorism.

I have been to the Navy SEALs school, which was under Downing's command. I have personally spent time with the leaders he helped develop. And I have seen them interact with him. Even in retirement, he remains a leader/teacher to them. I am convinced that much of the success of the SOF goes to his leadership as a teacher.

• Eleanor Josaitis, who co-founded Focus: HOPE in 1968 in Detroit with Father William Cunningham. She has been unstoppable in her pursuit of its mission, which at its essence is "intelligent and practical solutions to racism, poverty and injustice." Her leadership, along with that of her co-founder, the late Father Cunningham, has built a 600-person organization that is emulated around the world, but so far never to the same scale.

Focus: HOPE provides food for 70,000 people a month, trains machinists, runs a for-profit machine tool business, has a program allowing students to earn bachelors' degrees in engineering, runs a child care center and a Montessori school, offers remedial education to high school graduates and dropouts, and has an information technology training center as well. It does this on a modern forty-acre campus created in the bombed out, burned out area of inner-city Detroit.

Eleanor Josaitis teaches every day of her life. She starts each morning by walking the factory floor at 6:00 A.M. She also makes sure that she interviews every new colleague, with whom she shares her Teachable Point of View on poverty, racism and the role of Focus: HOPE. She does this over and over again with all stakeholders. She *lives* the Virtuous Teaching Cycle.

Eleanor Josaitis and Wayne Downing are two of the leaders you will meet in this book. They are among a very diverse group of leaders from a variety of organizations whom we cite. It is my experience that people learn most when they reach out beyond their everyday world. I hope you will benefit from the broad range of experiences and settings of the leaders in this book.

Are You Ready to Build a Cycle of Leadership?

So why should you as a leader take the journey to build a Teaching Organization? It's a lot of work and demands great personal courage. You will encounter resistance, and there is the potential for failure. But, the alternative is worse—not creating a Teaching Organization to develop leaders at all levels marks the beginning of the end for your organization. It means that you have mortgaged its future by not providing for the needed leadership.

To take the journey affords you the opportunity to look back on your career with unbelievable satisfaction and pride, because you will have a leadership legacy. Larry Bossidy, the former CEO of Honeywell, said it so well:

> *You won't remember when you retire what you did in the first quarter . . . or the third. What you'll remember is how many people you developed, how many people you helped have a better career because of your interest and your dedication to their development . . . When confused as to how you're doing as a leader, find out how the people you lead are doing. You'll know the answer.*

Chapter One

The New DNA of Winning: A Virtuous Teaching Cycle

■ Winning Organizations Are Teaching Organizations
- Everybody teaches. Everybody learns.
- Practices, processes, values all promote teaching.

■ They Are Built Around Virtuous Teaching Cycles
- Teaching isn't one-way. It's interactive.
- Interaction generates knowledge. It makes everyone smarter.

■ They Create Attributes Needed in the Knowledge Economy
- Maximum use of everyone's skills and talent.
- All-level alignment needed for smart, speedy action.

For fifteen years, Jack Welch drove the GE transformation from his teachable point of view that every business in GE needed to dominate its market. "No. 1, No. 2, fix, close or sell," was the mantra by which every GE executive lived or died. Then, in 1995, a group of middle managers in a class at GE's Crotonville leadership development institute sent Welch a startling message. The No. 1 or No. 2 vision, they told him, was stifling growth. Instead of scrambling to grow, leaders in GE were gaming it. GE was missing opportunities because its business leaders were defining their markets too narrowly so that they could be No. 1 or No. 2.

Welch's response to this "punch in the nose," as he described it, was to revise his thinking. In not very long, he came out with a new declaration: Define your business in such a way that you have less than 10% market share. Then direct your creativity and energy to finding new ways to attract customers. This change in outlook, according to Welch, was a major contributor to GE's double-digit rates of revenue growth in the latter half of the 1990s.

This story illustrates what I call a "Virtuous Teaching Cycle" at work. In the process of teaching, the teacher, Welch, learned something valuable from the students, which made him smarter and prompted him to go out and teach a new idea. Such interactions are an essential reason why GE has been so successful over the past two decades and why it is likely to remain one of the world's most valuable companies for some time to come.

Jack Welch handed over to Jeff Immelt a world-class Teaching Organization in which everyone teaches, everyone learns and everyone gets smarter every day. The Virtuous Teaching Cycle is the dynamic process that keeps it working. Jeff Immelt, the new CEO of GE, is a product of that Teaching Organization, and he believes that the most important core competency of a GE leader is to be a teacher.[1]

■ ■ ■

In Fort Benning, Georgia, my colleague, Eli Cohen, while doing the research on *The Leadership Engine* book, watched a platoon of Special Operation's Rangers conduct a raid on a terrorist camp. The Rangers team entered a compound of terrorists (actually, army role players) who were well armed and also had chemical weapons. As the simulation unfolded, Eli saw that it was anything but the well-orchestrated ballet he expected. It was chaos. But, such simulations aren't, as some people might think, opportunities to become perfect in choreographed maneuvers, which seldom if ever work on the battlefield. Instead, they're meant to season soldiers to make split-second decisions in difficult circumstances. They are designed to develop functioning leaders, able to accomplish their mission despite the obstacles, rather than lock-stepped martinets. So, after the exercise came the After Action Review.

In the After Action Review at Fort Benning, one of the NCOs said:

> Don't forget: What gets the job done is bold, aggressive leadership. Nothing went according to plan. We were sup-

posed to face a chain-link fence: We faced triple-strand razor wire. The enemy wasn't supposed to have night vision goggles, but they did, so we were compromised before we breached the fence. Our radios were supposed to work: They didn't.

That's going to happen. But we got it done because some men stepped up and made decisions. When the alpha leader went down, his team leads took charge. When the communications didn't work, the lieutenant didn't fiddle with the radio or yell at his communications specialist. He ran around to find out what was going on and gave orders. When the fence turned out to be razor wire, the bravo squad leader changed his approach and commandeered two men to help get everyone into the compound.

Throughout the After Action Review an observer facilitated the dialogue, asking questions such as: "What were the conditions that caused you to do this? Why did you make that decision? Knowing what you know now, what would you have done differently?"

In a later conversation, General Pete Schoomaker, former head of SOF, explained the process to us. After an exercise "we stop and say, 'Now let's go back to the beginning.' So, we go through the mission phase by phase, using a formal process called an After Action Review. From privates to generals, everyone who had anything to do with the operation sits down and reviews what happened." Everyone contributes and learns from the others. It is a Virtuous Teaching Cycle.[2]

The Virtuous Teaching Cycle

In *The Leadership Engine,* I wrote about the importance of leaders developing leaders. A key theme of that book was that winning companies win because they have leaders at all levels, and those companies have leaders at all levels because their top leaders make developing other leaders a priority. They personally devote enormous amounts of time and energy to teaching, and they encourage other leaders in the company to do the same. This book builds on that work and adds a critical element.

Winning leaders are teachers, and winning organizations do

encourage and reward teaching. But there is more to it than that. Winning organizations are explicitly designed to be Teaching Organizations, with business processes, organizational structures and day-to-day operating mechanisms all built to promote teaching.

More importantly, the teaching that takes place is a distinctive kind of teaching. It is interactive, two-way, even multi-way. Throughout the organization, "teachers" and the "students" at all levels teach and learn from each other, and their interactions create a Virtuous Teaching Cycle that keeps generating more learning, more teaching and the creation of new knowledge. Virtuous teaching cycles are what keep people in winning companies getting smarter, more aligned and more energized every day. Teaching Organizations make them possible.

Figure 1 on page 5 captures the essence of the thesis presented in this book: Namely, the key to creating knowledge and aligning people in organizations is this Virtuous Teaching Cycle embedded in an ever expanding spiral. This interactive teaching, engaging more and more of an organization's members, expands knowledge while it also aligns people. Examples in the book include GE, which has 15,000 full-time teachers called black belts, who take two years off from their regular jobs to teach Six Sigma[3] (the 3.4 defects per million quality methodology). The black belts teach all 300,000 employees how to use the tools of Six Sigma, and the employees then teach the black belts by applying the Six Sigma methodology to projects that generate new knowledge and new products, streamline processes and enhance quality. Other examples include how Virtuous Teaching Cycles are being used by biotech firm Genentech to improve and accelerate the launch of new biotherapeutics via interactive teaching in the commercial organization, by the consulting firm Accenture to gather and share information among partners around the world, and by Home Depot to forge partnerships with its suppliers and customers.

Everyone Gets Smarter

It takes very tough-minded and disciplined leaders to create these virtuous spirals. All too often, the spirals found in organizations are the opposite kind. Command-and-control hierarchies, with their cram-down, one-way communication, create vicious cycles in which information is hidden, gamesmanship is raised to a high art, and trust is destroyed. As a result, the leader learns nothing, the organi-

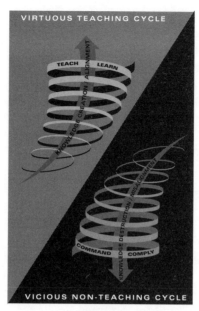

Figure 1

zation gets dumber, and there is an ever expanding spiral of knowledge destruction and misalignment.

Creating value is still the game. Despite all the turmoil in the world—from the 9/11 tragedy and ensuing war on terrorism, to the bursting of the new economy bubble with Enron as the poster child for that era, and a worldwide recession, coupled with incredible advances in digitization, biotech and other technological innovations—the fundamentals of leadership and business have not changed. Successful leaders add value. No matter what level or what type of organization, the true measure of a leader is whether he or she has made the assets under their control more valuable today than they were yesterday.

A leader is given stewardship over assets, in the form of people, capital, information, and technology. Their job is to make them more valuable and to keep making them more valuable into the future.

For the leaders of publicly traded companies, the long-term market capitalization of the company is the indicator. I use as my barometer the research of Professor Larry Selden at Columbia University. He found that the companies consistently in the top quartile of the S&P 500—whom I count as the winners—maintain annual growth rates of 12% in revenue and a 16% operating return on assets. These numbers are not just financial abstractions. They are the real measure of whether a company is pleasing customers and making a profit, the two things that ultimately determine whether it stays in business and employs anybody.

For non-publicly traded organizations, the same rules apply. The metrics are a bit trickier, but they hold. I like to teach people that as a professor at the University of Michigan Business School, I have the same assignment as the CEO of a publicly traded company. As a leader, I must figure out how to add value, how to make the Business School assets more valuable tomorrow. There are two ways I can do that. One is profitable new revenue, which could be achieved through new executive programs, new degree programs, expanding our services, etc. The other is better asset utilization, being more productive off the same asset base, such as leveraging more student throughput through larger classes, better use of technology, etc. The point is, all leaders must drive these two dimensions.

While there is no "new economy," there are some new rules. What it takes—the assets and the abilities needed to grow profitably—have changed drastically in recent years. There is a new environment. Technology has accelerated globalization. Intangibles have replaced physical goods as the primary conveyors of value. Change has revved up to a fast, pass-and-shoot continuum.

In this new fluid, rolling game, the assets needed to win are people with brains and energy. They must be aligned and empowered, able to quickly figure out what needs to be done, and then get it done, efficiently and effectively. Old, football-style teams with a coach on the sidelines calling the plays are doomed. Basketball and soccer are the new metaphors. Winning still means scoring, but there is no time for huddles, no pauses for strategizing, and set patterns won't work.

In this environment, the key to winning is a leader's ability to raise the collective intelligence of his or her team and keep its members aligned, energized and working to please customers. This last element is a critical one. In today's world, a company's people are its most important value-producing assets. Their brains create the ideas and intangible goods that draw customers to their door. To keep creating new value for the customers, team members must get smarter every day. But pulling them off-line for training more than intermittently is not an option. The teaching, the learning, the aligning and the energizing must be done on an ongoing basis *while* they are on the job, doing things to please customers.

The Teaching Organization

The way to do this, which we will describe in this book, is by building a Teaching Organization, one in which everyone is a teacher, everyone is a learner, and reciprocal teaching and learning are built into the fabric of everyday activities. The CEO must assume the role of head teacher. He or she must set the direction, shape the culture and share the valuable insights and knowledge in his or her head.

But while it is critical that everyone in the organization, from the top down, teach, the teaching cannot be one-way. It must be interactive teaching, where the leader who is teaching is at the same time drawing on and learning from the knowledge and experience of the students. As in the GE and SOF examples, the people on the front lines often have valuable information ahead of senior management. Capturing and utilizing that information can create significant competitive advantages for the leaders who figure out how to do it.

In a Teaching Organization, the learners at all levels are also teachers, both up to the leaders above them as well as down into the organization where they lead others. This creates a Virtuous Teaching Cycle, a self-reinforcing teaching and learning process that is what keeps winning organizations learning and improving every day.

This is not a New Age, feel-good approach to winning. A real Teaching Organization is anything but a soft, touchy-feely kind of place. The Teaching Organizations we describe are interesting, fun, enjoyable places to work, but that's because they engage the brains of the workers and allow them to contribute to a winning team. A Virtuous Teaching Cycle generates smarter team members, who become aligned and emotionally energized through the interactive teaching and learning process. This, in turn, is what leads directly to the delivery of results.

The environment of a Teaching Organization is perhaps best described as one of controlled freedom, or disciplined fun. It is what professional athletic teams, orchestras and the Navy SEALs achieve when they are at peak performance. They have the freedom to be creative because they are in a flow and a process that is demanding, disciplined and energizing.

It is at the core of what Jack Welch created at GE. The discipline of attending regular teaching and learning sessions at GE's Crotonville leadership development institute is not optional for senior leaders.[4] The quarterly Corporate Executive Council meetings at Cro-tonville, where the members of the top team teach one another, are never missed. The succession planning reviews that are held three times a year are very closely scripted.

It is the structure that is built into the processes that allows the content to be creative and free-flowing. GE's very disciplined, teaching-and-learning environment invites humor, constructive conflict and dialogue with the understanding that effective action will follow. Jeff Immelt, the current CEO of GE, is both a product of this system and the new head teacher.

World's Largest Teaching Infrastructure: GE

Teaching Organizations have Virtuous Teaching Cycles operating not just at the top, but throughout the organization. Yum! Brands is cascading teaching to all of its 750,000 workforce, employed by both the company and franchisees, through formal programs and thousands of coaching sessions. Home Depot will train 40,000 new leaders for positions in its stores.

The world's largest teaching infrastructure is at GE.[5] The elements include the following:

1. The top team holds quarterly workshops at Crotonville to share best practices and to think about how to make all of the GE businesses the best in the world. These Corporate Executive Council (CEC) meetings are true Virtuous Teaching Cycles where everyone is a teacher and everyone a learner.

2. More than 15,000 high-potential middle managers are assigned for two full-time years as "black belt" teachers of Six Sigma. They are teaching all 300,000+ employees at GE and leading over 20,000 Six Sigma projects. The Six Sigma program is a Virtuous Teaching Cycle, with the black belts teaching the quality tools to the workforce, who then use them to generate new ideas and, in turn, teach the black belts.

3. Work-Out: Starting in 1988, Welch required line managers to run town hall meetings as problem-solving teaching and learning sessions. Leaders held three-day sessions to solve actual problems that employees felt would improve their organizations and work lives, and the boss had to respond real-time. Over 300,000

employees went through at least five Work-Out sessions in the late 1980s and early 1990s. In 1999, Welch mandated a new round of Work-Out sessions for everyone in the company as an antidote to bureaucracy creeping back into the company.

4. Change Acceleration Program: The top 10,000 GE leaders are trained to teach and lead change projects throughout the company. This is essentially developing the teaching capability in the top levels of the company.

5. Crotonville: The leadership development center is a fifty-acre campus overlooking the Hudson River in Ossining, New York. It enrolls more than 5,000 GE leaders a year, ranging from entry level to senior executives. It is a place where knowledge is generated, where ideas and values are taught, and where leaders teach and learn. In the mid-1980s, I ran Crotonville and led the effort to transform the center from a traditional one-way teaching infrastructure to an action-learning Virtuous Teaching Cycle, where everyone teaches and everyone learns.

6. GE's operating mechanisms, the processes through which it runs its business, succession planning, financial planning and strategy, are designed as teaching and learning sessions, not as bureaucratic reviews.

For all their rejection of top-down, one-way teaching, Teaching Organizations are seriously disciplined environments. In all cases, the discipline includes consequences for non-delivery of results and for not living up to institutional values.

High-performing teams do not carry C players for long. In the NBA, 20% of the players are traded out every year. At GE, Jack Welch required that the bottom 10% be cut every year. One of the surest ways to raise the level of a team is to cut from the bottom and add to the top.

The Navy SEALs are another great example of a solidly based Teaching Organization. The military discipline and the demands for top physical performance are predictable and obvious. More than half of the men and women, who are already carefully screened before entering the six-month Basic Underwater Demolition training program, can't measure up and drop out or are dropped out before graduation.

But the training isn't the only reason for creating this tightly disciplined society. Equally important is the building of a high level of trust and respect among all of its members, so that each one, no matter what level in the hierarchy, will be able to teach others the things they learn that will make the collective IQ go up. Underwater, in tight situations, everyone must, and must be allowed to, contribute 100%, regardless of rank.

Brains and Alignment

The success of institutions in the new millennium will be determined by how much smarter they can become every day, through knowledge creation and through aligning members of the organization around new knowledge. The bursting of the new-economy bubble, the tightening of the capital markets, the death of many dot-com darlings, and the accounting debacles at Enron and other companies only reinforce our certainty about this.

The world has definitely changed. Markets are truly global. Intangibles carry premium value.[6] New technologies create new capabilities every day. The revolving doors of the labor markets spin at the speed of turbines. In this lightning-fast world, old strategies and processes won't work. New ones that are much more versatile and that function much more smoothly are needed. But the job of a leader has not changed. Enhancing the value of assets and sustaining growth are still the ultimate goal.

Developing others to be leaders, creating leaders at every level, and getting them aligned and energized is how you get there. The company that fields the better team with the smarter people and has them working most often on the things that create the most value will win out over its competitors.

What is new in this book is a critical insight about how leaders create and maintain such teams. It is: To create organizations that get smarter and more aligned every day requires an interactive teaching/learning process. It isn't hierarchical teaching. You teach me, and then I teach the people below me. It isn't about alternating roles. You teach me something, and then I'll teach you something. Rather, it is a process of mutual exploration and exchange during which both the "teacher" and the "learner" become smarter. It is synergy. $1 + 1 = 3$.

In *The Leadership Engine*, the big "aha" for me was that it was up to the leader to be the teacher. He or she had to develop a Teachable

Point of View and then personally teach it to others. This was why Roger Enrico's leadership school at PepsiCo was so successful.[7] He ran it himself, with no consultants and no professors. It was just Enrico, twelve hours a day for five days straight with ten rising leaders in the company. Then he'd send them back home to work on projects, and bring them back in for follow-up sessions.

Jack Welch's secret was the fact that he was constantly teaching. He ran sessions at GE's Crotonville leadership development institute every couple of weeks. He ran workshops with senior executives in the CEC. But perhaps most importantly, he was always teaching, no matter what else he was doing. If you had a meeting with Welch, no matter what the topic, you could expect a quick coaching clinic at the end.

The Key is *Interactive* Teaching

What we missed in *The Leadership Engine* was the need for the teaching to be interactive. We included Roberto Goizueta because he had a clear Teachable Point of View and was building leaders at Coca-Cola. We also included Eckhard Pfeiffer at Compaq. Yes, they had points of view that were very clear, and they made sure that they were taught very well. But they were missing the critical element. The two-way nature of great teaching, where the teacher is also a learner and becomes smarter through interaction with the students.

Pfeiffer was a one-way teacher. He was a brilliant man who did not seem to understand that he would have been smarter and his people smarter if he had been more open to learning. The people would also have become more bought in and aligned around executing his strategy. The Compaq chairman, Ben Rosen, who led the board coup to fire Pfeiffer told *Fortune*, "The change [will not be in] our fundamental strategy—we think that strategy is sound—but in execution, . . . Our plans are to speed up decision making and make the company more efficient."

One element of the Compaq strategy that was not executed well was the acquisition and integration of Digital. Pfeiffer bought Digital Equipment to acquire the people and skills Compaq needed to compete in the new service-oriented market. But, rather than listening and learning the things that he and Compaq needed to learn from Digital, he set about directing them as if he already had the expertise that he paid $9.6 billion to purchase. In discussions I have had with Digital leaders, they said it was clear that the Compaq leaders, starting with Pfeiffer, were not going to listen to their ideas. The result is that the good Digital leaders left and the others went underground.

In doing this, Pfeiffer distanced himself from the real deal and the problems he needed to address. He did not learn from the people at Digital, and he set the tone for other people at Compaq to disregard what the Digital people brought to the table as well.

Evidence of Pfeiffer's lack of interest in interaction was the fact that he outsourced his leadership development program to Harvard rather than develop an in-house program with a lot of teaching and interaction between him and other senior leaders. Can you imagine Jack Welch or Jeff Immelt closing Crotonville and sending their people to Harvard to be taught by professors? No way. Welch knew— and Immelt has learned from him—that not only was it his job to develop the other leaders, but also that teaching was the best way for him to learn and get smarter himself. Pfeiffer saw the value of developing leaders, but he didn't do it himself and he was rarely in the room with the participants, thus there was little or no opportunity for him to grow and learn. One of the participants in the program told me that when Pfeiffer did come to the program, he talked to the participants and did not listen to them.

In this book we'll talk about both how to build a Teaching Organization and why it is more important today than ever before that leaders build them. One reason is that we are in a post-industrial era. Knowledge, human enthusiasm and brainpower have replaced physical plants and equipment as the critical assets in competitive markets. More than ever before, the abilities of the people in a company, and how effectively those abilities are used, are the keys that determine whether a company wins or loses.

Attracting those smart, talented people and raising their level of play, therefore, becomes a core competence. Yes, Intel invests billions in building state-of-the-art plants to produce microprocessors, but once a new chip is on the market, it is only a matter of months before the competitors are producing almost precisely the same thing. The differentiator, and the thing that keeps Intel on the top of the heap, is the knowledge, creativity and energy of the people who work at Intel and keep coming up with the new products.

As GE has moved from a maker of products to a more global services organization, the boundaries between suppliers and customers have blurred. In order to deliver services to hospitals, the people at

GE Medical Systems must teach. They must transfer knowledge to the hospitals' personnel, ranging from how to run a radiology department more effectively to helping set up a learning center like Crotonville, as it did for Long Island Jewish Hospital.

At Home Depot, CEO Bob Nardelli's new strategy includes adding services such as installation. It is also increasing sales to professional builders. To do this means that new partnerships must be forged that require a teaching and learning interface.

Another example is Cisco, which is the largest supplier of computer networking gear in the world, but does very little of its own manufacturing. Rather, it designs the technology, markets the products, and maintains the customer relationships, but it assigns most production, fulfillment and on-site customer service to its partners.

Networking Requires Teaching

This points to another reason that teaching and learning are becoming increasingly critical abilities. In a networked world, temporary alliances and partnerships perform crucial functions that were once done almost entirely in-house.[8] Although Cisco depends on its suppliers to build machines and perform services for customers, John Chambers and his colleagues have no direct authority over the people who are doing the actual work.

If GE, Home Depot and Cisco aren't pleased with their partnerships, they theoretically end an alliance and find a new partner. But in reality, the people at these companies need to be able to reach into partners' organizations and interact with their employees as if they were on their own payroll. They need not only to influence ideas, values and behaviors in the partner organization, but also to collect and use the intelligence generated by people in the partner organization.

I think that command-and-control is generally an ineffective way to manage. It is the mark of a weak leader who doesn't have the self-confidence to face criticism or grow, and it doesn't generate the excitement or energy needed to win. But within an organization where a leader has the authority, it is an option. In networked situations, however, it is not an option. A leader who wants to lead people over whom he has no authority must have the ability to do it through teaching.

Winners Must Be Big, Fast and Smart

The companies that win in the post-industrial knowledge economy will be the ones that are big, fast and smart. Teaching Organizations foster all three of these characteristics, and, critically, they do it in a way that intensifies, rather than diverts from attention to, the ongoing business of pleasing customers.

For young companies in a stage of hypergrowth, teaching is an absolute necessity. Not only must the people streaming in the door be assimilated into the company and directed to meaningful work, but also cadres of new managers must be developed. If a company is growing 100% a year, that means 75% of its employees have been there less than two years—and that's only if everyone sticks around, which is a very unlikely circumstance. Even though the dot-com bubble has burst and there are fewer hypergrowth companies in the digital high-tech sector, there are still sectors such as biotech where rapid growth is occurring, and there will be many more start-ups in the future across a wide range of industries.

With these kinds of human development needs, teaching and learning can't be spun off and left for HR trainers. And, the processes of teaching and learning can't be relegated to specific designated locations or circumstances. Instead, teaching and learning must happen on an ongoing basis. Leaders must make sharing ideas and information a central part of their everyday work.

For example, Mary Tolan, the group chief executive of Accenture's 12,000-person resources operating group that services the energy utilities and chemical industries, sees teaching as central to making her consultants able to provide new value to clients. She runs action learning development programs for emerging partners, holds large-scale workshops for salespeople to share best practices, and dedicates over half her calendar to teaching. At Genentech, Myrtle Potter, COO and head of the Commercial Group, is building a teaching organization to ensure that there is new knowledge generation and alignment. This will be critical as the company enters its greatest commercialization phase and prepares to launch new products.

It is the routine gathering and sharing of information and ideas that allows Teaching Organizations to be faster and smarter than their competitors. There are a number of reasons for this that we will explore later in the book. One of them, for example, is that Teaching

Organizations are better at collecting information and getting it to the people who can use it.

It's About Collecting and Sharing Knowledge

In every organization there are enormous amounts of wasted knowledge. A service tech who goes into the offices of customers every day collects a lot of information about those customers. He or she often learns things that even people higher up in the customer's organization don't know. Some of that information and those insights, about the goals, the values and the needs of the customers could be useful to people back in the office. But often it is lost because the service tech doesn't recognize its value and/or because he or she isn't able to get it to the people who could use it.

If the service tech is part of a Teaching Organization, however, he or she is more likely to understand his or her own company's business well enough to make some decisions about which knowledge is useful, and to have the ability to input it usefully into the company's knowledge pool. This is just one of the ways that being a Teaching Organization allows a company to be both smarter and faster. Later chapters will explore many more.

Building a Teaching Organization requires a subtle and complex combination of many elements. Members of senior management must have the mind-set that teaching is a core competitive competence. They must invest the intellectual energy to develop clear Teachable Points of View, and they must become role model teachers themselves.

Teaching Organizations have cultures in which everyone is expected to teach, and they have compensation systems that reward teachers. The teaching covers both the ideas and the information needed to run the business and also offers coaching and mentoring on how to be a better leader and teacher. When the right dynamic balance is achieved, the result is the creation of a Virtuous Teaching Cycle and an environment of disciplined excitement in which everyone learns, everyone teaches, and everyone gets smarter every day.

There is no one blueprint or precise recipe for creating a model Teaching Organization. In part, this is because the processes, the style and the culture of the organization will reflect the personality, ideas and interests of the leaders who build them. And in part, this is because Teaching Organizations are agile and flexible and adapt quickly to changing circumstances.

We will cite examples to illustrate our points from General Electric, Trilogy Software, Cisco Systems, Home Depot, Yum! Brands, Southwest Airlines, Accenture, Limited Brands, 3M, the United States' Special Operations Forces, Focus: HOPE, Genentech, and a number of other companies. But we are not holding any of them up as model organizations. Rather, what we are offering in this book is the intellectual framework and a collection of examples and best practices that will help leaders figure out how to build their own unique Teaching Organizations.

Leadership Benchmarks

Benchmarks are for learning, not direct copying. Each leader must invent his or her own Teachable Point of View and take full ownership for teaching other leaders, thus, the examples in this book are to stimulate learning, they are not meant to be copied.

When I teach benchmarking to leaders, I ask them to get a mind-set like a professional musician or athlete may have. If you talk with a violinist, pianist, opera singer, tennis pro or golf pro, they all benchmark, but they rarely copy. In fact the opera singer may say, "I can't stand the way she sang that." Or the tennis pro, who says after watching a Pete Sampras, 128-mile-an-hour serve, "That's a weird way to grip the racket." But then they set about learning from and figuring out how to do better than the benchmark. The point is, professionals do not willy-nilly try to copy. Rather, they learn from others. The point of the benchmarks in this book is to stimulate learning. You may dislike a benchmark, but you can and should still learn from it. This book is meant to stimulate your development as a leader.

What we are offering in this book is the intellectual framework and a collection of examples and best practices that will help leaders figure out how to build their own unique Teaching Organizations. The benchmark practices we will look at include:

COMPANY	LEADER	LESSONS FOR OTHERS
ACCENTURE	Mary Tolan, head of Accenture Resources Group	• Large-scale knowledge creation • Action learning model

CISCO	John Chambers, CEO	• Virtuous Teaching Cycles with employees, communities through the Cisco Networking Academies
DELL	Michael Dell, founder, CEO	• Entrepreneur founder became head teacher with a very clear Teachable Point of View
EDS	Dick Brown, CEO	• Rapid transformation of a company using teaching as the core process
GENENTECH	Myrtle Potter, COO and head of the Commercial Group	• Biotech firm using teaching cascade to align and accelerate competitive capabilities
GENERAL ELECTRIC	Jack Welch, former chairman and CEO Jeff Immelt, chairman and CEO	• World's most fully scaled Teaching Organization Redefining leadership for the 21st century
FOCUS: HOPE	Eleanor Josaitis, founder	• Civil and human rights organization transforming thousands of inner-city youth into high-tech workers • a world class Teaching Organization • leader/teachers at all levels
LIMITED BRANDS	Les Wexner, founder, chairman and CEO; Len Schlesinger, COO	• How to develop a Teachable Point of View and develop leaders
3M	James McNerney, CEO	• Transforming old-line company into agile Teaching Organization
HOME DEPOT	Bob Nardelli, CEO	• Transition from founders to a leader/teacher who is building a huge teaching infrastructure
NOKIA	Jorma Ollila, CEO	• Building a top-to-bottom global teaching organization • Senior level action learning
ROYAL DUTCH/SHELL	Cor Herkstroter, former chairman, Committee of Managing Directors	• Global scale and cascade teaching

(continued on next page)

COMPANY	LEADER	LESSONS FOR OTHERS
SOUTHWEST AIRLINES	Herb Kelleher, founder	• Using fun and positive emotional energy to drive learning and teaching
SPECIAL OPERATIONS FORCES	Gen. Wayne Downing, retired, head of SOF, former Assistant to the President and Deputy National Security Advisor for Combating Terrorism	• Developed SOF culture to be a 24/7 Teaching Organization
YUM! BRANDS	David Novak, CEO	• Recognition and teaching culture for global restaurant organization (750,000 team members at Taco Bell, Pizza Hut, KFC, Long John Silver's and A&W All American Food) • Building leaders at all levels
TRILOGY	Joe Liemandt, founder, CEO	• Young software company shows how GE concepts can be built into a startup • Trilogy University • Digital Virtuous Teaching Cycles

Simultaneity and Return on Time

Building a Teaching Organization does not require any magic. It is complicated, like writing a sophisticated software program or building an aircraft engine. A lot of pieces have to be put in place and set to work in harmony. But what makes it difficult is not that any of the pieces are particularly complex, but rather that there are so many distractions and obstacles that keep leaders from doing enough of them.

The distractions may come—as they did for many dot-com executives—in the form of bedazzling success and celebrity or from a downturn or business complication that becomes all consuming. Especially in young companies, so many things need to get done seemingly all at once, it is easy for leaders to fall into the trap of thinking that planning ahead and building for the future is an incredible luxury. It is not. It is an absolute necessity.

An entrepreneur may not be able to get all the right pieces in place from day one, but he or she needs to have an eye on the future even while dealing with the demands of today. What this means is making sure that the right stuff gets put into the DNA of the embryonic organization so that it can take hold and grow later. Otherwise, if the organization gets built around expedient values, practices and structures, it is almost certain to fall apart at some critical moment down the road. Enron and MicroStrategy are just two examples of what happens when companies don't build in appropriate values and controls.

With markets and technology changing daily, new products and new competitors popping up everywhere, and customers demanding satisfaction immediately, leaders often push human and organizational development issues to the back burner. Creating products, responding to customers and staying solvent are so pressingly urgent that even the leaders who understand that building a strong organization and developing leaders are important tend to let it slip. They figure that they can worry about it later, when the company is bigger, there are more people to do the work, and things feel less chaotic.

The problem with this line of thinking is that the anticipated slower and less chaotic "later" never arrives. In fact, as a company struggles to get or stay on top of the market and grow to viable scale, the only thing that is going to get the company through is developing a well-coordinated team of A+ players and getting them into the game where they can make a difference. Over time, it's the ability to attract, develop and effectively utilize talent that separates the winners from the losers.

The mistake that many people make is in thinking that winning the game today and building a team for tomorrow are two separate activities. Either you respond to the exigencies of the moment or you send your assets off-line for maintenance. The truth is that winning today and upgrading the organization to be a bigger winner tomorrow does not have to be an either/or trade-off. Rather, it requires a return-on-time mind-set.

Making the Most of Every Minute

Leaders with a return-on-time mind-set are always thinking about getting the most out of every minute. Andy Grove was famous at Intel for his fanaticism about starting meetings on time. "Just as you would not permit a fellow employee to steal a $2,000 piece of office equipment," he says, "you shouldn't let anyone walk away with the time of his fellow managers." Leaders with a return-on-time mind-set consciously design processes and structures that simultaneously accomplish more than one goal.[9]

With carefully architected business processes, for example, it is possible to develop leaders and lay firm foundations for the future while dealing with the pressing issues of today. In fact, combining the two often improves the results achieved on both fronts. There is no better way to train leaders than to put them to work grappling with real-life, real-time issues. And the responses to those issues are improved for having lots of leaders focusing attention on them.

Simultaneity is very different from the multitasking that drove so many dot-coms down the tubes. Multitasking often simply means that a person attempts to do more than one thing at once and as a consequence does each of them less well. I remember sitting in one very serious senior management meeting of a dot-com after its stock had lost 50% of its value. The leadership team was holding an all-day meeting in an attempt to wrestle out a new strategy. There were only twelve people at the meeting, and at one point I counted no fewer than three members on their BlackBerry electronic assistants doing e-mail. The purpose of the meeting was to figure out if and how the company was going to survive, and only two participants made it through the day without tuning out and reading their e-mail. By the way, the company is now in Chapter 11 bankruptcy proceedings.

Unlike multitasking, the concept of simultaneity requires no such sharing of attention or dilution of results. Rather, it is the design of processes or activities that when pursued wholeheartedly further the achievement of more than one desired result. For example, Trilogy Software uses its college-hire orientation program to partner with customers and come up with new business ideas. The exercise provides a framework for teaching kids to think about business while picking their brains for new cutting-edge ideas. Home Depot's sales assistants are gathering valuable ideas from customers at the same time they are advising them on their home-improvement projects. And at GE, Jack Welch ran every meeting, whether with employees, customers, suppliers or the press, as a teaching and learning workshop.[10] His successor, Jeff Immelt, does the same. The agenda of a GE meeting may say that the session is about budgeting, but the way it is conducted—as a dialogue instead of a one-sided I'll-tell-you-what-I-want presentation—is designed to make sure that everyone leaves the room smarter businesspeople and better contributors for GE.

The old way of thinking about operations vs. development is that it is a zero-sum game in a linear world. But, if that were ever true, it cannot be now. Trade-offs do have to be made, which is one reason, as we discuss later, that achieving scale is important. You must have enough resources to meet many demands at once, but increasingly leaders must figure out how to accomplish several things with the same resources at the same time. Teaching Organizations not only do that, but they generate a steady stream of new ideas, even including ways to do it.

A Virtuous Teaching Cycle: David Novak and Yum! Brands's Strategy

A Virtuous Teaching Cycle is created when a leader commits to teaching, creates the conditions for being taught him or herself, and helps the students have the self-confidence to engage and teach as well. It is a continuing cycle that requires conviction and courage to implement.

Yum! Brands was created in 1997 as Tricon Global Restaurants when PepsiCo spun off its Pizza Hut, KFC and Taco Bell restaurant divisions. David Novak, a former PepsiCo executive, is the CEO. In the first month of Tricon's existence, Novak developed a workshop that he and other Yum! Brands leaders continue to run called "taking people with you." The purpose of these workshops was first to teach the top 500 leaders of Tricon and its franchisees the new company's business model and core values. (One of those core values is having fun. Hence, the playful stock symbol YUM and renaming the company Yum! Brands in 2002.) Then they went out and began teaching and energizing the rest of the 750,000-member workforce about the new strategy and values.

During the three-day session, Novak models his fourteen leadership principles. One that is particularly critical is a mind-set that wipes out "not invented here" thinking. The message is: You must learn from anybody and not be arrogant.

Novak has clear content to be imparted to the students. He spends more than a day teaching a framework of strategy, structure and culture, followed by teaching the Yum! Brands business model and values. But it is run with a lot of dialogue and interactivity.

The purpose of these workshops is four-fold:

1. Teach the 600 leaders of YUM! Brands and its franchisees the new organization's business model and core values.
2. Share Novak's personal learnings on leadership.
3. Teach a set of principles designed to help build and align teams that would drive results with their sense of ownership.
4. Develop action plans to apply the lessons learned in the workshop. These plans covered both leading growth initiatives and teaching and energizing the rest of the 750,000-member workforce about the strategy and values.

To make sure that his message is getting across and also that the teaching flows both ways, Novak sits down for an hour at each table of seven participants to hear their views of the business and their responses to the lessons being taught in the workshop. Novak recalls this from one session:

I laid out a vision for multi-branding. In fact, we wanted the franchisees to become big advocates for putting two brands into a restaurant. Ned Kirby, a Taco Bell franchisee, said, "Hey, David, I love what you're talking about, you know. It just really makes a lot of sense, but your people in the companies are not cooperating. You may want me to be two brands, but the people of the individual brands want me to just focus on one brand. And when I try to find out about how to execute multi-branding, I go back and forth from one company to another company and phone calls get passed from here to there. I think we need to have a central source in terms of where we can really go to in terms of contract administration and find out what the opportunities are and really get a better understanding of that.

The other thing is that you've got two training manuals. You've got the KFC training manual and the Taco Bell training manual. You need to have an integrated back-of-the-house system as we go forward and you need to make this a lot simpler.

For David Novak, this was a punch in the nose. He thought he was executing his strategy, but Kirby was telling him that his organization was all screwed up, and it was getting in the way of his strategy. As a result, he had to rethink, reorganize and ultimately teach a new set of strategy implementation guidelines. One result of this new information was to put all the contract administration under one person at Tricon. Ultimately, says Novak, "We put together a complete new operating team, which could really focus on our back-of-the-house processes so we could make things simpler and more efficient as we go forward."

Chapter Two
Two Roads to Winning: Hypertransformation and Hypergrowth

■ The Knowledge Revolution
  • Intangibles; brains replace physical goods, equipment as main sources of value.
  • Winners must figure out how to be big, fast and smart—and do it quickly.

■ Hypertransformation: The Challenge for Established Organizations
  • Older companies are often big, but need to become fast and smart.
  • Processes and mind-sets must be changed to encourage risk-taking.

■ Hypergrowth: For Start-Ups, Achieving Scale Is Critical
  • New employees must be brought on line and up to speed efficiently.
  • Structures and systems must be established to avoid chaos.

I go out every day and talk about trust. . . . Trust has been broken. Enron is a small piece of this. Trillions of dollars have been lost in the dot-com meltdown in the last few years . . . I don't blame investors for being pissed. It's a world where you have to get up and talk about your company every day . . . I have to lead for tomorrow's world.

Jeff Immelt, CEO of GE

The Knowledge Revolution

We are living in a revolutionary era. The hardware era is giving way to the software age, and as a result, the economic and social landscape of the world is undergoing seismic changes.[1] The world is also struggling with massive geopolitical turmoil, as evidenced in the 9/11 attacks, not only in the Mideast but around the world. Right now, more than fifty ethnic wars are occurring. We are entering a twenty-first century where our optimism must be tempered with the realities of a very uncertain and violent world.

Times of transformation like this are always messy. Inevitably, they involve errors and excesses. As corporate leaders and investors grapple for new and better ways to deploy assets, the pendulum swings too far and it suddenly reverses course. One day Ariba was planning to double in size from 2,000 to 4,000, practically the next it was laying off 35% of its workforce. All over Silicon Valley the story was repeated. "New economy" companies from Cisco to Yahoo flipped the switch from wholesale hiring to major cutbacks. For many eager entrepreneurs, dreams of hypergrowth suddenly morphed into nightmares of sudden death. The Enron debacle was the most visible symbol of the end of this era of excess and greed. In the "old economy," companies such as Procter & Gamble, General Electric and Charles Schwab, got caught in the recoil as well.

In our eagerness to move ahead, we tend to forget that while some things change, not all things change. Human nature does not change. Business cycles still happen. People still get greedy, or overexcited. They get carried away with their own press clippings and fall under the spell of their own hubris. They go to excess. So we experience booms and busts that cloud the overall picture. But through these cycles, the world sometimes does move on to new trajectories. And despite the messiness of the locomotion, we are clearly on a new trajectory now, as biotech and digital technologies alter the landscape of business and everyday life.

There are many ways to describe the challenges that leaders face in the new millennium. Peter Drucker talks about an era of overwhelming information, in which both enterprises and individuals "will have to learn to organize information as their key resource."[2] Don Tapscott, David Ticoll and Alex Lowy talk about networking and the ability to create and manage alliances as core competencies in a fluid world.[3] Stan Davis and Christopher Meyer have written about value creation and human capital in a world of efficient markets. Lester Thurow sees a knowledge economy in which genetic re-engineering, new materials, robotics and other knowledge-based technologies will have increasingly profound impacts.

All of these things, and many others, are true. Like the industrial revolution, the knowledge revolution is reordering the ways that people relate to one another and to work. The instant availability of information has broken down the walls separating individuals, institutions and economies. Intangibles have replaced physical goods as the primary source of customer value. And brains and energy have replaced plant and equipment as the resources most critical to producing that value.

Further, in an always-on, 24/7 world, everything is constantly in motion. Not only are there new technologies, new applications and new effects every day, but our vantage point changes each moment as we get deeper and deeper into new territory.

During the tech-stock boom in the late 1990s, the old, the physical and the predictable lost value, while investors clamored for the new, the virtual and the volatile. Solidly profitable industrials were squeaking out price/earnings ratios in the single digits, while IPOs with no profits in sight pulled down price/*revenue* multiples in the hundreds. It appeared that start-ups were about to take over the world. Then in March 2000, the bubble burst. Wall Street did a 180 degree turn, and almost overnight tech stocks went from darlings to dogs.

In the euphoria that led up to the spring 2000 sell-off, a lot of entrepreneurs were able to attract investors with nothing more than hope and hype. These ventures were among the first to die when the capital markets tightened. A lot of other companies that had good ideas but bad timing or bad management also got squeezed out. And even many of the fundamentally sound and profitable companies in the e-commerce and high-tech sectors saw their valuations fall by 50% or more. But the fact that the capital markets overinflated a lot of prices in the late 1990s and then overcorrected in 2000 doesn't mean that it was all just Tulipmania.

The fact is that the world has been fundamentally changed by information technology. Quick reversals in the capital markets are simply emblematic of the new environment. The new reality, in which all companies are going to have to compete, is one of constant communication, continuous transformation and rapid-cycle change. In technology, customer markets and the labor market, as well as in the capital markets, movement has become the status quo. Success in this world requires dealing with change. It requires recognizing shifts and mobilizing networks of smart, energetic people to react quickly and intelligently.

It's a New Game for Everyone

In this new knowledge-based economy, it's clear that the practices, systems, policies and mind-sets that won in the old industrial economy will not do the job. So leaders, whether they are starting with four friends in the basement or as the head of a corporation with hundreds of thousands of employees, must build, or rebuild, teams that can win in the new game.

It's as if the International Olympic Committee has just invented a new sport for the next round of games. There are no world-class players yet, but in a very short time competitors will have to develop the needed skills. For the leaders of companies like GM, P&G and Kodak, the challenges are obvious. Like overweight, out-of-shape athletes, they need to develop agility, flexibility and speed. Meanwhile, new, upstart high-tech companies may have agility, flexibility and speed, but they are like preadolescent kids. Most of them are skinny, weak and totally out of control. They may have moments of dazzling brilliance, but neither the muscle nor the discipline to go the distance.

So, it is no foregone conclusion, as many believed in the late 1990s, that the scrappy start-ups will emerge as the winners in the new millennium while the old behemoths face extinction. And it's not the other way around, either, as investors were betting by the spring of 2001. Experience, marketplace recognition and financial resources won't automatically assure that the older established companies will be able to absorb or knock off all of the new entrants.

Rather, the issue is going to be who is best at generating knowledge, harnessing the energy of workers and making sure that it is targeted to the most productive uses. The winners in the future will be organizations that are big, fast and smart. And they will be that way because they will be Teaching Organizations.

The challenges that leaders will face along the road to building them will depend on where they are starting. But at the end of the day, whether they are starting with a three-person or a 300,000-person organization, they will all be competing on the same playing field and will need the same qualities to win.

The Destination

The ultimate destination for all leaders is sustainable value creation. This is reflected in the value of assets over time. Are the people, capital, information and technology worth more today than yesterday? Will they be worth more tomorrow than today? For publicly traded companies, this is reflected in the long-term market capitalization of the company.

What is new and makes this particularly tricky in today's world is that sustained value creation requires an organization to be both big and fast.

Jack Welch went on a twenty-year journey to try to make GE a "big company with the soul of a small company." Over and over again, he would repeat that he wanted GE to be a big company that operated with the speed and agility of a small company.

In his final letter to shareholders in GE's 2000 annual report, Welch gave his view of size:

> One of the biggest mistakes large institutions can make is indulging the compulsion to "manage" their size. They become impressed with how big they are and at the same time nervous about the need to control their size, to get their arms around it. This often leads to layers, structure and bureaucracy—and eventually stifled and frustrated people.
>
> We see size differently. We understand its inherent limitations—on speed and on clarity of communications, among other things—and we fight every day to create the quickness of a small company. But we appreciate the one huge advantage size offers: the ability to take big swings, big risks, and to live outside the technology envelope, to live in the future. Size allows us to invest hundreds of millions of dollars in enormously ambitious programs . . . Our size allows us to do this knowing that we do not have to be perfect, that we can take more risks, knowing that not all will succeed. That's because our size—far from inhibiting in-

novation, the conventional stereotype—actually allows us to take more and bigger swings.

Until now, most leaders have been willing to settle for making a trade-off between big and fast. In fact, the principles of good management taught in the leading business schools prescribe layers of controls that increase with the size of the organization. The best managed companies have been considered to be those with the best controls. But today, the trade-off between speed and scale is no longer acceptable. To be a winner, a company must have both. The key to achieving this is creating a Virtuous Teaching Cycle because effectively generating, sharing and utilizing knowledge is what lets a company achieve scale without losing speed.

The diagram on page 30 shows how these components relate.

The ultimate goal is to deliver *results* in the form of profitable growth and sustained value creation.

In order to do this an *organization* must have scale and speed.

Attaining the scale and speed to stay ahead of the competition in delivering value to customers requires *people* who are aligned, energized and smart. These three attributes are what lead to the ability to scale the organization, whether it be the alignment and scaling of a 300,000+-person GE, or a 30,000-employee Cisco or a small Trilogy at 1,000.

A *Virtuous Teaching Cycle* (VTC) helps people stay aligned, energized and smart. The process of interactive teaching at all levels is the primary mechanism for getting people aligned. The process of teaching and learning is energizing and helps everyone to be smarter.

Starting from the other direction: A Virtuous Teaching Cycle ▶▶ People who are aligned, energized and smart ▶▶ An organization that is both big and fast ▶▶ Profitable growth and sustained value creation.

A Teaching Organization is one that creates the conditions and sets in motion the Virtuous Teaching Cycle.

The Need for Speed

In a world of commoditization, speed is the No. 1 competitive differentiator. The company that figures out what a customer wants and provides it to him or her the fastest wins the customer for that trans-

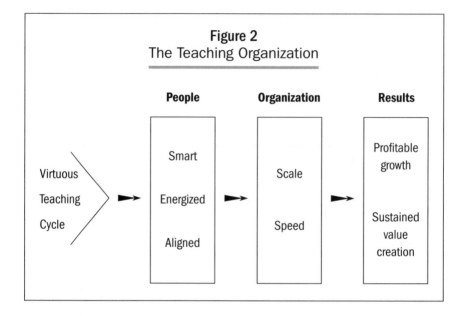

Figure 2
The Teaching Organization

action. The company that consistently figures out what the most (or largest) customers want and delivers those things fastest becomes the industry leader.

Consistently figuring out what customers want and delivering it ahead of the competition is what creates growth. And it requires efficiency and speed in just about everything a company does, not just the processes that directly impact the creation and delivery of products. The companies that win will be fast not only in filling an order, but in everything else that they do, including the following:

• **Developing new technologies and products.** Winning isn't just about getting current products out the door. It's also about coming up with new ones ahead of the competition. Taking cycle time out of developing new cars is critical for automakers. The companies that push the envelope the furthest the fastest in creating new applications for genetic, wireless and other technologies will win in their arenas, too. The same is true in all industries.

• **Developing human assets.** The goal is to have the best assets and to have them most effectively deployed. This means improving people's leadership abilities as quickly as possible. It also means having people in positions where they can make meaningful contributions for as much of the time as possible. Trilogy, for example, has its new hires developing new products and customer solutions within six weeks of joining the company.

• **Data gathering and communication.** Real-time collection of information and fast effective communication of knowledge are also key competitive factors. The faster information is collected and transmitted, the faster it can be acted upon. The more efficiently people within a company can share ideas and insights, the better they are at pulling together toward shared goals.

• **Transformation.** One of the hardest things for leaders to do is recognize changes in the environment and respond appropriately. This often requires revamping business ideas and redeploying resources. It means throwing out ideas and businesses when they stop producing value, and coming up with new ones. For Trilogy, it meant closing down its dot-com spin-offs when the business model no longer worked. For Cisco, Dell and Amazon, it meant implementing layoffs, when just months earlier, growth was everything.

The Need for Size

In a global economy, by just about any measure, success implies scale. If you aren't No. 1 or don't have a shot at it, investors lose interest, customers lose interest, you die. Starting small is fine. Staying small is not. Even if smallness isn't fatal, a company that hasn't proven its ability to grow cannot be classified as a success.

But scale is more than just a metric of success. Large companies have the resources to do things that smaller ones can't. In an era when speed is so critical, companies must be able to meet the needs of many customers at once. Asking customers to delay gratification is not an option in a hypercompetitive world. At the same time, companies must do the research and development to come up with the products and services that will keep attracting and satisfying customers. Or if a company hasn't done the R&D, it better, like Cisco, be large enough to have generated the financial resources to acquire somebody who has done it.

Further, while many big companies are slow and deliberative, their deep pockets actually give them the opportunity to play faster and looser than smaller companies. Lou Gerstner has been able to use IBM's size to great advantage in its revitalization. He has had the resources to develop a new portfolio of innovative services and products while creatively destroying much of the old IBM's stultifying bureaucracy.

The problem with big companies is not that they are big. Scale is a plus, a positive attribute that companies must attain in order to have long-term success. Rather, the problem with big companies is that their bureaucracies and cultures often keep them from seeing new ideas or acting on them in a timely fashion. In other words, big companies are often slow and stupid. The challenge that the leaders of older, established companies face, therefore, is to transform their cultures and structures so that they can use their big-company resources to please customers with smart, innovative products and services.

After twenty years of fighting bureaucracy, Jack Welch was still fighting it to the very end. In the annual report letter cited above, he wrote:

> *We cultivate the hatred of bureaucracy in our Company and never for a moment hesitate to use that awful word "hate." Bureaucrats must be ridiculed and removed. They multiply in organizational layers and behind functional walls—which means that every day must be a battle to demolish this structure and keep the organization open, ventilated and free. Even if bureaucracy is largely exterminated, as it has been at GE, people need to be vigilant—even paranoid—because the allure of bureaucracy is part of human nature and hard to resist, and it can return in a blink of an eye. Bureaucracy frustrates people, distorts their priorities, limits their dreams and turns the face of the entire enterprise inward.*

Knowledge Is the Critical Asset

In the knowledge era, it's brains and motivation that make the difference. Winning companies will be the ones that are filled with smart people who can quickly figure out what needs to be done, and then make it happen without lots of direction from above. Not only is knowledge a critical asset with its own intrinsic value, but also the collection, creation, dissemination and use of knowledge is a key ability in increasing the value of other assets. That is why we are focusing on the continuous generation and deployment of knowledge in this book.[4]

One way to describe the fundamental job of leaders today is as the generation and dissemination of valuable knowledge. This knowledge falls into two broad categories. The first type is knowledge about markets and customers. It relates to figuring out what goods or services will attract the most customers at the best prices. The second type of knowledge is about how a company operates, how it produces those goods and services, and how it enhances operating return on assets. These are the age-old concepts of effectiveness and efficiency.

The twist in the knowledge era is that the gathering of raw data and the application of human intellect to turn that data into valuable knowledge must be done on a constant and cumulative basis. Once Henry Ford designed the Model T, he left it practically unchanged for twenty years. The assembly line was a design breakthrough that remained the model in many industries for more than half a century. Today, innovations remain unique and cutting-edge for approximately a nanosecond, and then they are superseded by something newer and often better. The challenge for leaders, therefore, is to design and build organizations where everything gets better and everyone gets smarter every day.[5][6]

As Peter Drucker points out, the proliferation of information in the Internet-enabled world means that organizing information becomes increasingly important. Gathering data, while important, is not enough. The critical competence is making sure that that information flows to the people who need it and will turn it into usable knowledge, and does not flow willy-nilly to overwhelm and distract those who don't need it.

Tumbling Walls: A New Global Ecosystem

Shortly after becoming CEO of General Electric in 1981, Jack Welch began removing layers of management and tearing down functional silos within the company. His idea was that walls impeded the free flow of information and created competition among various groups within the company. Tearing down the walls, he reasoned, would increase cooperation and help GE respond more quickly and effectively to customers' needs. By the early 1990s he had coined a term for what he was seeking to achieve: "boundarylessness."

In trying to make GE a boundaryless company, Welch instinctively was preparing it to compete in a boundaryless world. In the twenty-first century, walls and friction are increasingly being removed from business. As a result, the middlemen, the brokers who use inefficiency and ignorance to make money rather than add true value to the end-user customer, are going to lose. The organizations that are able to use speed and transparency to create value will be the winners. And the key to doing this will be the ability to generate and quickly disseminate useful knowledge.

For Welch, creating a boundaryless GE entailed a massive effort and a huge demolition project. Today, technology is tearing down walls at a rate that many people find alarming. And, in the process, it is vastly changing the competitive playing field.[7]

The walls won't all disappear. And new ones will pop up as the old ones go down. But the new barriers will be more flexible and their height and placement will be constantly shifting. Think about a basketball game. The basic court is flat, but barriers—the opposing players—are constantly moving. This new, ever-changing field creates new kinds of competition and requires new abilities for success.

In 1987, when Wal-Mart and Procter & Gamble linked up their computers so that P&G could monitor Wal-Mart's sales and replenish its inventories, it was a breakthrough use of technology. Previously, computers had been used to keep track of customers' and suppliers' performance, but now Wal-Mart and P&G were using them as an interactive management tool. Almost no one realized the impact that this new use of technology would have on management and the shape of organizations in the future. In the years since, the walls that have traditionally divided and supported both individuals and institutions have been rapidly falling. This has meant the demise of traditional notions of inside and outside, near and far, your place or mine.

In this fluid new world, the challenge for leaders will be to create a new kind of organizational architecture that provides strong structural support without confining walls. Sound structures are even more essential in a fast-paced world than in a slower-paced one. That's because there isn't time to stop, coordinate and refigure what you want to do. People must be able to respond instantly to new information, knowing that their decisions and actions will be in accord with those of their colleagues. In the past, this has been accomplished by building walls that limit people's area of action and restrict their options.

The winners in the future, in a world where the walls are falling down, will be the organizations that are built around internal frameworks of shared values and knowledge. Not only will they have the strength, focus and flexibility to consistently create value for customers, but they will have the skills and the aptitude to reach beyond their own organizations and build effective alliances with others.

The dismantling of walls is most obvious in the development of global markets. Nearly instant access to information and speedy delivery systems put suppliers around the world in direct competition with one another. But this is only one of many ways in which walls are disappearing.

Added to the Internet's ability to span distance is the fact that for many products, the Internet has made distance simply irrelevant. Software, information and entertainment are increasingly delivered electronically, so it doesn't make any difference where the supplier or the customer is. The same is true for services. A technician halfway around the world can talk me through a computer crash or e-mail me a software patch as easily as one across town. Or a doctor halfway around the world can listen to my heart or look at my knee, make a diagnosis, and even perform long-distance surgery.

Redefining Competition

At the same time, technology and the need for speed are putting into competition products or services that might not have been considered competitors in the past. Substitution is not a new concept. For every need or problem, there have always been ranges of solutions that creative people have tried. Whether you raise the bridge or lower the water, you've still solved the problem of crossing the river.

There are two forces at work in the digital era that are fueling cross-competition. One is that with speed, a critical competitive factor, the "best" solution is not necessarily the one that most *perfectly* resolves the problem. Rather, it is more likely to be the one that resolves it *adequately* the fastest. Before the competition comes up with a more adequate one, the game will probably have moved to somewhere else.

Another force that is taking down barriers and opening up competition is the fact that technology makes experimentation so much easier. It isn't exactly the million monkeys with typewriters eventually producing Shakespeare. But, when you can try something out on a computer without having to build a prototype to find out if it works, a lot more people can afford to get in the game.

It isn't just consumer markets that are losing their clear definitions and blending together. All along the value chain, suppliers and customers are tearing down walls. Old, adversarial relationships in which the buyers push for lower prices and higher quality while sellers push for just the opposite are pretty much a hallmark of losers these days.

The companies that really want to operate efficiently and win customers have figured out that teaming up with suppliers is much more helpful than haggling with them. When they give up the notion of the I-win-you-lose zero-sum game and start working together, they find that they can please more customers down the line and create a win-win situation for both of them. So rather than just dicker over prices, quality and delivery schedules, many are working to align their process and eliminate the friction that costs them both time and money.

The benefits of tumbling walls are reaped, however, only when the parties on both sides open up and share their knowledge. General Electric actively draws on the expertise of its various suppliers when designing new products. It also works with suppliers to teach them what it knows about building winning organizations.

Another result of the need for speed and flexibility is the rise of alliances. Rather than take the time to develop new abilities internally, increasingly, companies are seeking out partners for specific competencies when needed. Some of these are short-term, based on the completion of a single contract. Others come close to being long-term mergers.

The key to success both inside winning companies and in these networks of alliances is a new breed of leader/teachers, ones who can both generate new knowledge and disseminate it through interactive teaching. The old-style, command-and-control leader is a dinosaur rapidly going into extinction. The successful leaders of the future will be much more self-confident. They will have the courage and the intellectual and emotional strength to continue to grow and learn.

In the remainder of this book, we will describe the type of organization that we believe leaders must build to succeed in this fluid and boundaryless world. It is a Teaching Organization. That is an organization in which everyone is a teacher, everyone is a learner, and where every human interaction is viewed as an opportunity to acquire and share knowledge. It is an organization in which dialogue, debate, self-improvement and leadership development are built into the fabric of everyday activities.

The destination is the same for everyone. The roads to getting there, however, will be very different.

Framework

The diagram below depicts a process that is occurring as leaders prepare their companies to compete in the new millennium. It shows that "old economy" and "new economy" companies are on different paths. The destination is the same, but the older companies will have to deal with one set of problems during a period of hypertransformation, while the new ones will face a different set as they go through a dizzying time of hypergrowth. It isn't that the new tech-savvy start-ups are ahead of the old behemoths, or that the old guys with depth of capital and in-place management structures are ahead. Rather, the winners will be new entities that combine the best attributes of both. And the one challenge that leaders at all companies face, no matter where they are starting, is the need to travel quickly.

Figure 3: Two Roads to Winning

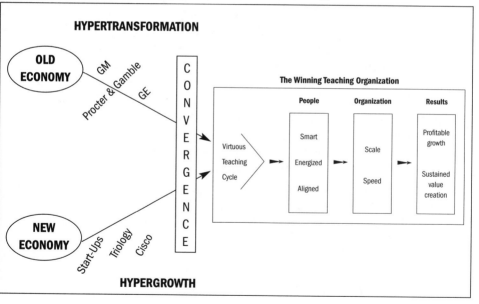

Hypertransformation Road

For older, established companies, existing cultures, processes and bureaucracies present the biggest obstacles. In very short order, they must develop new mind-sets in hundreds of thousands of employees about which kinds of decisions and behaviors are valuable. They must also creatively destroy and rebuild all of the organizational systems that have reinforced the old ways of doing business. The fundamental challenge for old economy companies is transforming themselves from "old way" machine-age companies to "new way" information age—knowledge economy companies.

The "old way" paradigm of the twentieth-century corporate organization was built on a machine-age mentality. Business institutions created rational, nonemotional, "scientifically" sanitized bureaucracies. It is an anti-knowledge generation model. People in the organization are not expected to have original ideas. Rather, ideas and knowledge are built into the bureaucracy through a variety of "scientific" practices. The century-old time-motion studies and concepts developed by Frederick Taylor that prescribed each physical move a worker was to perform can still be found in many companies, especially including fast food restaurants.

Until very recently, AT&T was notorious for its volumes of policy and practice manuals specifying how almost everything was to be done. GE had a five-volume set of "Blue Books," each hundreds of pages long, created in the 1950s and taught until the 1980s on how to plan, organize, integrate and measure. The larger the bureaucracy, the more ideas and knowledge generation were stifled. The focus rapidly became how to perpetuate the technical status quo in the organization, which, in turn, led people to dwell increasingly on the politics of turf protection and careerism.

The challenge for the old economy companies is to tear down and rebuild their institutions without killing themselves in the process. Half of the companies on the *Fortune* 500 list in 1980 were off the list by 1990. Among the casualties that failed to pull off successful transformations were Westinghouse, Digital Equipment and Chrysler.

Transformation: It's a Three-Act Drama

In order to pull off a successful transformation, leaders at older companies must execute a tricky set of maneuvers. It is a drama with three distinct acts, but they have to be played out simultaneously.[8] They are:

Act I: Waking up the organization to the need for change and dealing with resistance. This awakening entails making the case and convincing everyone at all levels that things cannot continue as they are. This means getting people to face reality as it really is, rather than as they are used to seeing it or as they would like it to be. Because change is threatening, there is always resistance. So the alarms must be sounded repeatedly, and new alarms must be set off when people stop listening to the old ones.

Some people resist deliberately because they don't believe in either the need for or the direction of the change. Others may be intellectually on board but emotionally stuck in the past. Leaders must be vigilant in ferreting out both kinds of resistance and dealing with it. Those who can't be coaxed into embracing the change must be removed from the organization.

Institutional resistance to change is one of the most difficult challenges for any leader. At P&G, Dirk Yeager could not overcome it and was fired. At AT&T, both Bob Allen and John Walters lost the battle and were removed as CEO. Embattled Mike Armstrong is still fighting. AT&T's entrenched bureaucracy appears willing to kill the company rather than take the actions required to survive. Thus far, the wake-up call has not been sounded clearly enough. This is what occurred at Westinghouse, which disappeared in its merger with CBS. It is the challenge that leaders at Kodak, Xerox, GM and other old-line once-blue-chip companies are struggling with.

Jack Welch and Lou Gerstner are successful exceptions, but the price, both emotionally for themselves and professionally for members of senior management at GE and IBM, was high. In 1986, Welch had to change out 14 of 21 senior leaders to cut through the resistance. At IBM, Gerstner had to bring in key leaders from the outside to get a team of players who were enthusiastically committed to his change agenda.

Leadership is not a popularity contest, and a leader who wants to effectively sound a wake-up call cannot be fainthearted or concerned about being liked. An anecdote that I often tell about running GE's leadership development center in Crotonville, New York, is about walking into a room where a group of fairly new managers were debating a proposition they had written on a flipchart. It said: "Jack Welch is an asshole."

Creative destruction and rebuilding of an established institution does require the willingness to be called an asshole. I often have people reflect on the fact that the reactions to Gandhi and Martin Luther King Jr. were even worse. They were killed by people who didn't approve of their vision and their activities as change agents. Many of the leaders who are failing at hypertransformation are unwilling to accept unpopularity. As a result, they fall into playing with the bureaucracy, rather than fighting it with sufficient vigor to win.

Act II: Crafting a new vision and aligning people to it. Transformation involves not just tearing away from the past, but moving into a new and better future. Leaders must craft a vision for that future, and they must communicate it in a way that is so compelling that people will want to attain it.

When Jack Welch took the reins as CEO of GE in 1981, he had the main elements of his vision for the company. He knew that he wanted to build the world's most competitive enterprise. He figured that it would need to combine the muscle of a big company with the agility of a small company, and he believed that the surest way to succeed was to have only businesses that were number 1 or 2 in their industries. But figuring out how to pull all the pieces together and get them articulated with the proper balance and emphasis took years of practicing.

By 1985 he was able to write a simple 350-word document for all of his 300,000 employees explaining a more complete vision. But he never quit working on refining and improving the vision or his articulation. He kept revising and revising it right up to his retirement, adjusting it to new learnings and changes in the world. Yet, throughout it all, the fundamental vision of the most competitive enterprise never changed. One of the ways he got buy-in was to challenge leaders throughout GE to craft visions for their units, because as CEOs in their own arenas, they had the same leadership challenges that he did.

In his early days at IBM, Gerstner was roundly criticized for not having a vision. He was brought in to replace a CEO who had overseen the loss of $60 billion in market value, but beyond not being John Akers, he didn't seem to have a clear path in mind. In fact, Gerstner was busy with Act I, making sure that people both inside and outside of IBM were totally clear that he was not John Akers, and that Lou Gerstner's IBM was not going to be John Akers's IBM.

In IBM's highly conformist environment, Gerstner realized that the resistance to change would be massive, so his initial steps were aimed at seizing control of the "police, the media and the schools." As all revolutionary leaders know, success depends on bypassing the old chains of command and getting into the hearts and minds of the people who have been commanded. In political revolutions, this is done by controlling the people with the guns, printing presses and broadcast towers, and those running the educational system.

In a company, the police are the people controlling the finances and the HR functions. Among Gerstner's first acts was hiring new people to head these departments. The media is both the internal communication and external communication with the press and Wall Street. Gerstner personally devoted a lot of time to these. The "schools" are all the training programs. In these he systematically changed the curricula, and he actively involved himself in teaching as a way to interact with people from all over the company at all levels.

As Gerstner worked through Act I, he simultaneously started crafting the new vision for IBM. But it was two years before he began clearly enunciating his vision of IBM as a service company. While Gerstner got away with the two-year lapse between his arrival and focus on a new vision, leaders today don't have the same luxury of time. To become winners—versus merely hanging on as not-dead-yet survivors—they must move much more quickly. In fact, the reason that I have chosen to use the awkward word "hypertransformation" is that speed is a critical element in the process.

Just as entrepreneurial companies must deal with hypergrowth to achieve the necessary scale, older companies must move quickly to shed the old cultures and practices that hobble them. Increasingly, they must deliver on all three acts of the transformational drama, simultaneously rather than serially.

At Ford, Jac Nasser found himself caught in a race against time. He created a new vision for Ford that ignited the imagination of thousands of Ford leaders. These leaders were working excitedly and energetically to change mind-sets and redeploy resources. But Ford is an organization of not thousands of people, but hundreds of thousands of people, and his change efforts also ignited massive resistance, which ultimately led to his dismissal. The antibodies from the one hundred-year-old bureaucracy killed him before he could overcome them.

Act III: Re-architecting the organization. Old structures and processes that hinder achievement of the new vision must be torn down and new ones that foster it must be built. At GE, for example, Jack Welch re-architected the planning process when he got rid of the staff of 200 strategic planners and replaced the old presentation-and-review sessions with informal give-and-take discussions around his conference table. In addition, new cultural values and new kinds of working relationships within the organization must be established. This is a massive job that requires constant attention.

In this re-architecting process we have "old economy" companies struggling all over the map. At the farthest end we have companies like General Motors, with a still-bloated bureaucracy, and slow-moving behavior. These companies have the farthest to go. GE is one of the best positioned. Under Jack Welch, it became a fast-moving, boundaryless, customer-focused company with a market cap that makes it the most valuable enterprise in the world. But even though GE is about as fit as any company to survive and thrive in the knowledge economy, as Jeff Immelt puts it, his job is "to lead GE in a new set of circumstances" including the fact that "post 9/11 is a different world."

Hypertransformation Derailers

In addition to the challenges inherent in dealing with hypertransformation or hypergrowth, there are some other serious, potentially fatal, problems that basically arise for older companies out of having too much experience, and for younger ones from not having enough. These are cultural or attitudinal problems that are particularly pernicious because the sufferers are often not aware that there is any problem. While navigating through the stages of hypertransformation or hypergrowth, leaders must also be vigilant about creating and maintaining cultural environments that aren't toxic to success.

In older companies, years of tradition-building often result in the development of certain kabuki-like behaviors. When an organization has been successful, the impetus within it often is to hang on to what has worked in the past. In these cases, maintaining the status quo and playing to the system become the driving forces behind people's actions, while serving the customer becomes an afterthought. This is what killed Westinghouse and Digital Equipment and is now killing Xerox. For a company where such inside-out thinking is the norm, it is almost impossible to achieve the level of customer responsiveness needed to survive the knowledge economy's highly competitive global markets.

One of the biggest advantages that start-ups enjoy over most established companies is that they tend to be what Jack Welch calls boundaryless. Because they are so small and so new, they don't have the layers of administrators and the bureaucratic walls that divide many older companies into self-competing fiefdoms. Workers in these older companies waste tremendous amounts of time and emotional energy dealing with bloated corporate staffs, protecting the interests of their own units, and positioning themselves for the next step up the corporate ladder. And, while they are doing this, they lose sight of the customers, and they either lose touch with or fail to develop the partnering relationships with suppliers that would allow them to compete successfully in a fast-paced marketplace.

This single factor alone opens the door for the start-ups to sweep in and develop huge new markets in the backyards of the established giants. While workers in the older companies are focused inside-out, responding to the demands of the bureaucracy and the internal processes, workers in new companies are more able to be focused outside-in. If they aren't distracted by other problems, such as those listed below, they are more likely to be listening to customers, figuring out what they need or want, and getting it to them.

Some of the attitudinal problems that characterize older organizations are the following:

Individual motivation	Power/Security
Organizational structure	Stultified
Leadership style	Bureaucratic
Teamwork style	Hierarchical
Customer attitude	If they were here before, they will come back.
Capital markets	We've been here forever. We'll survive.

The demise of Digital, Westinghouse and Chrysler and the struggles at GM, P&G and AT&T can all be traced to the problems listed above. These companies turned inward. Their people became more interested in themselves and the power bases of the different leadership factions than in pleasing customers—customers weren't half as important as the next promotion. The motivating goals became the perpetuation of bureaucratic perks, and the symbols of achievement were rank, not success in the marketplace.

Hypergrowth Road

The bottom line of the chart on page 37 is the path from the embryonic couple-of-friends-in-the-garage stage on the left toward the right-hand side with the Ciscos, Microsofts and Sun Microsystems. If it's lack of speed, flexibility and creativity that are most likely to kill off the big, old companies, it's either the failure to grow or the inability to handle growth that is the biggest threat to small companies.

In order to provide the level of service demanded by customers today and, at the same time, develop the new products that will win them again tomorrow, companies need critical mass. A couple of

Cisco Systems: A Classic Case of Hypergrowth

Cisco Systems has done as good a job as any company of dealing with hypergrowth. A company that had four employees and shipped its first product in 1986, by 2000, it had nearly $19 billion in revenue and a market capitalization of $575 billion that ranked it the highest valued company on the planet. To achieve these numbers, it had sustained a compound annual growth rate of 100%+ for fourteen years.

Year	Number of employees
1986	4
1987	10
1988	48
1989	174
1990	254
1991	506
1992	882
1993	1,451
1994	2,262
1995	3,479
1996	8,259
1997	10,728
1998	14,623
1999	20,657
2000	34,617
2001	43,000
2002 (1/02)	36,786

hundred, even a couple of thousand, people, no matter how smart and energetic, just can't get everything done quickly enough. So while delivering world-class customer service and developing dazzling new products, the leaders of start-up companies must also create organizations that can grow at rates of 100% or more a year.

This means not only finding and hiring the right people and effectively putting them to work, but also building the leadership pipeline and organizational structures needed to support a large, self-sustaining organization. Here again, speed is a critical issue.

Compounding the challenge on the hypergrowth route is the fact that increasing size brings with it some of the problems that older companies face. Hypergrowth quickly creates bureaucracy and resistance to change. Thus, the entrepreneurs must learn to play out the three act drama, albeit at a much smaller scale. And they must do it while still dealing with the hypergrowth issues.

They also must deal with the same general economic issues as older companies. In response to the downturn in early 2001, many entrepreneurial companies had to begin laying off people. Cisco was among them. Even as he continued to hire and build for the future, John Chambers and his team announced the layoff of 8,000 people. This event required another set of skills, selecting the people, implementing the downsizing programs, and redeploying and keeping energized the people who remained.

Interestingly, there are many lessons that the leaders of older companies need to learn that successful entrepreneurs are going to learn through hypergrowth. Most important, they must learn how to build and maintain a smart and effective workforce in a world where workers think nothing of changing employers every two years.

The entrepreneurs who survive the hypergrowth phase do so only by becoming very skilled at hiring, developing and deploying people. In the digital age, when brains, creativity and energy are a company's primary assets, this will be a critical competency.

Another thing that older companies need to learn from the new ones is how to quickly change directions and launch new businesses to keep up with technology.

Hypergrowth Derailers

The cultural pitfalls, or bad attitudes, that occur in newer companies are often the flip side of the ones that plague older companies. They generally arise out of having too few structures and controls and too little respect for the past.

The technologies that "new economy" companies either have created or on which they are building their businesses are so powerful that people working in these companies fall into the trap of thinking that they are invincible.

Further, because the "old economy" folks didn't come up with the new technologies, or didn't come up with brilliant ways to use them, people in the upstart companies tend to arrogantly discard everything—the rules, the ideas, the practices—that the established folks value. A culture that disdains everything from the past is just as misguided as the one that clings to all of it.

Some of the dangerous attitudes that characterize new organizations are:

Individual motivation	Get rich quick
Organizational structure	Chaotic
Leadership style	Anarchistic
Teamwork style	Instrumental (what's in it for me?)
Customer attitude	Customers are dumb. We know better.
Capital markets	We are "new economy," so we win. (This notion lost credence in the high-tech meltdown of 2000, but it remains a cyclical danger.)

Any one of these problems can be serious inhibitors of success. In combination, they become potential killers. For example, the "get rich quick" self-interest motivation at the dot-coms led to many "rest and vest" employees who decided that they didn't need to work very hard. This created schisms between the pre-IPO old-timers and more recent hires. When this was coupled with weak "anarchistic" leadership, companies such as Webvan and Northpoint were destroyed.

The two single quickest killers are lack of respect for customers and poor leadership. Being arrogant and treating customers with disdain led to a serious backlash and the self-destruction of many dot-coms. Add to this immature, chaotic and inconsistent leadership that allows the other bad attitudes to persist, and death is almost certain.

Conclusion

The rest of the book focuses on how to create a winning Teaching Organization, regardless of where you are starting. It is important to know which road you are on and how far you have to go. Just moving along the road, however, does not automatically get you into the winner's circle. There are some quantum changes that have to be made to truly become a Teaching Organization with Virtuous Teaching Cycles throughout the organization. That is what we will tackle now.

Chapter Three
Building the Teaching Organization: Knowledge Creation Through the Virtuous Teaching Cycle

■ The Virtuous Teaching Cycle: A Self-Perpetuating Positive Spiral
- Leader/teachers invite dialogue, seek to draw on knowledge of student/workers.
- Everyone becomes smarter, gains new knowledge to share with others.

■ The Mind-set: Teaching and Learning Are Key Competitive Factors
- Leaders build time into their calendars for teaching and reflection.
- Routine processes are built on teaching/learning rather than command/control.

■ The Infrastructure: It Creates Opportunities for Everyone to Teach and Learn
- Building a teaching/learning infrastructure signals commitment.
- It assures that everyone is included, maximizes available talent.

About eighteen months before he became CEO of PepsiCo, Roger Enrico began to run workshops for rising senior executives at the company. For five days at a time, he would take nine people off-site and, from early morning to late night, he would talk with them about the business and what he knew about how to be a successful leader.

The executives each brought with them a project to cut costs or produce top-line growth in their business unit. The group would discuss and analyze them all, then the executives would go back to their jobs to implement them and return in sixty days for a three-day follow-up.

The original idea for starting the workshops was that Enrico, a highly acclaimed leader, would pass on his knowledge and insights to future leaders of the company. But in the process, Enrico discovered that he was learning as much as the "students." Without intentionally setting out to do so, he created a Virtuous Teaching Cycle in the workshops.

They turned out to be so valuable to him that as CEO, he continued to make time on his calendar to run them. Not only did they hone the abilities of the rising leaders, but they helped Enrico become a better leader himself, let him get to know an important group of leaders a couple levels below him, produced some good business ideas, and generated revenue. Eventually, a total of 110 executives went through the program, and their projects delivered $2 billion in top-line growth for the company.

One story that Enrico tells is from an early Building the Business workshop. After the initial five-day session, the students had gone back to their business units to try to implement their projects. When they returned, he asked about how they had fared. One student responded that what he had learned was that, even if you were working on something really important, there was no way to make it happen unless you get it into the top five positions on the priority list.

When he said this, some of his colleagues chimed in, saying that they had the same experience. "My project isn't important enough to get to the top five," one of them said. "It's an important thing to do, but I can't get to the president."

Enrico was so far up in the company at that time that he rarely had this problem. His priorities, essentially, were the company's priorities. But he recognized that it was a serious issue and Pepsi was wasting the talents of lots of bright people and missing lots of opportunities to do smart things. So he began to explore the issue with them. When he asked one student why his project didn't get up on the priority list, the student replied, "Well, because there were other people working on this and this and this."

So, says Enrico, "I thought about it, and I said to him, 'Aren't these things connected? Isn't there a knee bone connected to the thigh bone kind of thing here?' He said, 'Well, yeah, there could be.' And I said, 'Well, why don't you guys band together?' "

Enrico says as they explored, they realized that many of the things that others were working on were, in fact, aspects of the same problem. "So, together we came up with this concept of 'bundling,' " he explains. "What you've got to do is bundle these things into a business proposition, which in fact will make money ... but you can't ... get the components by themselves over the hurdle. So, now part of what we do is we talk about bundling.

"I've decided," he says, "that bundling is one of the biggest ideas in leadership."[1]

■ ■ ■

In recent years, the concept of the learning organization has been a really hot item in management circles. Over the past decade, executives at thousands of companies have invested vast amounts of money trying to build organizations in which everyone is open to and continuously learning. It's a great idea, as far as it goes. Unfortunately, it doesn't go far enough. Learning is only half of the equation. The organizations that win in the future will be Teaching Organizations.

The difference here is not just a matter of playing with words. Teaching Organizations differ from learning organizations in a number of very significant ways. While both espouse the idea that in order for a company to succeed, its workers must continually acquire new information, new ideas and new skills, a Teaching Organization adds the critical expectation that everyone will be a teacher as well as a learner. When set in an organizational framework that approaches every activity as a teaching and learning opportunity, the result is a powerful self-sustaining cycle that keeps collecting, generating and spreading knowledge to players at all levels of the organization.

The Core DNA: A Virtuous Teaching Cycle

Teaching Organizations work because they set in motion and sustain what I call a "Virtuous Teaching Cycle." A virtuous cycle, or circle, operates the same way as a vicious cycle, or circle, except with the opposite results. Where a vicious circle is a negative spiral of events, a virtuous cycle is a positive one. In a virtuous cycle, each event triggers a repeat of the preceding causative events in a form that is better and more beneficial than before.

There is no one model and no paint-by-the-numbers formula for building a Teaching Organization. Each one will reflect the ideas, values and personalities of the people within them. Teaching Organizations can be large or small and can be created in any industry. Good non-profits are often Teaching Organizations. At the heart of each one, however, is the dynamic of the Virtuous Teaching Cycle at work.

At all levels of the organization this core process is replicated.

The Jack Welch story that opened this book and the Roger Enrico story that opened this chapter are examples of Virtuous Teaching Cycles at work. Welch and Enrico learned from those they were teaching and in turn developed a new Teachable Point of View (TPOV) that they then went on to teach others. This continuous learning and teaching chain is fundamental if an organization is to make the best use of available knowledge and generate new knowledge.

Another great Teaching Organization with strong Virtuous Teaching Cycles is the U.S. military's Special Operations Forces. The SOF,

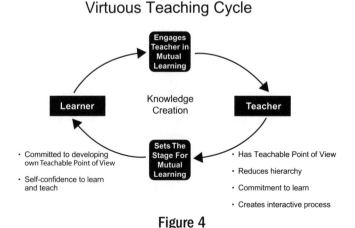

Virtuous Teaching Cycle

Figure 4

which includes the Army Rangers, the Nightstalkers, Green Berets, Navy SEALs and Air Force special operations squadrons, takes young enlistees and seasoned veterans and trains them to lead both combat and peacekeeping missions in hot spots around the world.

The military stereotype is that of the ultimate command-and-control organization, but for the SOF, that couldn't be further from the truth. The 57,000 SEALs, Rangers and other members of the SOF work in small autonomous groups around the world engaging in both humanitarian and military actions. Its members have to be leaders, able to think on their feet and make smart decisions, often without even contacting their superiors.

Because each one must be prepared to make life-or-death decisions in an instant or take actions that could have worldwide geopolitical implications, they are encouraged from their first day in the command to learn and share their knowledge. This applies up and down the chain of command.

General Wayne Downing (U.S. Army, Ret.), described a "typical" field visit while he was the head of SOF from 1991 to 1996.

> *I was visiting a Special Forces team working with the Kurds in the mountains of northern Iraq. They had been working in villages across the region for over four months when I got there. I was going to fill them in and tell them about the larger geopolitical picture. But after I had been talking for a while, they began to chip in with what they were seeing on the ground and talking about some geopolitical shifts that they could see locally. As a result, we put our two sets of knowledge together, problem solved about what they needed to be doing there, and I came away with a new set of assumptions about where the next hot spots in the region were likely to emerge.*

Downing left the unit better able to do its job, and he came away with a new world view to share with both other teams out in the field and senior colleagues from all branches of the government back in the United States. According to Downing, this kind of give and take happens all the time nearly everywhere the SOF is deployed. It is essential to maintaining the readiness and versatility of the Special Operations Forces, and updating our national policies.

In a Virtuous Teaching Cycle, each act or event of teaching improves the knowledge and abilities of both the students and the teachers and spurs them both to go on and share what they have learned with others. It creates a cascade of teaching and learning, where, eventually, everyone is always playing the dual roles of recipient and imparter of valuable knowledge. Virtuous Teaching Cycles work to make people smarter every day, align them around shared goals, and give them a sense of self-confidence as valued and contributing members of the community.

Teaching Organizations are faster, smarter and make better use of their assets than non-Teaching Organizations. This is in part because they have more and better leaders. They have more leaders because they make a conscious effort to teach people to be leaders. And they have better leaders because in order to teach, people must think through their ideas and develop the ability to communicate them, both of which hone their own leadership abilities.

Further, organizations that view everyday activities through the lens of teaching and learning are less likely to become complacent. Working in an environment where seeking new knowledge and insights is an expected norm makes people much more inclined to look for and recognize changes in the marketplace, and to accept the need to seek new responses to them.

Vicious Cycles Make People Dumber

At the other end of the spectrum are organizations that deplete their intellectual capital and actually become less smart, less aligned and less energized every day. These are organizations that are caught in vicious non-teaching cycles where there is little or no knowledge transfer, intelligence is assumed to reside at the top, and everyone below senior management is expected to check their brains at the door.

Not only do these organizations waste valuable information by not getting it to people who need it, but they alienate workers and destroy their self-confidence, so that they stop thinking that they have anything to offer and stop trying to be contributors. Workers in such organizations rarely understand the business plan and therefore are unable to make smart decisions in alignment with the goals of the company. Unfortunately, for a variety of reasons, most companies are closer to this end of the spectrum.

In newer hypergrowth companies, vicious non-teaching cycles tend to be the product of overwork and arrogance. There are so many demands and so many crises in start-ups that leaders often just jump from handling one potential disaster to the next. In the early days, an entrepreneur may not have anyone else to make decisions and handle problems even if he or she wanted to hand them off. Later, when the company is a bit larger, the crises come so quickly that, unless the founders have been able to build some organizational structures, it just seems faster for the senior inner circle to deal with them.

In order to hand them off, other people would have to be designated and then brought up to speed, not only on the problem, but on how a resolution would fit into the company's overall agenda. Thus, as more problems arise, the top leaders find themselves doing more and more of the front-line work and having less and less time to share information and create the knowledge base that would allow others to contribute.

The Perils of Arrogance

This already vicious cycle is often exacerbated by arrogance. Successful entrepreneurs generally are successful because they are able to see or do things that other people can't or haven't. In order to do this, they must have the self-confidence and determination to overcome odds that others have not. But, while self-confidence and determination are valuable assets, they become detriments in the absence of a healthy dose of humility.

People who think that they know it all are not only not interested in learning anything from anyone else, but they are unlikely to share power, authority or even information with their inferiors, i.e., anyone else. And, when people have no information and no opportunity to contribute, their talents are wasted.

■ ■ ■

Michael Saylor, CEO and founder of MicroStrategy, fit this profile.[2] He rode the Internet bubble to amass a personal net worth of $13.5 billion, but he had total disdain for anyone else's ideas. In an interview in early 2000, when the market for technology stocks was at its peak, I mentioned, in the context of asking something else, that there currently was a "bubble" in Internet stocks. He replied that "The only people who really think we're in the middle of a bubble are the people that don't get it, that don't really understand what's going on, the GE people," and, of course, me.

One week later MicroStrategy's auditors made it restate its earnings reports, and the SEC charged it for fraudulent revenue recognition practices. The settlement included a personal fine for Saylor of $10 million and indirectly led to his relinquishment of day-to-day authority in the company. A few weeks later, after MicroStrategy's stock had plummeted 62%, Saylor was still the know-it-all.

"The accounting rules are very technical, and in some cases, arbitrarily pedantic," he told a reporter. "I can't imagine a reasonable person would not agree with us [on our original accounting]. . . . If it was to be tried in a court of law with a bunch of educated citizens, we'd probably win. They'd probably say, 'You guys were too conservative the first time, and you should increase your revenues in 1999.' "

There were some later indications in the press that the loss of $23 billion in market value finally taught Saylor a few lessons, but as his comments indicate, at the time he was unable to listen even on the most superficial level. Learning from others was not a possibility, and that was what led to his downfall. He pushed his finance people over the edge, and his refusal to hear conflicting opinions made the company dumber and more vulnerable.

Bureaucracies Impede Learning

A different kind of vicious non-teaching cycle occurs in organizations, where control has traditionally been exercised through hierarchy and rules. In these, everyone's sphere of influence is rigidly limited, and the notion that "knowledge is power" prevails in its most sinister form. Everyone is competing with everyone else to grab and hang on to power, so no one wants to share knowledge because it is tantamount to giving away power. Further, in these rigidly top-down environments, seeming to disagree with the boss, or even to pass on something he or she might not want to hear, is considered disloyal and career-limiting. When the orders go out from the top, subordinates are expected to follow them, if not blindly, at least silently.

While such command-and-control structures are politically incorrect in today's world, the cultures they build continue to do damage. The difference now is that the boss proclaims that he or she wants things to be open, but the same old strong-arming, punishing and brow-beating continue, just in more subtle, passive-aggressive ways. People still end up compromising their ideas and values and sub-optimizing the organization. To this day in GM, there is a never-challenge-your-boss-in-public attitude, meetings are rehearsed so that there are no surprises, and people sacrifice their personal lives and their weekends preparing sanitized presentations to make the boss look good.

Even at Hewlett-Packard, a company known for its enlightened people practices and people development processes, the famous "HP Way" evolved into a leave-me-alone-to-do-my-thing culture. When bosses began to set up their own fiefs and protect people rather than hold them accountable, the collective IQ and alignment went in a downward spiral. This is one of the things that prompted the bringing in of a new CEO, Carly Fiorina, who may have arrived too late. It is the nature of bureaucracies, if unchecked, to turn people inward and focus them on power and careerism, rather than customers, competitors and the outside world.

The *Challenger* disaster in 1986 was an example of an information-withholding culture at its worst. The leadership at NASA did not want to learn about the O-ring problem because it would stop the launch and hurt their careers and reputations. So the engineer working for a subcontractor who did know about the problem was browbeaten, pressured until he eventually stopped pushing the issue. It was a vicious cycle of "non-learning" and "non-teaching of each other." The result was a lowering of the collective team IQ, a lack of alignment and negative emotional energy that led directly to the disastrous crash of the space shuttle.[3]

Building Blocks of a Teaching Organization

Because they reflect the personalities of the people within them, and because they are continuously adapting to changes in the environment and adopting new ideas, Teaching Organizations are continuously changing. There are, however, certain characteristics that good ones all share.

I. The Teaching Organization Mind-set

Building a Teaching Organization starts with a mind-set that teaching is a valuable core activity. This is a mind-set that is firmly held by top leaders who make teaching an explicit goal within the company and development of people a top priority for everyone.

There are several related beliefs that come together to create this mind-set. One is that companies that actively promote the sharing of

Traits of Virtuous Cycles vs. Vicious Cycles

Obviously no one organization is a normative case of a perfect VTC and there are probably no pure vicious non-teaching organizations. There are, however, a number of contrasting dimensions.

VIRTUOUS TEACHING CYCLE	VICIOUS NON-TEACHING CYCLE
Leadership at all levels	Leadership top down
Teach and interact	Command and control
Open communication	Defensive communication
Teamwork	Passive-aggressive behavior
Grows self-confidence	Reduces self-confidence
TPOVs at all levels	Rigid top down TPOV
Collective knowledge at all levels	All intelligence assumed to be at the top
Everyone's brain counts	Brains of the masses checked at the door when work starts
Organizational knowledge grows	Organizational knowledge is depleted
Positive emotional energy grows	Emotional energy sucked out of the organization
Boundaryless	Boundary-ful and turf oriented
Mutual respect	Fear of boss
Diversity valued	Homogeneity of thought

knowledge and experience gain a competitive advantage by helping everyone in the company work smarter and faster. A second is that teaching is the most effective means through which a leader can lead. A third is that teaching develops leaders, and the more good leaders a company has, the better it will succeed. And a fourth is that the job of a leader is to increase the value of an organization's assets, and the way to increase the value of human assets is by teaching them to be smarter, more productive and better leaders.

As a result of this mind-set, Teaching Organizations have not only a culture that values teaching but strong infrastructures to facilitate teaching throughout the organization. In addition, the day-to-day operations of the company are designed to promote teaching. Organizational structures assume a teaching environment. Processes are set up to function not through chains of commands, but through the exchange of ideas, skills and information. Everyone in the organization is expected to be constantly in a teaching and learning mode. Performance evaluations and rewards reflect the expectation that each person will teach what he or she knows to others, and teaching skills are explicitly taught.

The passion and commitment of the CEO is an absolutely essential requirement. Someone else may plant the idea, but the CEO and the top leadership team must completely buy in and act on it. That's because true learning takes place only when the leader/teacher invests the time and emotional energy to engage those around him or her in a dialogue that produces mutual understanding. Autocrats can command behaviors by issuing orders. But developing an organization of genuine leaders who will continue to teach others requires a serious commitment to teaching.

If you look at the leaders who have had the best success building Teaching Organizations, you will see that they are all dedicated teachers themselves. They all take on classroom or seminar teaching assignments. Jack Welch met classes at GE's Crotonville leadership development institute at least twice a month for the whole time he was chairman. Andy Grove taught new hires at Intel. They seek out informal opportunities to interact with employees. That's why John Chambers roams the halls at Cisco and holds monthly birthday breakfasts. They give him a chance to personally explain his Teachable Points of View to Cisco workers. And, like David Novak at Yum! Brands they turn budget reviews, strategy meetings and sales conferences into coaching sessions.

For these leader/teachers, sharing knowledge and helping others is their way of operating. It is a leadership style that usually has helped their rise to the top. Or if it hasn't, it is one that they have adopted and found to be effective since they arrived.

II. The Leader Learning Mind-Set

Great teachers are also great learners. People who value knowledge enough to put the time and effort into communicating it well to others also value it enough to want to keep acquiring it for themselves. They are as avid about learning as they are about teaching,

Success Factors

The figure below is one that I use to show the importance of leaders teaching. It provides the basis for long-term organizational success because it ensures that a company will have a supply of leaders who have developed their points of view and are ready to act on them. By setting up a Virtuous Teaching Cycle, this model keeps improving the talents and skills of everyone and renews the company by bringing in fresh ideas. There are four critical factors to consider.

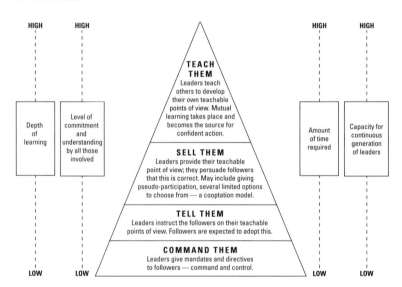

1. Depth of Learning

The depth of learning that occurs both for the leader and the follower varies significantly depending on the leader's approach. At the most superficial level, a command-and-control leader does not create much learning for himself or herself or the follower. At the other end of the spectrum, both the leaders and the students learn from each other.

The exchange of information and learning is critical to creating a Virtuous Teaching Cycle. It is an interactive circle—it is not a one-way street. So, it is particularly important that senior leaders set the example as listeners and learners.

You could see Jack Welch doing this at every meeting he attended as CEO of GE. You can be sure that he came in to the meetings with some pretty definite ideas, but he constantly tested them out on the other people in the room, and he revised and refined them based on what he learned. One of the concepts that Roger Enrico developed and taught in his Building the Business leader program was taking an idea "off Broadway," to get responses from other people before implementing.

2. Commitment

Commitment is another critical factor. Teaching entails a serious commitment on the part of the leader to nurture individuals and a serious commitment on the part of followers to wrestle with the teacher's point of view and develop their own.

3. Time

It takes little time to command and much time to teach.

4. Continuous Generation of Leaders

When there is genuine teaching, a positive cycle is created. Learners have developed their own points of view and are energized to help others as they have been helped. They consequently make good teachers. By contrast, the command model launches cycles that range from blind obedience to open revolt.

---

which leads them to see everyone they meet as a potential teacher and every situation they experience as a learning opportunity.

This is not a trivial issue. Many executives close off learning. In their day-to-day interactions with staff they are usually either issuing instructions or making judgments about the ideas or performance of others. Think about the typical budget meeting in which the subordinate comes to the boss with a plan he or she has carefully developed, complete with a thick binder of backup data and a glossy PowerPoint presentation. The presenter is personally invested in the plan and prepared to defend it, while the boss's job is to be the evaluator and critic. It is an inherently adversarial encounter where there is little chance that there will be any pooling of brainpower, generation of knowledge or positive emotional energy.

Even executives who participate as teachers in formal development programs are often little more than lecturers. They come in and do a show-and-tell and answer a few questions of the crowd, but they are not in a learning mind-set. Worse yet, many find little or no time to even participate in the sessions. Contrast this with Roger Enrico who literally moves in and lives with a small group for five days, teaching and talking about leadership and the business. By the end of the five days. Enrico himself is a lot smarter, having learned, if nothing else, about his people, their organizations and the quality of ideas for growing the business.

Michael Dell is a world-class leader/teacher who says that his basic approach to the world is "to get to the guts of why things happen."[4] This is why Dell teaches all of its employees about economics and finance and encourages them to ask questions.

"Asking lots of questions opens new doors to new ideas, which ultimately contributes to your competitive edge," he says. When Dell employees understand the cost structure of Dell, its suppliers and its customers, they can find the relevant information, make decisions and enter into relationships that keep all of them healthy.

Dell is also a big believer in learning from everyone in the company. It does this systematically by polling people around the company. "We also learn a lot by asking the same question in similar groups across the company and comparing the results. We do this to share the best ideas throughout our various businesses because we're all working on the same team, toward the same goal. If one team is having great success with medium-sized companies, we cross-pollinate their ideas about the world. If another team has figured out how to sell into law firms, we share their learning throughout the organization. Our best ideas can come from anywhere in the world and be shared instantly. They help us develop the broad-reaching mind-set required of a global company. We exchange ideas through e-mail and the Web and through councils where we bring different groups from around the world together to exchange information."

Dell also encourages idea-sharing on a more informal basis. "Information in its raw form doesn't present itself in neat and tidy packages. That's why you must encourage the free-flow of information at all levels. . . . If an engineer in one of our product groups has an opinion about something, and it just so happens that customer input confirms his suspicion, I want to know. Random bits of information from sources both inside and outside the company won't always lead you to the answer, but they will assist you in focusing in on an emerging problem or opportunity or new idea," he says.

The teaching and learning mind-sets are reflected and reinforced in a variety of other ways in Teaching Organizations.

• **Time for learning, reflection and teaching.** This is a tough one for many CEOs. The demands of the job, especially in a fast-moving 24/7 world, often combine with a just-do-it personality to put many executives into a constant attention deficit mode. The fragmented time often crowds out the quality time needed for thinking and modifying and improving one's Teachable Point of View. Leader/teachers, such as Welch, regularly put aside big blocks of time for writing, thinking and working alone.

• **An informal environment.** Informality is a prerequisite if teaching and learning are to flow in all directions. If people who have "rank" are aloof or dismissive, they will miss the opportunity to learn from others because few people will risk opening up to them. The higher people are in an organization, the more they must be approachable. Leader/teachers invite substantive exchanges and make clear that they want to know what people really are thinking. They encourage openness by listening and taking other people's ideas seriously, while dismissing comments that ring of saying-what-you-think-the-boss-wants-to-hear.

Hierarchy and bureaucratic barriers between the learners and the teachers can also keep issues from being raised. Jack Welch often cites GE's informality as one of its core strengths. It "breeds an endless search for ideas that stand or fall on their merits, rather than on the rank of their originator . . . [it is] a culture that brings every mind into the game." Without informality, he says, people would not have had the nerve to tell him things he needed to know. He cites in particular, the "punch in the nose" that the middle managers at Crotonville delivered in telling him that people were playing games to meet his No. 1 or No. 2 goal. The No. 1 or No. 2 message had been a key theme of Welch's leadership, but as soon as they pointed out the weakness, he revised it.

• **Use of authority to promote flow of knowledge.** Although they encourage informality, leader/teachers abdicate neither their responsibility nor their authority. Teaching Organizations use teaching and learning as the means for coordinating and controlling their activities, and the leaders who build them do avoid flamboyant displays of power. But they do not take any tools out of their toolbox, and they can be quite creative in using their authority to promote teaching and learning.

Jack Welch did this when he ordered the top 1,000 managers at GE to get mentors and learn e-business. In his letter to shareholders in the 1999 annual report, Welch described the process—which, despite the polite word "asked," was not optional:

> We took the top 1,000 managers in the Company and asked them to become "mentees" of 1,000 "with it," very bright e-Business mentors—many brand new to GE—and to work with them three to four hours a week, traveling the Web, evaluating competitor sites, and learning to organize their computers, and their minds, for work on the Internet. It was this mentor-mentee interaction—which in some cases resembled that of "Stuart" and his boss in the Ameritrade commercial—that helped overcome the only real hurdle some of us had—fear of the unknown.

This is a great example not only of the use of authority to open up new channels of learning, but also of an interactive Virtuous Teaching Cycle at work. Jack Welch's young mentor was clearly nowhere near his level in the company, but she was his teacher. She knew a lot more than he did about navigating and using the Web, so she was able to have a huge impact on his learning and hence the company's success with e-business. But, while she was the official "teacher" in this case, you can be sure that she learned a lot hanging out with Welch for several hours a week. The same was true with most of the other mentor-mentee pairs. In the give and take of the sessions, both parties were teaching and learning.

• **Nurturing a healthy self-confidence.** Self-confidence is like the use of authority in that a certain amount of it is essential, and too much of it is fatal. Self-confidence is absolutely critical to learning. People who don't have self-confidence may hide it in different ways. Some may cling to the past because they are frightened by change or don't trust themselves to sort through and judge new options. Others brash it out and imitate the people who have too much self-confidence by refusing to admit that there might be something that they don't already know. Senior executives tend to follow this model. Bureaucracies tend to encourage the cling-to-the-status-quo model not only in the bureaucrats, but also for everyone in the organization.

Each of these models is inimical to both learning and teaching. People need self-confidence to open up their minds to new knowledge, and they need it in order to appreciate that they have knowledge worth teaching to others.

Informing and underpinning all of this is a burning desire to, as Michael Dell puts it, "get to the guts of why things happen," or as Jack Welch says, "seeing the world the way it is, not the way we hope it will be or wish it to be." Winning companies are winners because they are attuned to constant changes in the marketplace, in technology and in society. The leader who really wants to know what is going on and wants the people in his or her organization to know what is going on builds a Teaching Organization.

III. Building Teaching into Everyday Operations

The mind-set that teaching and learning were primary competitive competencies guided Jack Welch as he set out to redesign and rebuild GE in 1983. In the old GE, rule-making and conformity were guiding principles. All of its managerial systems and its corporate values were designed to deliver adherence to a rigid code of rules. In the new GE, teaching and learning are the organizing rules. Its systems, processes, operating mechanisms and cultural values all revolve around the sharing of information, knowledge and experience.

Eliminating bloated bureaucracies and tearing down walls that impede the flow of information actually creates competitive advantages beyond the simple transference of skills and knowledge. The digital, global economy punishes slow, inward-looking, dumb-acting organizations. Companies must be not only fast but also smart about figuring out what customers want and then getting it to them. In traditional companies, the bureaucracies and the walls tend to foster what Ram Charan and I call an "inside-out" mentality. Pleasing the bureaucrats and doing the things that will make your particular business unit look best become overriding considerations.[5]

The internal politics eat up energy, while the walls keep people from looking beyond the interests of their own small group. Instead of asking: What do the customers want and how do we get it to them?, they ask: What can we make profitably and how do we get people to buy it? This inside-out orientation is what provides opportunities for the start-ups.

By definition, the start-up organization looks from the outside-in. Entrepreneurs really are outsiders who are trying to get in, so that is the perspective that they naturally bring. Further, they don't have elaborate organizations that eat up time and attention, and they don't have the walls that keep them from looking beyond their own little piece of territory.

The problem is that in the past, as companies have become successful and have grown, the precepts of good management practice—the ones epitomized by the pre-Welch General Electric—have encouraged them to build the bureaucracies and walls. The structures created to manage a sizeable organization were corsets that restricted action. In a Teaching Organization, there still are structures, but they are skeletons designed to support growth and protect the guts of the company without confining it.

In addition to having an organizational design that doesn't divert attention or limit sightlines, Teaching Organizations also actively encourage exploration and inquisitiveness. Interchanges at all levels in Teaching Organizations are routinely approached as learning opportunities. Meetings are not simply presentations of facts and conclusions made by one side for the purpose of selling predetermined courses of action to the other side. Rather, they are occasions for the participants to contribute their knowledge and experience to help reach the best possible solution.

At GE, teaching is firmly embedded in almost all of the operating mechanisms through which the company is managed. The strategy process, the operational planning process and the succession planning process all have coaching, teaching and learning elements built into them. It started with Welch making sure that all sessions are informal, around his conference table, with five to eight people wrestling with a problem, jumping up to the flipchart to sketch an idea, debating, tossing out ideas, and with Welch—and now Immelt—always looking for real-time coaching opportunities.

At Yum! Brands, David Novak had teaching as well as customer satisfaction in mind when he decided to give front-line servers in Taco Bell, KFC and Pizza Hut restaurants discretion up to $25 to respond on the spot to customer complaints. This delegation of authority serves the primary purpose of winning customers. At the same time, however, it gives responsibility and decision-making authority to people in jobs where rote adherence to rules has been the norm. In the process, they not only gain self-confidence, but they learn about customers, about managing problem situations and what it takes to please customers and avoid problems in the future.

The individual amount of money may not be much, but it gives these bottom-tier employees, who are already the primary contact points for customers, the opportunity to take a leadership role. Further, the reporting and reviewing of the expenditures create opportunities for the managers to discuss the business and coach workers.

This environment in Teaching Organizations, which says that engaged exploration is better than the selling of canned ideas, encourages people not to limit their horizons to the boundaries of the company. Thus, they are far more likely than people in traditional companies to listen to customers, to watch competitors, to ask for the opinions of suppliers, to steal good ideas from other industries. As Jack Welch exulted in the shareholder speech cited above: "We purged NIH—not invented here—from our system . . . a company that isn't searching for the best idea isn't open to ideas from anywhere, will find itself left behind with its survival at stake."

IV. The Teaching Organization Infrastructure

Even with a strong culture and operating processes that promote the sharing of knowledge, a company cannot maintain a Virtuous Teaching Cycle without a well-developed teaching infrastructure. In addition to making a public statement about the importance of teaching, infrastructure is needed to meet the challenges of speed, leverage and scale.

In order to have a Teaching Organization that delivers impact, information must flow quickly and accurately. Leaders need to receive information from the field and communicate corporate initiatives and strategy changes fast enough so that the responses and actions will be effective in a rapidly changing world. They also need the ability to reach deep into the organization and deliver messages so that everyone hears the same thing without the dilution and distortion that comes from relying on layers of hierarchy or the rumor mill.

Once an organization gets over a couple of thousand people, the Friday beer parties and the all-hands meetings with the leader and the bullhorn in the cafeteria can't do the job. One of the reasons that Scott McNealy of Sun MicroSystems says he wanted to get to know Jack Welch was that "Jack has seen a movie I haven't seen. All of a sudden we're at 37,000 employees, we're growing at 20%+ growth rates . . . the kinds of things that Jack has done, I'm beginning to have to deal with. It's a vast organization. You can't just call everyone into the lunchroom and stand on a chair and tell them, 'Here's plan B.' That's what I used to do. It's a very, very different process. Jack has developed a learning organization that can spin on a dime, because he's got these black-belt, Green Beret–type folks infiltrated throughout the organization. So when the word comes down that this is the new initiative, away they go."[6]

Further, as an organization gets larger, it needs to become more systematic about making sure that everyone in the company gets the appropriate teaching and learning opportunities and that no one is inadvertently overlooked. This requires the development of a variety of teaching capabilities and a human resources department that sees its job as facilitating teaching—as opposed to just enforcing policies and administering benefits.

Trilogy Software has a world-class new-hire program in its Trilogy University. It also has a very effective virtual teaching venue called Leadership.com. In addition, founder Joe Liemandt tries to put people in job assignments where they grow for the future as well as add value today. "What we still need, and will need even more as we go through future cycles of growth and contraction," he says, "is a system and a systematic way to make sure that all of our people are groomed to be as valuable as possible to Trilogy in all environments and under all economic circumstances." Maintaining this level of preparedness requires development of a variety of teaching capabilities, ranging from the virtual, such as Leadership.com, to brick-and-mortar corporate campuses, to seminars run out of hotel conference rooms around the world.

Leverage is the other key issue. For example, how does Jim McNerney at 3M leverage his TPOV to 100,000 people, or how does David Novak at Yum! Brands get to influence the ideas and values and emotional energy of 750,000 people? New technologies that allow the creation of Websites that are available 24/7 with streaming videos and interactive mechanisms for collecting and disseminating information help. But careful thought must also go into designing a teaching infrastructure at all levels of the organization, from entry level "boot camps" to total company teaching cascades, to driving initiatives like Six Sigma quality programs, to the creation of leadership development programs for different career stages.

GE has the most infrastructure and the largest scale Teaching Organization in the world. In the mid-1980s, even as the company was cutting thousands of jobs, Jack Welch spent $50 million on new facilities at its Crotonville leadership development center. He did this in part because he wanted to make a clear statement that teaching and people development was important at GE. He also needed the leverage that the Crotonville programs provided in implementing the changes he wanted to make in GE's business and culture. More than

8,000 leaders a year go through programs at its fifty-acre campus, ranging from new managers training up through a senior executive development course.

I had the opportunity to run Crotonville in the mid-1980s and help transform it into a "staging ground for revolution." To make it much more focused as an instrument of change, we jettisoned traditional programs in favor of action learning. We scrapped the Harvard teaching cases and engaged rising leaders in solving real problems that GE faced. We began to send teams out into the field to solve both operational and strategic issues that were hampering the company, and we asked them to bring to class problems from their own workplaces.

In tandem with the Crotonville offerings, GE also has company-wide teaching programs that run in offices, training facilities and off-site locations around the world. Work-Out, which was first instituted in 1988, was designed to bring the spirit of Crotonville to everyone at GE. Today, it is one of the primary developmental mechanisms deeply embedded in the GE culture.

Work-Out started as a series of fairly free-form workshops. Leaders throughout the company were required to hold "town hall" meetings so that the people working for them could speak up and identify the situations, processes and procedures that were slowing them down and hassling them. The rules were that the bosses then had to respond and make changes happen. The idea was that the employees knew best where the problems were, so giving them a voice would help GE run more effectively.

I ran my first workshop session at GE Medical Systems in the latter part of 1988, where John Trani had us work with one hundred middle managers to try to improve the organization. By 1989, Welch had mandated Work-Out for the whole company. Every business had a small consulting team helping facilitate it and literally thousands of meetings have taken place since that time. In the fall of 1999, as part of his pre-retirement housecleaning, Welch mandated a new ninety-day round of Work-Out. He said the purpose of it was to fight the reemergence of bureaucracy. It's about "throwing out the crap that keeps creeping in—tons of meetings, getting rid of reports that aren't needed, getting rid of crap."

GE has a Crotonville program to develop the senior leaders as teachers, called the Change Acceleration Program. This program was developed in the late 1980s and continues to be used to make sure that the leaders are equipped to run and teach their own change programs.

The biggest part of GE's teaching infrastructure today is Six Sigma training. GE spends more than $500 million a year teaching everyone in the company the tools to attain Six Sigma quality (3.4 defects per million). It is a monster teaching machine, with more than 10,000 GE leaders serving two-year stints as full-time "black belt" Six Sigma teachers. They teach and lead projects to improve quality. GE is teaching all 300,000+ of its employees Six Sigma methodology, and everyone is assigned to a Six Sigma project to improve quality.

Cisco is another company that has a large-scale teaching infrastructure. And, as might be expected, much of it is Web-based, including its innovative You Have a Friend @ Cisco program that pairs job seekers with Cisco employees. The recruits provide Cisco employees with valuable information about trends and events outside of the company, while the recruits get to hear what Cisco is like from front-line, non-HR staffers.

As we discuss in Chapter 10, the use of interactive technology will increasingly be a competitive factor as the companies that Web-base their management systems become smarter and faster than their competitors.

Web-based programs are particularly conducive to teaching and learning because of their 24/7 availability and their ability to allow transparency and interactive connections among thousands of people. Streaming videos allow leaders to reach deeply into the organization and present the same information in the same words to people at all levels. And their easy and open feedback mechanisms spur dialogue and the sharing of information among people who might otherwise never come in contact. The Cisco in-house programs also serve as beta tests for the thousands of programs it offers to non-employees to teach them the skills they need to use and service Cisco systems.

Virtuous Cycles Keep Generating Knowledge

The creation of a Virtuous Teaching Cycle is the key to building a Teaching Organization. A Teaching Organization is one in which everyone is a teacher, everyone is a learner, and as a result, everyone gets smarter every day. Teaching Organizations are better than non-

Teaching Organizations at figuring out what customers want and how to get it to them quickly and economically. This is because the collection and dissemination of information and the sharing of the insights and experiences that turn raw data into valuable knowledge are routine activities. In addition to a strong teaching infrastructure, teaching and learning are built into the culture and into the everyday processes through which the organization conducts business.

A Virtuous Teaching Cycle is what keeps the teaching and learning continuously happening. It requires not only the mind-set throughout the organization that teaching and learning are valuable core activities, but also an interactive style of teaching that engages both the teacher and the student to contribute knowledge and learn from each other. It is this interactive teaching, in which teaching and learning flow both ways, that is the hallmark of Teaching Organizations.

Leaders who lecture or engage students only through Socratic baiting are not interactive teachers. They may be imparting information, but they are not interactive teachers because while their mouths may be open, their minds are shut.

Interactive teaching occurs when the teacher respects the students and has a mind-set that they probably know things that he or she doesn't, and when the students have the mind-set that they have something to say and that the teacher would be interested in hearing it. These are developed and maintained in an open, informal environment where people have confidence in the knowledge and abilities of others, as well as self-confidence.

To break the code and build a teaching machine, leaders must understand, embrace and enact the Virtuous Teaching Cycle. Building such cycles at all levels of the organization is a way to keep regenerating people and generating knowledge. It is the key to a smarter, aligned and hence faster value-creating organization.

The Art of Leadership: Good and Bad Teachers

During the first twenty years of our lives, most of us are exposed to upwards of one hundred teachers. The average high school graduate has had about seventy classroom instructors. By the end of college, that number has risen by another thirty or forty, not to mention the coaches, private instructors, camp counselors, scout leaders, grandparents and older siblings who offer guidance and instruction to help us develop into healthy, mature adults.

The point is we all have very large databases of teachers. And when I ask people to assess these databases and describe the qualities of good and bad teachers, the results are incredibly consistent.

• Bad teachers are not well prepared with a Teachable Point of View or they have a rigid point of view that they refuse to modify.
They lack a clear set of values.
They do not energize themselves or others.
They have very little capacity for interactivity with their students.
They have low self-confidence, which they often manifest by becoming autocrats.

(My personal worst-case example was an English teacher who was a drunk ex-boxer who hated teaching. All I recall of his classes was that either he was diagramming sentences on the board, or we were doing exercises at our desks while he slipped out of the room to nip at his flask. He wasn't engaged. We weren't engaged. There was no energy and little learning.)

• Good teachers are just the opposite.
My best was Charles Kadushin, a sociology professor at Columbia University in my Ph.D. program. He was a world-class researcher and a well-published academic who always made both of us smarter as a result of our teaching interactions.

Kadushin gave me my greatest epiphany as a learner and prepared me to be a teacher. He did this by role modeling the essence of the VTC. He came to me in my second year as a Ph.D. student and asked for my input. In 1968, he was studying communist elite in Yugoslavia and was using social network analytic techniques to map the power and affinity relationships among the elite, to understand how decision making took place.

He had his TPOV on how to analyze social network data among the communist elites. He taught it to me, but said there was a hole in the sociological and political science literature when it came to understanding how cliques formed and operated. He knew I was studying micro-organizations and was interested in the informal systems in organizations. He wanted me to teach him everything in the organizational literature that might help him with his work. I said I would take a look.

A couple of weeks later I went back to him and said I was sorry that there really wasn't much in the literature. He thanked me and then gave me my lesson. He suggested that since there wasn't much literature, why didn't I create a theory and take a lead in the field. That way I could help him and help my field by developing a theory and publishing it. I did that. I developed my own TPOV and turned this first into a qualifying paper for my Ph.D. and then a refereed article for the most prestigious academic journal in my field, *The Administrative Science Quarterly*.[7]

I have never forgotten this experience and have tried to role model it with all of my Ph.D. students. I try to get them to develop their own frameworks. I teach them what I know, and then I ask them to teach me.

■ ■ ■

Kadushin had a Virtuous Teaching Cycle because:
He had a TPOV.
He was self-confident enough to say what he did not know.
He reinforced my self-confidence.
He gave honest tough-love feedback—he had me rewrite the
      article at least twenty times.
He changed his own TPOV in the process.
I, as a learner, became a teacher as well.
I developed self-confidence.
I developed a TPOV in the area or "field."

Chapter Four
You Must Start with a Teachable Point of View

■ A Teachable Point of View: Making Your Knowledge Available to Others
- Step 1: Sorting through ideas and beliefs to figure out what you know.
- Step 2: Developing ways to communicate it clearly to others.

■ The Elements: Ideas and Values
- The ideas are about a plan for success.
- The values are ones that support achieving success.

■ The Elements: Emotional Energy and Edge
- Leaders must generate excitement about the ideas and values.
- Making tough decisions and teaching others to do so, too, is essential.

"Whether you are hiring someone in an entry-level position or to run one of your largest groups, that person must be completely in sync with the company's business philosophy and objectives."[1]
Michael Dell, founder and CEO of Dell Computer

I often challenge executives with the following situation: You've just been hired to coach a high school tennis team. Fifty kids have shown up to learn tennis. You are standing out there on the court. Now what do you do?

You are an excellent tennis player. You went through college on a tennis scholarship. You have even played in the U.S. Open. But can you teach these high schoolers? Can you take the knowledge that you have inside your head and your muscles and convey it to them in a form that they can use? Do you have a Teachable Point of View?

A tennis coach has to have ideas about how to teach the serve, the backhand, the forehand and all the elements of the game of tennis and the intellectual framework. A good coach also has a set of values about the behaviors he or she expects of the team. Often, these are simple things like showing up on time, dressed a certain way, with a certain set of ethics on the tennis court.

A coach also needs a Teachable Point of View regarding emotional energy. It is not sufficient just to have the ideas and values. You have to have ways of positively energizing the players, getting them committed to the ideas and values.

Finally, a good coach has to have edge, the courage to make yes/no decisions. He or she has to decide: You are playing or not playing. You are on the team or off the team. The decision may be based on abilities, but often it's based on values. A coach does not call consultants and set up committees to make the edge decisions. The same should be true for business leaders. They must have all the elements to lead a business: ideas, values, emotional energy and edge.

A Teachable Point of View is a cohesive set of ideas and concepts that a person is able to articulate clearly to others. The difference between an excellent solo player and a world-class leader is the ability to teach others. Roger Enrico, the former CEO of PepsiCo, built a stunningly successful career by repeatedly proving his talents as a daring marketer and savvy strategist. He clearly had a point of view about how to build and run successful businesses. But it wasn't until he figured out how to articulate his instinctive knowledge so that he could teach it to others that he became a true leader.

The essence of leading is not commanding, but teaching. It is opening people's eyes and minds. It is teaching them new ways to see the world and pointing them to new goals. It is giving them the motivation and discipline to achieve those goals. And it is teaching them to share their own knowledge and teach others.

Having a Teachable Point of View is absolutely critical to creating a

Virtuous Teaching Cycle. A leader must not only have implicit knowledge, but must be able to make it explicit so that others can understand, interact and build on it. Experience isn't enough; a point of view isn't enough. A leader must have a Teachable Point of View.

Leaders must be able to share their experience. And in order to do that, they must externalize the tacit knowledge within them. They must draw lessons from their experiences, and then convey those lessons in a form so that others can use it. Having a Teachable Point of View is both a sign that a person has clear ideas and values, and a tool that enables him or her to communicate those ideas and values to others. It is also a vehicle for improving leaders' self-awareness and the starting point for revisions and improvements.

The Elements of a TPOV

Leaders must have a Teachable Point of View around four basic building blocks. These enable the leader to create dynamic and engaging stories that detail where their company is, where it is going, and how they will get there.

Ideas

Great companies are built on central ideas. By passing ideas to others and teaching others how to develop good ideas, leaders create organizations that are finely tuned toward delivering success. The ideas provide the answer to: Where are we going? What are we aiming to accomplish?

Values

Winning leaders articulate values explicitly and shape values that support business ideas. For example, GE's Jack Welch articulated the value of "boundarylessness" in order to facilitate speed-to-market, the generation and sharing of ideas across a vast complex company, and the sharing of best practices. The values element guides the organization in the kinds of behavior required to be a member of the organization.

Emotional Energy

Winning leaders have a clear set of beliefs and actions for motivating others to buy into and internalize the values of the organization. Winning leaders are also motivated and they motivate others about change and transitions. Leaders energize others when they personally interact with them.

Edge

Great leadership is about making tough yes/no decisions. Winning leaders face reality, and they make decisions about people, products, businesses, customers and suppliers.

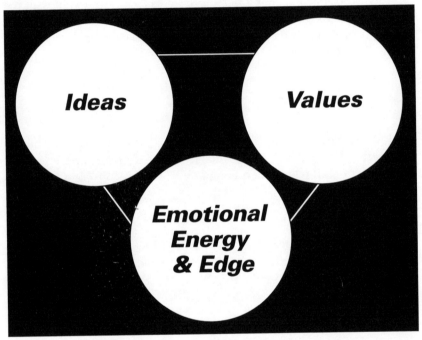

Figure 5

Ideas: The Organizing Principle

The primary ideas that a business leader needs to develop and teach throughout the company are about how it is going to make money and win in the marketplace. A leader's central idea or business theory lays out his or her concept for organizational success in terms of products, services, distribution channels, customer segments and the like. It states a set of assumptions and beliefs the leader holds about what will make the company profitable.

Success Reflects Clear Business Ideas

• A century ago, Theodore Vail organized American Telephone & Telegraph Company around the idea of "universal service." The goal of the company would be to provide every home in the United States with basic, standard telephone service. For nearly a hundred years, this idea drove all of AT&T's behavior and decisions about running a regulated monopoly, about technology development, and about organizational structure.

• Barney Kilgore, the editor responsible for building *The Wall Street Journal* into America's first national newspaper, had the idea that business people in Portland, Oregon, needed the same news as business people in Portland, Maine. The *Journal* would sell advertising in regional editions across the country, but would deliver the same editorial content throughout.

• Sam Walton built Wal-Mart around the idea of bringing big company economies and efficiencies of scale to small-town markets.

• Michael Dell's idea was to sell custom computers directly to customers. Dell Computer would make money by eliminating the middlemen and the inventories in the selling chain.

• Bill Gates launched Microsoft with one central idea: PCs were taking off, so he wanted to "own the operating system."

• Tom Monahan's idea in founding Domino's Pizza was to deliver a hot pizza to your house or office in thirty minutes or less. The thirty-minute goal has been relaxed because of car accidents, but the central focus of all Domino's operations remains speedy delivery of fresh, hot pizza.

The Home Depot's Central Idea

• Low prices/High volume
• Volume derived from:
   • Low prices
   • Big inventories and wide variety
   • World-class customer service

The idea that guided Bernie Marcus and Arthur Blank in building The Home Depot was low-price, high-volume.[2] In 1978 the hardware industry was a chummy little fraternity of independent stores and regional chains. They carried a similar selection of the top two or three brands of each item. They bought from distributors and tacked on a more-or-less standard markup. As a result, the prices and selection at all the hardware stores in a town were pretty much the same, and loyalty tended to be geographic. There wasn't much reason to shop around, so people bought from the neighborhood store.

The idea that Marcus and Blank came up with was to revolutionize the business. They would cut prices by eliminating the middlemen in purchasing and by reducing their profit margin to about 30% from the industry norm of more than 40%. Then they would make up for the lower margins by generating huge volume. The lower prices would be just one of the attractions for customers. A second would be that Home Depot stores would be huge warehouses stocked not only with much larger inventories than their competitors, but also with a wider array of goods.

The third piece of the strategy for generating volume was a unique brand of customer service. Before Home Depot came along, people hired contractors to do most home improvements. In part, this was because the individual homeowner didn't have access to all the necessary materials, but mostly it was because there was very little support or encouragement for do-it-yourselfers. Most nonprofessionals were unsure of their abilities and uncomfortable taking on big projects. So, in addition to offering a wide range of materials at low prices, Home Depot would expand the market by giving more people the skills and self-confidence to take on home improvement projects.

Home Depot would hire sales associates who were professionals or had professional-level skills and build a culture of partnering with customers. Home Depot would say to its customers, "You aren't alone. We will help you." At Home Depot, sales associates would work with customers in planning their projects and then tell or show them how to do what they needed to do. They would run clinics on how to install a toilet or build a deck. They would advise customers on what to buy, and how much to buy, and the store would take back anything they didn't need. They would also suggest simpler or lower-cost alternatives to what the customer had come into the store planning to do. For example, if a customer came in to buy a water heater, the first thing a Home Depot sales associate would do would be to see if there were a way to fix the old one.

Winning organizations are always firmly grounded in clearly stated ideas. The ability of their leaders to develop and articulate those ideas is the foundation for their success. Winning in any business depends on getting a team of people pulling together to reach a common goal. It also depends on the ability to improve on and change those ideas in response to new market conditions or new information.

In order for this to happen, everyone in the organization has to know and understand what the ideas are. By defining the game and setting the rules, leaders provide every member with an intellectual framework and an internal yardstick for measuring the validity of the ideas and the appropriateness of his or her actions. Understanding the ideas allows each individual to act independently and to take actions that will move them together toward success. This understanding also allows them to be partners in the interactive teaching and learning that keeps the whole organization getting smarter and more productive every day.

Values: Behaviors Need to Support the Ideas

Just as winning leaders use ideas and strategies to move their companies ahead, they also know that having the right values can make a critical difference. So they pay just as much attention to developing and clearly articulating their Teachable Point of View on values as they do on ideas.

When people talk about values, they often have in mind a set of moral principles with broad social meaning. Some of these are the big immutable values like honesty and integrity. While people may argue over what constitutes honesty or integrity or about who has them, there's not much argument about the need for them. These foundational values are the basis for all societal interaction.

Others value sets, such as the highly politicized "family values" and the self-assertive "libertarian values" are very subjective, and often the basis for divisive debate. Winning leaders always embrace and embody the first kind of value and, unless they are leading a cause-related organization, rarely take public stands on the second kind of values.

There is a third kind of values, however, and good leaders are both closely attentive and highly vocal about them. These are what I call "operational values." They are the ones that relate directly to an organization's business or its marketplace. They support the fulfillment of the central business idea. And, far from being immutable, these values can, and in most cases should, change whenever the business model changes.

AT&T

The old AT&T, for example, was a regulated monopoly, so its growth and profitability didn't depend on speed or low cost. Rather, its keys to success were providing reliable service and satisfying the regulators. In this environment, it isn't surprising that predictability and not taking risks were corporate values.

One of the big problems for the Baby Bells after the breakup of AT&T was that suddenly they were in a new environment where they needed to be nimble, innovative competitors, but they were filled with slow-moving, risk-averse bureaucrats. Even when their top leaders came up with new business models for winning in the new, competitive marketplace, they were hampered by cultures that worked against them.

IBM

Before Lou Gerstner came along, IBM almost went under. In part, that was because John Akers and his colleagues moved too slowly to come up with new business ideas to respond to changes in the market. But the failure of that homegrown team of IBM veterans to let go of the past and move ahead was largely a values problem.

From day one, Tom Watson had built IBM around the values of consistency, conformity and reliability. For several decades, these values served the company well. The world wasn't moving as quickly as it is today, and since business machines were just entering the market, it was important to establish their reliability. IBM's army of buttoned-down, crew-cut sales reps, whose behavior and responses were almost totally predictable, was just the right team to implement Watson's strategy.

Then, in large part thanks to IBM's efforts, the computer age arrived, bringing with it a rapid increase in the pace of business. In this environment, the values of conformity and lock-step predictability became hindrances. IBM was unable to compete against companies like Dell, which had such values as avoiding hierarchy, embracing change and delighting customers.

Speed and agility were now the critical qualities essential to winning. The old culture of conformity and predictability not only slowed IBM down, but it drove away the curious and creative types who might have seen and responded to the changes in the marketplace sooner. When Gerstner joined the company as CEO in 1993, the first thing he did was clean house and bring in other outsiders to create a culture of speed and excitement.

Home Depot's Culture of Customer Service

At The Home Depot, Bernie Marcus and Arthur Blank knew from the start that creating the right values and culture were critical to their strategy. Their low-price model required extremely high volume to generate the level of profit they would need to attract investors and to grow. While low prices and big inventories were essential pieces of the model, it was the customer service element that was going to make or break the company. And this meant building an organization that valued serving the customer ahead of everything else.

"You can copy a Black & Decker drill and sell it for the same price that we do," says Blank, but "we're very difficult to emulate without believing in the same values that we do." Competitors can "copy almost everything we do, from store design to marketing," he says. "But the reason they still only achieve about 60% of our volume is that they don't understand the essence of what we do: Take care of the customers."

As a start-up in 1979, Home Depot didn't have an old culture that it needed to change. But it did need to build a culture that was different from the rest of the hardware industry and most other retailers, as well. In most companies, salespeople are taught that their primary job is to make sales, and this value is reinforced by paying them on commission. In these organizations, some good salespeople realize that they can win customers' loyalty not by pressuring them, but by helping them find just the right things that they need. But they don't get paid for being nice, and they don't get paid for helping the customer save money. They get paid for making sales, so that is what they focus on.

At Home Depot, Marcus and Blank realized that they couldn't

achieve their volume goals without strong customer loyalty. They couldn't have customers who just came in once, or only dropped by when they were in the neighborhood. They needed customers who were drawn to Home Depot. They needed customers who would go out of their way and go past other stores to get to a Home Depot. So cultivating the customer became a primary corporate value.

"The key is not to make the sale. The key is to cultivate the customer," says Blank. "We teach our associates that if you can save a customer money, do it. We're not looking to fleece the customer. If I can save them $100, why not do it? That reflects one of our values: caring for the customer. Care for them today, and they'll be back tomorrow." To reinforce this, the corporate motto became "whatever it takes," meaning that a Home Depot employee should always do "whatever it takes" to satisfy a customer.

In addition to this value of cultivating the customer, Marcus's and Blank's Teachable Point of View on values included a number of others that tie in and are related. In their book *Built From Scratch* they list them as:

- **Excellent customer service.** Doing whatever it takes to build customer loyalty.
- **Taking care of our people.** The most important reason for The Home Depot's success.

If you want your front-line people to focus on doing whatever it takes to get customers to trust Home Depot, then those front-line people have to trust Home Depot. They have to trust that the company will back up their promises to the customers, and more importantly, they have to trust that the company will support and look out for them.

Recounting a story about an associate who told a customer that he didn't need a new $200 faucet because he could fix his old one for $1.50, Arthur Blank explained: "If this sales associate didn't think he was being taken care of, he probably wouldn't have taken the trouble to do all the right things with that customer. But the single most important reason for The Home Depot's success is our effort to take care of our associates."

- **Developing entrepreneurial spirit.** This encourages associates to take responsibility and make on-the-spot decisions needed to respond creatively to customer needs.

- **Respect for all people.** Talent and good people are everywhere, and we can't afford to overlook any source of good people.

  Respect gives people the self-confidence to take risks in making decisions.
- **Building strong relationships with associates, customers, vendors and communities.** Strong relationships create loyalty.
- **Doing the right thing, not just doing things right.** This will build strong relationships.
- **Giving back to our communities as an integral part of doing business.** This will also build strong relationships.
- **Shareholder return.** This is the key metric of success.

Lots of companies have values statements filled with platitudes that they hang prominently in the front lobby. But winning companies have values that are designed to support a specific set of ideas about how to make money and win in the marketplace. Winning leaders always think about values in this context, and they developed Teachable Points of View that allow them to articulate their values to others.

As Arthur Blank puts it, "Hourly associates really do lead The Home Depot. Every day, their decision making and independence makes our stores better, and that reinforces our customer loyalty . . . It's all about trust. With the right value system and the right knowledge to do their job, people can be trusted to make the right decisions."

Emotional Energy: Enthusiasm Makes Winners

Ideas and values unify people and allow them to act independently, but still in support of a common goal. The ideas and values are themselves strong motivators. In fact, one of the reasons they are so important is that they inspire people to action. However, ideas and values alone can't carry the day.

Winning organizations do their jobs better than others. And in a highly competitive world, this means that they work faster and with greater energy. Therefore, winning leaders not only encourage people to have good ideas and develop strong values, but they also take deliberate actions to generate energy and to channel it to productive uses.

A leader's Teachable Point of View on creating positive energy contains his or her thinking about how to motivate other people. In small companies, leaders can do this in casual meetings and through informal encounters. Larger companies need formal programs to make sure that no one is overlooked.

Yum! Brands

David Novak has a challenge like few other leaders in the world. Novak is CEO of Yum! Brands, the parent company of Pizza Hut, Taco Bell, KFC, Long John Silver's and A&W. Novak's challenge is to lead 750,000 workers, most of them hourly workers, in the highly transient fast-food business. Many of these people work for franchisees and aren't even employed directly by Yum!.

In the fast-food business, there is only one point of contact with the customer—at the counter or drive-thru window—and if everything goes right, the contact is brief. So the enthusiasm of the frontline people who serve the customers is critical to the customers' experience.

Building energy in a workforce that is far-flung and widely diverse—ranging from teenagers to grandparents—takes a lot of energy from Novak and his colleagues in senior management.

What many would find hokey, Novak finds essential to Yums!'s success. He takes every opportunity to create positive emotional energy through recognition, fun and camaraderie. To outsiders, the rituals and symbols of any institution can look silly. But when they are sincere and linked to the values of the organization, they fulfill a deep human need to be connected and energized.

Novak is an avid believer in laughter and playful celebrations of accomplishment. When he was president of KFC, he made a big deal out of giving the "Floppy (rubber) Chicken" award to outstanding performers. For the star performers at Pizza Hut, his presidential award was a "Big Cheese" like the ones worn by Green Bay Packers fans. Taco Bellers get the "Royal Order of the Pepper." He even chose the company's name and New York Stock Exchange (YUM) symbol to be memorable and fun. And he has a leadership development program that he calls Building the YUM Dynasty.

David Novak's Teachable Point of View on emotional energy is that he believes that a "recognition culture" is how to get it. "While the practice of saying thank you and recognizing people for good work wasn't necessarily new to us," he says, "the idea of identifying those things as a way to grow our business was a little different. . . .

We're a company full of awards, from stars to smiley faces to boomerangs to magnets to crystal trophies to CHAMPS cards. And that's just a small sampling of the tangible stuff. We're also overflowing with smiles, applause, cheers, thanks, high-fives, handshakes, voicemails, e-mails, thank you notes, banners, kudos and so much more."

As frivolous as this may sound, Novak is sincere, and his people know it and love it. It generates a lot of emotional energy, and he personally coaches his managers on how to do the same.

The Energy Grid

People have the most positive energy and work most eagerly and productively when five conditions exist. Leaders don't always have to actively create all of these conditions. External events, for example, can create a sense of urgent need with no prodding from the leader. But whether outside forces create the conditions or leaders generate them themselves, leaders need to make sure that they exist. A leader, therefore, must have a Teachable Point of View on each of them. They are as follows:

- **A sense of urgent need that is clear and palpable to everyone in the organization.**

This is created by conveying the message that certain things have to happen if the organization is going to succeed, and if those things don't happen, the organization is in serious trouble.

At The Home Depot, for example, the urgent need is for great customer service. The idea of great customer service is part of The Home Depot business model that is explained to every associate. It is also an explicit corporate value that is fostered at all levels of the company. But much of the sense of urgency and the energy behind it comes from the actions of senior leadership.

In the early days of Home Depot, Marcus and Blank would deliver products to customer's homes. They would go out into the parking lots and ask the customers leaving empty-handed why they hadn't bought anything. And if the reply was that the store didn't have what the customer wanted, they would find the item, even if they had to buy it from a competitor, and get it to them that day. They would give refunds on items that Home Depot didn't even sell.

The repetition of the injunction to do "whatever it takes" to please the customer, combined with the lengths to which they personally went to support it, did more than anything else to drive home to everyone the supreme importance and urgency of the goal.

• A mission that is inspiring and clearly worth achieving.

People are energized when they feel that they are helping to accomplish something worth accomplishing. Money is important. People need money to support themselves and their families, and they want to receive a level of compensation that recognizes their contributions to the organization. But money alone cannot buy most people's hearts and energy, or at least not for long. People get excited and energized when they feel that they are working toward something important and making a positive difference in the world.

Jack Welch had a wonderful speech that he gave over and over about creating a GE that would be "the world's most exciting enterprise. Where ideas win. Where people flourish and grow. Where the excitement of their work lives is transferred to their whole lives." He talked about speed not just as a competitive weapon, but as an "organizational energy giver. People love speed. Think about fast cars, fast boats, fast planes. People get excited by speed. I want us to have that excitement," he said.

Herb Kelleher of Southwest Airlines talks about building a low-cost carrier that makes air travel available to people who might not otherwise be able to afford it, where it is fun to fly, fun to work, and employees are appreciated and rewarded.[3] And Home Depot is a company where every person is charged with building the skills and self-confidence of customers.

The mission doesn't have to be worthy of a Nobel Prize. It doesn't have to be eradicating poverty, curing AIDS or eliminating world hunger. It can simply be building an organization that provides valuable services to customers, a decent quality of life for its workers, and, at worst, doesn't harm the wider community. The important thing is that leaders describe it in sufficient detail and act so that it comes alive for everyone else.

• Goals that stretch people's abilities.

Setting stretch goals can be an excellent energy builder. Obviously, there is some level at which a goal is ludicrous. At this point, it becomes, if not demoralizing, then simply, laughably irrelevant. But the risks of setting one's sights too high are far less than of setting them too low. Nobody has any energy for doing things that are too easy.

Everyone wants to feel that they have accomplished something. Despite Woody Allen's oft-repeated comment that "eighty percent of success is showing up," most people don't find doing only that a very exciting prospect. A runner may be energized and excited about simply completing his or her first marathon. But after that, the energy comes each time from trying to beat the previous time.

Another reason for setting stretch goals that Jack Welch talks about a lot is that even when they aren't met, stretch goals get people to accomplish more than they would have without them. A group with a realistic goal of, say, a 10% increase in sales for a year will pat themselves on the back, throw a big party and stop pushing when they reach that goal. That same group with a stretch goal of a 40% increase may not reach it, but they are more likely to come up with a 25% increase than the group that was aiming for only 10%. Sometimes, goals do get exceeded, but not all that often, and not by all that much. In most cases, low goals mean low results.

Winning leaders set goals that people think are impossible to achieve, and then help them to achieve them. They do this, in part, by building a spirit of teamwork that lets people know that they have a role to play and then giving them the self-confidence to do it.

Decimal Points Are a Bore.
They Inspire or Challenge No One.

Jack Welch has the best Teachable Point of View on goals that I have ever seen. Most world-class winning leaders share Welch's basic bias toward creating stretch goals, but few have the explanation—the teachable part—down so well. Here's how he described it in a letter to GE shareholders. Welch wrote most of these letters himself, so the words are his:

Stretch . . . *essentially means using dreams to set business targets—with no real idea of how to get there. If you do know how to get there—it's not a stretch target. We certainly didn't have a clue how we were going to get to ten inventory turns when we set that target. But we're getting there, and as soon as we become sure we can do it—it's time for another stretch. The CEO of Yokogawa, our Japanese partner in the medical systems business, calls this concept "bullet train thinking," i.e., if you want a ten-miles-per-hour increase in train speed, you tinker with horsepower—but if you want to double its speed, you have to break out of both conventional thinking and conventional performance expectations . . .*

We used to timidly nudge the peanut along, setting goals of moving from, say, 4.73 inventory turns to 4.91, or from 8.53% operating margin to 8.92%, and then indulge in time-consuming, high-level, bureaucratic negotiations to move the number a few hundredths one way or the other. The point is—it didn't matter. Arguing over these petty numbers in conference rooms certainly didn't inspire the people on the shop or office floor who had to deliver them—in most cases, they never even heard of them. We don't do that anymore. . . . decimal points are a bore. They inspire or challenge no one, capture no imaginations. We're aiming at ten inventory turns, at 15% operating margins, and at the introduction of more new products in the next two years than we've developed in the last ten. In a company that now rewards progress toward stretch goals, rather than punishing shortfalls, the setting of these goals, and quantum leaps toward them, are daily events.

As Welch emphasizes, his point of view isn't about precisely what the goals should be or about the strategy for reaching them. Rather, it is about using goals to energize the company and his understanding of how stretch goals do that.

• **A spirit of teamwork.**

When many people think about the importance of teamwork, they think of it in terms of how much energy it saves when people aren't working at odds or playing politics with their colleagues. But a sense of teamwork has a value far beyond simply eliminating ineffi-ciencies. A good leader who can make people feel that they really are contributing members of a team that is working toward a shared and worthwhile goal can unleash huge stores of positive energy. Welch called them "rewards for the soul." (Which, he pointed out, also needed to be accompanied by rewards for the wallet.)

In recent years, companies have increasingly tied financial rewards to performance by making stock options a routine part of compensation packages and other programs that encourage employee stock ownership. Even though the late 1990s saw massive abuses of these rewards, creating wealth based on luck and being in the right spot at the right time, and even though many people's wealth was destroyed by the dot-com bubble in the tragedy of Enron and other greedy leaders, the use of stock options or ownership plans makes sound sense.

Dell, Southwest Airlines, GE, Yum! Brands, Genentech, 3M and Home Depot all have programs to make employees owners within a few months of joining the company. In spite of the market downturn, General Electric and Home Depot claim to have millionaires working on the shop floor and the sales floor. The idea is that the financial incentive will get people to work harder and with more energy, especially when they are seen as fair and linked to actual performance, not just luck.

That is certainly true. An equity stake in the financial results does encourage people to conserve resources and produce results. But the kind of ownership that really generates energy is not economic. It is emotional. It is the kind that gives people a sense of responsibility. It is the kind that makes them feel that their actions make a difference. It is the sense that they are a valuable member of the team.

One of the key ways that leaders generate this spirit of teamwork is by having a Teachable Point of View that gives each person an understanding of the role that he or she needs to play and a sense of his or her own importance. It is creating a feeling that "we are all in this together, and we will succeed or fail, based on the actions of each person."

Bad leaders are often too busy proclaiming their own importance to think about how energized the organization becomes when other people feel important. A person who feels either unnecessary or ineffective has no positive energy, and over time can generate a sizeable store of negative energy. A person who feels needed is usually ready and eager to pitch in.

Yum! Brands

Yum! focuses on building teams in every store. Each of the 32,000 store managers is trained to be a team leader, to create a culture of customer mania and to energize each and every employee. The goal, of course, is never fully achieved, but they persistently pursue it.

David Novak, CEO, makes it clear that everything they do at Yum! is geared to a set of drivers that will lead to consistent sales and profit growth year after year. He calls this "building the YUM Dynasty." He explains the term: "When Tricon was started we said our passion was to put a Yum on our customers' faces at Taco Bell, KFC, and Pizza Hut around the world."

Novak has five major drivers that constitute his Teachable Point of View on how to build the YUM Dynasty. They are:

1. Winners will create a culture where everyone in the company and on the team knows that they can make a difference. The formula is simple, says Novak. "People first . . . satisfy customers . . . make more money. This is our recipe for success that started at the Restaurant Support Center in Louisville and is now worldwide."

He translates this into three factors to drive top performance:

- Managers do a good job of casting the right shadow of leadership.
- People know what goals we have to improve performance.
- They feel appreciated and recognized.

Novak points out that, "Good people leave for two reasons. They don't get along with the boss. That's why we believe in coaches. Or, they don't feel appreciated. That's why we recognize people. It's the soft stuff that drives hard results."

2. Focus the culture on making people what Novak calls customer and sales "maniacs." "I'm convinced," he says, "that no matter how well we innovate with great products, or produce memorable advertising, nothing, absolutely nothing brings customers back time and again more than the service they experience in the restaurant . . . our goal is to train 750,000 people on the customer mania mind-set."

To do this, Yum! Brands has taken all of its executives through the team member training. "We're requiring all our leaders to have a Teachable Point of View on customer mania and cascade the message to their team members." Part of the Teachable Point of View is to ensure that all associates develop important life skills: empathize, listen, exceed expectations within the team, and recover when necessary.

3. Competitive brand differentiation. "We must give them an experience they can't get somewhere else—the best people, best quality, friendliest service, best drive-thru times, best facility."

4. Continuity in people and process. Novak says: "There is no substitute for experience and keeping people in position. . . . when our regional general managers and the core team are in place for more than a year, sales and profitability are always higher. They know what really matters, so they have process and discipline around what really matters."

5. Consistency in driving growth versus a year ago. "Year over year improvement has to be our battle cry."

- **Self-confidence and a realistic expectation that the team members can meet the goals.**

The fifth condition needed to evoke positive emotional energy is self-confidence, the sense that if I exert myself, I can make a difference. Unless it's a life-or-death struggle, people lose energy pretty quickly when they think that either a goal is unattainable or they don't have the ability to have an impact. In business, there are very few life-or-death struggles, so leaders must find ways to instill confidence.

Building a spirit of teamwork is one way to do this. Simply knowing that they are needed makes people want to pitch in and help. And the feeling of mutual reinforcement gives them confidence.

A goal that seems out of sight to a lone individual becomes a lot more achievable when viewed from the perspective of a team member. Where the line is between stretch goals that are inspiring and ones that are demoralizing depends not so much on the goals themselves as on how people in the organization feel about them. Team members gain confidence and energy from one another.

Self-confidence energizes people to take the kind of independent action that companies need from people at all levels if they are going to be winners. For this reason, building people's self-confidence is one of the most valuable things a leader can do.

In order to succeed in the marketplace, companies must respond to changing customer demands quickly and creatively. This means that people throughout the organization must be able and willing to think, make decisions and take risks. In today's world, timidity and fear are serious competitive liabilities.

Home Depot

"Building self-confidence is absolutely essential," says Bob Nardelli, the current CEO of Home Depot. "World-class customer service is a critical piece of our business model. Our sales associates must know that when we say, 'Do whatever it takes to please the customer,' we mean it. And they must have the self-confidence to listen to each individual customer and then give that person the individualized response that he or she needs.

"We can't write rules about every situation, and we can't make the customers wait while an associate goes off to find somebody else to make a decision. Each associate has to decide and do something on the spot. If they don't have the self-confidence to believe that they can come up with a good solution or they don't think that we have confidence in them and will back them, then we are sunk."

Southwest Airlines

At Southwest Airlines, encouraging self-confidence and risk-taking is both a customer-service issue and a strategic tool for outsmarting the competition, says Herb Kelleher. "We've never tried to be like other airlines. From the very beginning, we told our people, 'Question it. Challenge it. Remember, decades of conventional wisdom has sometimes led the airline industry into huge losses.' "

Babe Ruth, The Strike-Out King

Winning companies recognize, reward and promote people who take risks. If the risk pays off or the creative idea pans out, that's all the better. But the key message is that if you don't swing the bat, you won't hit the ball.

Fact: In six of the twelve seasons that he was the home-run king, Babe Ruth was also the strike-out king.

Many leaders, especially in the high-tech world, encourage self-confidence and risk-taking by building what I call a "beta test" culture. It means taking a leap with something that you know isn't perfect with the assumption that you will fix it when the flaws pop up. Joe Liemandt describes his Teachable Point of View on product development at Trilogy as "Good is good enough to get started. If you wait for perfect, you will miss the market. Ship it now, and then fix it to do exactly what the customer needs. Make it work!"

Michael Dell calls it planning for "course corrections." "We're forced to innovate to stay ahead of the competition. And, when you're dealing in an industry that's changing so dynamically, there are often more unknowns than knowns.

"You also need to embrace an experimental attitude in making decisions. Sometimes you can't wait for all the data to present themselves before making a decision. You have to make the best decision you possibly can . . . We have deliberately shaped our culture to accept continual 'course corrections' on the learning curve because in order to thrive, we need an environment in which people feel it's okay to experiment."

Building positive energy is something that too few leaders have a Teachable Point of View about. They work hard on coming up with a business plan that will squash the competition. Or they figure out a strategy to get the organization out of a crisis. But they don't have a Teachable Point of View about how to get everyone else energized to rally around it. So the big idea goes nowhere.

You may be able to order people to do things, or even persuade them intellectually that a strategy is appropriate, but to get the speed and creativity to win, you need their energy. You have to engage their hearts and emotions as well as their minds.

Edge: Making Tough Decisions

The fourth area where leaders need to have a Teachable Point of View is edge. Edge is the ability to make difficult yes/no decisions. Leaders' Teachable Points of View about edge enable them to explain their thought process for making those decisions.

Easy decisions usually don't require much explanation, and most people don't need to be taught how to make them. But the tough ones need explaining, and most people must be taught to make them.

Leaders who have a Teachable Point of View can take others through the thought processes that lead to tough decisions. This helps others accept the decision and stay energized and pulling together. Teaching others in the organization to make tough decisions is also a critical leadership skill. A leader who is unable to walk others through the process will have a hard time teaching them.

Demonstrating edge is the most difficult thing a leader has to do because it requires courage. For most leaders, that courage comes from having clear ideas and values and a keen sense of fidelity to them. The question boils down to this: If you really believe that X business strategy and Y set of values are the ones that are going to lead to success, then can you allow situations that don't fulfill that strategy or adhere to those values to persist?

A leader with edge will say "no" and does something. A leader without edge will find a way either to avoid seeing the inherent conflict in the situation or decide that it is something to be lived with. When the rest of the organization sees that the leader's actions don't back up the ideas and values, those ideas and values are dead.

Edge decisions are often painful. The layoff of thousands of people, the sale of a unit that has been in the company for decades, or the cancellation of a project that people have been working overtime on for months are all painful. But the amount of pain involved in a decision is not the test of edge. It's the courage. A leader who is willing to face reality, see that projects or units are not working out as hoped, or that additional activities are needed, and to then take action, is demonstrating edge.

Intel

Andy Grove is a leader with a lot of edge. Especially when Intel was younger, every time he decided to shell out a couple of billion dollars to build a new plant, he was risking the company. But if he believed in the company's technology and its strategy of staying on the cutting-edge, he had to do it.[4]

Perhaps his edgiest decision came in 1984. In the 1970s, Intel had built a great business providing semiconductors, primarily memory chips, to the computer industry. As Grove puts it, the company's total identity was tied up in memories. Then the Japanese began producing chips, undercutting Intel in the market. Intel would invest in the R&D to come up with a new semiconductor, and within months the Japanese would be producing high-quality copycats.

Finally, Grove describes one day when he was staring out the window of an office at the company's campus in Santa Clara. The only two people in the room were Grove and Gordon Moore, another of Intel's founders. Grove knew that everything he had helped to build was on the line. He asked Moore a very tough question, "If we got kicked out and the board brought in a new CEO, what do you think he would do?" Moore responded, "He'd probably get us out of memories." Grove reflected for a moment. And then he said, "Why shouldn't you and I walk out the door, come back and do it ourselves?"

The solution they ultimately reached was to abandon Intel's biggest business. Memory chips had become a commodity to which they could add little value, so they decided to start out almost entirely new, designing and building the best microprocessors in the world. It was a painful and gutsy decision, but one that probably saved the company.

General Electric

There are numerous Jack Welch examples of business edge, ranging from the one hundred or so acquisitions that GE made each year in the last decade of his tenure, to the divestitures of GE Small Appliances, Semiconductors, TVs, Aerospace and Kidder Peabody, to name a few. And when it came to cost-cutting, he exhorted everyone to edgy decision making. I have one video clip that I use all the time in which he warns his managers that he does not intend to pay anyone for easy across-the-board cuts:

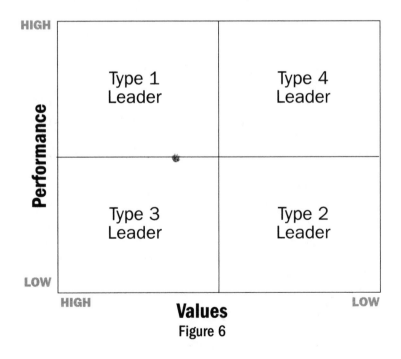

Values

Figure 6

There is too much share-the-pain mentality in our management. How can we add global service? How can we add IT resources, when we are cutting back [by saying] "Let's get 5%.

Let's get 10% out from everyone." Any manager in this room who we find saying 10% across the board, share the pain, if we find you, is in big trouble. Your whole job is to differentiate. Your whole reason for being is to say "yes" to some and "no" to others, to pour the coals to some and squeeze the others. Your kid can come in a rocking chair and say "10% across the board." That ain't the game. The game is to differentiate around opportunities. No share-the-pain discussions. We have to add quality resources, IT resources while we slash the hell out of overhead. . . . no share-the-pain discussions.

The toughest kind of courage is around people. Welch perhaps set the gold standard when he began in the late 1980s to fire some of GE's top performers for failure to live up to the company's values. He explained his Teachable Point of View with a chart that he drew up and printed in GE's 1991 annual report.[5] The chart is a simple 2 x 2 matrix with four cells and values and performances as its axes. Welch described the type of manager that goes in each cell:

The first is one who delivers on commitments—financial or otherwise—and shares the values of our Company. His or her future is an easy call. Onward and upward.

The second type of leader is one who does not meet commitments and does not share our values. Not as pleasant a call, but equally easy.

The third is one who misses commitments but shares the values. He or she usually gets a second chance, preferably in a different environment.

Then there's the fourth type—the most difficult for many of us to deal with. That leader delivers on commitments, makes all the numbers, but doesn't share the values we must have. This is the individual who typically forces performance out of people rather than inspires it: the autocrat, the big shot, the tyrant. Too often, all of us have looked the other way—tolerated these "type 4" managers because "they always deliver"—at least in the short term."

But, in the future, he said, these people would have to go.

Edge is one of the most difficult leadership abilities to teach. In part, that is because it is the one most dependent on a person's inherent personality. Some people are naturally gutsier than others. In part, it's also because motivation plays such an important role in determining whether a specific action is brave and edge-ful, or cowardly and cruel.

Jack Welch and "Chainsaw Al" Dunlap[6] both fired thousands of people. Welch did it in accordance with his ideas and values for building a better GE. He had edge. Dunlap didn't have any business ideas or values for building companies. He just cut costs quickly, even if it destroyed the company. There was no edge in his decisions. He was just cruel and greedy.

Nonetheless, edge can, and must, be taught. A leader who fails to have edge or teach others to have edge cannot build a winning company. Winning demands good ideas and values, the focused energy to carry them out, and the edge to stay on course. The pain associated with many edge-ful decisions makes teaching it to others extraordinarily difficult. But a determined leader with a clear Teachable Point of View can do it.

The Value of TPOV

The value of developing a Teachable Point of View is multifold:

1. The very act of creating a Teachable Point of View makes people better leaders. As they step back from the day-to-day ferment of business and reflect on what they know, leaders come to understand their underlying assumptions about themselves, their organization and business in general. When implicit knowledge becomes explicit, it can then be questioned, refined and honed, which benefits both the leaders and the organizations.

Roger Enrico says: "A Teachable Point of View is worth fifty IQ points."

2. A Teachable Point of View expedites one of the leader's most difficult and mission-critical tasks: developing people. Many leaders try to develop other leaders by example. That can take a long time and leaves many insights unarticulated. Learning only from role models is a pretty dull instrument. Imagine trying to learn golf by only watching Tiger Woods play.

The power of the Teachable Point of View is that it gives leaders an explicit body of knowledge to impart, debate, modify and pass on to others. It also helps the learner construct a framework for how the ideas, values, emotional energy and edge fit together.

3. A Teachable Point of View is a vehicle for assuring that the same set of messages gets transmitted throughout the organization. This allows leaders at all levels to create alignment through a clear and consistent storyline. This keeps everyone working toward the same goals and operating with consistent values. It also speeds up learning and change in an organization.

Chapter Five
How to Develop a
Teachable Point of View

■ Developing a TPOV Is an Essential Job for Leaders
  · It's an iterative process of reflection, writing, testing and
    amending.
  · Feedback from others will help refine it, but the leader must
    craft it first.

■ It Starts with Willpower and Taking a Hard Look
  at Reality
  · What are your fundamental, core beliefs? And what shaped
    them?
  · What's the business environment? How equipped is the
    company to succeed?

■ Crafting a Compelling Plan for the Future
  · Where do you need to get, and how will you get there?
  · Come up with a storyline that makes it vivid and exciting.

The question became, how do you make your theory of the
business substantially more explicit? And then how do you reinforce it? In large part, that's what I've worked on in the 1990s. *Les
Wexner—founder of Limited Brands*

■ ■ ■

Developing a Teachable Point of View is not a simple process. It requires first doing the intellectual work of figuring out what your point of view is, and then the creative work of putting it into a form that makes it accessible and interesting to others. It is both time consuming and challenging.

The process involves digging into often tacit knowledge and crafting it into explicit teachable concepts. Most of us don't know what we know. We live our lives and do our jobs based on a huge internal database of assumptions and ideas, but we usually aren't very aware of what they are or how they shape our behavior. As artisans and practitioners, we have not taken the time and discipline to examine the underlying principles that guide our success. To become effective teachers, leaders must figure out what elements lead to what outcomes and develop the underlying principles that guide their successful activities.

Once they have figured out the principles behind their actions, then they must figure out not only how to articulate them and make them teachable, but how to do so in a way that is engaging and exciting to others. This requires pulling all the various elements into a cohesive narrative. It requires creating a story that hangs together and flows so that other people can take the internal knowledge that the leader has made explicit and then internalize it themselves.

Developing a TPOV is an iterative process of wallowing in reality, self-reflection, writing things down, and testing them out. Les Wexner, founder and CEO of Limited Brands, says that he began to work on it seriously when he realized that he couldn't successfully scale the company by relying just on the apprentice model that was the norm of the fashion industry.

"The organization was built on the mental model that said that great merchants are artists. You learn to be a merchant by working behind a master merchant. . . . If you sit next to me, you will figure it out. The problem is that it doesn't work. You can't have the apprentice just watching the master. The master really has to teach the apprentice. Otherwise, they don't develop quickly enough, and they often learn the wrong things.

"For example, if you ask someone who's been sitting at someone's side for fifteen years why do they do X, you often get an entirely inappropriate logic for why X was done. This is because there was never any dialogue about it. So the question becomes, how do you make your theory of the business substantially more explicit? And then how do you reinforce it?"

Even if the apprentice model did work, says Wexner, it was too inefficient. Eventually, the company got too big for him to have the time to teach through osmosis.

In addition, Wexner realized that being a merchant—which he defines as being able to predict and select fashion, the artistic part of the job—was necessary but not sufficient for the company. He also needed more fully rounded business leaders to run the company. "That's when I realized," he says, "that I was going to have to start teaching them."

Wexner says that his new Teachable Point of View on developing leaders for Limited Brands is, "I think the artistic part of it, the sixth sense that design architects, that artists and merchants have, is highly intuitive. It's not a skill you can really develop. So I don't try to teach it. You select for the basic talent, the ability to see around corners, the ability to know it's purple . . . what length skirts are eighteen-year-old girls going to wear a year or eighteen months from now, etc. Then I have to teach them to be leaders and business people.

"There are two skill sets that creative people typically don't have. One is respect for organization and organizational development of people and leadership skills. The other is the financial part. Do you have respect for numbers? Do you understand what a balance sheet is? Do you understand what happens if you run out of cash? . . .

"Let's face it," he says. "Let's move from the notion of implicit contact. It doesn't lead to explicit knowledge." He had to develop a Teachable Point of View.

Step 1: Personal Willpower to Develop a TPOV

Coming up with the initial TPOV really is hard work. It starts with the leader taking a mental inventory of the stuff inside his or her head. It requires a total commitment of head, heart and guts.

The head part is the intellectual work of taking decades of implicit internal knowledge and making it explicit. It means examining your own thought processes and behaviors to figure out why you do the things you do. It means framing the various ideas and beliefs that underlie your actions, and then tying them together into a cohesive whole. Basically, it involves examining the entire contents of your brain, figuring out what is important, and then expressing those things in a way that is clear enough for others to take them in *and* respond.

The heart part is generating the enormous amount of emotional energy required to do the job thoroughly, and also dealing with the surprising memories and feelings that are almost certain to be uncovered in the process.

And the guts are about opening yourself up and letting others see what really is, or isn't, inside of you. The discipline to do this requires a commitment and willpower that few leaders have. For a variety of reasons, from intellectual laziness to a lack of self-confidence, to simply not recognizing the need for it, few leaders invest the time and energy needed to develop Teachable Points of View.

Some get excited and eagerly embark on the project, but then get distracted with other less demanding or more enjoyable activities. Others never get into it at all. But either way, what happens is that staffers and consultants end up doing the thinking, and the executive just signs off on it. In essence, these executives are outsourcing their brains.

It's possible to get by if you manage a business on a day-to-day basis this way. But being a leader, teaching others to be leaders, and building a Virtuous Teaching Cycle requires full participation and ownership. The leader needs to be totally in the game, and this only happens with the investment of lots of personal energy.

A prime example of a leader who wasn't totally in the game is John Akers, the CEO who presided over the loss of $60 billion in market value for IBM shareholders in the years 1987–1993. Under Akers, IBM was a consultant's paradise. Lacking his own Teachable Point of View, Akers relied on outsiders and staffers to come up with ideas and operating plans. But because he didn't fully own them, he was unable to implement them. The organization clearly saw his lack of deep understanding and commitment and resisted him.

The result was a constantly changing "flavor of the month" menu that encouraged and reinforced cynicism throughout the company. I remember being in the European IBM training center in LaHulpe, Belgium, in 1990, doing a workshop with all the European presidents, and they were openly contemptuous of Akers's various initiatives and programs. This lack of commitment ultimately contributed to his downfall.

Write it Yourself

General Electric: Jack Welch

One of the hallmarks of Jack Welch was that he actually wrote all of the speeches he gave and the documents that appeared over his signature. He had staffers help him with some of the details, but the basic content was pure Welch. He followed a disciplined regimen of personal reflection, writing, reviewing and revising. He actually used the crafting of his annual report letter as a means for articulating the TPOV by which he was currently running the company.[1]

He would start in the fall, working on his ideas and testing them out in a senior management meeting in October. Then he would revise them based on the responses he got and use the new version as the centerpiece of the big operating managers meeting in Boca Raton, Florida, in January. After that, he would write the final draft for publication, which he also referred to and used throughout the year in working with and teaching GE's 300,000+ employees.

There are two important points here:

The first is Welch made himself sit down and put his thoughts in writing. I strongly believe that writing is an essential part of the process of developing a TPOV. The cognitive act of putting words on paper and trying to make sense of them helps create the necessary intellectual rigor and clarity.

The second point is that he integrated the development of the TPOV into the fabric of running the enterprise. In other words, he used the cycle of routine management meetings to create the Virtuous Teaching Cycle on his TPOV.

Get Feedback

The process of articulating one's Teachable Point of View is not a one-time event. It is an ongoing, iterative and interactive process. It follows the principles of the scientific method: Develop a set of constructs and hypotheses, test them out, then revise them.

You might also describe it as the "beta test" method. You come up with the product, float it on the market, then fix it based on the responses. The Virtuous Teaching Cycle is the process through which leaders test and improve their Teachable Points of View. The first step, however, is developing the Teachable Point of View. And this must be done by the leader.

Jack Welch often used classes at Crotonville to test his thinking and get dialogue and feedback. When I was running Crotonville, one of the most important things to do every time Jack came was to make sure that he got written feedback on his time with the group. We would have everyone at Crotonville join Jack in the "pit," a big case room that holds 120 people. There were almost always multiple programs going, so GE professionals at all levels, from twenty-five-year-olds to senior leaders in their forties, across all the businesses, would be there. Welch would spend several hours with the group both sharing his TPOV and answering their questions. At the end we would have everyone write Jack a memo answering three questions:

As a result of the session with Jack:

1. What issues were resolved?
2. What issues are still unresolved? What troubles me?
3. This is my number one takeaway from the session:

We made sure that Jack got these handwritten notes with no summary and no editing. He got 100 to 120 feedback memos every time he came, every week or so. He read them all.

The VTC that Created the GE Shared Values

Successful leader/teachers are very disciplined and committed to repeatedly creating and engaging in Virtuous Teaching Cycles. The way that Jack Welch developed, reshaped and taught the GE values illustrates this ongoing journey.

In 1985, while I was heading up Crotonville, a small group of staff met regularly with Welch and his top team in the office of the CEO to craft, debate and formulate a statement of GE values. After several multi-hour sessions, Welch would tell me to take a draft to Crotonville and discuss it with all participants, literally hundreds over a several week period. Then we would come back and see what we had. He also came to Crotonville and discussed the values.[2]

After several years of dialogues about values with thousands of Crotonville participants, discussion with officers coupled with CEO presentations, there was still a long way to go in really instilling the values throughout GE. One milestone event, which came out of frustration on Welch's part, was in 1988 when he saw that the teaching of values was still not getting through the organization.

So he created a set of teaching notes for his leaders. He sat down and tried to articulate his TPOV on the values. Again, the discipline and writing are important elements here.

This is just one artifact of a journey that continued until he retired:

Welch's 1988 TPOV on Values

Business Characteristics

Lean
What: Reduce tasks and the people required to do them.
Why: Critical to developing world cost leadership.

Agile
What: Delayering
Why: Create fast decision making in a rapidly changing world through improved communication and increased individual response.

Creative
What: Development of new ideas—innovation.
Why: Increase customer satisfaction and operating margins through higher value products and services.

Ownership
What: Self-confidence to trust others. Self-confidence to delegate to others the freedom to act while, at the same time, self-confidence to involve higher levels in issues critical to the business and the corporation.
Why: Supports concept of more individual responsibility, capability to act quickly and independently. Should increase job satisfaction and improve understanding of risks and rewards. While delegation is critical, there is a small percentage of high-impact issues that need or require involvement of higher levels within the business and within the corporation.

Reward

What: Recognition and compensation commensurate with risk and performance—highly differentiated by individual, with recognition of total team achievement.

Why: Necessary to attract and motivate the type of individuals required to accomplish GE's objectives. A No. 1 business should provide No. 1 people with No. 1 opportunity.

Individual Characteristics

Reality

What: Describe the environment as it is—not as we hope it to be.

Why: Critical to developing a vision and a winning strategy, and to gaining universal acceptance for their implementation.

Leadership

What: Sustained passion for and commitment to a proactive, shared vision and its implementation.

Why: To rally teams toward achieving a common objective.

Candor/Openness

What: Complete and frequent sharing of information with individuals (appraisals, etc.) and organization (everything).

Why: Critical to employees knowing where they, their efforts, and their business stand.

Simplicity

What: Strive for brevity, clarity, the "elegant, simple solution"—less is better.

Why: Less complexity improves everything, from reduced bureaucracy to better product designs, to lower costs.

Integrity

What: Never bend or wink at the truth, and live within both the spirit and the letter of the laws of every global business arena.

Why: Critical to gaining the global arena's acceptance of our right to grow and prosper. Every constituency: Share owners who invest; customers who purchase; community that supports and employees who depend, expect and deserve our unequivocal commitment to integrity in every facet of our behavior.

Individual Dignity

What: Respect and leverage the talent and contribution of every individual in both good and bad times.

Why: Teamwork depends on trust, mutual understanding and the shared belief that the individual will be treated fairly in any environment.

Step 2: The Hand You Have Been Dealt Personally

The best leader/teachers start by looking in the mirror. People develop their values and beliefs through their life experiences. So a direct look at those experiences is a good place to start figuring out what those beliefs and values are. After hearing Warren Bennis remark that world-class leaders are world-class at learning from painful experiences, I began to ask the people I work with to actually draw journey lines that show the high and low points in their lives.

The exercise is simple and often provides people with surprising insights. Take a piece of paper and draw a line from left to right showing your emotional ups and downs from childhood up to the present. Then look at what was going on at those times, and think about how those events or situations shaped who you are as a person and a leader. Think about them specifically in terms of what impact they had on your ideas, on your values, on how you generate emotional energy, both in yourself and in others and on how you approach tough edge-y decisions.

The point of the exercise is to focus on the events that have been significant in developing the implicit points of view that you now need to turn into explicit Teachable Points of View.

Learning from Life Experiences

Genentech: Myrtle Potter

Myrtle Potter, the COO of Genentech, is one of the clearest people I know when it comes to talking about how her life created her Teachable Point of View. She grew up in a large African-American family in New Mexico. When she talks about her journey line, it is a series of huge challenges with successes achieved by working hard, maintaining her focus and building teams. Her core belief, she says, is: "I truly do believe that you can do absolutely anything with the

Myrtle Potter's Leadership Journey Line

right team focused on the right goal, all together working toward a common place. And that philosophy has served me well throughout my career." Here's her drawing of her leadership journey line.

Potter can point to clear events and situations that shaped these beliefs. She says, for example, "I now know I was poor as a kid, but certainly when I was growing up I didn't realize just how tough we had it! I say that with a laugh because in many respects it was a life lesson from the standpoint that you make the best of your circumstances, and your circumstances are what you make them."

After retiring from the military, her father owned a small business that became successful. So when she was in the seventh grade, the family moved into a nicer neighborhood. This exposed her not only to a new world of opportunity, but also to a new world of overt racism. "It was really incredible. Neighbors wouldn't speak to us. Things were thrown at the front of our house. . . . But, I clearly remember what my parents said to me about that. Here they were, they had a hard time finding a home they were allowed to buy. Their kids were going to schools where they were sometimes mistreated, and the perspective of my parents was, 'They're just ignorant. It has nothing to do with you. They are just ignorant.' There was no hate. There was no anger. There was no 'We're going to get back at them.' . . . It was just simply ignore them."

Potter says that this wasn't easy, given that she was one of only four African-American kids in a 500-person middle school. But she followed her parents' advice as best she could and focused on her school work and extracurricular activities. As a result, she was accepted into the University of Chicago after finishing high school.

Potter says that she knew that her education in New Mexico wasn't very challenging, but she was stunned to find out how ill-prepared she was compared with her fellow students at Chicago. But, she says, "My parents had always been very clear that you can do anything. There's no limit to what you can do with hard work, discipline and focus." So with that core belief, she persevered and successfully completed her studies at Chicago.

She also traces her feelings about teamwork to her childhood. "Not having the luxury of having a lot of money, we learned to really sacrifice for each other. If child number three had a school dance to go to, everybody readily gave up whatever they needed so my parents could take the money to buy the dress for girl number three. If my brother needed a new set of drums, we all sacrificed so my brother could get his drums. So we really did learn to sacrifice and give and really work as a team. And I think that's where my value of teamwork really comes from. . . . I don't believe we can do it by ourselves. I think we're not intended to do it by ourselves, and it's generally out of inexperience or ego that people choose to take on challenges alone. I think leveraging high performing teams nine times out of ten gets you ten times further than doing it by yourself."

But Potter says that overcoming one huge challenge in her life has made everything else seem comparatively easy. Potter's challenge was the diagnosis of her son at age three as having serious developmental challenges. "I will never forget how I was told about his diagnosis. As a parent, times like this are heart-wrenching. We went in for an evaluation. It was a full week of testing. We were completely on edge. When it was all over, we were taken into a conference room, white coats sitting all around the table, giving department reports. . . . neurology, otolaryngology and so on. I'll never forget what the attending finally said to me. She said: 'Mr. and Mrs. Potter, you must understand that he will likely never be able to even place an order at McDonald's' . . . I will never forget that statement."

The outcome has been very different. "Thankfully, with a lot of intervention, we were able to fundamentally change his prognosis," she says. "I'm happy to say that he's doing really well, extraordinarily well, and I'm proud of him. He excells academically and musically."

And the lesson she has learned was, "I've had many people describe me as fearless, and I guess it's because when you've lived through this [her son's challenges], you say, 'Hey this is real life. Let's talk about things that really makes you fearful.' So it's easy for me to maintain perspective about what's important and what's not important.

"I also learned from my son that I had one job. I have pursued it in my personal life as well as in my professional life. My number one job is to help people grow, to help them achieve their greatest potential, and to help them bring out the best that they have. And if I can do that, I feel like I would have made a huge, huge contribution."

Learning from Work Experiences

Yum! Brands: David Novak

David Novak, CEO of Yum! Brands, can point to a number of events on his journey line that have defined his leadership TPOV. His father was a surveyor. He lived in a trailer and moved to a new school every three months. So he got lots of lessons about dealing with changing circumstances and taking the initiative, such as in making friends fast and quickly sizing up a situation.

One event that had the most direct and conscious impact happened while he was working for PepsiCo. Novak built his career in marketing at PepsiCo, but at one point he persuaded Craig Weatherup, then CEO of Pepsi Cola, to give him a line position, running operations. In operations, he said: "I did these roundtables where I'd go out with the front line and meet with the sales guys and sales women, and the people who worked in the warehouse. So, one day, I'm in this meeting and I'm asking these route salesmen about the power of merchandising and who's really good at it.

"So, they all started talking about Bob. Everybody started talking about how good Bob was. They were saying things like, 'This guy taught me more about merchandising in six hours when I went out with him than I'd learned in nine years.' Well, Bob was at the other end of the table, and when I looked over at him, he's crying. And I said to him, 'Bob, why are you crying?' And, he said, 'Look, I've been in this company for forty years and I never knew these guys felt this way about me.'

"Now, I'm sitting there, and he's crying. And I said to myself, 'If I ever have a chance to be president or leader of a company, I'm not going to have any Bobs if I have anything to do with it. I want to make sure that I, as a leader, understand the impact that I really have."

Yum! Brands' culture of recognition, with all its awards and celebration, is a direct outgrowth of that epiphanic moment. Novak says that was the moment when he realized that people need to be given recognition and rewards real-time, very clearly and visibly. Thus, not only are there rubber chickens and plastic cheeses all over the place, but Novak's office is filled with pictures of Tricon performers. It is a citadel of recognition, with floor to ceiling pictures of workers in stores around the world receiving the Floppy Chicken, Cheese Head, Royal Order of the Pepper, and the Chairman's Walking the Talk Award—a set of plastic teeth that chatter. The lesson that David Novak learned from Bob has been embedded in Novak's point of view from the day that it happened. But it took reflection and effort to come up with the articulation that brings it alive and makes it clear to other members of the Tricon team.

Step 3: The Hand You Have Been Dealt Organizationally

Examining the hand you have been dealt means not only looking at yourself, but also looking at the world around you. It means taking a no-nonsense look at the organizational problems facing you both on the hard, business side of the ledger as well as the soft, people and cultural side. And it means keeping a sharp eye on the constantly changing external environment. The assignment, as Jack Welch used to say, is "facing reality, not as it used to be or as you would like for it to be, but as it really is." A leader must have a firm grasp of reality and have a TPOV that enables him or her to keep everyone else focused on reality.

General Electric: Jeff Immelt

The new CEO of GE, Jeff Immelt, describes the hand he was dealt this way:

I'm following the best manager of the last century. I get the job on September 7, 2001, and then 9/11 happens four days later, and I watch, it's an unspeakable tragedy. I lost a friend in that, and it was extremely sad. From a business standpoint, I saw planes with our engines and buildings we insured covered by NBC, four days after I become chairman. Then things like Enron hit, and the world just changed. . . . I've never thought about my job as replacing Jack. My job's to lead GE in a new set of circumstances. The fact is, post 9/11, it's a different world. Even Jack would have had to change his style if he'd stayed with the company and this environment.[3]

But Immelt says that his philosophy is that "you stay true to who you are. Stay true to what you want to get done. Stay focused on what the job is, and the time you're in today passes . . . GE gives me staying power. It's a 120-year-old company. It's been around a long time, we have got great people and we've got a business model and values that work."

In terms of how the business operates, Immelt has an equally clear picture. He says he inherited a company that "works because we have a business model that consists of four things . . .

The first thing is diversification. Basically we run a multi-business company that has one culture, one financial system, and we make it work . . . When it all comes together, we're number one in medical. We've got the number one network [NBC]. We've got the biggest financial services company. It works when it comes together.

The second part is initiatives, cross company, cross business . . . It's the way you make the whole exceed the sum of the parts. We drive things like digitization or Six Sigma. We make them work in our medical business, our power business and across the company. And the ideas get shared, they allow us to capitalize on our diversity. Digitization was worth a billion dollars to us last year.

The third part is we generate cash. We've got great financial mechanisms and disciplines . . . so you can use your balance sheet. GE is all about using size to drive growth. We leverage size to grow fast.

Fourth is people. We recruit. We train. We educate. We coach. We have consequences. We spend a ton of time developing people. I probably spend 40% of my time leading the company, selecting, coaching, deciding who gets which jobs. People are a big part.

As noted above, Jeff Immelt realizes that the world changes every day and that his job is to keep GE competitive in that changing world. But his ability to take the company where it needs to go is greatly facilitated by the fact that he has a clear understanding of where he is starting.

Reality Keeps Changing

Cisco: John Chambers

The reality that John Chambers had to face in 2000–2001 was a particularly harsh one. Chambers was one of the most outspoken champions of the "new economy." He was a believer, and a Pied Piper for millions of others. Encouraged by Chambers' enthusiasm, a lot of people put their life savings into Cisco stock. At the height of the Internet bubble, Cisco was growing at rates of more than 100% a year, and had a market cap of nearly $600 billion, which made it the most valuable company on the planet. In just 12 months, it crashed to $80 billion, giving Chambers the dubious honor of having presided over the largest destruction of market value in history.

The problem that leaders often have is that they don't, or won't, see that the world has changed. Some may criticize Chambers for taking too long, but there is no question that he is facing reality. In mid-2002, GE still had a value of $300 billion, Microsoft was at $280 billion, and Cisco at $100 billion. John Chambers is aggressively leading Cisco through this tough recession. Through his leadership, we can expect to see a Cisco that has come to grips with a new reality and is able again to be a world-class leader.

Yum! Brands: David Novak

For David Novak, the reality was that when PepsiCo spun off KFC, Taco Bell and Pizza Hut to create the company that is now Yum! Brands, it spun off about $5 billion in debt as well. So the challenge that Novak had to deal with wasn't just on the building the business side. At the same time that he was trying to blend the three units into one multi-brand, he also had to reduce debt fast. This meant creating a real operating company rather than a holding company of three unrelated brands. He had to look for economies of scale and ways of sharing best practices and talent development.

Home Depot: Bob Nardelli

When Bob Nardelli arrived to be CEO of Home Depot after losing out on the top job at GE in 2000, he had to face a couple of new realities. One was that the consumer-oriented Home Depot was in a very different market from the industrial businesses he had grown up in at GE. The other was that the powerful growth engine that had propelled Home Depot from a non-existent to a $30+ billion company in twenty years was not going to work forever. Both the company and its customers were maturing.

"When you come from an industrial sector," he says, "typically your factories would shut down on Saturday and Sunday, unless you were out of balance with capacity. Here, we build to a crescendo on Saturday and Sunday. We basically only close our stores a couple of days throughout the year for major holidays. Other than that we're running full speed, and so the demands, the spontaneity, the speed, the need for flexibility and decision process have to be almost visceral. You need a lot of intuition and a lot of data, and you need to execute at top speed."

In this case, the fact that Nardelli himself was new to the business actually helped him frame the issues that faced the company. Because he wasn't steeped in the business, it was all new to him. He brought fresh eyes to the situation, and after years of grooming by Jack Welch, he was an eager and avid learner. For senior executives brought in from the outside, learning is a critical skill. The trick is to be open to learning from the people who know more about the company and the business than you do, without losing the freshness that allows you to see things that the old-timers may be missing.

When I talked to Nardelli in late 2001, after he had been on the job for several months, here was his TPOV on the corporate hand he had been dealt:

"The founders, Bernie Marcus and the rest of the team, have done a phenomenal job. They overcame all the adversity of a start-up. When you think about this, four stores twenty-some years ago, now we have 1,400+ as of today, and in 2001 we did $53.6 billion in sales. Think about the vertical growth. Now what got us here won't get us there. So we understand that the growth scenario that our co-founders gave us is one that we have to build upon. But now we need a new formula for a world that has been changed by having Home Depot in it."

Developing the Ideas TPOV: Drucker's Business Theory

A framework that I recommend to leaders for thinking about their business ideas is one developed by Peter Drucker that he calls the "business theory." Drucker's point is that successful businesses are built on a central concept. This concept is based on assumptions about the "outside" and the "inside" of the company. The assumptions about the outside relate to customers, markets, distribution channels and competition. The assumptions about the inside are about core competencies, technology, products and processes.[4]

Drucker stimulated me to develop a set of questions that I use to help leaders work through the ideas portion of their Teachable Point of View. I usually start by using Microsoft as an example.

Drucker asks leaders to examine three fundamental questions about the present and the future. These are tough questions that are made all the more difficult to answer by their simplicity.

Question 1:   What is the environment you are operating in now? What will it be in the future?

Question 2:   Given the environment, what is your business theory? In other words, how do you make money today? And how are you going to be able to make money in tomorrow's environment?

Question 3:   How well do the people in the company truly understand the business theory? What do you need to teach them to change the business theory for tomorrow? And how are you going to do that?

Microsoft Embraces the Internet

Microsoft is a great example because Bill Gates changed his business theory in 1996. The answers below show Bill Gates's old, pre-1995 TPOV and the new one he has pursued since then.

Question 1:   The old environment for Microsoft was the advent of the PC era. Microsoft would be operating in a world of rapid growth in the use of PCs.

Question 2:   The business theory that Bill Gates settled on was "own the operating system." This was how Microsoft would make money.

Question 3:   How well understood is the business theory? Everybody got it. It was a period of rapid growth for Microsoft. Employees joined the company, and suppliers and customers did business with it fully understanding that Microsoft's purpose was to own the operating system.

Bill Gates Post-1995 Business Model TPOV

Question 1:   The environment in the future would be Internet-based. Bill Gates was famously slow to embrace the Internet. In fact, he publicly maintained that Microsoft would *not* become an Internet company before changing his mind—a hallmark of a good leader— in 1996. After that, he began aggressively pursuing a new business theory.

Question 2:   The new business theory for Microsoft is "own the Internet" with a host of products and services. This has resulted in the hiring of new software people, a search for content ownership, and involvement in actual hardware ventures.

Question 3:   While most people intellectually get the new theory, many don't have a firm grasp on the implications.

The old Microsoft was very customer un-friendly. Because it did own the operating system, it was able to get away with products that were late, unreliable and difficult to use. But the Internet is a wide-open place full of competition, so "owning" it is going to require speed and responsiveness to customers. This means not just hiring people with those values, but also changing the values of the people who have been part of the company for a decade or more.

The point of the Drucker-derived questions for me is that they force leaders to take a hard strategic look at their organizations and develop a clear business model that they can teach to others.

General Electric Becomes a Services Company

At GE in the mid-1990s, Jack Welch made a fundamental change in his business model TPOV for GE, moving it from a global products company to a global services company. Now Jeff Immelt is refining that model. Using the Drucker framework, here's how the GE business models look:

The Pre-1990s GE model

Question 1:   The traditional environment for GE had been mostly industrial markets, in which people paid for hard goods and companies competed on the basis of price and quality of those goods.

Question 2:   GE made money on margins. The business theory was to sell products with as much margin as possible.

Question 3:   Everyone at GE in the product organizations knew this, and all of the processes, metrics and teaching reinforced this business theory.

Welch's Model for the 1990s

Question 1:   The new environment was one of commoditization, deflationary pressure and overcapacity. As a result, it was very hard to get price increases. Airlines were pushing for price-cuts on engines. Hospitals bought CT scanners solely on price. The only way to maintain profitability with the old model in this environment was cost cutting, but that can only go so far.

Question 2:   Welch decided that GE's growth would have to come from a massive transformation from a product company to a global services company. Here's how he explained it:

"Customers will always need high-quality hardware, but what they must have more than ever are productivity solutions that help them win in their markets. Our challenge in the years to come will be to continuously find new ways to help them fight their competitive battles, by providing more sophisticated added-value services."

Question 3:   At the 1995 meeting of operating managers in Boca Raton, Welch announced his new business theory for GE. "Services is so great an opportunity for the company," he told them, "that our vision for the next century is a GE that is a global services company that also sells high-quality products." This began five years of teaching to everyone in GE. It is reinforced and taught by Jeff Immelt to this day.

For his part, Immelt isn't changing Welch's global services growth engine as much as he is souping it up. He says that he remains convinced that the Welch model is still essentially correct. "But," he says, "we are not happy to stay there."

Immelt says that there are two things he wants to do to make the model work better. "First of all, I want to make the company leaner, faster and more focused on the customer. The businesses of the twenty-first century need that to win. When I look at GE today, 60% of our resources are in what I call 'front rooms,' touching the customer and driving growth. Engineers, manufacturing, sales people are touching the customers. Forty percent are in what I call 'back rooms,' administrative centers, support centers and things like that. In the next three or four years within GE, that back room, that 40%, is only going to be 10%."

The second thing he plans to do to make GE a better services company is to leverage the Internet and information technology. "Digitization and the Internet are just beginning, so what I am trying to do is drive a much more customer-facing, growth-oriented company, and a much more externally focused company."

With new technologies, in aircraft engines, for example, he says GE can continue to grow its maintenance services to airlines with such things as remote monitoring of jet engines while the planes are in flight. Power systems may be able to help clients forecast demand and maximize productivity. In the medical markets, GE already monitors the equipment for efficiency and delivers software upgrades over the Internet. Immelt intends to make this intellectual content a bigger piece of GE's business:

"Technical excellence is a linchpin of GE's long-term growth strategy. We plan to increase our Six Sigma designed product launches by 25% in 2002, and we will advance in new areas—such as molecular imaging, distributed energy, advanced composites and sensors, with much of the research led by the GE Global Research Center."

Home Depot: A New Model for a New Market

Bob Nardelli is also crafting a new business theory for Home Depot. The old Home Depot model followed these lines:

Question 1: The economy was strong and baby boomers were in their prime.

Question 2: The old Home Depot business model was to expand the retail market for hardware by helping everybody in America become a do-it-yourselfer. It would offer them the widest array of goods at the lowest prices.

Question 3: Teaching customers was built into the fabric of the company. Hiring was based on an applicant having skills that he/she could teach.

The new Nardelli model sees:

Question 1: The future environment for Home Depot is dramatically different. The economy is less buoyant, and the baby boomers are aging. Also, Home Depot is no longer an upstart with lots of room to grow. It is now the dominant player in the consumer hardware market.

Question 2:   Home Depot is pursuing two new lines of business. One is expanding Home Depot's sales to professional contractors and builders. Home Depot has been "playing only modestly" in this $280-billion market, says Nardelli. So he has targeted an initiative "to make sure that we are growing the opportunity to serve our professional customers.

"We also understand that our customers are maturing," he says. "Home Depot really grew the do-it-yourself market. We taught a lot of people and helped them do a lot of projects. But now they are getting older and maybe have some more money, and they are changing from a do-it-yourself concept to a do-it-for-me concept. There is a huge opportunity, a $150- to $160-billion opportunity in services. We are only modestly in that business right now. We did about $2 billion last year. We ought to be targeting 25 to 30% compounded average growth rate."

Question 3:   Nardelli, along with the help of his HR executive, Dennis Donovan, has launched a set of teaching mechanisms to reach out to hundreds of thousands of associates and get the new business theory taught. In addition, Home Depot is holding workshops with suppliers to get them to understand its changing needs.

Developing the Values TPOV

After leaders have developed their business models, they then have to take a hard look at the organization's ability to deliver on that model. The framework above touches on this when it talks about making the business model widely understood. This understanding, however, can't be just intellectual. It has to be at a level where it affects behaviors. And this is where values come in.

The values of an organization need to support achievement of the business model. In the Microsoft case, I noted that the people who, in the past, have not placed much priority on being customer friendly are going to need to develop that value if they are going to win customers in the highly competitive Internet market. A value that focuses on customer satisfaction is new for Microsoft.

Thinking about how people need to behave in order to deliver on the business theory is the essence of getting the values component right. Leaders create, shape and reshape culture. They must do this very consciously by developing the values component of their TPOV and teaching it just as assiduously as the ideas component of the TPOV.

The process I have leaders use for developing a values TPOV is similar to the ideas exercise. You start by looking at the reality of what the present values are. Then you decide:

1. Which of the current values are still helpful and should be retained?
2. Which ones are detrimental to achieving the new plan and need to be weeded out?
3. What new values need to be added?

General Electric: Jeff Immelt

Jeff Immelt took the period of transition at GE, the first half of 2001 while Jack Welch was still around, to reflect on how the GE values needed to change to support his TPOV on ideas.

Immelt concluded that in order to succeed as a services company, the core values of GE needed to more strongly focus on the customer. He also concluded that with the ever increasing demands on workers, especially in technology companies, GE needed to become more concerned about the quality of its workers' lives. This would include explicitly working to instill values related to giving people more balance in their lives and a greater connection to the broader community. When I talked with Immelt in October 2001, a month after Welch's retirement, he said:

> In terms of putting my spin on the GE values, they should be more on customer, more on innovation, more on community . . . on the need to lead in the community. . . . I think we're too internally focused. So [we need to get] the leaders of our businesses more in front of customers, more in front of normal employees, out in the community, out with leaders in industries. . . . We need to become a bigger advocate for things like diversity. The good part of globalization . . . probably means being more focused with respect to how we deal with the community, as well as better environments for our people, more flexibility, more cultural respect . . .

This was a very preliminary statement. At that point he still needed to figure out how to articulate these values more clearly and then to operationalize them so that they can be taught throughout the company. But the hard part is what he had already wrestled with, which is how the shift in the business theory calls for a shift in the values.

He has a strong sense of what he wants in GE leaders: "I'm trying to change the leadership. I'm trying to create leadership for what I consider to be the next generation." Immelt says that he thinks the next generation of leaders at GE has to have four traits.

The first two are ones that Welch also strongly nurtured. "First," says Immelt, "you have got to be able to perform. There is nothing that replaces people who know how to perform in cycle after cycle, in good times and bad. Performance is absolutely critical. You can't go anywhere without performance.

"Second, you want people who know how to learn every day. The people who drop out in GE are the people who stop learning."

But, he sees the need for an added emphasis on diversity and global teamwork. "Third, great people are going to have the ability to work in diverse global teams. At GE you're going to have to learn how to work with diversity and global teams and be able to energize people to do better."

And a new trait he believes will be necessary is what he calls "heart." "Fourth," he explains, "we have got to find a way to attract people who want to give back, give back to the environment, back to the community, give back to the workplace. Now more than ever before, people want to win, but they want to do it with heart, and both things are important in the twenty-first century."

Crafting Your TPOV into a Compelling Story

Understanding the concept of the Teachable Point of View and the value of each element is important, but having each of the elements isn't enough. They need to be woven together into a story that people can understand, relate to and remember. It is *not* enough to have slogans and mission/values statements. People don't sign up for that. People follow leaders who can make them part of something exciting.

Think about all of the boring seminars you have sat through and the exciting, inspiring speeches you have heard. The boring seminars were probably taught by people with decks of dry, analytical PowerPoint slides. The people with the inspiring speeches were painting pictures with their words and telling stories.

In his book *Leading Minds,* Howard Gardner, the noted Harvard psychologist, points out that as early as the age of five, humans understand the world through dramatic stories. Children relate to the stories of Robin Hood and Cinderella because they feature individuals with whom they can identify, and they portray dramas of life that reflect the world around them. This is also the reason software designers build computer games around plots and specific, identifiable characters.[5]

As people mature, their views become more complex. Nonetheless, he says, "Adults never lose their sensitivity to these basic narratives." Therefore, the leader "who can draw on or exploit the universal sensitivity" to the classic storylines is the one who most often "succeeds in convincing an audience of the merits of his or her program, policy, or plan."

Generating an interactive exchange of ideas and insights and creating a Virtuous Teaching Cycle requires that information and ideas be presented in a way that people can easily grasp and respond to. In *The Leadership Engine,* I talked about the kinds of stories that winning leaders tell in order to get people to let go of the familiar past and move into a transformed future. These stories are powerful because they tap into people's emotions and instincts as well as their intellects. And they are also essential to creating Virtuous Teaching Cycles.

Who Am I?

There are three basic types of stories that winning leaders tell. The first of these are "Who am I?" stories. These are the personal stories that explain the real-life experiences that have shaped a leader and his or her Teachable Point of View. These stories not only give power and authenticity to a leader's TPOV, but they also help build the bonds of trust and affection that permit open exchanges between people.

Cisco: John Chambers

A central element of the "Who am I?" story that John Chambers, CEO of Cisco, tells is that he has a learning disability. He talks about how kids in the third grade in West Virginia made fun of him because he couldn't read. He was told by teachers that he would not graduate from high school. He said, "It hurt, because there is nothing worse than being laughed at because you can't read. You think you are dumb."

Chambers says that three things happened as a result of that experience. "First, once you overcome a challenge like a learning disability, you can face anything in life. Business challenges are not anywhere near as hard." Second, "you learn to treat others as you want to be treated." Being made to feel dumb and having his self-confidence undermined taught him the importance of empathy and caring. Finally, "you learn the value of education."

John Chambers's Teachable Point of View on leadership and his shaping of Cisco and its culture are deeply rooted in his "Who am I?" story. When Chambers talks about his TPOV about diversity and about appreciating and using the talents of everyone, people know where he is coming from and that he really means it.

Who Am I? Examples

- Jack Welch—the stutterer. Never, ever going to let anyone best him.
- Andy Grove—the Hungarian immigrant. Fought his way out of his country during the Russian occupation; always a fighter, always paranoid.
- Myrtle Potter—overcoming son's illness made her fearless of business issues.

Leaders' "Who am I?" stories help them clarify and understand their own deeply held beliefs.

Who Are We?

While leaders' "Who am I?" stories explain and ground their TPOVs and build bonds with others, there are two other types of stories that convey the content of a leader's TPOV and provide the basis for discussing, revising and/or acting on them. These are the "Who are we?" stories, and the "Where are we going?" stories.

"Who are we?" stories are similar to leaders' "Who am I?" stories, except instead of being about the personal experiences and frame of mind of the leader, they are about the joint experiences and attitudes of the people within the organization and also about their shared beliefs.

Home Depot

At The Home Depot, for example, the "Who are we?" stories revolve around being people who "do whatever it takes" to please customers. The people at Home Depot see themselves as customer advocates and partners, and the stories that they tell are about individual instances when they have helped people accomplish goals and improve their lives.

Southwest Airlines

At Southwest Airlines, the "Who are we?" story is about a team of rebels who take their jobs but not themselves seriously. Led by fun-loving Herb Kelleher, they identify themselves as people who "make travel fun and affordable."

The message at both Home Depot and Southwest Airlines is that the people who work there are "special" people, who have a shared history of success and who can and will attain greater victories in the future by following their traditions.

"Who are we?" stories weave together the values of an organization into a dynamic vision that serves as both a guide and an inspiration. By grounding people emotionally as members of a special team, they create the bonds that make them want to keep improving the organization and make them eager to open up and participate in interactive teaching and learning.

Where Are We Going?

The third type of story that winning leaders tell is the "Where are we going?" story. This is the story that embodies the corporate Teachable Point of View about what the organization is aiming to do and how it is going to do it. It starts with the leader's TPOV about the business that the company is in and how it is going to succeed in that business. As the Virtuous Teaching Cycle revs up, however, it quickly becomes a shared product. As each leader teaches it and elicits the students' responses, the story gets refined and improved.

The "Where are we going?" story is the battle plan, but taken off the slides and flipcharts and made into a live action movie. It is the translation of the plan into narrative form that makes it available for everyone to respond to, both on an emotional, action level and on an intellectual, conceptual level.

"I Have a Dream . . ."

Martin Luther King, Jr.'s "I have a dream" speech is the gold standard for laying out a Teachable Point of View and transforming it into a compelling narrative.

Here's the TPOV.

- Ideas: "One day this nation will rise up and live out the true meaning of its creed: 'We hold these truths to be self-evident; that all men are created equal.' "
- Values: "We must forever conduct our struggle on the high plane of dignity and discipline. We must not allow our creative protest to degenerate into physical violence."
- Energy (teamwork and urgency): "We all have come to this hallowed spot to remind America of the fierce urgency of now. . . . Now is the time to rise from the dark and desolate valley of segregation to the sunlit path of racial justice."
- Edge: "There will be neither rest nor tranquility in America until the Negro is granted his citizenship rights."

Here's the narrative, the call-to-action movie:

- Ideas: "I have a dream that one day on the red hills of Georgia the sons of former slaves and the sons of former slave owners will be able to sit down together at a table of brotherhood.

I have a dream that one day even the state of Mississippi, a desert state sweltering with the heat of injustice and oppression, will be transformed into an oasis of freedom and justice.

I have a dream that my four little children will one day live in a nation where they will not be judged by the color of their skin but by the content of their character.

I have a dream today.

I have a dream that one day down in the state of Al-

abama, whose Governor's lips are presently dripping with the words of interposition and nullification, will be transformed into a situation where little black boys and black girls will be able to join hands with little white boys and white girls and walk together as sisters and brothers.

. . . When we let freedom ring, when we let it ring from every village and every hamlet, from every state and every city, we will be able to speed up that day when all of God's children, black men and white men, Jews and Gentiles, Protestants and Catholics, will be able to join hands and sing in the words of the old Negro spiritual, "Free at last! Free at last! Thank God almighty, we're free at last!"'

• Values: "With this faith we will be able to hew out of the mountain of despair a stone of hope. With this faith we will be able to transform the jangling discords of our nation into a beautiful symphony of brotherhood."

• Energy and Edge: "With this faith we will be able to work together, pray together; to struggle together, to go to jail together, to stand up for freedom together, knowing that we will be free one day."

Jack Welch, A Master Storyteller

In the business world, Jack Welch was the master of storytelling. He has a clear analytical mind that dissects situations and creates strategies with line-by-line bullet points. But when it came to waking up a complacent organization of 300,000+ people and getting them to embrace new ideas about their markets and new values about how to win, he did it by crafting stories.

On a tape I have from the 1983 annual meeting in Boca Raton of the top 500 GE leaders, Welch told a story he repeated in various forms and at varying lengths for twenty years:

Our objective, without question, is to become the most competitive enterprise on this earth. Don't ever forget it. It's going to be absolutely what we're going to be. We're going to take the Japanese and run them right into the ground on head-to-head competition where we face them. We can take on the best in this country or anywhere else. And we are going to be the most competitive enterprise on this earth. We're good enough. We've got the resources. And the only way to do that is to be sure we understand this idea of being number one or number two, or driving to get there. We can't stand the three or four positions. We can't be fat. We can't be bureaucratic. We can't be slow moving. . . . Don't stand for anything less than the best. You have great responsibilities, but you also have tremendous opportunities. Being the very best will be an incredibly rewarding experience for this total organization of close to 400,000 people.

Welch repeated this storyline for twenty years, over and over, embellishing and expanding it.

In 1985, he said in his annual report letter:

As we look to the next five years, our combination of different business cultures and shared values gives GE the ability—the flexibility—to win in world markets. It provides the bond that stimulates our people, the most important asset of any organization, to pursue a common goal—achieving excellence in everything we do.

In the 1992 annual report letter he wrote:

Our unending drive to build a boundaryless, high spirited company is moving us faster every day in the direction of what we want passionately to become—the world's most competitive global enterprise.

At the end of his tenure as CEO he wrote the continuation of the same story in his 2000 annual report:

The GE of the future will be based on the cherished values that drive us today: mutual trust and the unending, insatiable, boundaryless thirst for the world's best ideas and best people. But the GE of the future will be a faster, bolder GE whose actions will make the Company of today appear slow and tentative by comparison, a GE whose every employee will understand that success can only come from an inextricable link to the success of our customers.

Jack Welch's GE Story

For the year 2000, Jack Welch was able to write a letter in the GE annual report that wove many of the elements of a complex TPOV into a comprehensive story.

The Business Ideas

• "Globalization has transformed a heavily U.S.-based Company into one whose revenues are now 40% non-U.S. Even more importantly, it has changed us into a company that searches the world, not just to sell or to source, but to find intellectual capital: the world's best talent and greatest ideas."

• "A services focus has changed GE from a company that in 1980 derived 85% of its revenues from the sale of products to one that today is based 70% on the sale of services. This extends our market potential and our ability to bring value to our customers."

• "Six Sigma has turned the company's focus from inside to outside, changed the way we think and train our future leaders, and moved us toward becoming a truly customer-focused organization."

• "Digitization is transforming everything we do, energizing every corner of the company and making us faster, leaner and smarter even as we become bigger."

Values

• **Teaching and learning.** "Our true 'core competency' today is not manufacturing or services, but the global recruiting and nurturing of the world's best people and the cultivation in them of an insatiable desire to learn, to stretch and to do things better every day . . . values and behaviors are what produce those performance numbers, and they are the bedrock upon which we will build our future."

• **Integrity.** "It's the first and most important of our values. Integrity means always abiding by the law, both the letter and the spirit. But it's not just about laws, it is at the core of every relationship we have."

• **Relishing change.** ". . . learning to love change is an unnatural act in any century-old institution, but today we have a company that does just that: sees change always as a source of excitement, always as an opportunity, rather than as threat or crisis . . . We strive every day to always have everyone in the organization see change as a thrilling, energizing phenomenon, relished by all, because it is the oxygen of our growth."

· **The customer.** "Bureaucracies love to focus inward. It's not that they dislike customers: they just don't find them as interesting as themselves. Today we have a company doing its very best to fix its face on customers by focusing Six Sigma on their needs."

· **Annihilating bureaucracy.** "We cultivate the hatred of bureaucracy in our company and never for a moment hesitate to use that awful word, 'hate.' Bureaucrats must be ridiculed and removed. They multiply in organizational layers and behind functional walls—which means that every day must be a battle to demolish this structure and keep the organization open, ventilated and free."

· **Self-confidence, simplicity and speed.** "One leads to the other. . . . We see, day after day, people's lives—and not just their business lives—utterly transformed by the self-confidence born of meeting big challenges.

"Self-confidence in turn allows one to communicate simply and clearly—without the business jargon, busy charts, convoluted memos and incomprehensible presentations that insecure leaders use to mask their self-doubt. Leaders who lack self-confidence use their intelligence to make things more complex. Self-confident people use it to make things simpler.

"Simplicity clarifies communications and enhances the chance that everyone in the organization gets the same message. Those clear, simple messages energize people and inspire them to action; thus simplicity leads to speed, one of the key drivers of business success."

Emotional Energy

"Leadership is about the four E's we've been using for years as a screen to pick our leaders. 'Energy': to cope with the frenetic pace of change. 'Energize': the ability to excite, to galvanize, the organization and inspire it to action. 'Edge': the self-confidence to make the tough calls, with 'yeses' and 'noes' and very few 'maybes.' And 'Execute': the ancient GE tradition of always delivering, never disappointing."

Edge

"It's about the four 'types' that represent the way we evaluate and deal with our existing leaders. Type I: shares our values; makes the numbers—sky's the limit. Type II: doesn't share the values; doesn't make the numbers—gone. Type III: shares the values, misses the numbers—typically, another chance or two.

None of these three are tough calls, but type IV is the toughest call of all: The manager who doesn't share the values but delivers the numbers; the 'go-to' manager, the hammer, who delivers the bacon but does it on the backs of people, often 'kissing up and kicking down' during the process. This type is the toughest to part with because organizations always want to deliver—it's in the blood—and to let someone go who gets the job done is yet another unnatural act. But we have to remove these type IVs because they have the power, by themselves, to destroy the open, informal trust-based culture we need to win today and tomorrow . . . until an organization develops the courage to do this, people will never have full confidence that these soft values are truly real.

". . . Not removing the bottom 10% early in their careers is not only a management failure, but a false kindness, a form of cruelty, because inevitably a new leader will come into a business and take out the bottom 10% right away, leaving them sometimes midway through a career—stranded and having to start over somewhere else . . ."

It Must Start with the Leader

Having a dynamic TPOV is key to leading a Teaching Organization. It is what drives the collective IQ of the organization. In a dynamic changing world, the leader/teacher must continuously learn while teaching. This is the essence of a Virtuous Teaching Cycle.

The initial step in building a Teaching Organization is for the leader to develop a Teachable Point of View. He or she must do the intellectually and emotionally hard work of sifting through a lifetime of learning and experience and extracting the valuable lessons. This process of examination and articulation not only makes the leader's implicit knowledge explicit and available to others, but also forms the basis for new learning on the part of the leader. It is also the first stage in building a personal Virtuous Teaching Cycle that keeps the leader continuously articulating, testing with others, revising, teaching and revising the TPOV by which the company is run.

At the same time that leaders are creating and constantly improving their TPOVs, they must also craft them into stories that are not only intellectually clear, but emotionally engaging, so that other people will be eager and willing to participate in the Virtuous Teaching Cycle that will make everyone smarter and faster and more aligned.

Chapter Six
The Paradox of Power: Overcoming Resistance on the Top Team

❚ Building a Teaching Organization Is a Radical Act
  - The top team must be unified and enthusiastic role models for change.
  - The top leader must work to build that unity and enthusiasm.

❚ Moving Along the Power Continuum
  - Leaders must be willing to command participation and open to hearing others.
  - Effective use of power requires a constant cycling through different roles.

❚ Leadership Failures Are Often Power Failures
  - Autocrats: They refuse to learn. Their organizations get dumber.
  - Abdi-crats: They fail to take needed actions. Their organizations lack discipline.

■ ■ ■

I have worked with dozens of CEOs over the past twenty-five years helping them wrestle with developing a vision, mission and values for their organizations. They have ranged from school superintendents in the 1970s, to health system administrators, to the CEOs of some of the world's largest companies. In all these years and experiences, when these top leaders have taken their senior teams off-site to focus on the future of the company for several days, I cannot remember one single instance when all the members wanted to participate.

This seems incredible to me. You would think that the top leaders of major institutions would relish the opportunity to work together, setting an agenda for the future of their institutions. But in every group there are always resisters, people who don't want to join the game and, often, who don't want the game even to take place at all.

In each of these instances, the process has gone ahead and worked only when the senior leaders have firmly taken command. Although the purpose of the meetings was to have a free and open dialogue, these dialogues occurred only when the leaders used their authority and power to command both attendance and participation.

This paradoxical use of power, issuing orders so that people will do things that are voluntary, is often needed to get Virtuous Teaching Cycles going. In order for Virtuous Teaching Cycles to work, people must be open to sharing. They must be willing to teach what they know and to learn from others. These are generous, self-reflective behaviors that cannot be commanded. However, they are also behaviors that generally have not been valued or rewarded in most organizations. Leaders who want to foster these behaviors, therefore, must be willing to exercise their power to overcome resisters and to create environments where the benefits of the desired behaviors can be experienced.

Overcoming Resistance

Uniting the members of the senior team around a common Teachable Point of View and then getting them to engage in the behaviors that create a Virtuous Teaching Cycle is an immense leadership challenge. It is as important as it is difficult. A leader who fails to crack the code on this and who doesn't succeed in unifying the top team will be unable to create a Teaching Organization.

Failure to develop solidarity within the top team is the single biggest stumbling block to successful transformations of any kind. Ultimately the lack of team formation at the top led to the demise of CEOs Bob Allen, formerly of AT&T; Eckhard Pfeiffer, formerly of

Compaq; Richard McGinn, formerly of Lucent; Jill Barad, formerly of Mattel; Lloyd Ward, formerly of Maytag; and Jac Nasser at Ford.

The issue basically boils down to the effective use of power. The leader who is too dictatorial encourages resistance and stifles creative engagement. The would-be leader who is unwilling or unable to exert authority at critical moments loses, or never attains, control, and thus is unable to carry out any long-term change.

Getting the power equation right is tricky in most circumstances. But the toughest place for a leader to do it is with his or her immediate team. Exercising power face-to-face with close associates is much harder than the non-personal exercise of power through rules, rewards, punishments, guidelines, etc.

There are two primary reasons for this. One is because of the close interpersonal dynamics. Face-to-face encounters require interactivity with other emotional beings. The potential for emotionality makes many leaders uncomfortable. So they avoid it, sometimes by becoming domineering, but most often by being too laissez-faire.

This first reason relates to the psyche of the leader. The second relates to the psyches and positions of the other team members. By definition, the top team includes the biggest power players in an organization. These are the people who have the biggest axes to grind and the most turf to protect. They are also used to exercising power in their own spheres and are often covetous of the CEO's job.

CEOs I have advised and observed are inevitably always wrestling with power and their top team. Cor Herkstroter's job at Shell was particularly difficult because its governance structure made his role of chairman similar to that of the Chief Justice, first among equals. I remember Jack Welch's struggle with Gary Wendt, CEO of GE Capital, who was generating half the profit of the company and thus had a huge power base. Wendt continuously argued with Welch and resisted him much of the time. Ultimately, Wendt headed for a business he could run himself. These dynamics never disappear—they are part of the power dynamics of leadership.

Aligning the Top Team

Power mistakes at any level, but especially at the highest levels of an organization, are very costly. Great leaders understand this, which is why they are very conscious and conscientious about exercising power within their top management teams.

Failed transformations and failures to build winning Teaching Organizations can almost always be traced back to the failure of leaders to use power appropriately. The root cause in most cases has *not* been the brain power of the CEO, but his or her political failure to appropriately use power and at the same time empower the team.

When political failures occur, teams fall apart, and the leader is almost inevitably doomed. One CEO I know started out with a very strong political hold on the top group. Through a judicious mixture of ordering, cajoling and persuasion, he got them to participate in a series of workshops to develop their team TPOV. Then he got them to teach their teams. But, over time, the CEO lost his focus. He got involved in acquisitions and outside commitments and took his attention off of maintaining the team. A power vacuum emerged. Some resisters took this opportunity to rebel and undermine the CEO. Ultimately, he lost control of the organization, the top team splintered, and he was fired.

Another charismatic CEO I know started out with a similar fervor, but got seduced by success and high-visibility outside activities. Thus, he not only failed to maintain the political support of the top team, but he failed to notice that he had lost it. He caught on when he was faced with a difficult set of business issues that resulted in the team undermining his power and the board ultimately firing him.

In contrast, Jack Welch never forgot the importance of keeping the top team on his side. Every day for twenty years, he worked at it. He viewed the world through the lens of building an inspired, able and energized team. People who weren't working 1,000% for his side had to be won over and excited . . . or fired. He knew that if he could maintain a top team of several hundred leaders at GE—all with the same TPOV and all out teaching—the battle was more than half won.

Power is one of the most written about topics in all of the social sciences. Management literature abounds with theoretical treatises on the sources and uses of power. And, in the popular press, power lists (the most powerful world leaders, women in business, people under thirty, fashion setters, etc.) are perennial favorites. But despite all the academic analyses and the popular glorification of the people perceived to be powerful, there is very little serious discussion about the concrete power issues that face leaders on a day-to-day basis.

In the very same circles where demonstrations of power confer status on the power wielders, straightforward discussions of power are often considered crass. It is as if power were evil and to admit to an interest in it is to concede a moral failing. Unfortunately, that is a very damaging way to look at it. The issue isn't whether a person exercises power, but whether he or she exercises it appropriately and productively.

In discussions with Jeff Immelt, the CEO of GE, he was very clear about how he uses power. He is very participative in seeking the input of his senior team. He meets weekly with them to hear their ideas, but then he says:

"I make every decision. I get lots of advice, but I don't delegate. I ask, What do you think? What do you think? from everyone, then boom, I decide."

When a leader uses power clearly and appropriately, there is usually tremendous support for a decision and a cohesiveness in the team. When the use of power is seen as inconsistent, capricious or manipulative, the seeds of team disharmony and resistance are sown. Immelt, as with all CEOs, is continuously faced with this cycle of control and participation. It is a paradox, not one or the other, but both.

Resistance: It's a Power Play

A person who doesn't have the power to positively change a course of events will often try to do so negatively, through resistance. It may be covert, but it's still a power play. It needs to be recognized as such.

Occasionally, resisters can be diverted and/or converted through indirect means. But most of the time, it takes a strong leader who is willing to use his or her power in direct opposition to win.

People who become resisters have a variety of motivations. But what they have in common is that they feel threatened. In workshop settings, they may feel threatened either by the setting itself or by the results that it might produce.

At the extreme end of the political spectrum are the people who want to topple the leader and are out to thwart anything he or she tries. But there are many other kinds of resisters who are not as clear or overt about their intentions.[1]

- People who hijack power by using pocket vetoes usually don't like anything that takes decision making out into the open.
- Bureaucrats who get their power from writing and enforcing regulations don't like activities that bypass their checkpoints.
- People who don't have much self-confidence try to avoid being put on the spot, either to contribute their ideas in a workshop or carry out the resulting plans.
- People who benefit from the current power structure are simply reluctant to change it.

In these situations, it doesn't matter whether it is the resisters' motivation to perpetuate their own self-interest or timidity that makes them fearful of change. Winning leaders all do the same thing: They exercise their own considerable power to overcome the resistance. While their ultimate goal may be to promote an open interactive non-hierarchical sharing of ideas, they do not hesitate to slam dunk the opposition to make it happen.

It's a Cascade that Starts at the Top

Ultimately, the most successful organizations are the ones that create Virtuous Teaching Cycles and become Teaching Organizations from top to bottom. These are the ones in which people at all levels share information and learn from each other. Teaching and learning behaviors that permeate the environment and daily business transactions are based on mutual exchanges of valuable knowledge. But organizations like this don't just spring up spontaneously overnight. They are always created by a team of zealots in top leadership positions who are dedicated to creating them. And these teams, in turn, are built only when there is a senior leader at the very top with the focus and guts to build them.

The process for building a Teaching Organization is a progression that flows from the CEO to the top management team, then throughout the organization. First, the CEO, or whoever is at the top, must develop his or her own Teachable Point of View about how the company will succeed in the marketplace. He or she then works with the senior management team to share and improve that TPOV by creating a Virtuous Teaching Cycle. Those leaders then cascade the ideas and the teaching throughout the organization. The scale shifts from the individual to the small team to the whole organization, but the basic elements of creating the teaching and learning cycle are the same.

Principles For VTC Team Workshop

These are the guidelines that I have used for years to help leaders work with their teams to develop a shared Teachable Point of View. Understanding the principles for running the process helps the leader get the input of the team and helps the team collectively reach a jointly owned TPOV. It is a cycle that is repeated routinely in Teaching Organizations.

Step 1: Concepts   Frame the issues for the team. Give them the conceptual framework, whether it be how to think about business ideas, values, emotional energy or edge.

Step 2: Benchmark   Share benchmark examples of other leaders. Elicit benchmarks from the team as well.

Step 3: Individual written work   Have the team members think and commit to their thoughts in writing before opening the dialogue. This maximizes diversity of ideas.

Step 4: Group sharing and debate   The leader runs a very open dialogue, which gets out the diverse individual written work as well as generates new thoughts.

Step 5: Final decisions on TPOV   This is where the leader exercises power to bring closure. Participation and input must result in closure. It is up to the leader to make the summary of what gets decided, hopefully with as much consensus as possible, but the call ultimately is the leader's.

The leaders who succeed in building Teaching Organizations—or in implementing any change, for that matter—are the ones who recognize the importance of building a team at the top. And, paradoxically, they are willing to exercise all of the power they have to issue orders, to coerce, to reward, to punish, even to fire people, to make sure that they get the teamwork they need.

NBC: Bob Wright

When Bob Wright was named CEO of NBC in 1987, he faced a particularly difficult challenge. Even though he had been president of Cox Cable Communications earlier in his career, he was a lawyer whose job immediately preceding this assignment was the head of GE Financial Services. The people in both the entertainment and news divisions at NBC were skeptical about his understanding of and commitment to the business.

We met with the team for an off-site meeting at the GE guest house, an ultra-modern forty-bed conference center on the GE campus in Fairfield, Connecticut. Wright knew he was despised by half the team, several of whom had been passed over for his job. But, after commanding that the senior NBC management team attend the meeting, he lay back and let the arrows fly.

For many people, a turning point came when we did an exercise in which each participant wrote a mock magazine article describing what they would like for NBC to be three years in the future. We then went around the room and the participants read their articles to the group. When they heard Wright's, they realized that he wasn't just out to wring money from the unit and that, like them, he wanted to create a world-class network.

This three-day meeting laid the foundation for the teamwork under Wright's leadership that made NBC a winner. The meeting by itself didn't resolve the doubts about Wright in the minds of the NBC veterans or end their resistance. In fact, he ultimately had to use his power to fire several players who wouldn't change, but it was the beginning of building a team with one common Teachable Point of View.

If Wright had been unwilling to exercise his power to command attendance and participation, and ultimately to get rid of the people who refused to join his team, he would not have been able to build the momentum needed for change. But, if he had been only the rigid command-and-control guy that the NBC veterans expected him to be, he would not have been able to get the support he needed to get the changes implemented. It was the combination of using his power while at the same time opening himself up to share his hopes and hear the hopes, fears and ideas of others that allowed him to get a team that was both aligned and energized.

Ameritech: Bill Weiss

After seven years as an able manager at Ameritech, Bill Weiss turned in a bravura performance as a power manager in the two years before he retired as CEO in 1994. During the 1980s, he had just tinkered with the former Baby Bell, "because our performance was solid and life was comfortable."[2]

But in 1991, he realized that big things had to change if the company was going to survive, and someone had to make those changes happen. So, over the next two years, he skillfully used both his authority as CEO and his considerable personal skills as a coach and teacher to find his successor and to transform the company.

On the power side, he removed the four people who had been considered the top contenders for his job. They didn't see the need for change. They, rightfully, were threatened by the possibility of significant changes in how the organization operated. So they resisted participating in even the discussions about change. When Weiss saw this response, even though these were old friends of his who had risen through the ranks right behind him, he knew what he had to do. He, to use his own words, "Separated them on the most kindly terms possible."

The process that Weiss went through with these four people was similar to what winning leaders almost always do. First he tried to convert the resisters. When that failed, he took them out of the game and moved ahead with a new team of potential successors to lead a massive cultural change effort that they called "Breakthrough Leadership."

Weiss tore up his own calendar and devoted 50% of his time to coaching and teaching. He worked with the four people on the new Lead Team, who were now the candidates for his job, to teach them what he had learned about leadership and to help them learn to be effective teachers for the rest of the organization. They in turn taught him about the future of the business and their views on leadership. Together, they became a very powerful teaching team for transforming the company.

Weiss also role modeled the kind of personal transformation that he was seeking in others. He did everything that he asked his people to do, whether it was outdoor team-building activities, 360 degree feedback, or standing up in front of a workshop and sharing his Teachable Point of View. With the Lead Team as the head teachers, the Breakthrough Leadership program involved hundreds of leaders and task forces and intensive development activities in 1992, and it expanded to thousands of Ameritech managers in 1993.

Exercising Power to Build the Team

The single most important and difficult-to-master issue for a leader/teacher is how to effectively exercise power to the betterment of the organization and of the individuals in the organization. In academic terms, the question is: How does one manage the mutuality of power in an asymmetric power relationship? In lay terms, the issues are: How do leaders, who do have power to direct, reward and punish followers, use that power to generate the kind of teamwork that diminishes their need to use that power? How do they encourage members of the team to act independently on their own? And how do they elicit feedback, even pushback, from the people over whom they have formal control? It requires a careful and continuous cycling through a variety of power roles.

People like to talk about achieving a "balance" of power among competing groups and in their own relationships with others. But the notion that a leader should seek a balance is misleading if it implies that there is some ideal, static equilibrium that once found can, or at least should, be maintained. The truth is that organizations and relationships are dynamic. When "balance" is achieved, it is the sort of balance that a tightrope artist achieves when riding a bicycle across the wire. She remains upright and moves ahead only by constantly shifting from left to right.

Winning leaders recognize that the challenge is to move dynamically along the continuum of power from authoritarian to empowering and through a variety of roles—teacher, learner and coach—rather than to maintain a singular static position. Role modeling this behavior, first to senior management and, ultimately, to everyone throughout the organization, is how they build Teaching Organizations.

Power Failures

The two extremes of what I call "power failure" are easy to point out. On one end of the spectrum are the autocrats who have a Teachable Point of View, but who cram it down into the organization. Autocrats drive ahead without accepting feedback or input from others.

At the other end of the spectrum are the abdi-crats, who are so much into empowerment and listening to others that they don't make the decisions that need to be made. By abdicating their leadership responsibilities, they create power vacuums that result in anarchy and political chaos. These two extremes are exhibited first and foremost with their immediate team.

The Autocrat

Eckhard Pfeiffer is a person who got many of the elements of leadership right, but lost his job and damaged his company because he did not use his power well. In *The Leadership Engine*, I cited Pfeiffer as a good leader because he had a clear Teachable Point of View about how Compaq was going to win in the marketplace. He understood the need to create values in the Compaq culture that supported his business model. And he was effective in getting his TPOV to people throughout the company. What I missed in *The Leadership Engine*, however, was the need for interactivity, for teaching *and* learning.

Pfeiffer was extremely effective in executing a turnaround of the company based on his very clear Teachable Point of View. But what he did not do was create a power setting where he was able to build Virtuous Teaching Cycles.

His dissemination of knowledge was one-way, and the message for those who might disagree or have suggestions was, "It's my way or the highway." A leader can, in the short-term, get away with a one-way, top-down rigid Teachable Point of View. However, when the world began to change, Pfeiffer wasn't able to change quickly enough to keep up with it.

Pfeiffer saw that buying Digital Equipment would give Compaq workers the skills they needed. But after he spent $9.6 billion buying Digital, he did not let those people teach him. He continued to insist on his own ideas. Valuable ideas and information that Digital workers brought to the table were not only not utilized by the people in Compaq, but the Digital people were discouraged from acting on them as well. Several months after the acquisition took place, one of the Digital leaders told me that he was totally out of the loop on key decisions, and that the Compaq leaders, starting with Pfeiffer, had little regard for the Digital team's ideas or input. What Pfeiffer created was a vicious non-teaching cycle in which everyone actually got dumber instead of smarter.

Some autocrats are smarter and more noble-minded than others.

Pfeiffer really did want to make Compaq a winning competitor. He just didn't understand what he needed to do. Other autocrats, such as the almost cartoonish "Chainsaw Al" Dunlap late of Sunbeam, aren't even trying to improve their organizations. They have other agendas, usually related to making lots of money fast and/or feeding their own inflated egos.

But the defining characteristic of autocrats is not whether their goal is self-serving, but how they use their power in trying to reach that goal. Autocrats weaken, and if given the opportunity, will ultimately destroy their organizations because they are narrow-minded. They cram orders, strategies and ideas down into the organization and they don't learn.

At any given moment, a command-and-control organization may be able to move more quickly than one that is more decentralized. But over time, the organization that utilizes the eyes, ears, brains and energy of 30,000, or 300,000 people, instead of relying on one powerful person at the top, will find smarter things to do and do them better and faster.

Dot-Com Power Failures

Arrogance and hubris are at the core of most autocratic power failures. People who think they know it all invariably flame out. No place in recent memory has been more conducive to such fatal arrogance than the dot-com world. The scenario was played out time after time.

• **It starts with luck.**   People make a lot of money being in the right place at the right time.

• **Luck translates into an illusion of invincibility.**   Success comes so easily that failure doesn't seem to be even a possibility.

• **Celebrity seduction sets in.**   The calls, the board offers and the attention from the President, legislators and journalists all reinforce the illusion.

• **A "smarter than everyone else" attitude takes hold.**   The top team begins to attribute the creation of the wealth and power to their own intelligence and superiority. Nobody else is smart enough to "get it." One early warning sign, in retrospect, was a comment made by one CEO I worked with in 1999 about how Dick

Stonesifer and Ram Charan—two of the smartest and most seasoned business people I know—probably couldn't help him because they really did not understand the new economy and were too old-fashioned.

· **Basic business discipline is lacking.**   Internal controls are weak. The capital markets were throwing money at the dot-coms. How fast you burned cash did not really matter when the markets allowed you to keep getting more capital.

In one dot-com I worked with, the CEO was surprised to discover that his company had overspent its capital budget of $100 million. A disciplined manager would not have been surprised, but if by chance he or she had been, a crisis would have been called. In this case, that didn't happen. Three months later there was another more serious surprise that destroyed the company's credibility with investors and billions of dollars in market capitalization.

· **Teamwork splinters at the top.**   When the finances fell apart, so did the top teams. Team members were hurt, emotionally, financially and sometimes professionally, but the pain was uneven. Founders often slipped only from being incredibly wealthy to being very wealthy. More recent arrivals sometimes had margin calls that threatened them with bankruptcy.

· **Organizational cynicism begins.**   It spreads like a cancer, often unstoppable.

The Abdi-crat

Whereas autocrats hold power too closely and exercise it too forcefully, abdi-crats do just the opposite. They wimp out. They don't enforce discipline and they don't make decisions that need to be made. Bob Allen never controlled his team at AT&T, and neither did his successor John Walters. Allen tried to play the autocrat at times, but the system and the players on his own team resisted, and he never reined them in. This was also John Akers's problem at IBM and Mikhail Gorbachev's problem in the Soviet Union.

A misguided trend away from the importance of strong leaders began developing among organizational behavior theorists in the 1950s, and it continues in some circles today. The foundation for this was the work of Kurt Lewin, a social scientist who fled Nazi Germany. Lewin dedicated his research to how the social and behavioral sciences could build more democratic societies. This led directly to the establishment by many companies in the 1960s and 1970s of sensitivity training workshops. In these multi-day sessions, employees engaged in a variety of team activities including individual feedback to each other, self-reflection shared in the group, and learning about group dynamics.[3]

Since then, there have been several highly visible schools of thought among both academics and practitioners that are ambivalent, at best, about power and leadership. They portray change as something that must grow from the bottom up, grass roots. In more recent years, a stronger anti-leadership bias has emerged.

The argument is made that companies win because they have strong, cohesive cultures that support winning behaviors. This represents a bias against strong leadership that is dead wrong in my analysis of the same data.

I agree that winning companies do have strong cohesive cultures that support winning behaviors. But those cultures don't just happen. They exist because they are built and changed when necessary by strong and determined leaders, as underscored by Edgar Schein in his book on culture.

Arguments have been made that GE, IBM, HP, 3M and Motorola are companies whose cultures—as opposed to their leaders—have made them great. First, they have not performed equally, and some like Motorola and HP are floundering. Second, the same data show me a different picture. IBM, HP and 3M all had to hire new leaders from the outside because they failed to produce them internally. And, those new leaders have had to creatively destroy and remake the cultures.

Lou Gerstner at IBM has succeeded, but Carly Fiorina at HP is struggling. Under John Young and Lew Platt, a leadership vacuum developed at HP. Without a focus and a disciplined plan for moving ahead, fierce territorialism developed within the senior ranks. The result was increasing anarchy. Fiorina's big challenge was to build a teaching team at the top, regain control over the divided factions, and provide a TPOV for regaining market share. So far, she has definitely not succeeded.

Jim McNerney, new from GE to 3M, is off to a good start. At Motorola, there is a serious probability that Christopher Galvin, a family member, may not make it. At GE, the story is about how Jack Welch, a revolutionary from the inside, totally remade the culture to become a faster and smarter competitor.

The truth is that the notion of "bottom-up" leadership is naïve. It is true that to be successful and to effect real change in an organization, a leader must win the hearts and minds and energies of people throughout the organization. It is also true that in order to get this, a leader must empower those below him or her and give them a sense that their participation is valued. But the achievement of any mission or plan comes only with the focus and discipline of leadership from the top. It is the leaders who create the environment in which grass roots support grows.

Power Framework for Leader/Teachers

Sociologist Amitai Etzioni has a helpful framework that looks at both the source of a leader's power as well as the consequences of using that power on the others. It provides a useful way of looking at the interplay between how power is used and the level of commitment it generates.[4] This, in turn, makes it easier to figure out the conditions necessary for the successful exercise of power. This is particularly important for leaders attempting to build Teaching Organizations, in which both firm use and generous sharing of power are important elements.

According to Etzioni, there are three fundamental sources of power:

- Coercive   The use of force
- Utilitarian   The use of incentives
- Normative   The use of values

Coercive organizations, like prisons, get very little psychological commitment from their members. Prisoners comply because of the threat of punishment. They do not buy into the values of the leaders exercising the power.

Utilitarian organizations get a bit more commitment. Businesses are, to a greater or lesser degree, utilitarian. The relationship between a factory owner and a piece-rate worker is utilitarian. The worker assembles X number of blouses, running shoes or dolls, and the owner pays him or her Y amount of money. It is a straight exchange of labor for wages. It produces a little more commitment than coercion. People are willing to trade a certain set of behaviors in return for money, but they are not highly committed to the organization or the leadership.

Normative organizations exercise power through commitment to a set of values. A religious organization is a good example. Missionaries thousands of miles away from the home church behave according to a set of values to which they are highly committed. These values are internalized, and the power relationship is neither coercive nor utilitarian.

Businesses over the years have used all these sources of power, but predominantly have relied on the utilitarian exchange of pay for performance. As jobs have become a larger part of people's lives, the use of normative control has played a bigger role. Work has increasingly been used in a secular society as a means for fulfilling a broader range of outcomes for members—not just money, but self-esteem needs, social needs, and, in some cases, the highest order need, self-actualization, or the realization of one's creative potential.

In a knowledge economy, where companies need to creatively tap into people's ideas and get them to commit to 24/7 pressures, a combination of utilitarian rewards and normative power works best.

Power Cycles for Teaching Organizations

The challenge for leaders, then, is to use power in a way, or in ways, that, on one hand, focuses people on a course of action and enforces the discipline to achieve it; and, on the other, empowers, involves and engages the rest of the organization. In order to do this, leaders must be aware of how they use power in its various forms. Leaders must have a clear Teachable Point of View about both the forms and the uses of power. This includes having a TPOV about edge—when and how to make the tough yes/no decisions necessary to support their values and ideas.

Jack Welch used to say that rewards and incentives needed to be "both in the pocketbook and in the soul." You can't have people feel great about doing meaningful and important work and then reward them with a slogan and no financial incentives, nor can you get the emotional energy out of people through pure financial incentives and no meaningful feeling about the nature of their work. In addition to incentives, the leader needs to know when to push and punish.

Welch described his approach as "hugs and kicks." The ideal, obviously, is to motivate people through utilitarian and normative means. To achieve this, Welch personally reviewed incentive compensation and stock options of the top 500 leaders in the company, while at the same time, he worked hard to get them normatively bought into the values of GE. But he recognized that coercive power is sometimes needed, and he didn't shy away from using it when he thought it appropriate.

One of my favorite Welch qualities was his comfort with paradox. He spent a great deal of time coaching his leaders to have the edge to fire the bottom 10%, especially those who were not living the values. The paradox: threat of coercive power, of being fired, if you did not buy into the normative values of the company.

Even people who turn out to be strong team players sometimes have to be coerced into initially getting into the game. And there are always some people who just won't get on the team.

Each leader has to figure out the appropriate time period for "tryouts," which will vary according to the situation. Despite his reputation for toughness, Jack Welch was slow. He was CEO for more than five years before he made the "varsity" cut in 1986. At that time, having tired of trying to get all the leaders to buy in to his TPOV, he removed fourteen of twenty-one business heads. Dick Brown, CEO at EDS, got rid of more than half of his officers when he came in and was able to build his team at the top within a matter of nine months. They then became a cohesive teaching unit. Brown determined that the half that he let go were not going to be leader/teachers who embraced his philosophy of creating Virtuous Teaching Cycles.

David Novak also made development of a teaching team at the top of Yum! Brands a major priority from day one. The company was new, created from the restaurant division spun off by PepsiCo. He had a Teachable Point of View around building great brands and excellent customer service. His aim, he said, was to staff each store with a team of "customer maniacs."

So, even with all the demands of heading a new company, he personally ran ten weeks of workshops all around the world each year. The purpose of the workshops was to teach both managers in company-owned stores and franchisees how to build teams at the store level, how to reward people, and how to celebrate success. Nonetheless, for all the upbeat tone of his TPOV and the hundreds of hours he invested in coaching and cajoling, he still had to replace several members of the top team. If he hadn't done that, he says, "There is no way that we could have grown this business so fast and prepared it for the future."

The point is that building a Teaching Organization is not about being soft and fuzzy. It is about building high-performing teams of leader/teachers. A leader who doesn't use power appropriately does a disservice to the whole organization. All three kinds of power—coercive, utilitarian, and normative—exist, and failure to use or over rely on any of them can be fatal.

Chapter Seven

Building the Leader/ Teacher Pipeline: Developing Leaders for the Future

▮ A Special Need: Grooming Leaders for the Senior Team
  · Most companies wait until it's way too late to find a CEO successor.
  · Winners don't find successors—they create them.

▮ The Pipeline Should Run from the Entry Door to the CEO's Office
  · The apprentice method isn't efficient.
  · Leaders must be systematically taught.

▮ Design Principles: Develop a Core Curriculum
  · Create developmental goals for every level.
  · Use all available teaching tools—on the job, off the job, stretch assignments.

When Les Wexner, founder and CEO of Limited Brands, tells the following story about himself, he does it in a wry, lighthearted manner. But the lesson he learned was a very serious one. If he hadn't learned it, he probably wouldn't be laughing today.

Wexner says that he did a little survey, asking Jack Welch at GE and Wayne Calloway at Pepsi what they did every day. Do you look at sales? Do you monitor them every morning? Both of them told him no. Selling stuff and keeping track of sales were other people's jobs. They told him that what took the largest portion of their time and the most important thing that they did was review and develop people. At GE, Welch tracked the top 500 people. Calloway focused on the top 250.

Hearing this, Wexner decided that he would follow their example. "After I thought about this for several months, pondering how they spent so much time doing this, I said, 'Well, we should do this, too.' I asked my HR VP to organize a meeting about the top 100 people. He showed up in my office with a yellow legal pad and said, 'Okay, start talking.' I said, 'Where is your list?' And he said, 'We don't have one. You wanted to talk about it so I'm here to talk.' So, then I said, 'Well, who are the top 100 people?' And he said, 'You will have to pick them.'

"It was a frustrating hour or two because we just kept going around and around in this vein and nothing happened, but it did get me to thinking about things I should have been thinking about before. It really was appalling. I realized that I had no concept even how to think about people, no conceptual frame. I began with some pretty primitive stuff, strengths and weaknesses, and did I think that they had a future here? That started the process."

Leadership Test: Who Is Your Successor?

The primary reason for creating a Teaching Organization is to develop leaders. Leaders are people who can think and act intelligently on their own and who can teach others. In order to win in the marketplace, organizations must have leaders who are able to recognize customers' needs and fulfill them quickly and efficiently. And, in order to sustain that success, those leaders must be constantly teaching others to be leaders.

This means broadscale teaching that raises the level of play and improves the leadership abilities of everyone, everywhere in the organization. It also means building a pipeline to develop the abilities needed for future generations of senior management. Building this pipeline is critical to long-term corporate survival.

As I have said for many years, a company's success is directly tied to its ability to create leaders. The companies with the most leaders are the most successful. And companies get leaders by consciously creating Virtuous Teaching Cycles that constantly improve the abilities of people at all levels of the organization.

One of the biggest failings of any institution is the failure to develop leadership bench strength. This is highlighted when large companies with hundreds of thousands of employees have to go outside to find a CEO. This is a manifestation of a disastrously broken leader/teacher pipeline.

Some leadership failures are quite obvious. These are the ones that often lead to the firing of the CEO. In the early 1990s, AlliedSignal fired CEO Edward Hennessy and brought in Larry Bossidy, former vice chairman of GE. Soon afterward, IBM sacked John Akers and hired Louis Gerstner; AT&T pushed out Bob Allen, went outside to hire John Walters from Donnelly, then fired him and brought in another outsider, Mike Armstrong from Hughes. Kodak fired Kaye Whitmore and brought in George Fischer from Motorola. Other recent CEO firings that required outside replacements include Jill Barad at Mattel, and Richard McGinn at Lucent.

But sometimes the failure of a CEO doesn't become apparent until succession crunch time is reached. At Merck and Hewlett-Packard, CEOs Roy Vagelos and Lew Platt appeared to be successful. The companies were not in trouble and neither were Vagelos and Platt, but neither had a successor. Not only had they failed to take the steps to assure that the companies would have sound leadership in the future, but by failing to teach others, they had also deprived the companies of their own decades of knowledge and insight.

But whether the failure costs the CEO his or her job or becomes apparent only when he or she decides to leave, the lack of at least one strong internal candidate for succession is a clear sign of leadership failure. A leader who doesn't prepare for the future has flunked an essential leadership test.

GE: A Leadership Academy

The most notable success in developing leadership talent is General Electric. Shortly before Jack Welch retired from GE, he had more than a half dozen viable candidates within GE to replace him. These included current vice chairmen Bob Wright, Dennis Dammerman and Gary Rogers as well as the obvious finalists, Bob Nardelli, Jim McNerney and Jeff Immelt who got the job, plus several younger GE leaders. And that doesn't count a number of GE executives who had already been hired away by other companies.

GE's CEO Graduates

Among the Welch-era GE graduates who went on to head other companies:

Home Depot	Bob Nardelli
3M	Jim McNerney
Albertson's	Larry Johnston
Polaris	Tom Tiller
TRW/Honeywell	Dave Cote
AlliedSignal/Honeywell	Larry Bossidy
SPX	John Blystone
General Dynamics	William Anders
Calpine	Peter Cartwright
Conseco	Gary Wendt
Stanley Works	John Trani
Pentair	Randy Hogan
Iomega	Bruce Albertson
Primedia	Tom Rogers
Great Lakes Chemical	Mark Bulriss
Intuit	Steve Bennett
Terra Lycos	Joaquin Agut
Comdisco	Norman Blake
Owens Corning	Glenn Hiner

General Electric is not a leadership academy company by accident. Jack Welch consciously made leadership development a top priority. In 1985 when he hired me to head the Crotonville leadership development center, one of my primary assignments was to help him develop a leadership pipeline. With then vice chairman Larry

Bossidy, we spent many hours designing a series of developmental activities to give everyone in GE the opportunity to acquire the skills and experience to move ahead.

In addition to the formal development activities, Welch built a culture and business practices to keep everyone at all levels participating as teachers and learners in Virtuous Teaching Cycles.

When I recently asked Welch how it was that he succeeded where others had failed, he told me essentially what he told Les Wexner. He said that what was most important for him at GE was knowing and developing people, not knowing the details of every business. This goes back to the Teachable Point of View, "people first, strategy second," that he expressed in 1981. He saw his job as picking and developing the right leaders, and then it would be up to them to develop the strategy and know the details of the business.

Welch can be funny and self-deprecating when he explains this philosophy. But like Les Wexner, he is very serious about his point. He once told me, "One of the things that helps us at GE is that I couldn't possibly know how to build a jet engine, make a CAT scan, pick a *Seinfeld* program, or build a refrigerator. The senior team and I aren't smart enough to run the businesses, so we have to focus on getting people who are."

In a more serious vein, he went on to explain, "Every day we are developing and assessing people, in the hallway, in meetings, at Crotonville, on the job, trying them in new jobs. We carry out extensive people reviews three times a year. We see this as our single most important job . . . I am proud of having so much leadership talent."

The Leader/Teacher Pipeline

Almost as soon as he took office, Jack Welch began planning for succession. Barring health problems or a colossal screw-up on his part, he knew that he probably had about twenty years until his retirement. But he saw this as simply giving him enough time to do the job right.

The first thing he did was zero-base the planning. He announced that whatever got him to be CEO would not be what would get his successor there. The company was going to be different and the world was going to be different. So, rather than replicate his own path for others, he set out to figure out what values and capabilities people would need to be successful in the future, and then how to develop them.

The leadership pipeline that we designed in the mid-1980s was based on the needs and values that we could discern then. In the subsequent years, the content and some of the processes have evolved in response to changing times. The framework, however, covers the design principles for creating a leader/teacher pipeline with Virtuous Teaching Cycles at all levels. It provides a useful way for thinking about how to build a pipeline.

Designing a leader/teacher pipeline is a strategic duty of the CEO. It is not a one-time task, and it cannot be assigned to functionaries or consultants. It is essential to the health of the company and it therefore must be a primary concern of the senior leader.

Yum! Brands

At Yum! Brands, for example, David Novak has set up a leadership development council that meets with him six times a year to work on the design of the Yum! Brands leader/teacher infrastructure. The group includes Novak and six key leaders who meet one day every other month to discuss leadership development issues and make sure that the pipeline is producing the results the company needs.

Accenture's New Leadership Model

Mary Tolan, a member of the executive committee at Accenture, is taking the lead in designing a new leader/teacher development architecture for the consulting firm. In the past, leadership development at Accenture has been basically an apprentice model. The firm's primary business was implementing large business process change and technology projects for blue-chip companies, and its leaders were people who excelled at handling the complex details that such projects required.

But in the past few years, Accenture has changed its business model to place more emphasis on becoming a strategic partner with its clients and coming up with innovative ideas for clients. This new TPOV requires new key traits in Accenture's managers and partners. It still needs people with top-quality implementational skills, but it also needs, as Tolan says, "the kinds of people who know how to celebrate the ideas of the client more and understand the role that we have in helping the client bring their ideas to life, while we play the role of improving the ideas. The best outcome is probably going to be the great ideas the client has, augmented by expertise that we can bring and help in getting all of that implemented."

This shift in emphasis for Accenture is requiring a revamping of who gets hired in the first place, both off-campus and mid-career. Tolan says, "We now want to hear confidence, but we also want to hear humility in the course of the dialogue. We want to see that they can be influenced by ideas of others. It is difficult to find the balance of confidence and humility."

It also requires different kinds of developmental activities. Tolan's goal is to build a leader/teacher pipeline at Accenture that produces leaders who are also strong collaborators. "We want people who say, 'I've got a lot to contribute, and I know I'm going to, but you've got a lot to contribute too.' These leaders tend to be the best collaborators both internally and with the client. They also tend to be people who build big client relationships because they are a pleasure to be with."

In line with its decision to become more proactive business partners with their clients, Accenture has changed its own organizational structure to admit many more younger partners. This has made the need for formal leadership training even more acute.

"We wanted to make partner status more accessible to people at a younger point in their career," explains Tolan. "In the past, it had been very strictly based on demonstrated performance. This meant multiple-year generation of $15 million or more in business for the firm. The change was to make being a partner more accessible to people at a younger stage based on talents and potential . . . We wanted to find younger people with energy and things they wanted to contribute, and to give them more responsibility and stretch them . . . The result is that we have a huge challenge, because it means we have 1,500 high potentials who need a ton of coaching and development from their fellow partners. They need to learn how to be successful entrepreneurs, how to lead, and how to grow client relationships.

"Historically," she says, "partner development was very much an apprenticeship model. There was a good deal of generosity. Partners would actually vacate pieces of the business to give it to a younger partner, and older partners would begin to judge themselves on their ability to be a king maker, to create more successful partners behind them. That was a very positive virtuous circle that really drove us. But now we're over stretched with so many new partners. Everybody is looking at all the ways in which we can crank up this cycle of development."

As part of the Accenture leader/teacher pipeline, Tolan and her team launched an action learning program for high-potential pre-partner managers. Tolan and her team created a Virtuous Teaching Cycle where they frame projects for five teams of five to work on over a six-month period. The projects have ranged from finding acquisitions for Accenture to coming up with value creation plans for mid-cap clients and ideas for dealing with major oil companies' huge cash reserves. The top team frames the projects, then learns from the young team members who pursue them. The junior team members learn by doing the projects and from interacting with the senior partners, while the partners get new information and ideas from the young managers.

Results Must be Measurable

Developing leader/teacher pipelines and keeping them tuned to produce leaders with the capabilities needed to succeed requires most senior leaders to develop a new mind-set and a new repertoire of skills. Good leaders have always considered coaching and development a part of their role, but when push comes to shove in a time-scarce world, it is often what goes first.

Leaders, therefore, must find ways to maintain the discipline and commitment to developing leaders even when other demands seem more pressing. One way to do this is to focus on some metrics that show whether the pipeline is performing as desired.

The metrics for success are as follows:

Leaders at All Levels

The measurement here is both quantitative and qualitative. The quantitative measure is simple: Are there slates of candidates to fill leadership positions at all levels of the organization? The qualitative measure is: How good are the candidates?

Leaders with a TPOV

Do the leaders have a clearly articulated Teachable Point of View? Can they explain it in writing? More importantly, how good are the leaders' TPOVs? This is measured over time by how well the organization, or the part of the organization the leader is driving, performs in the marketplace.

Leaders Who Develop Other Leaders

Track the number of leaders each leader has played a major role in developing. The concept is simple—most organizations do not take the time to track this or try and measure it. At a macro level, the press has done this with Jack Welch in remarking on all the leaders he produced at GE. At a micro level, it is tracked informally at GE in the Session C succession planning process where the question is repeatedly asked: Who has the person developed, and how well are they doing it?

The Ultimate Metric

When you retire, you won't remember what you did in the first quarter of 1994, or the third. You'll remember how many people you developed—how many you helped have a better career because of your interest and dedication to their development. When you're confused about how you're doing as a leader, find out how the people you lead are doing. You'll know the answer.

—Larry Bossidy, former CEO of Honeywell and a former GE vice chairman

---

Leaders Build VTCs

Are leaders eager to learn from others as well as to share their knowledge? Have they created systems that institutionalize interactive teaching and learning? Examples of such systems are the Special Operations Forces' notoriously bloody and frank, but productive, "after action reviews" that engage everyone, regardless of rank, in benchmarking and seeking ways to improve. GE's Six Sigma programs, which have 15,000 middle managers serving full-time as "black belt" teachers and facilitators, are another. At Accenture, Mary Tolan's three-day partner meetings are VTCs. These 500-person meetings held every six months are designed to share best practices and help the partners learn from each other.

Designing a Leader/Teacher Pipeline

The architecting of a leader/teacher pipeline is a critical strategic issue for the CEO and the top team. It requires tough intellectual work, the crafting of a Teachable Point of View regarding the kind of leaders the company needs for the future, and then a framework for how to develop them.

Because it is a tough and time-consuming job, this often gets assigned to outside consultants or HR staffers. Sometimes this is because the senior leader feels that he or she just doesn't have the time to do it. Sometimes it is because someone in HR recognizes the need for it but can't convince the senior leadership. Unfortunately, the result is almost always just an expensive report that gets tossed aside or a futile HR exercise. This is because successful pipelines only get built when the senior leadership is passionately committed to doing it. And this commitment comes only when the senior leaders are intellectually and emotionally invested in designing them.[1]

At GE, for example, shortly after he became CEO, Jack Welch spent about eighteen months working with me and his top team, Larry Bossidy, Ed Hood and Paul Van Orden, designing a new leader/teacher pipeline for GE. The process involved innumerable sessions, many of them lasting a half day or longer, in which we discussed ways to build a pipeline that would not only produce a successor to Welch twenty years hence, but populate GE with leaders to improve its performance in the shorter-term. In notes that we made to document the process, we explained our reasoning as:

> The competitive challenges driving the cultural change process at GE requires that we have many leaders, at every echelon of the structure, in every function, in every business, in every location and across all ranges of experiences. True, we do need a few leaders capable of managing huge organizations of many thousands of people. But at the same time, we need a very large number of leaders, each capable of effectively maintaining a small number of people better than they have ever been managed before.

As a first step, we defined the various career stages that would take a GE employee from an entry level position up to the very senior-most ranks of the company. Not every person would climb all the way. In fact, very few would, but we wanted to create a process that would give everyone the opportunity to acquire the skills and experience to take them to the next level. Individual interests and performance would determine how far each person got, but we wanted a system that would maximize the capabilities and contributions of everyone.

Interestingly enough, we created ad hoc Virtuous Teaching Cycles to help us with the process. Often the heated debates with the office of the CEO would result in Welch saying: "We can't seem to agree. Noel, take this to some of the classes at Crotonville and let's get their feedback." As a result, we had literally dozens of meetings with leaders at all levels of GE at Crotonville that debated the framework and provided input as to both what was really happening in the organization as well as new ideas about development.

Ultimately, Welch and Bossidy took total ownership of the new leadership development framework that went from individual contributor all the way up to the contenders for Welch's job. The process was as important as the product because it forced Welch to articulate a clear Teachable Point of View regarding the development of leaders at all levels. And in the process of doing this, he became excited and invested in the importance of systematically developing leaders, and he built leadership development into the fabric of GE.[2]

The leaders discussed in this book are all wrestling with designing the next generation leadership pipeline for their organizations. This is not a one-time task, it is and should be an ongoing strategic issue for leaders who are developing the next generation of leaders. For example, Les Wexner of Limited Brands now clearly understands that as chairman and founder, his whole legacy is tied up in building a Teaching Organization with a systematic pipeline for developing new leaders for the company. Although he tells the story at the beginning of this chapter with a lighthearted, ironic tone, he knows that it is a tragicomedy. Failure to deal with his leadership legacy will mean failure to build a sustainable company. So, albeit late in the game, Wexner has begun a multi-year process to define leadership for Limited Brands and to build a pipeline.

Architectural Guidelines for VTC Pipelines

When architects design buildings, they follow a set of design principles—some are aesthetic and some are structural. Without these principles we get ugly buildings that are structurally unsafe. The same goes for social architecture. Without solid design principles, we end up with flawed organizational processes that don't work very well and when they do work, often produce the wrong results.

The design principles that apply to building leadership pipelines include:

The 80/20 rule: 80% of leadership development comes on the job and through life experience. Formal development experiences have the potential to deliver only about 20% of the knowledge and capabilities needed. Therefore, the architecture of the pipeline should be weighted much more heavily toward work experiences than formal programs.

Find teachable moments: The key to leveraging development is to find those unique transition points where there is the maximum opportunity for imprinting new learnings. I use the example of ducks to make this point. When a duck is hatched, the first moving thing that it sees becomes its "parent." In the duckling's perceptual system, birth is a receptive "teachable moment," which explains why it is possible to "trick" a duck into having a dog as a parent figure.

People are not quite so genetically programmed, even though I have seen some tricked into accepting a dog for a boss. The point is there are some very predictable transition points where formal development has a higher probability of making a difference than others.

Many of these are not surprising. Entry into an organization is a classic one. When people join an organization, they are inevitably imprinted by what they see and hear in the first few weeks. What they observe and are told about the culture, how the place operates, and how to do their job sets the pattern for the rest of their time with the organization. These impressions can be changed, but only with great effort. It is much easier to give people a firm grounding in the leaders' TPOV for the company at the beginning, which is why smart leaders invest in "boot camps."

Other teachable moments include the transition into management. The first time a person has to manage others, he or she faces a whole set of new demands. The need to master the arts of hiring, firing, appraisals, rewards, and developing and leading teams creates a teachable moment when they are more open than normal to learning. Because the move from individual contributor to manager is a quantum step, many institutions have formal programs at this transition point. Unfortunately, many of them are not well thought out as to what needs to be taught.

Develop a curriculum: At GE, we designated standard career periods. For each of these we needed TPOVs about the capabilities to be developed and how to develop them. We actually started out with nine periods, but eventually combined some of them to get down to five. For instance, we combined the "trainee" career period with the "individual contributor" period because the developmental tasks were essentially the same. But the developmental tasks for a new manager were so unique that we found that focus became diffused when we tried to combine new manager and experienced manager. We ended up with five levels: individual contributor, new manager, experienced manager, general manager and business leader.

Once the leadership levels are determined, next comes the defining of the learnings and developmental tasks for each level. The categories of the TPOV—ideas, values, energy and edge—are built into the learnings. A new entry-level, off-campus hire at GE, for example, was expected to start learning the business ideas and the values of GE, to begin the process of energizing themselves and others, and to start understanding how to make edge decisions.

Four levels later, by the time a GE leader was running a business, the business ideas category was focused on developing a vision and strategy for a large business as well as having specific business ideas for driving execution. The values tasks included teaching and aligning thousands of people around the core GE values. The emotional energy component was now focused on learning how to energize thousands of people around the leadership ideas and values. And, edge at the business leader level includes tough yes/no investment, acquisition and divestiture decisions, as well as yes/no people decisions that might include layoffs, the firing of key people, and making key promotion and hiring decisions.

The TPOV categories are very much like the elements of a school curriculum. When laying out a K through 12 curriculum, the categories remain the same: math, English, science, social studies, whether for first grade or sixth or twelfth grade. At each level, the developmental tasks and challenges become harder, more complex, as cumulative learning is assumed. Math in first grade sets the stage for math in second, and so on up the grade levels. The same is true for leadership. The four curriculum elements are:

Ideas: This is the mastery of intellectual content and skills. For a new college hire, the ideas component is largely related to mastery of specific functional job skills and the disciplines for accomplishing them. At the division head level, the ideas component means mastery over setting the business strategy and business model for the division.

Values: At the individual contributor level, it means learning the organizational values and reflecting on how one's own value set relates to the organization. For a division president, the role is to be the teacher of values for thousands of people and to evaluate and revise the values for the organization as the world changes.

Emotional energy: This component is about learning how to energize oneself and others. An individual contributor needs to learn to bring positive emotional energy to the job and begin to learn how to energize those around him or her. A division president must master ways of energizing thousands of people. This involves learning a whole array of leading/teaching mechanisms that range from running workshops to holding meetings with people at various levels, to establishing developmental programs to re-architecting the operating mechanisms of the company.

Edge: This is learning to make tough and courageous yes/no decisions. The individual contributor must learn how to deal with edge regarding workload and work planning, and how to meet deadlines when he or she is overloaded. Even though still not managers, individual contributors must also begin learning about people edge and how to make decisions regarding the performance of their colleagues.

At the division president level, edge is one of the most critical elements of the job. A business head must be able to make tough decisions on investments, strategy and acquisitions/divestitures. The hardest type of edge to master relates to people, especially when it comes to evaluating and possibly removing members of the senior team who all have power bases and often have long tenures and are personal friends.

Use all available tools: Once you have the curriculum for what you want people to learn, the next job is figuring how they are best going to learn those things. Here we go back to the 80/20 rule. It's 80% on-the-job experience and 20% formal training.

The framework that GE uses has five basic categories of tools:

Primary position assignment: The normal range of assignments a person could expect to have during that career period.

Enrichment assignment options: An assignment outside the normal path that presents unusual perspectives or developmental

Figure 8
Yum! Brands Leadership Pipeline

Position	Is a customer maniac	Knows and drives the business	Builds and aligns teams
Individual contributor	• Applies understanding of HWWT: Can describe the principles, uses the language and is put into practice. • Understands the end customers is why we exist: Applies Customer Mania principles of acting like an owner, making it user-friendly, doing it right the first time, sense of urgency, and taking accountability.	• Has knowledge and passion for the restaurant business: Can speak about the industry. Understands Balance Scorecard drivers. Takes a visible interest in food, restaurants, and competitors. • Takes accountability for excellence in achieving blue chips: Achieves a high standard of results. Recovers and learns from taking risk. Gains expertise in a particular functional area.	• Demonstrates positive energy AND productive conflict in team settings: Collaborates well with others. Contributes and enables others to team results. • Has effective communication skills: Clear and concise messages, both verbal and written. Develops comfort in presenting in front of a group.
First time leader of people/process	• Recognizes and reinforces Customer Mania behavior: Ensures that work from team supports our restaurants with user friendly, cost effective programs that are right the first time. • Actions reflect words in Walking the Talk of HWWT: Identifies and reinforces use of HWWT.	• Relies on others to accomplish Blue Chips: Selects the right opportunities to delegate instead of doing it yourself, but accepts accountability in either case for results. Through their own actions, motivates team to be self-starters. Coaches others to achieve excellence and accountability. • Recognizes results: Reinforces progress, even small steps in the right direction. Uses both formal and informal settings to recognize achievements.	• Can lead a diverse team: Understands and deals with own strengths and weaknesses. Achieves own clear leadership style but applies situational leadership. Can play on multiple teams. Helps the team connected to a vision. • Develops an eye for talent and team building: Selects the best talent. Able to articulate and act on individual strengths and weaknesses. Enables productive conflict to achieve stretch team results. Provides immediate and actionable coaching for non-performance. Effective at handling conflict and negative feedback.
Broader coach	• Uses Customer Mania to package and communicate strategy: Frames AOP Blue Chips, etc. around serving those who serve the customer. Acts like an owner and recognition are a regular part of doing business. • Casts the shadow, in good times and challenging times: Enforces and inspires HWWT across the organization.	• Brings team focus to the vital few: Cuts through clutter. Tolerant of uncertainty. Simplifies complex information into a teachable point of view. Through selling, not telling, connects team to company direction. Passionately removes bureaucracy/obstacles to projects. • Allocates limited resources: Identifies and partners to obtain essential resources. Properly executes using existing processes. Drives improvement by constantly raising personal and team bar.	• Builds People Capability: Sponsors promising individuals to grow them for future leadership roles. Prioritizes the development of their managers. Coaches and supports two-levels down. • Influences across a broad range of stakeholders: Gains credibility through relationship building, deliver of results, and adaptable communication. Applies learning to influence organizational strategy.
Senior leader	• Casts the shadow of Customer Mania, even in challenging times: Makes customer mania the core of his/her leadership actions. Uses customer mania and HWWT to work through personal and team challenges. Views leadership as a privilege. • Mobilizes and energizes customer maniacs: Can make the big speech, which drives and inspires Customer Mania, change, and passion for the business.	• Broad business knowledge and financial acumen: Applies and teaches "One System Approach". Drives understanding of business levers deep into the organization. Seeks and embraces best practices which continually raise the bar. • Decisive thought leadership that sets current and future course: Able to anticipate stakeholder needs. Develops and gains consensus on solutions which are global, equity-blind, and highly adaptable. Makes change happen.	• Ensures clock-building, not time-telling: Views development of next generation of leadership as their personal legacy. Holds their leadership accountable for the development and sharing of talent within YUM. • Has influence over internal AND external teams: Communicates effectively to a broad audience. Gains credibility and respect through relationship building, and confidence in making "edge" decisions. Creates a large network of internal and external contacts to discuss issues, and benchmark.

opportunities. For example, a star in a technical specialty might be assigned to a customer contact role to give him or her new insights about how to be a better technician.

Perspective broadening experiences: Experiences afforded within the scope of an assigned position, such as special projects, attendance at certain meetings, membership in certain groups, etc.

Coaching emphasis: This lists what kinds of coaching would be most helpful at each career stage and by whom.

Educational options: Educational opportunities that can be made available while the person is on the job. These could be programs offered by the company or by an outside school, university or consultant.

Fixing Broken Pipelines

Older companies all have some sort of leadership pipeline. Otherwise, they could not have operated at scale. The issue for them is not to build a totally new one, but to transform it into a leader/teacher pipeline. This means sorting out what to keep, what to discard, and what to add for the new leader/teacher pipeline.

For the newer companies like Trilogy, Genentech and even the larger Dell, the issue is getting a pipeline that can deal with hypergrowth. Even though the ups and downs of the economic cycle may temporarily slow these companies' growth, longer term they will be struggling with doubling and tripling their size. When that happens, their scarcest resource will be good leaders to run the organization. One factor is new for everyone, and that is creating Virtuous Teaching Cycles at all levels.

3M: The Pipeline Needs Revitalization

Historically 3M had a leadership pipeline that was quite good, as far as it went. It took fresh young college hires and moved them through progressively more challenging and responsible jobs around the world. Because the company had forty-one separate business units, it wasn't uncommon for high-potential players to be heading businesses by the time they were in their late thirties. This system produced a cadre of well-developed leaders with a wide range of experience and capabilities.

But, over time, leadership development in the top ranks slowed down. The tradition at 3M had been to bring mid-career candidates who had done well as the heads of small business units or geographic areas back to headquarters to give them significant staff or line jobs. At this point, a major shift occurred for them. Out in the field, there had been a rich flow of learning derived from their hands-on leadership roles, but at headquarters, their focus became coordinating across the company.

This led to an emphasis on breadth of experience and resume-building. Over time, these became overly valued at the expense of learning to run bigger and bigger businesses. The result was that young managers were clogging the career paths at headquarters while they waited in line to get bigger jobs, and they were spending time in jobs that weren't doing enough to develop them as leaders.

When Jim McNerney arrived from GE to become CEO in 2000, he described the situation this way:

> *The good news is that you have mid-career men and women who can run big businesses. The bad news is that too many stand in line too long. They are often moved laterally to jobs and experiences that don't stretch them enough. Momentum and learning are lost."* In the future, says McNerney, *"broad and deep experience will not be the only criteria that drive why we promote people. Demonstrated leadership potential and performance will play a bigger role in why people move forward.*

When we talked, McNerney had been on the job only a few months, but he had already started building a Teaching Organization. The new 3M leader/teacher pipeline will include new definitions of what is considered good leadership, opportunities for rapid movement based on performance, and a set of VTC opportunities, including the creation of Six Sigma Black Belt teaching positions. McNerney is also building a leadership institute with action learning programs and extensive teaching by the 3M senior leaders.

Home Depot: The Ad Hoc Pipeline

In its first twenty years, Home Depot had a remarkable record of growth and success. A linchpin of its then-unique business model was outstanding customer service, and its associates, especially in the early years, were often models of ingenuity and initiative. They were leaders of the highest order when it came to listening to customers and making fast, smart, independent decisions. But while the company had a wide array of training programs to help its associates become even better at helping customers solve their do-it-yourself problems, its development of future leaders for the company was primarily through informal on-the-job training.

This was in part because the company was growing so quickly. As is common in hypergrowth situations, founders Bernie Marcus and Arthur Blank were so busy figuring out where and how to open new stores and staff them with top-flight associates, that long-term leadership development never quite made it onto the radar screen.

This situation was likely exacerbated by some confusion, which is common, between the people who are operationally excellent and the people who can lead a company of thousands of people. Les Wexner at Limited Brands talks about having lots of "merchants" but few leaders. At Home Depot the customer-oriented creativity of so many associates produced such strong results that the lack of leadership depth wasn't a serious concern.

Now, Home Depot's head of HR Dennis Donovan and Bob Nardelli view the key to their success as developing a new kind of leader at Home Depot at all levels. These will be people who are able to develop and retain leaders around them. They are also starting the process, a good decade in advance, to think of Nardelli's successor. "My goal," says Nardelli, "would be to have somebody in place and well entrenched with the organization for acceptability and continuity so that you don't run the risk of dislocation."

To meet its human development needs in a more systematic manner, Home Depot is organizing four institutes: a leadership institute, a Six Sigma institute, a customer service institute (which includes product knowledge, business knowledge and selling knowledge), and an enterprise institute that covers corporate management issues such as finance, human resources, supply chain and safety. Although only one of the institutes is labeled "leadership," all four of them provide skills and capabilities needed to be a well-rounded leader.

The institutes will provide the formal structure for the leadership pipeline, but their classroom component is only the 20% portion in the 80/20. The rest will be supplied through assignments and the creation of other on-the-job learning opportunities.

Donovan talks about the need to create "classrooms" in the context of everyday work.

The classroom is anywhere, training room to selling floor. Step one is to provide individuals with new thinking. Then, you test for understanding. Next apply it away from the floor and get feedback. Then, go to the floor and observe others, and finally, apply it on the floor and get more feedback. This is our adult learning model and how learning takes place.

Limited Brands: An Entrepreneur Who Got Religion

The broken leadership pipeline at Limited Brands is typical of many entrepreneur-led companies. Entrepreneurs usually have a mental model of leadership development based on their own experience. They often mistakenly believe that others will develop as they did—through some combination of Darwinian selection, apprenticeship and God-given gifts. That was definitely the case with Les Wexner at Limited Brands.

Wexner is one of the most talented entrepreneurs of the latter half of the twentieth century. From one store in Columbus, Ohio, in 1963, he built an empire of almost 5,000 stores around the U.S. out of his vision, energy and charisma. As he says in the story that opens this chapter, for many years he never thought much about developing leaders. He figured talented "merchants" would somehow figure out the leadership part of their job through trial and error and a Darwinian sorting-out process.

But in the last decade, he has realized that he was dead wrong about that and to sustain his legacy, as well as the company he has built, he needed to work on systematically developing leaders. Without leaders at all levels of the company who would teach other to-be-leaders, the company was doomed. So he began the process of building a leader/teacher pipeline.

Following the design principles above, he started by developing his own Teachable Point of View on leadership for Limited Brands. This meant personal reflection and thinking about what kind of leaders Limited Brands would need in the future.

He began by critiquing what he had done in the past. His first bad assumption, he decided, was that a good person would succeed if only given an opportunity. "If you are an entrepreneur and you see yourself as lucky, and you can't really define your own skills, or you think it will be there for everyone who gets the opportunity, then what you need to do is find people that are just like you. Just give them exactly the same opportunity. So as the business grew, I tried to give other people the same opportunity that I had had. I imagined that I could replicate myself that way." But to Wexner's disappointment, they did not replicate.

As he began thinking about building a leadership pipeline, he realized that part of the problem was the way the company was structured, or rather *not* structured. As he looked closely at what was going on, he saw that while he thought of Limited Brands as a multi-divisional company where he could orchestrate the development of people and assets, the reality was that it was a hodgepodge.

"I used to describe us as a large multi-division company," he says, but "we weren't a multi-division company. We were a very bad venture capital company, because there were no processes, no refined capabilities. Nothing was defined, and it was deliberately not defined because I was an entrepreneur . . ."

So before he could build the pipeline, Wexner had to fix the company. But rather than building the multi-divisional specialty retailer that he thought he had, he changed the business model to one that he thought would be more successful in the future. Limited Brands would become a "designer brand that is carrying and controlling its retail channels, having its retail stores."

In the context of this transformation, he rethought the issue of leadership talent. He started with a series of benchmarking visits with other CEOs, set up by Len Schlesinger, who is now chief operating officer of Limited Brands but was a professor at Harvard Business School at the time. Welch and Calloway visits were also especially helpful, he says.

As he began the process of articulating his Teachable Point of View on developing the leaders who could carry Limited Brands into the future, Wexner says that he developed a list of qualities that he thought were necessary and then began to think about which could be taught and how.

"In the fashion business and the entertainment business, a big piece of your success quotient is a God-given skill. If you're color blind, if you have no sense of style, or size, or proportion, then you just can't cut it in the fashion business," he says. But once you select for those talents, there are other "non God-given skills" and abilities that can be taught.

"You can teach people accounting and finance and process, so I began going around the business to learn what my presidents knew," he says. The results of this little research project were shocking. "I would ask them things like, 'Did you ever take an accounting course? When do you have a P&L meeting?' And weird things came back to me. They'd say things like, 'No, there is no reason to have a special meeting to discuss profit and loss, we discuss it every day.' Or, I'd say, 'Does span of control mean anything to you?' and some would respond by asking, 'Is that a fabric?' "

The leadership pipeline that Wexner is building with Schlesinger, who is now COO of Limited Brands, starts with a totally new focus on who gets hired. With Wexner's new Teachable Point of View on leadership, the company screens for different people.

When Wexner interviews people for leadership positions, he starts by asking candidates about their personal journey lines: "I typically ask them, 'What did you do in junior high school and high school?' Sometimes, they were president of their class, or treasurer of the class, or president of the Spanish club or something. They wanted to lead. When they were a Boy Scout, they were a patrol leader. When they have it, I believe that the pattern of natural leadership shows up very early and gets exercised in different ways."

Les Wexner and Len Schlesinger are committed to building a Teaching Organization. As they work through the process described above, they are simultaneously working to figure out creative ways of building Virtuous Teaching Cycles throughout Limited Brands.

Wexner has personally committed to being the role model at the top of the company, regularly teaching and learning. In addition, Len is bringing to base his considerable experience with other companies, including the GE Work-Out and CAP experience, which will ultimately lead to Limited Brands having its own curriculum, as well as programs that touch every single leader at Limited Brands.

Action Learning as a Virtuous Teaching Cycle

A well-designed leadership pipeline, discipline, and commitment are absolutely essential in order for an organization to assure that it will have the leaders it needs when and where it needs them. Without a deliberate and formal pipeline structure, leadership development is only random. Some leaders will emerge, but their emergence will not be predictable, there will not be nearly enough of them, nor will they have the diversity and level of skills of those who have been systematically taught and tracked.

But, having a plan, a structure, and even the right curriculum and discipline don't guarantee an abundance of smart, agile leaders. For decades, IBM and AT&T spent incredible amounts of time and money on staff development programs. But the programs were fairly static and they were backward-looking. They were designed to reproduce the leaders the companies already had, rather than developing ones with the capabilities that would be needed in the future.

The key to making leadership pipelines that actually do produce the needed results is the creation of Virtuous Teaching Cycles. The teaching can't be a one-way cram-down from the top. It can't be assigned to the HR staff and outside consultants like me. And it can't be based on dry, theoretical exercises. The process must be interactive. The teachers must be active and proven leaders in the organization. And the teaching and learning must be based on real business situations that engage students and give them the opportunity to make a difference while they are learning.

When I look back at the two years in the mid-1980s that I spent working with Jack Welch running GE's Crotonville leadership development institute, I realize that what we were doing was setting up Virtuous Teaching Cycles. At the time, I hadn't developed the specific concept of the VTC. I was focused on taking leadership development out of the classroom and creating "action learning" opportunities. But I now see that the interactive teaching and learning component was the key piece of why it worked so well.[3]

I was lucky that Welch was a natural leader/teacher. In fact his self-image is as a teacher. "When all is said and done," he says, "teaching is what I try to do for a living . . . whenever I went to Crotonville, I never lectured. I loved the wide-open exchanges. The students taught me as much as I taught them." Therefore, introducing "action learning" to Welch and GE was a natural.

In his book, *Jack: Straight from the Gut*, Welch describes the impact of action learning and how it created Virtuous Teaching Cycles:

> *Tichy, who became head of Crotonville from 1985 to 1987, brought great passion to the job and introduced 'action learning' . . . Tichy's 'action learning' concept of working on real business issues became the heart of the more advanced BMC (Business Manager Course) and EDC (Executive Development Course) classes. Projects were focused on a key country, a major GE business, or the progress the company was making on an initiative like quality or globalization. Interestingly enough, we had BMC classes in Berlin the same day the Wall came down and in Beijing the very day of the Tiananmen Square protest. The students watched both events, but all came out safe and sound and smarter for the experience.*

In essence, what we did was turn the students into consultants for more senior leaders in the company. "In every case, there were real take-aways that led to action in a GE business. Not only did we get great consulting by our best insiders who really cared, but the classes built cross-business friendships that could last a lifetime," says Welch.

The result of sending the students out to be the eyes and ears for senior leaders was the creation of first-rate Virtuous Teaching Cycles. "Our most valuable teachers there became the students themselves. Through their classwork and field studies, they taught the company's leaders and one another that there often was a better way . . . ," says Welch.

The students learned from both the work they did on the projects and from the senior leaders with whom they interacted. The senior leaders learned not only the information gathered by the students, but they also learned from the thinking the students contributed. And the company benefited by getting more and smarter leaders in both the senior and junior ranks. It also began to infuse the GE culture with the idea that teaching is a key component of leading.

In recent years, the concept of action learning has caught on at other companies. But without the engagement of senior leaders and the resulting interactivity between teachers and students, it doesn't work.Well-run action learning operates with a VTC. The top team frames the project and stays involved while the learners go out and work on the project. Then the senior team members sit down face-to-face with the students to hear the results and learn from them. The process produces a much deeper level of learning than didactic or case study approaches, because it requires not just intellectual mastery, but action and doing. Its holistic approach drives both emotional and intellectual development.

Jorma Ollila, the CEO of Nokia, for example, leads an action learning program every year for his high-potential senior leaders just below the officer level. He and his team frame a set of strategic projects. Leaders are assigned to teams, and they work on the projects over a six-month period, supported by three workshops, one at the beginning, one in the middle and one at the end.

Ollila and his team all teach in the program, are all engaged with the projects and all spend several days in the last workshop hearing the recommendations of the teams, but more importantly learning and then deciding on the actions to take. These projects range in focus from new technologies for Nokia to how to enter new geographic markets, to how to improve the internal functioning of Nokia. The important thing is that this is a high priority for the company and that it engages Ollila and the senior team in a Virtuous Teaching Cycle.

Chapter Eight
Scaling the Teaching Organization: Get Everyone in the Game

▋ Virtuous Teaching Cycles Must Reach Throughout the Organization
  • Pipelines are for the top leaders of the future.
  • Cascades are for everyone.

▋ You Can't Have Only Half the Team Playing
  • Teaching and learning behaviors must be organizational values.
  • You must move quickly to build energy and trust.

▋ Competitive Advantage Comes from Maximizing Everyone's Contribution
  • People on the front lines will be smarter, more eager and aligned.
  • Staff people will be more supportive team members, less bureaucratic.

When *Fortune* senior editor Geoffrey Colvin asked Jack Welch why someone who had been so negative on quality-improvement programs had become a zealot about Six Sigma and was now spending hundreds of millions of dollars to implement it. Welch had an interesting reply:

"Once Larry Bossidy convinced us that Six Sigma was not BS, and my own people in a survey told me we needed to deal with quality, we jumped on it . . . [but] I couldn't just come out and say, 'Quality is good. We need to do quality.' I have to be nuts about it. I have to say no one gets promoted without doing it, [and] that you have to be a black belt to get ahead in the company. You just have to go nuts, because in a big company, to get change you have to go overboard to get them to turn partially. . . . GE now spends over $500 million a year on Six Sigma training and projects and has 15,000 full-time Six Sigma black belt teachers. We have people take two years off the job to do nothing but Six Sigma, leading over 20,000 projects and engaging all 300,000 people in the learning and teaching."[1]

■ ■ ■

There are two important ideas embedded in the Jack Welch quote above. The one that he states most directly is that you have to move quickly and forcefully in order to build or change anything significant in an organization. The other idea is about scale. Teaching Organizations don't engage just a few members in virtuous teaching and learning cycles. They try to engage everyone.

I say "try" because you never get 100% of anything. But the point is that in Teaching Organizations, teaching and learning are a way of life and their modus operandi. Therefore, they can't have just a few members of the elite engaged in Virtuous Teaching Cycles, while everyone else is living by the old bureaucratic rules. Without a critical mass of well more than 50% of the workforce living and breathing the values, the actual daily practices that leverage knowledge and make everyone smarter don't happen, and you don't get the momentum that will keep the Virtuous Teaching Cycles going.

Building a leadership pipeline as described in the last chapter is a critical element both in perpetuating the Teaching Organization and in maintaining the quality of the teaching. In order to compete in a fast-paced and rapidly changing world, a company must have people with highly developed leadership skills. But pipelines have a specific purpose, which is to groom the best talent for senior management positions and produce the next CEO.

Pipelines, therefore, narrow pretty quickly. At GE, for example, by the third of the five levels, there are only a few thousand people still in the pipeline, out of a total of 300,000 employees. By the next level, it narrows to a very elite group of fewer than 200.

So, in addition to the leadership pipeline, Teaching Organizations must have other processes and systems that bring everyone into virtuous cycles of teaching and learning. This is a huge challenge. For Yum! Brands, the target is more than 750,000 employees of the company and its franchisees. For Wal-Mart, it's more than a million people, and for Accenture, more than 70,000 consultants.

In fact, many of the abilities that leadership pipelines cultivate revolve around getting as many people as possible in the organization involved in collecting and sharing knowledge. That's because it is the job of the elite senior management and high-potential leaders developed in the pipeline to teach other people and get the whole organization to be smarter. In other words, the qualities that make people leaders are the ones that will enable them to leverage knowledge and scale the teaching/learning opportunities in the company.

Incrementalism Doesn't Work

When I talk to people about building Teaching Organizations, I generally talk about the need for speed and scale. You need to build programs and systems that engage everyone in the organization, and you need to build them quickly. Incrementalism just doesn't work. Programs that dribble out over a multi-year period get diluted, and often "refined" and "improved" until they have morphed into something else, or into nothing at all. This breeds cynicism, because to the people in the organization, it seems that each program is just a "flavor of the month." Even if a program seems like a good idea, it's hard to generate much enthusiasm if history shows that it will soon be gone.

So building a Teaching Organization requires a leader who is not only dedicated to the concept but who is willing to move quickly and to press on multiple fronts to make it happen. By this I mean waging a full-scale campaign with a maximum time horizon of six months. Otherwise, as Welch points out in the quote that opens this chapter, the inertia and bureaucracy win every time. In order to energize the organization, everyone must be engaged in Virtuous Teaching Cycles quickly.

3M

To do this, the top leadership must kick-start the process. The leader must have the courage to push through the inevitable resistance and force the scaled teaching. In addition, the top leaders must role model the teaching. Jim McNerney, for example, launched Six Sigma across 3M in three months—starting less than a year after he arrived as CEO—personally going out to teach it and to coach throughout the company.

The program had been in use in some of 3M's forty-one businesses, but until McNerney personally jumped into it, it wasn't going anywhere. McNerney started with a three-day workshop that he co-led with a Six Sigma consultant. The top 150 3M executives got to experience McNerney as the leader/teacher helping them understand and get aligned around this important initiative.

Yum! Brands

At Yum! Brands, for David Novak this means allocating time on his calendar to run Customer Mania workshops around the world. He took his top several hundred leaders through a workshop to prepare them to make sure the teaching cascade went to all 750,000 Yum! Brands employees, both company and franchisees.

Scale and Speed at GE

While I was running Crotonville for GE, Larry Bossidy, then vice chairman, kept asking me, "What the hell are we going to do for all of the people at GE who don't get to come to Crotonville?" He pointed out that we did not run the company with only the select few who were in the leadership development programs.

The people really doing the work of the company were the folks running the plants, making things happen in GE Capital call centers and in operations around the world. There were hundreds of thousands of them, and they needed a Crotonville experience. At first, Welch's ears were deaf to this talk, but in the fall of 1987, when his efforts at cultural change were stalled, he came around.

Work-Out   In the fall of 1987, Welch had gathered together all of the outside professors who taught at Crotonville. They were hired to teach the tools of their specific disciplines, but he figured that they could do a better job and teach more effectively if they really understood the new GE business model and values. So he had them brought together so that he could teach them personally.[2]

What happened in the session was that after he had clearly explained his point of view, the professors were very enthusiastic. But in effect, they said, "You have a great model and some wonderful plans. It's too bad that not many other people in the company get them." Their students, they said, showed very little evidence of having heard, or adopted Welch's message.

At this point, Welch realized that if the students coming to Crotonville hadn't gotten his message, there was little chance that the hundreds of thousands who weren't high enough in the organization to be coming to Crotonville had gotten it either. He concluded that his leaders weren't doing enough to help them and the bureaucracy was getting in the way. He intuitively knew that he needed to re-create the Crotonville Virtuous Teaching Cycle experience for everyone.

On the way back to GE headquarters in Fairfield, Connecticut, Welch and Jim Baughman, who headed up Crotonville after I returned to the University of Michigan, were reviewing the session and talking about the frustration of not being able to change the organization fast enough. That's when Welch hit upon the idea that he would require all of his business leaders to create workshops and hold town hall meetings to work on changing the culture. He later dubbed the effort Work-Out, a play on words meaning both getting the bureaucratic work out of the system, and getting in shape for the future.

The creation of Work-Out is a good example of using power to create Virtuous Teaching Cycles. Welch issued the order that every one of GE's top leaders, the approximately 115 corporate officers, had to spend twenty-four days a year in workshops with their people at all levels. The workshops were to be multi-day events in which people told the leaders how the bureaucracy and business practices were slowing them down and keeping them from doing their best work. On the last day, the leaders had to respond. They had to make decisions on 75% of the problem issues on the spot and deal with the rest of them within thirty days.[3]

■ ■ ■

As with all major initiatives, there was the normal range of people who accepted and supported it, and there were those who resisted.

In 1988, about one-third of the business leaders thought that what Welch was requiring was great. Another one-third were watching to see how the wind would blow but played along, and the final one-third were resistant.

Some of the resisters were quite vocal, including one business head who said to Welch, "How the hell can you tell me to run these workshops and spend twenty-four days next year with my people doing this, when you talk about empowerment? I've got my own continuous improvement process going, so I don't want to do Work-Out." Welch's response to this head of a $9-billion, 40,000-person organization: "I don't mess with your strategy. I don't mess with your pricing, or how you are organized. This is too damn important. You are going to do it." It was the classic case of the leader/teacher exercising command-and-control power to create Virtuous Teaching Cycles.

Work-Out was extremely successful, and in the vast majority of cases it really became a Virtuous Teaching Cycle. The leader came to the beginning of the workshops and taught about the state of the business, the GE values, and how to use some simple problem-solving tools such as process mapping. They also taught a bureaucracy-killing tool called RAMMP, which was about how to get unnecessary reports, approvals, meetings, measurements, plans and policies out of the system.

The students then used the tools to identify problems that were getting in their way and causing the organization to be inefficient. Finally, they taught their leaders about the problems, and together, they made a huge number of changes in the system.

One example was a Work-Out session in GE Medical Systems in 1989. About forty middle and lower-level professionals were in a workshop with the head of GE Medical Systems Service. This unit services hospital-based MRIs, x-ray and scanning equipment, etc.

One process map that a team of six service people put together identified one step in the process where seven signatures were required to authorize the order of a part to fix a CAT scan. This translated to a delay of an average of seven days in getting the part, during which time the machine was out of service, patients may have died for lack of the machine, and the hospitals were losing revenue. As soon as the leader, who was head of GE Medical Systems Service, learned about this, he decided on the spot to eliminate the approvals. There have been tens of thousands of such bureaucracy-whacking examples since Work-Out began.

Ultimately, every GE worker around the world was involved in Work-Out sessions. They turned the pyramid upside down. The leaders learned about a lot of things that were wrong, and they fixed many of them. The Work-Out system continues to this day at GE, as leaders regularly hold several-day workshops for the people to identify problems and come up with solutions.

CAP (Change Acceleration Program):   In 1989, GE took Work-Out to a new level. Welch decided to eliminate the dependency on outside consultants and staff and to equip all leaders at GE with the skills to run their own workshops. Interactive teaching and learning would be a core competency of all GE leaders in the future.[4]

In order to do this, a team of faculty, of which I was a part, designed and launched the Change Acceleration Program. The program, which was to train the leaders to be teachers, was built on action learning and a VTC.

Each leader who came to CAP brought a team of his or her own people and a real business project that they wanted to accomplish. The projects had to be something to take costs out of the business or generate new revenue. We would then teach and coach the leaders as they worked with their teams.

The CAP program involved a series of workshops held over a four-month period. The leader and the team would first meet with five or six other teams in sessions where they learned new sets of concepts and tools, ranging from organizational diagnosis to tools for building boundaryless organizations—a framework for leading change, problem-solving techniques, and how to benchmark learnings. The faculty/staff taught everyone the concepts and the tools. The leaders then used the tools by practicing with their own people, and the team members used them to teach the leaders as they worked on the projects. In the year 2002, the top 15,000 leaders at GE were all considered proficient leader/teachers.

Six Sigma: In 1996, Welch launched the largest leader/teacher endeavor in corporate history, Six Sigma. Until this time he had thought all quality management programs were worthless fluff that delivered few results. But in 1996, when Welch went into the hospital for bypass surgery, he asked Larry Bossidy to speak at a meeting of the Corporate Executive Council that he was going to miss. A former vice chairman at GE, Bossidy knew all the players and they respected him. So when he got up and talked enthusiastically about Six Sigma, describing great things that had been accomplished at AlliedSignal using it, the GE leaders became excited. By the time Welch returned, there was a groundswell of support for it. They convinced Welch, and he embraced it with a vengeance.

Six Sigma (a measurement that amounts to 3.4 defects per million) is a quality process that has worked brilliantly at GE, not because of the uniqueness of its tools and techniques, but because of the incorporation of large-scale Virtuous Teaching Cycles. The tools it uses are old ones, such as variance analyses and other statistical measures, problem-solving disciplines, such as DMAIC (Define, Measure, Analyze, Improve and Control) and process mapping. But the key element that makes GE's Six Sigma program so effective is that it is driven by leader/teachers. Another way to look at it is that GE uses Six Sigma as the framework for creating Virtuous Teaching Cycles.

At GE, there are now 12,000 teachers. These so-called black belts, who spend two years in full-time teaching, are selected from the pool of high-potential younger managers. GE reports that its $500-million annual investment in Six Sigma produced a $3-billion return in 2000, $4-billion in 2001, and it was expected to yield $5-billion or more in the year 2002.

The Six Sigma Virtuous Teaching Cycles start with a black belt teaching a group of people the underlying idea, or TPOV, that is the basis of Six Sigma as well as its various tools. The people in the group then go out and use the tools to find and diagnose problems. They bring these back and teach them to the black belt, who then helps them mobilize the organization to change.

A good example of a Six Sigma Virtuous Teaching Cycle is the design for the Six Sigma process that was developed by GE Medical Systems (GEMS) when Jeff Immelt was its CEO. It is a Six Sigma process that is basically the same as the one used internally in GE, except it is used with customers. GEMS sends black belt teachers out to teach customers the tools of Six Sigma, and then the customers use them to figure out where their problems are, and, with the GE folks, what kinds of new equipment or services might solve them.[5]

GE's revolutionary Light Speed CAT scan is a product that probably would not have been developed, or at least not for a long time, without Design for Six Sigma. Previous scanners worked slowly and required the patient to lie still in a narrow tube. When the radiologists examined their practices through the lens of the Six Sigma that the GE folks taught them, they found out some obvious but previously ignored facts:

In addition to the economic fact that slower scans meant fewer scans and lower revenue, they were actually losing some patients, such as car accident victims, because it took too long to get an image done in the old product. Also, patient claustrophobia deterred some from getting needed scans. And when those who did start the scan had to be removed, schedules were disrupted, subsequent patients were inconvenienced, and the machine was out of use for extra time.

As a result of the findings that these were the big issues rather than image quality, the GE engineers developed an open-design scan that doesn't require putting the patient in a tube, and the whole scan can be completed in six seconds.

The GE engineers have now developed more than thirty innovative products using Design for Six Sigma.

Accenture Scales the Teaching Organization

At Accenture, Mary Tolan is the group chief executive of the 12,000-person Resources Operating Group that serves clients in the energy, utilities and chemical industries, and she is also a member of the senior leadership team for the 70,000+ person firm. In both capacities, she is working on building a leader/teacher pipeline and a wide-scale leadership development program.

Communities

In the Resources Operating Group, she is leading an effort to build VTCs throughout the organization. For a number of years, every Accenture consultant has been assigned to what they call "communities." These are groups of about one hundred people, from entry level to senior consultant, who meet periodically. This infrastructure was designed to keep those consultants who often spend most of their time in the field tied into their colleagues and the firm. The infrastructure is old, but Tolan is using it in Resources to create Virtuous Teaching Cycles that will involve everyone in the group. As she explains it:

> One of the things we're doing is comprehensive for the entire workforce, 12,000 employees. And it's really this notion of getting the Teachable Point of View articulated in the most powerful way and then making it really accessible . . . We are actually training a group of leaders who can leverage the Teachable Point of View and bring this into communities. It's a long-term com-

mitment. *We don't want this to be a one-time shot, a one-time in-oculation.*

Tolan took what was an existing part of the infrastructure at Accenture, namely, the communities, and turbo charged them into Virtuous Teaching Cycle sessions. In doing this, she took advantage of the fact that participation was already required in these teaching and learning forums. As Tolan told me:

> *In these communities we were already having meetings and what was happening is that each one of the community leaders would look around the firm, try to get leaders in the firm to come in and speak about something that was topical. They would try to figure out a really good agenda for that quarter, but it wasn't really being shared consistently on a global basis so that everyone got the highest-quality content and curriculum. There was a bit of "do your own thing" on a local level.*
>
> *So we decided, "This is crazy." We're putting a ton of investment into this, and we're losing an important platform for really getting that alignment of the brains on where we're going. So instead of waiting for some sort of annual venue where everybody might see and hear the leaders speaking, we could be using this every quarter to really be reinforcing and advancing knowledge. And so that really motivated me to put a lot of time and investment in the Teachable Point of View because we had an existing place to leverage it immediately.*

Tolan and her team have transformed these quarterly face-to-face sessions into lively workshops for teaching each other best practices, getting the senior people to share Teachable Points of View, and encouraging a variety of interactive teaching and learning opportunities.

Book Clubs

One such mechanism is the "book club." The purpose of the book clubs, Tolan explains, is to "stimulate people to have a habit of looking outside the firm as well as inside." In addition, they give people a forum for grappling with new concepts that may be complex and difficult. To augment the reading, the book clubs sometimes work through exercises and assignments to see how the new ideas and information in a book will relate to real work situations that Accenture consultants face.

"As we go on, we think we're actually going to have a more formal assignment of cases," Tolan says, because "this has really been powerful, and the feedback that we've been getting from our communities has just been astounding. People are saying, 'Yeah, this is exactly what we needed,' which is nice to hear because the stuff that was being put together before was often not the most important thing that the firm was emphasizing."

Partner VTCs

At Accenture, the book clubs and the communities are two effective vehicles for scaling Virtuous Teaching Cycles. Another example of the investment in teaching infrastructure at Accenture is what Tolan and her team are doing with the 400 partners in the Resources group.

"We have sort of standardized that every sixty days, partners from all over our business will be at growth meetings. Those meetings have nothing to do with administration, nothing to do with financial data about the business, nothing to do with any sort of issue that doesn't have to do with bringing exciting ideas to clients. They are there with their other partners, and the things that get on the agenda are the latest sales and successes with clients. It's a real opportunity for us to celebrate those people who are achieving, and have ideas shared across the business much more rapidly. We think it's going to be much more of an opportunity for young partners to be coached by senior partners.

"The notion is to make sure that the partners feel that they are a very special population who control their own destiny and the destiny of the firm. Then we want to give them the confidence that they are armed with the killer ideas and aware of somebody else's recent success in an area." The partners also are expected to go back and teach the new ideas and best practices to all of their people, so that ultimately they reach all 12,000 professionals.

Diamond Council

Another Accenture mechanism for teaching and learning is the Diamond Council, which is an elite group of partners who have the largest and most successful clients.

These are big accounts, some generating as much as $500 million a year. The purpose of this council is knowledge creation for Accenture. The group gets together every sixty days to teach and learn from each other.

One purpose of this council, Tolan explains, is to acknowledge the importance of these partners and put them on an equal ranking with partners in the managerial ranks. It is a means for collecting and sharing the best ideas of its most successful and proven partners. "They've all been tremendously successful in growing the size of the client relationships. And frankly, when you have those really sizeable ones that keep growing, it means the clients improve, too. So getting those guys to share the secrets of their success is really valuable to the firm."

The Diamond Council meets every sixty days for a day. The infrastructure exists, but the members set the agenda and decide how to spend their time. They learn from one another, and, because they report out directly to the CEO/COO, they give top management a window into the market and what is really going on. "It's an incredible resource," says Tolan.

Sales Meetings

Accenture is also creating Virtuous Teaching Cycles in other ways. What used to be "rah rah" sales meetings with talking heads are now "teach-ins." "Everybody's looking at all the ways in which we can crank up this cycle development," says Tolan. The meetings now are "really all about getting alignment of our Teachable Point of View, but then letting our partners have access to each other and getting out of their way so they can share their innovations and their market successes."

After she had described one sales meeting for 550 partners, I asked Tolan if she personally had left the meeting smarter. She replied: "Absolutely. I was really surprised and much more convinced at the value of these investments. You know, I was sort of a big contrarian in the sense that this is a huge time and travel expense. Yet I took the mentality that this is an investment in growing the business. It was surprising to me just how effective it was, what I learned, and how important it is to get messages directly to the partners and not filter through layers.

"I also learned a lot of things about just where certain partners are and where the business is in different parts of the world. I understand the market and their opportunities better, so it gives me a lot of insight in terms of how to help them next, and what's the next thing to do to help that piece of the business."

The sort of multi-effort approach that Accenture is pursuing is precisely what is needed to build a real Teaching Organization. Each company will build infrastructures and programs unique to their situations and the personalities of its leaders. But the ones that succeed will all reflect a mind-set and Teachable Point of View that says that teaching and learning are critical core competencies. So they will actually follow through and make the needed investments to build Virtuous Teaching Cycles at various levels and with different constituencies throughout the organization.

Yum! Brands: Building a Teaching Organization in 32,000 Stores

In a consumer environment, the moment of truth is with the customer in the store. For Yum! Brands, the store is 32,000 Taco Bells, KFCs and Pizza Huts with more than 160 million customers a week around the globe. To please those customers and keep them coming back, 32,000 managers must energize and align 700,000 workers, many of whom are employed by franchisees and not directly by Yum! Brands. How do you do this when you have turnover rates of well over 150% a year, and most of the workers aren't on your payroll and earn only slightly more than the minimum wage? This is the challenge.

McDonald's approach is a regulatory one. It has traditionally relied on systems, rules and one-way teaching to control people. The store managers are carefully trained to follow a paint-by-the-numbers approach.

Yum! has a full set of systems and policies as well. But David Novak and the team are working on developing a more normative one in which it has leaders at all levels who share the values of being "Customer Maniacs" and who have the tools to teach and learn and energize other people. Novak recognizes that the task is a big one, but that it is critical to differentiating Yum! outlets in the market and building a company that will succeed in the long haul.

"We have over 32,000 stores with an average team of twenty-two, so we have well over 700,000 people out there. I will know that our company is great when our customers feel our culture and our work environment . . . and frankly, that's not where we are today," he told me in early 2002. "That's the reality that I am painting for our people, and I think the reason why we haven't penetrated with the restaurant general managers is that we've rolled out some of the concepts, but we haven't given them the tools to take to the front line so that they can truly get executed. In the past we haven't had the process and discipline around making that happen to the team member level. And holding people accountable for getting that done . . . I think we understand that now and we'll fix it."

To do this, he has developed a huge teaching infrastructure. Novak himself runs about six three-day workshops a year for 300 to 400 leaders. Aylwin Lewis, COO, focuses on teaching "high-impact coaching," and developing thousands of regional coaches who then teach the store managers. They have also developed a portfolio of Yum University programs for both company-owned and franchise operations. All of Novak's team is expected to teach on a regular basis. Cheryl Bachelder, CEO of KFC, held a series of multi-day sessions to get her team aligned on the KFC Teachable Point of View, and then they cascaded the process to the store level in 2002.

Yum! Brands's programs, which are all taught by leaders from within the company, are built around the framework of a Teachable Point of View that is summarized in a one-page document:

Our passion   Act as one system to put a Yum on customers' faces around the world.

Our formula for success   People capability first . . . satisfied customers and profitability follow.

How we lead	1. Be a Customer Maniac.
	2. Know and drive the business.
	3. Build and align teams.
How we win	1. Run great restaurants.
	2. Differentiate the brand in everything we do.
	3. Drive explosive global expansion.
	4. Lead the way in multi-branding innovation.
	5. Drive equity growth; convert cash flow into high value.

How we work together   Our how-we-work-together principles (customer mania, belief in people, recognition, coaching and support, accountability, excellence, positive energy, teamwork), along with our franchise partnership pact. (Because so many of its 32,000+ stores are franchises, it is important that Yum! Brands and the franchisees have a clear agreement on how we work together. The partnership pact articulates this.)

Among the programs that support that framework is one led by Lewis that is called Run Great Restaurants. It includes how to hire the right people, how to train them, how to manage teamwork, how to evaluate and reward, as well as how to build a Customer Mania culture.

David Novak has a very clear vision of what a good restaurant is all about, and he has created an infrastructure to teach it. But the formal programs go hand-in-hand with his own personal role modeling. Novak explains:

> Good restaurants have positive energy. They're fun. The restaurant managers recognize people. It's the soft stuff that drives hard results . . . if you go into a restaurant and you see people not having fun, the customers feel that . . . If you have been in a good restaurant, there's energy. It's alive, and people are smiling . . . It starts with me as the leader casting a shadow . . . The shadow that I cast will spread throughout the organization. So I enjoy my job. You know, I'm passionate about my job. I have fun at my job. But having fun is a big part of the restaurant business—that's probably why I am in it.

A Global Best Practice: Royal Dutch/Shell

Cor Herkstroter and the top team at Royal Dutch/Shell began building a Teaching Organization in 1995. They started with the very first step of creating a shared TPOV for the company and its future, and by the end of 30 months had built a series of Virtuous Teaching Cycles to engage all 100,000 people in the company around the globe. A team of colleagues and I worked with them. Here is the framework we used.

Step 1: Create the TPOV

The first meetings were with just the four members of the Committee of Managing Directors (CMD): John Jennings, Mark Moody-Stuart, Maartin van den Berg and Cor Herkstroter, the chairman. We spent several days analyzing the company strategically, financially and culturally. Then, using the format of a magazine article, they each made the case for change and wrote up their vision of how the company should look in four years. When they read their individual articles aloud, a clear picture of the case for change emerged and a still-fuzzy vision of the future started to show through.[6]

The CMD decided to engage other people in helping to refine and further craft this vision and develop a company-wide "story" of what Royal Dutch/Shell would be in the future. The CMD members would be the leader/teachers in the process, but they would draw in other people.[7]

They also decided that they would be the head leader/teachers in developing a Teaching Organization to reach all employees. Over the next several months, each CMD member met with several hundred other leaders to teach the story and to listen to their responses. Through this exercise, the foundation for Virtuous Teaching Cycles was laid.

Several months after the initial meeting, the CMD called together the top fifty Royal Dutch/Shell leaders to get them involved. Using the CMD's initial TPOV statement, plus the input from the company-wide meetings and their own reactions, these leaders fleshed out the case for change, designed a "New Shell" vision and business strategy, defined shared values for the company, and identified how the company would drive large-scale change involving leaders teaching at all levels.

At this senior level in the company, there was the predictable resistance from a number of members. So Herkstroter mandated participation. His message: "This is important. You must attend, but we want open participative dialogue." For their part, the CMD members participated as teachers and learners, as they incorporated many of the elements proposed by the others.

Step 2: Develop a Change Team of Leader/Teacher Coaches

Although the CMD members were committed to personally teaching, the business case demanded rapid, large-scale change that senior management alone could not drive. Learning from benchmarking General Electric's Crotonville, Herkstroter created an internal change team. He first called on Mac McDonald, an American based in Amsterdam, who had been a long-time purchasing and operations manager but had exhibited both the straight-talking style and interpersonal skills to work with senior management.

McDonald's job was to build the infrastructure and team that would guide implementation of the leadership team's TPOV. He recruited ten high-potential line managers, intentionally without human resource or organizational development backgrounds, who had led major change efforts successfully. He reasoned that people with a track record of leading operational change in the company knew how to avoid pitfalls of the change process. Also, they could empathize with the leaders they would be coaching and offer insight into effective change techniques. Finally, he wasn't sure that HR and OD professionals had the leadership edge (courage) or the clout within the organization to drive real tough change.

The short-term imperative for McDonald's team members was preparing to teach others to be leaders and teachers.

Step 3: Engage the Organization

While McDonald was working on developing the internal change team, Herkstroter launched the initial phase of a program that would engage people at all levels throughout the worldwide Royal Dutch/Shell organization in cycles of teaching and learning. The ultimate goal was to transform the company and develop leaders who would be able to take the company into the future. To achieve this, there were three programs aimed at ever-increasing audiences.

1. Value creation: An action-learning program, operated at the global strategy level. Pulling together about 200 of the highest potential leaders from across the company, the CMD built cross-functional global teams designed to tackle major strategic challenges.

The process developed the participants' leadership capability through side-by-side work with the CMD members to understand, analyze and fix global problems such as worldwide branding, employee satisfaction and redefining the company's cost structure. Although the projects resulted in some important changes in how Royal Dutch/Shell operates, the process also had a profound effect on the culture and senior management. Senior leaders personally served as the teachers each time the process was run, which gave them new opportunities to interact with people they probably would not otherwise have gotten to know.

The selection of strategic projects and the decisions that the CMD members had to make based on their results served to test and reinforce their Teachable Point of View. Each time they had to ask: "Does this project (or decision) reflect our TPOV?" The entire process was based on the leader/teachers and the student/researchers teaching and learning from each other. The result was everyone becoming smarter and more aligned.

2. Business Framework Implementation (BFI):   This process was sponsored by Steve Miller, who had become a member of the CMD, and designed in conjunction with Columbia finance professor Larry Selden. The purpose was to work on both the "hard" (functional/operational) and "soft" (cultural/behavioral) issues necessary to change the organization. Using six-member teams, it directly involved about 600 people, who then went out and taught thousands more.

The three-workshop series began with a session, often taught by a CMD member, to engage the participants in the Royal Dutch/Shell vision and case for change. Activities included learning financial, team building, diagnostic and leadership skills. Using the tools, they were then given the job of building a business model for their organizations that would achieve unprecedented operating returns on net assets and top-line growth.

The second session was devoted to reviewing the progress on the business model and to developing the organizational and interpersonal dynamics to get the projects implemented. The third session was the review, in which senior leaders would decide whether to go ahead and fund the projects. Rather than formal presentations, these were held as collegial, high-energy debates in which ideas prevailed over hierarchy.

Throughout the BFI process, participants focused on developing leadership skills that matched the company's future direction. They debated the Royal Dutch/Shell mission and values and determined the implications for their personal leadership. The result was the creation of teams with reinforced leadership skills, who were aligned with the company's overall direction and had business plans that would contribute to Royal Dutch/Shell's bottom-line results.

Throughout, the process was a series of Virtuous Teaching Cycles. The senior leader/teachers taught the TPOV for the company and various skills. Then the students used them to study, diagnose their organizations and then report back with suggested changes for senior management.

3. Focused Results Delivery (FRD):   This two-workshop series was the process that really cascaded the new TPOV and introduced all corners of the company to virtuous cycles of teaching and learning.

In FRD, groups of forty to fifty members of a country organization would attend sessions in which they were organized in teams and asked to work on a project that would yield quantum improvement in the business. The projects were defined or approved by the countries' managing directors.

This drove alignment in two ways. First, it enabled the country's senior leadership team to ensure that the process would help it meet its business objectives. Second, because the managing directors team taught and worked with coaches from the parent company, they were kept constantly up to date on and aligned with the corporate TPOV.

When dialogue between the managing directors and their parent-company colleagues revealed an inconsistency, they often sought guidance from a CMD manager to clarify their own perspective or challenge the company's.

The Virtuous Teaching Cycle was a key component of why FRD worked. It got the country CMD member and the country head aligned on their TPOV. The fact that the country managing director was the head teacher put him or her in a position to get feedback from the people within the organization. It developed a new model for interactive dialogue as a process for running the operation.

A Case Study: Shell New Zealand

The downsizing of Shell New Zealand is a good example of how use of the Virtuous Teaching Cycles, started by the FRD process, helped one business come through a difficult period.

In 1997, when John Fletcher took over as managing director for Shell New Zealand, the country was facing new competitive entrants that planned to cherry-pick customers from Shell's most profitable territories. By benchmarking and learning from other markets, Fletcher says he knew what this would mean. "Competitors were opening a few well-placed sites at our most profitable areas that could do enormous damage to our margins. This would be death by a thousand cuts as they slowly squeezed us into a cost competition that we couldn't win, and that would leave us with a highly unprofitable margin mix."

Around this time, Fletcher saw a video that showed the output of FRD in South Africa. As he explains, "I saw the energy and involvement of a big group of people making change happen. I had been thinking that the horsepower of most companies' people is so underutilized, and we were no exception. I immediately rang the head of Shell Australia and said, 'We have to do this together.' "

In February 1998, a group of fifteen senior leaders from Shell New Zealand joined their colleagues in Australia for an FRD session. In this, they crafted a TPOV about where they were going and how they were going to get there. It included a 30% cut in head count.

When the team returned to New Zealand, they decided that they would implement the plan by using a Virtuous Teaching Cycle process for all of its employees. Twelve teams were organized, and the leadership team held a series of meetings and town halls to teach everyone the basic principles covered in FRD.

They also told them that the realities of the market demanded a cost structure that would require a 30% reduction in employment. But, they said, they had no concrete plan for where cuts would be made and that they wanted to work that out with participation from employees.

At first, nobody believed that management was really going to listen to them. "People just rolled their eyes," Fletcher says. But as the FRD process unfolded, and workers saw that their input really was desired, they joined in enthusiastically.

The FRD teams engaged people based on their interests and eagerness, rather than their job title or documented expertise. For example, one worker whose job assignment was to answer phones in customer service worked on a team looking at organization, rewards and employment contracts (ORE). When Fletcher and the ORE team agreed that the existing organizational structure was unsustainable, the worker ran a series of workshops that developed a set of new core values that would become part of every employee's performance contract.

With the ORE team's support, every job within New Zealand was posted for placement. Meetings and workshops throughout the company involved everyone in discussing and wrestling with the reasons for the reorganization and the criteria for "re-hiring." A significant part of the reapplication interviews involved the values the company wanted, and some people lost out on their old jobs because of inconsistent values. The FRD process gained enormous credibility when "people started seeing new heads of teams, not the same old faces. Leadership followed [the new recruiting process] to the letter to build people's trust," Fletcher explains.

The new organizational structure eliminated layers of bureaucracy. The new structure consisted of twenty-two flat teams with no more than two layers between Fletcher and the front line. A number of people chose to leave the company voluntarily because they didn't want, or saw that there wouldn't be, a position for them in the new structure. Those whose positions were eliminated or who failed to find a job after the initial reapplication process were invited to apply for up to five jobs. "Whenever someone was unsuccessful with an application, they would get feedback so that they could learn and improve their chances for next time," Fletcher observed.

As a result of ongoing coaching and dialogue with those who were unsuccessful, the company had only a handful of employees leave involuntarily. Achieving most of the reductions through voluntary departures was one benefit of the clarity of communication and the inclusiveness of the process. But more important, the reduction in force did not demoralize those who remained, as is often the case. In fact, the process left the people who remained with the company invigorated and excited.

Other FRD teams focused on commercial issues. A central group was created to manage customer contacts in order to free up sales people. Another team used process mapping to identify solutions for the customer contact center. As a result, Shell customer representatives resolve more than 90% of customer issues on the first call.

Overall, Shell New Zealand succeeded in reducing costs by more than 25%. "Margins did fall when competition came in," Fletcher says, "but [the competitors] got burned because they thought they were coming into a market with healthy margins."

The process not only drove alignment within Shell New Zealand and with Royal Dutch/Shell's center, it also changed the lives of many who were involved. By engaging employees in a highly structured yet empowering process, it offered senior management unique insights into the participants' capabilities and values in ways that could not be revealed through day-to-day work.

Learning from the Royal Dutch/Shell Experience

The results seen in Shell New Zealand are not unique. Gary Steele, who took over from Mac McDonald overseeing FRD, recalls an FRD project in Brazil that yielded $5 million in ninety days and generated more than $80 million in savings over five years. When the Brazilian management team asked their people why they had never identified the project before, Steele says, "They responded that they had never been asked."

Another program in Oman identified nearly $2 billion in un-tapped oil reserves. Steele says that at the end of the process, the managing director said he learned three very important things: "First, he didn't need to have all of the answers. Second, the best an-swers are within the organization. And third, if you build a plan with the involvement of 1,500 people, the organization will deliver."

Building teaching capability into an organization's leadership repertoire is no easy task. First, it requires a fundamental reframing of the role of leaders as teachers. Teaching requires a sincere open-ness to learning that is contradicted by the stifling air of the bureau-crat or power-monger. Second, some leaders appreciate the need for teaching but fail to make time to develop and align their TPOV with other organizational leaders. A multitude of teachers with different or conflicting messages can quickly create anarchy. Finally, the teach-ing must incorporate the Virtuous Teaching Cycle. The leader must have the guts to be vulnerable and open to learning while simultane-ously requiring participation.

Chapter Nine
Creating Virtuous
Teaching Cycles:
Operating Mechanisms

■ **Operating Mechanisms Are the Routine Processes for Running the Company**
- Because they are recurring, at many companies they become rote.
- Because they are recurring, they are great opportunities for teaching.

■ **The Big Three Are Succession, Strategy and Budget Planning**
- Old style, they are bureaucratic and adversarial.
- As Virtuous Teaching Cycles, they promote collaboration and innovation.

■ **The Leader Must Take the Role of Social Architect**
- Who participates in each process is a critical element.
- Activity flow and social interaction are also key design features.

Wal-Mart is headquartered in Bentonville, Arkansas, but members of its senior team spend most of their time on the road. Every week, the top leaders of the company fan out across the country.

They visit both Wal-Mart stores and its competitors' and return home at the end of the week with fresh information about what is going on in the marketplace—what is selling where, how the competition is trying to attack Wal-Mart, ideas for new promotions, etc.[1]

Back in Bentonville, they gather to share their findings with each other and revise their strategy for the coming week. On Saturday, they hold a videoconference with thousands of store managers to bring them up to date on the Teachable Point of View for the coming week's operations. Then, on Monday, they head out again.

This process has given Wal-Mart the agility that makes it a consistent winner in the marketplace. It is a huge company with the speed and flexibility of a small one.

The Power of Management Processes

All organizations have routine processes through which they coordinate and control their normal business operations. These operating mechanisms are what keep the organization functioning day-to-day, and year-to-year. The Wal-Mart leaders' weekly cycle of going out into the field and then returning home to share their findings is the operating mechanism through which they calibrate and refine their strategy on a weekly basis.

Although the people at Wal-Mart don't use the term, it is also a Virtuous Teaching Cycle. Out in the field, the senior leaders are taught by store managers, customers and competitors. At the same time, they also teach and coach the store managers. Then, when they get back home, the senior leaders share what they have learned with their colleagues, and together they revise their strategic point of view. The final step is that they teach it to the store managers before they head out to start all over again. Week after week, they go out and learn, come home to think and revise, teach their new conclusions, and then go back out.

This Wal-Mart operating mechanism is a key reason for the company's success. It is an informal and vibrant process that engages thousands of Wal-Mart leaders. It energizes them, raises the collective intelligence of the company, and generates incredible system-wide alignment.

Operating mechanisms are the means by which leaders calibrate and control their organizations. They cover everything from getting the doors unlocked in the morning to setting strategy and making sure that the company has the resources it will need five years hence to fulfill that strategy.

By definition, operating mechanisms are repetitive, and for that reason they are often allowed to become rote processes. But, because they are repetitive, and because they touch every significant area of the business, operating mechanisms have a huge impact on how and how well a company operates. If they are designed to be Virtuous Teaching Cycles, they will, every day, work to make people smarter, more energetic and better aligned behind good strategies. If they are poorly designed, they will do just the opposite.

Unfortunately, at far too many companies, they are poorly designed. When Jack Welch became CEO of GE in 1981, it was considered the best-managed company in the world because it had operating mechanisms and highly documented procedures for just about everything. But, as Welch knew, because he had struggled his way up through the system, many of them were dysfunctional. Rather than helping people make smart decisions and exciting them to energetic action, the GE operating system was a straitjacket that stifled creativity, sapped energy and wasted valuable knowledge that resided in the corporation.

GE's Cycle of Teaching/Learning Operating Mechanisms

When Welch became CEO in 1981, he immediately began to redesign the company's operating mechanisms. He didn't have in mind the explicit concept of building Virtuous Teaching Cycles. I didn't either when I joined GE in 1985. But in retrospect, in examining the things we did that were most successful, it is easy to see that they were all built on continuous cycles of teaching and learning.

Welch started by eliminating unnecessary reports and meetings. At the end of twenty years, he had succeeded in building a total system of operating mechanisms in which not only are individual functions performed far more effectively and creatively than anyone would have thought possible when he began, but that also feed into one another to reinforce teaching and learning across all the activities of the company. It is a model of finely tuned operating mechanisms fitted together to create a turbocharged engine.

Welch described what he called the GE Operating System, and

had it diagrammed in his last annual report letter. It is instructive to note how he fits all the pieces together and how each process feeds off of the previous one and into the next.[2]

How the GE Operating Mechanisms Build on One Another

The essence of the GE system is the degree to which the individual operating mechanisms build on one another. The teachings and learnings in one feed into and shape the next. The result is not only a collective enhancement of intelligence and alignment of leaders at all levels, but also follow-up that assures implementation of decisions and initiatives.

The diagram on the following page is basically a calendar that shows the progression and interweaving of the processes. It is centered on the three most far-reaching of an organization's operating mechanisms: setting strategy, formulating budgets and succession planning.

As the diagram indicates, the year is kicked off with GE's top 600 leaders convening in Boca Raton, Florida, for a three-day session. The meeting is designed to set the agenda for the company for the coming year. Welch used the meeting to share his Teachable Points of View, and to launch and reinforce initiatives such as Work-Out, Six Sigma and the shift to services, globalization and digitization.

Jeff Immelt continues the use of this operating mechanism, and in 2002 began sharing his Teachable Point of View, emphasizing deploying new technologies, using digitization and Six Sigma to become more customer centric, and preparing GE leaders for a tougher regulatory and investment environment in the wake of the Enron scandal.

The meeting also provides an opportunity to showcase best practices and let the leaders teach one another. On the final day of the session, leaders meet in their business or corporate functional groups to consolidate their learnings, decide how they are going to implement them in their units, and prepare to teach what they have learned to the people who work for them.

The Boca meeting sets the frame for the year. All of the company's leaders leave the meeting with a common Teachable Point of View that identifies the important priorities. As the year unfolds and the other operating mechanisms run their own cycles, the GE leaders weave the themes from Boca into all of these.

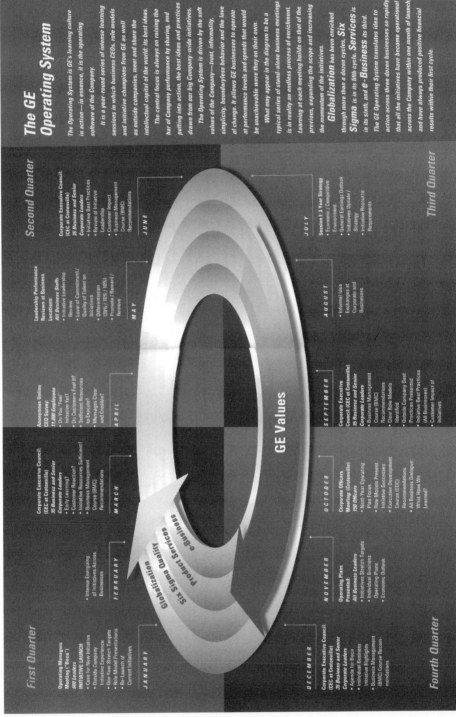

Figure 9

For example, in 1998 Six Sigma was a top priority, so each of the operating mechanisms built on that. Succession planning had a strong emphasis on making sure that the best talent was assigned to "black belt" leader/teacher roles. The strategy and budgeting processes also were built on using Six Sigma tools and furthering Six Sigma projects. In 2002, Immelt is driving his emphasis on customer centricity using Six Sigma and digitization through all the operating mechanisms.

In January and February, after the Boca meeting, the leaders who attended teach and cascade the learnings to the total GE population of 300,000+ people.

Every quarter, the heads of the businesses and the key corporate staff meet with the CEO at Crotonville for a day and a half session to teach one another about best practices, share new ideas, and figure out ways to collectively enhance the performance of GE. These sessions reinforce and build on the annual Boca Teachable Point of View as well as provide a way to bring in new ideas from outside the company through outside speakers, generally other CEOs.

The spring brings the beginning of Session C, the succession planning process at GE. It is a massive search and evaluation process that looks at the top 500+ positions in the company and comes up with several thousand candidates for those key jobs.

As in the other processes, the important thing about Session C is that it is done in a way to maximize teaching and learning. It is not just a mechanical process of checking boxes and filling out forms. The Session C process is designed to be an ongoing Virtuous Teaching Cycle, one in which leaders of the businesses and the CEO are in intensive teaching and learning interactions regarding the top 500 positions in GE along with the slate of candidates for those positions. This results in a review of several thousand people, with rigorous debate and learning.

After the meetings with the CEO are held in May, there is a follow-up videoconference in July with the CEO, the head of HR for the whole company, and the heads of the businesses and their top HR leader to get a status report on implementation of the Session C decisions. There is another follow-up review with the CEO in the fall in conjunction with the operating reviews.

In the summer, after the Session C process is completed, GE leaders turn their focus to reviewing their business plan and corporate strategy. At just about every meeting around GE, strategy is on the table. The Session C meetings are integrally tied into the company's business strategy. When senior leaders get together to follow up on the Boca meeting and talk about initiatives and ways to improve business, strategy is a critical piece of the conversation. But each July, the CEO starts a process of detailed review of the company's business strategy.

Unlike strategy reviews at many companies, the GE strategy reviews are freewheeling discussions and debates held around the CEO's conference table. This strategy operating mechanism is about ideas and plans for the future, not a lot about numbers. Again, like Session C, this is a Virtuous Teaching Cycle. The head of a business unit and his top staff are sitting down with the CEO and his top staff. At times, the head of the business is teaching the CEO, and at others the CEO becomes the teacher and the business head the learner.

The agenda starts with the Teachable Point of View from the previous Boca meeting, and incorporates the learnings from the executive meetings and Session C meetings held earlier in the year. The aim is to map out the fine adjustments and large-scale changes needed to keep each of the units successful in the future.

Corporate strategy is the focus of the officers' meeting that brings 135 top leaders to Crotonville in the fall. At the S1 strategy meetings in July, the CEO and the heads of each business have sorted out the priorities for each unit. Now, all of them come together to evaluate those priorities and start mapping out the corporate strategy and Teachable Points of View that will be the focus of the Boca meeting. It starts framing the new agenda for the coming year.

In the fall, the officers' meeting is both an opportunity to begin to draw closure to the year and make sure that GE delivers on what it set out to do at the Boca session, and also to start setting the stage for the next year. The themes for the new year are discussed at this session.

Throughout the year, the results of projects by classes at Crotonville and other operating mechanisms are also fed into the system. This provides a direct link between the learning that goes on at Crotonville and the management of the company. The leadership at GE learns from the work of the students, which is one more Virtuous Teaching Cycle.

The CEC Operating Mechanism at GE

Running throughout the year and building on all the other processes is GE's most powerful and unique operating mechanism: The Corporate Executive Council. This thirty-five-member group consists of the heads of each business unit, plus the senior corporate-level leaders. This collective of the best brains in the company meets four times a year to wrestle with business problems and help the CEO steer the company.[3]

Jack Welch created the CEC in the mid-1980s. It was a replacement for a very dysfunctional GE ritual in which the heads of the business would come to headquarters every month to report to the corporate staff. One after another, they each would get up and go through a slide-show presentation on the status of their businesses. The other business leaders would sit around and watch while the CEO and CFO asked "I gotcha, zinger questions."

The emotional energy was largely negative. There was defensive behavior all around, and people learned very little. In fact, it was a great example of a vicious non-teaching cycle. Because everyone was so guarded and afraid of attack, they mostly played hide-the-ball, and many people left the meetings knowing less about what was really going on in the company than when they arrived.

Welch redesigned the meetings and completely transformed this operating mechanism from a defensive cover-your-ass forum to a high-power teaching and learning centerpiece for GE. He changed the calendar so the group would meet only four times a year, but for a night and a day with a learning and teaching agenda. And he moved the meetings to the Crotonville leadership development center, a residential facility where they not only met in a workshop process, but also ate and drank together.

The primary items on the agenda at CEC meetings are the sharing of best practices and the working out of business problems. Each business head is expected to come with a best practice or idea that would be of benefit for others to learn about and help make GE a better company. The leaders each stand up and make a quick report on their business, but the numbers are handed out ahead of time so the purpose of the business reports is to see where things are going particularly well, so everyone can learn, and where there are problems, so everyone can think about ways to fix them. The atmosphere is one of sharing as team members rather than competition among rivals.

One of Welch's greatest crusades was to eliminate the not-invented-here syndrome at GE. Welch always said that he knew what he knew, and he wanted to learn what other people knew. So, to increase the learning, an outside CEO is often invited to come in the first night and share what is going on in their company and their Teachable Points of View about their businesses. Visitors have ranged from Scott McNealy of Sun Microsystems, to Bernie Marcus, co-founder of Home Depot, to Herb Kelleher from Southwest Airlines, to Joe Liemandt, the young founder of software company Trilogy.

Some of these outsiders have had a huge impact. Larry Bossidy, the then CEO of AlliedSignal who had been a vice chairman at GE, taught the group about Six Sigma. Don Soderquist, the COO of Wal-Mart, talked about the mechanism of having leaders go out into the field each week, share their learnings at the end of the week, and re-calibrate and re-teach their Teachable Point of View.

Welch and his team thought it would be a great idea to have GE's front-line sales people in direct contact with leaders of the business on a weekly basis, so he took the Wal-Mart Teachable Point of View and challenged each business to come up with their own version.

This led directly to the creation of GE's Quick Market Intelligence system. For more than a decade, every GE business head has had a face-to-face, or combination of face-to-face and telephone or video-conference, weekly war room to connect the sales organization to the leadership of the business. The result has been much better fast-cycle decision making.

During the heyday of the dot-com boom, Joe Liemandt of Trilogy challenged Welch's team by telling them about how he and thousands of other young entrepreneurs were out to destroy GE. The way they were going to do it, he said, was through cutting-edge applications of digital technologies.

So the GE team responded by having internal leaders in every business designated as "destroy your organization.com" leaders. These people were given the assignment to challenge old business models and come up with digital models. The result was an explosion of digital applications spread throughout GE, from a plastics trading business to a digital inventory tracking business in Medical Systems.

The CEC, as a collaborative teaching and learning forum involving the senior leadership, sets the tone as well as the agenda for the rest of the company. A small group that meets quarterly, the CEC functions as a team. Each brings learnings from running their own businesses as well as from participating in the succession, strategy and budgeting processes, and shares them in an informal environment of conversation and debate. As an operating mechanism, it raises the collective IQ of everyone on the team every quarter, it draws on their wide range of experience and knowledge, and it helps keep the many parts of the company aligned and moving together.

From Vicious Cycles to Virtuous Teaching Cycles

The overall GE operating system is turbocharged by the fact that each of the operating mechanisms builds on and feeds into the others. It is a mega-Virtuous Teaching Cycle in which the participants, in each operating mechanism, teach and learn from the participants in the others. The underlying power, however, comes from how each of the individual operating mechanisms is designed to generate knowledge, energy and alignment.

The CEC is an operating mechanism that Jack Welch invented to help him run the widely varied and far-flung businesses of General Electric. Although many other organizations could use such a mechanism, most do not have them. Most do, however, have processes for the other constituent elements—setting strategy, budgeting and succession planning—of the operating system. Unfortunately, few produce the positive results that they could.

The goal of the operating mechanisms should be to enhance the collective intelligence of the organization and create energized alignment of leaders at all levels. At far too many companies, however, operating mechanisms do just the opposite. They make the organization collectively dumber.

Because they are repetitive, in large companies these critical operating mechanisms are often institutionalized. They are put on autopilot and left to keep things moving without the benefit of thought. Thus, they become straitjackets.

At best, these rigid, often bureaucratic, structures are de-energizing. More likely, they are frustrating and induce apathy or rage. Further, in addition to depressing morale, they tend to slow decision making and stifle creativity. This was the case at GE when Welch took over in 1981.[4]

The good news is that if done well, operating mechanisms have the potential for having a huge positive impact on the organization. When run as Virtuous Teaching Cycles, the strategy, budgeting and succession planning processes produce smarter strategies, use resources better, and develop more and better leaders.

VTC Operating Mechanisms

Like all Virtuous Teaching Cycles, successful operating mechanisms are built by leaders who take an up-front role in creating them. The leader must take on the task of a social architect. He or she must do this by establishing several key elements:

People	Who gets involved.
Time	How often, for how long, and working on what issues.
Physical space	Where the meeting is held.
Social space	Processes, how people interact with one another.
Activity Flow	Phase 1—preparation. Phase II—face-to-face meeting. Phase III—follow-up.

In the preparation phase, the leader must provide the guidelines for who works on what to produce what output for the face-to-face meeting where key decisions get made. The face-to-face phase must be a carefully crafted meeting with the right people in the room, behaving in the right way, to make good decisions. Follow-up is critical to implementation. Failure to follow up renders worthless all the preparation and meetings. It invites cynicism and deflates morale.

Jack Welch intuitively understood from the start that he was a social architect. He knew he needed to creatively destroy and remake the operating mechanisms of GE. He started with an audit of the current functioning of the system.

The initial focus was on the strategy, budget and succession planning processes. While there are a wide range of operating mechanisms that facilitate day-to-day operations, these are the three most critical to long-term success. Other mechanisms, such as those for order fulfillment, supply chain management and maintenance of facilities, are essential to staying in business. But strategy, budgeting and developing leaders are the most overarching. They are the ones that have the broadest range, and which, if done wrong, inflict the most devastating damage.

Assessing the Social Architecture at the Top of GE

One of the key milestones for Welch's re-architecting of the operating mechanisms at GE was a study he did in 1987 to assess the operating mechanisms at the CEO level. He sought input from the board, from his senior leaders, and from staff. Don Kane, an organizational planning expert in the human resources area, conducted the study. The questions that Welch asked focused on how the operating mechanisms were really working and solicited ideas for change. Here are some of the actual audit questions.

Vision of what we want an operating business to be:

How much scope? How much autonomy? How much delegation to head of business? Does delegation vary by nature of the business, by our comfort with or the degree of tenure of its leader, or by the nature of the contemporary environment?

How much differentiation are we comfortable in allowing in terms of such factors as organizational structure, nomenclature/officer titles, motivation and reward systems, operating style?

How much communication laterally between businesses as opposed to vertically (CEO-Businesses)?

Vision of what we want the Corporate Executive Office to be:

What role and scope vs. operating businesses?

What added value should the CEO provide over and above the bare minimum necessary to satisfy corporate requirements?

If operating GE as a classic holding company represents one end of a spectrum and running GE as a highly integrated and centralized company represents the other end, where do we want to be on that spectrum?

Will "where we want to be" vary with the economic cycle, our comfort level with and trust of our Business Executives, or any other factor?

What decisions do we *clearly* want to make at the CEO level, what decisions *clearly* at the business level, and what decisions require the application of judgment (on whose part) before deciding at which level?

Given these visions of what we desire in the future, insofar as operating businesses, the Corporate Executive Office and Corporate Staff are concerned, to what extent are the following consistent with those visions:

Company *Policies* and the *Functional Procedures* that implement those Policies (including the delegations of authority contained therein)?

Any management *practices* we have installed (whether documented or unwritten) that are *not* in sync with our stated Policies/Procedures?

The recurrent annual *processes* that we utilize either at Corporate level, at Business level, or at both levels to manage the company?

How can we make the Corporate Executive Office more effective to manage a company one-third larger and significantly more complex than heretofore?

Should the CEO meet more/less/same as a collective body than at present?

On what things is it critical that we all see the same things/hear the same words? On what things do we trust one another's judgment sufficiently to rely on one individual for sole source inputs on some subject upon which the CEO must make a collective decision?

What factors seem to be important in reaching timely decisions we feel comfortable with? What factors intervene when we must reach a decision *more quickly* than we're comfortable with? When a decision takes *longer* than we're comfortable with?

When meeting collectively are we:

- too structured or rigid?
- too ad hoc and overly flexible?
- too disciplined and linear?
- all over the ranch?

Do we have enough "open" or "white space" days to allow us to carry our individual responsibilities effectively? Comfortably?

Are we oppressive, overly lax, or about right in our style of follow-up on operating matters over which we have approval authority?

How effective are we in utilizing our CEO staff? What do we need that we're not getting now? Ditto for those Corporate Staff Components whose role it is to service the staff needs of the CEO?

What is the optimum balance between the CEO interacting with the company on a hierarchical basis (i.e., through those reporting directly to CEO members) versus "meeting the people directly" via appearance at Crotonville courses, Elfun presentations, plant visits, roundtables, etc.? Are we presently doing too much or not enough of the latter?

These questions are illustrative of the level of attention to detail required to be a good social architect. In response to the input he received, he set about a massive rebuilding of GE's operating mechanisms.

The Strategy Process

Welch inherited the world's most complex, revered strategic planning system. GE had 200 strategic planners on staff at headquarters with a vast array of frameworks and quantitative models. The planners were a shadow government running the company. Welch himself was a master at playing the system. If he hadn't been, he would never have made it to be CEO. He produced the best strategic plan books of any of the business leaders. He had charts and graphs and went through the rain dance rituals at Fairfield without missing a step. But then he would return to Pittsfield, Massachusetts, where he was head of the Plastics division, and proceed to do whatever he wanted.

Because he was such a good player, Welch knew just how much time and money the system wasted. The old strategy process at GE was a perfect example of a vicious teaching cycle. No one got smarter. In fact, because everyone was playing games and putting window dressing on all the information, most people got dumber.

The face-to-face strategy meetings were events where, as Welch described it, "You went to a meeting. The lights went down. You read a script and then you got the hell out of the room." The strategic planners sat with the CEO and provided him with "gotcha questions" to show the business leaders that they weren't as smart as he was.

Business professors loved the GE strategic planning process because it looked so quasi-scientific. It had a lot of neat matrices and analytic frameworks that could be taught. There was a whole series of Harvard Business School teaching cases on GE strategic planning extolling its virtues. Generations of MBAs across the country were trained on the GE planning protocols. In fact, GE spawned an industry of strategic planners at other companies ranging from RCA to Westinghouse, from TRW to International Paper.

However, in a talk to a class at Harvard in 1981, the year he became chairman, Welch remarked that all the "nonsense you read in these books here and everywhere else is wrong. People come first then strategy." This was to be his guiding principle for the entire twenty years he was CEO. He went after leaders first, who would then formulate a straightforward simple vision for their businesses and clearly articulate it to everyone.

The transformation he effected was simple and stunning. First, he fired all but about six of the two hundred strategic planners at head-quarters. Then he told the heads of the businesses that the strategic session, the S-1 meetings held in July each year, were to be informal and interactive. They would be held at his round conference table.

The participants from headquarters would be the three members of the office of the CEO. In the beginning this was Welch, Ed Hood, and John Burlingame, who were vice chairmen. Later in the decade, Larry Bossidy replaced Burlingame. The head of the business could bring a small team including the finance head for the business, but there would be no strategic planners present.

The social architecture was totally changed. No big books were prepared ahead of time. Rather, the business head explained what was going on in the business and its markets, and together the team brainstormed about what would be the best strategy. What this did was to allow Welch and the other senior officers to participate in a meaningful way in the planning. Rather than coming in on the tail-end of the process with the role of critic, they got to contribute their brains and experience in the early creative stages.

The meetings were informal. No one stood up to present. Instead there was a team of people around a round conference table debating and discussing the business. The informality, as Welch describes it, "took the crap out of the system. The pontificating was gone and people could wrestle with real issues and ideas."

He created an environment where teaching and learning takes place.

The Budgeting Process

The budgeting process that Welch inherited in 1981 was also in-wardly focused and overly bureaucratic, and the changes that he made to it were also based on Virtuous Teaching Cycle principles.

When I worked at GE, I can remember business heads spending hours rehearsing their presentations and going over them again and again to try to address in advance every question the CEO might be able to think of. The general idea was that in the meeting with the CEO, the business head would be in the "barrel," and the CEO would fire questions at him. Although ostensibly playing only devil's advocate, the CEO and his staff in these meetings seemed more intent on showing up weaknesses in the business head and his budget than in mutual learning.

Welch did a couple of things to change that. One was to change the format of the process the same way he changed the strategy process. For example, the only participants in the meeting were the essential members. They were to talk about business ideas and focus on actions to drive the financials. He also changed the roles of the various players.

In particular, he changed the people in and the job of the finance organization that supported the process. Welch put Dennis Dammerman in as his head of finance in the early 1980s and started working with him to create a process of financial planning and budgeting that was focused on the outside world, on competitors and the marketplace.

He removed many of the old finance leaders and promoted a new generation of leaders, who developed a new kind of relationship with the front-line businesses. Dammerman told his people that their job was not, as it had been in the past, to be nitpicking bean counters and finance cops who tried to veto projects that the businesses wanted to do. Rather, their job was to partner with the people in the businesses and help them figure out how to carry out innovative strategies.

This required not only an entirely new mind-set on the part of the people in the finance department, but also new kinds of tools. One of the big projects when I was at Crotonville in the mid-1980s was to create a totally new set of finance programs to develop these new skills sets and attitudes in the finance organization. This support from the revamped finance organization provided the foundation to make the fall budgeting process interactive teaching and learning sessions.

Succession Planning

GE had a very systematic and much vaunted leadership development and succession planning system when Welch became CEO. The process was rigorous and the procedures were taken seriously. But it was more about ranking people than about coaching them. So performance reviews had become ritualistic exercises in which form was more important than substance. As a result, they lacked candor and the results were virtually worthless when it came to deciding on who really were the best people for promotions.[5]

So, as with strategy and budgeting, Welch redesigned the process. He changed the form of the meetings to make them into the interactive coaching and goal-setting sessions described above. He also changed the content of the reviews to focus explicitly on values and behaviors, not just performance and potential.

The Session C leadership development cycle starts in the spring with every professional doing a personal assessment, listing accomplishments of the past year and developmental goals and areas for desired development. The individual's supervisor writes a similar assessment, and then the two meet for a candid coaching session. This process is taken very seriously by the hundreds of thousands of individuals and their supervisors who actively coach and teach as they go through this process.

Each business unit conducts its Session C preparation, with thousands of potential leaders and their supervisors doing assessments and holding individual meetings. Then in May, the CEO goes out to each business for a full-day meeting that starts in the early morning and often goes late into the night. It is a very interactive Virtuous Teaching Cycle. The business leader teaches the CEO where the business is and how its strategy and structure are aligned. Then they have a detailed discussion of all the key players in terms of their performance, their alignment with the GE values, and their future potential.

Session C is one of GE's single most important operating mechanisms because it is how it keeps track of leadership talent, figures out ways of developing the talent, and plans career and developmental moves. The sessions are informal and intense, with candid debate and a great deal of edge exercised in deciding on promotions, firings and developmental assignments.

A typical Session C review includes a thorough discussion of key people's performance and leadership behaviors and action plans that will both develop individuals and take the business where it needs to go strategically. Often there is a specific initiative that the CEO wants to discuss, such as digitization or new technologies. In past years it has focused on the sales force and Six Sigma. The day's agenda is fluid and flows according to the interests and priorities of the CEO and the business leaders.

Building Digital Customer-Centricity

The future will mean more re-architecting for Jeff Immelt. As the world changes and as the leadership changes, so should the operating mechanisms. Building off the operating system created by Jack Welch, Immelt has launched into the next generation of re-architecting GE's operating mechanisms. The focus is to capitalize on digitization and the Six Sigma effort underway at GE.

As Immelt said he saw it in the fall of 2001:

> *The Internet allows every company to have fewer, more efficient and higher-value jobs. At GE, 60% of our resources are in the "front room," customer facing, growth-driving, manufacturing, selling and controllership. The other 40% of our resources are in the "back room," supporting as well as compiling and passing information. This will change. Digitized companies in the twenty-first century will have significantly smaller back rooms with more resources committed to growth and customer success.*
>
> *Digitization allows companies to change their shape, focusing only on those things that drive customer success, profit and growth. Across the company, we will take out $10 billion of costs over the next three years. Six Sigma, combined with digitization, will shape a leaner GE.*
>
> *The combination of Six Sigma and digitization is taking us into our customers' workflow. We are focused on three areas that make a difference to them: repeatable processes (span), sales force capacity and customer profitability . . . You have heard us talk about span, the "evil" variance our customers feel in our response to their requests for delivery, service or financing.[6]*

The result of Immelt's challenge to the organization is that every single function is revamping the way it operates and will end up shifting all of their operating mechanisms to be more customer facing, with more resources going to helping customers.

As simple as the concept sounds, there is tremendous angst over this at GE because it means that functions such as finance face major overhauls, which will result in both head count reductions and massive change in what the remaining people actually work on. Immelt has committed to a $10-billion cost reduction, and Wall Street is putting the whole organization under the gun to deliver.

One new set of operating mechanisms that Immelt is building is designed to integrate research and development more closely into operations. GE has a 100+ year history of R&D. In 1900, C. P. Steinmetz established the first industrial research laboratory in the United States in Schenectady, New York, and for years, GE was the world's No. 1 company for patents. So there have always been operating mechanisms for technology transfer. But over the years, R&D became more and more disconnected from the businesses.[7]

When Welch became CEO, he described many of the R&D labs as "hobby shops." And he began to use the budgeting and strategy operating mechanisms to alter the R&D to make it more accountable to the businesses. He did this, in part, by removing R&D from the corporate budget and making the businesses ante up the funding from their budgets.

Now, in a world where technology is becoming even more important, Immelt is trying to tighten the connection of R&D with business operations. To do this, he sees a need for a radically accelerated process for learning about new technologies at GE, so he is inventing a totally new set of operating mechanisms. These new mechanisms will revolve about the work of GE's corporate research and development center in Schenectady, New York.

In order to teach GE leaders about emerging twenty-first century technologies, such as nanotechnology, various biotech applications and new materials applications, he is building a new learning center as part of the R&D facility. The idea is that business leaders will participate along with scientists in training programs at the center. The business leaders will learn about new technologies from the scientists, who will learn about the marketplaces and real-world needs from the business leaders. It will be a Virtuous Teaching Cycle that will help GE come up with the products and services that customers need more quickly and efficiently.

Benchmarking VTC Operating Mechanisms

For any organization, the objective should be to build a system of operating mechanisms, all of which incorporate Virtuous Teaching

Cycles and reinforce each other. The GE case illustrates an extraordinarily high degree of integration and a large number of mechanisms involving hundreds of thousands of people.

Few other organizations have achieved such a degree of coordination, but increasingly, leaders are understanding the importance of Virtuous Teaching Cycles and building new operating mechanisms that incorporate them. The processes may well turn out to be the building blocks for innovative new operating systems.

One of those leaders is Dick Brown, the CEO of EDS, who is using a range of face-to-face and electronic methods to drive his operating mechanisms. At Home Depot, CEO Bob Nardelli is also implementing a massive new set of operating mechanisms.

EDS and Dick Brown's Operating Mechanisms

When Dick Brown left his job as CEO of Cable & Wireless to head troubled EDS in December 1998, he knew that he had no time to waste. He had to move quickly.

So he focused on two fronts. To make sure that he had a team firmly committed to change, he removed twenty-eight of the thirty-six officers who were in place when he arrived. Then he began to architect a new set of operating mechanisms that would make the company more flexible and agile.

The centerpiece, he decided, would be leadership development and succession planning. Since EDS is a consulting and services company, a key business driver is the quality of its people and leadership at all levels.

Succession Planning at EDS

Even before Brown's arrival, everyone at EDS knew that people were the firm's key asset, but nonetheless, the operating mechanisms for developing leaders were very weak, lacking discipline and integrity. Leaders went through the motions of evaluating performance. But the evaluations were perfunctory, and there was no vigorous debate and no edge in decision making. So too many mediocre players were being allowed to stay, either because they were not recognized as mediocre or no one had the nerve to send them away.

Brown made changing this a top priority. Brown's philosophy is,

"Picking people is the hardest task I ever have to do." But because it is so central to the success or failure of the organization, it is his job as CEO. "Picking leadership is a task you can't delegate to others, but it's a task you shouldn't do by yourself," he says. So he has set up a mechanism that he calls "team hiring."

"You have to be prepared as you pick leaders to get beyond the niceties and get into a real candid discussion of, not opinions, but examples where people can state what they did or didn't do in almost a clinical condition where you can evaluate. Do I think what they did was right, or do I think it was wrong? . . . People who are going to succeed and be real winners for you are not going to, all of a sudden, be winners for the first time. They're going to bring with them a pattern of winning that's been apparent . . . so you really have to get into . . . the pattern they've had of winning, and if you can't see it, beware."

The mechanism that Brown has set up to carry out this process is very informal, but disciplined. Each member of the top team comes up with candidates for the next level jobs just below them in their businesses. Then all the top team members have a free-ranging discussion. Those who know the candidates contribute their thoughts, while everyone digs for details and specifics. They try to push beyond generalities such as "this person lacks people judgment" to find examples and real situations where they have observed the qualities of the individual.

Brown's job is to keep the discussion on target. This is pressing to make sure they keep digging to uncover patterns and can collectively come to a conclusion, while at the same time, keeping it from becoming a witch hunt.

Two years after Brown started at EDS, I attended one such meeting and found all the elements of a Virtuous Teaching Cycle: honest data about the people being discussed, interactive teaching and learning about the people and what the organization needs to succeed in the future, and edge to implement the decisions.

Brown's belief is that a good succession planning operating mechanism starts with a "more robust, a more candid, concise, and constructive process of evaluation of performance and behaviors. And that becomes a platform to consider what more someone can do."

Teaching/Learning for the Top 150 at EDS

A new teaching and learning operating mechanism that Brown has launched at EDS is a thrice yearly meeting of senior management. The agenda is to share best practices, to talk about where the business is headed, and to hear what Brown is thinking. "Three times a year I bring our top 150 executives together from around the world for a day and a half roundtable, interactive, let's-talk-about-the-business session. It's an injection of religion. And you can see these top executives show their colors."

Brown also brings his team together in a monthly process that is much more time compressed, but has elements of the Wal-Mart business assessment. "Every month, we have an operating call that lasts less than one hour. It's basically to find out how things are going. It's just a check-up to keep us all informed. If somebody's doing a great job, they'll get accolades on the call, but if somebody's falling behind we'll schedule a meeting after class."

Like the three-times-a-year meetings, these calls are opportunities for Brown to get out important messages and to evaluate people in action. "It's an important mechanism and attendance is mandatory," he says.

Even though the calls are short, Brown's purpose is both teaching and learning. Sometimes he plays the tough teacher, putting people on the spot. "There was one time," he says, "when we were going through a particularly steep period for change. I had received quite a number of e-mails from people who expressed worry and concern . . . It wasn't from everywhere. It was from corners of the corporation. And so . . . on the call that day, I talked about leaders setting a tone, and I asked if anybody on the call was worried that we were undertaking too traumatic a change or that we were reckless in the process. And nobody spoke up. Then I said, 'It's okay to tell me you think we're wrong. It really is, try this again." Still nothing.

"So, finally, I said, 'Well a dozen organizations are worried. Those are people who work for a dozen of you, and people imitate their leadership. You worry and wring your hands, and your people worry and wring their hands, and I'm telling you twelve of you at least are worried and haven't said it. Now get religion, get strong, get into your organizations and stop this distraction or you can't stay effective.' And you know, it really did make a difference."

But toughness is only part of the equation. On other calls, Brown is the student, listening and learning from them about the marketplace, client issues and best practices. The important thing is he convenes the group, establishes the open environment, role models the behavior he wants, and repeats and repeats the process.

EDS Use of the Web to Teach

Another new operating mechanism that Brown has introduced at EDS is his bi-weekly e-mail to all 140,000 employees. "Every fourteen days, or more frequently, I send a message to the men and women of EDS around the world. . . . It's fabulous because it's fast, frequent, and filterless communication, and they hear what's on my mind twice a month at least."

Because of some of the responses he has gotten from his e-mails, he said that he has learned that "people are not afraid of change. They're afraid of the unknown, and the best thing that strikes at the heart of the unknown is communication." Brown says he particularly appreciates the two-way nature of e-mail. "It's become an electronic suggestion box. Because while I send these messages out, you know what I get back are thousands of well-intended and constructive responses.

"When I wasn't sure in the early days of EDS how to get our costs under control, I kept thinking, 'What do we do now?' I didn't know EDS that well, and it would have been easy to make a sudden bad mistake. I knew that, but no action was no option. So I sent an e-mail to everybody around the world and said, "I need you today!" Save $1,000 of expense, each and every one of you. Find a way to do it, and tell me how you did it. And we cut $100 million of expense in sixty days. It saved the first quarter. I just asked them. They knew where it was!"

This is a very powerful example of an electronic Virtuous Teaching Cycle. Brown taught the 140,000 workers about the need for and importance of cost-cutting, and they responded by teaching him $100 million worth of cost improvements. In the past, real interactivity at that scale would have been unthinkable. With new technologies, it is going to become a necessity.

Home Depot Operating Mechanisms

Bob Nardelli started re-architecting the Home Depot operating mechanisms shortly after arriving on the scene. He inherited some very good ones that he continues to build upon, but introduced several that I consider best practices.

One very important operating mechanism that goes back to the founders of Home Depot is the store walk. Store walks are how the leaders of Home Depot keep in touch with both customers and employees.

Leaders at all levels of Home Depot do store walks. CEO Bob Nardelli does at least one a week. Board members must do five a quarter. During a store walk, the visitor/leader puts on an orange apron just like any other associate and goes out into the store. He or she will visit with associates, wait on customers, and generally get a feel for what is going on.

On the morning that we interviewed him, Bob Nardelli had done a store walk in Kansas. While we were waiting for him to get back, we walked a store near the headquarters office in Atlanta with Gary Harvin, a district manager.

When we arrived at the parking lot, Harvin opened the trunk and pulled out his orange apron. The apron, he explained, was an important part of the walk. He wanted to be available and approachable to customers, and he wanted to be perceived as part of the team in the store.

As we walked through the aisles of the store, he role modeled the behavior he wanted to see in associates. When he stopped to chat with them, he asked both specific questions that showed what was on his mind, and probing ones to find out what was on theirs. The conversations they engaged in were easygoing, but substantive. Throughout it all, he was eagerly greeting customers.

Dennis Donovan says that when he joined the company in April 2001, Harvin was the person who took him through his first several stores. "When you do store walks, they are teaching experiences. Gary would go from one area to the other. He would look at the stats for a store before he went, so he knew where he wanted to focus his teaching. But he didn't just focus on things that needed improvement. He also found people doing things right, so there was a recognition element," says Donovan.

"He'd go around and, rather than give people the answer, he'd ask the questions, and he'd keep at it and keep at it. He'd make them think it through themselves, and then they'd get to a good answer, and he'd support it. And at the end of the day, he would get the people together from the store walk, and he'd go back through the learnings."

What really impressed Donovan was that "afterward, he would tell me what he learned, and by the time we got to the next store, he would have changed what he was going to do because of what he had learned in the last store. I remember in one store, he began discussing a problem with overdue returns of tool rentals. By the end of the conversation, he and the associates together had figured out that we actually weren't looking at the return of the tool. We were ready to start sending letters to customers telling them they had to return the tool. But we found the tool was already in the store. We weren't using our existing systems capabilities. Once you see the problem, it isn't that difficult to fix, so when he walked into the next store, he started with what he had learned in the last one."

When we visited the store with Harvin, he stopped to ask a couple of associates how well they were doing selling to contractors. Home Depot is trying to broaden its market from do-it-yourselfers to professionals in the construction business. So he was both gathering information and reinforcing the importance of the initiative when he made the inquiries. He also told them to "let me know if there is anything I can do from my end to make sure that you have the products and support you need."

His exchanges had the air of easy, open conversations. He repeatedly broke them off to speak to customers and offer assistance, but he was clear in his sincerity with both the customers and the associates. His openness and desire to help was what made his interactions both teaching and learning opportunities.

QMI at Home Depot

Nardelli brought the concept of Quick Market Intelligence, which GE had copied from Home Depot's competitor Wal-Mart, with him when he went to Home Depot. "Every Monday, regardless of where you are, from 12 to 2 we get on the phone. We talk about last week's sales figures and what's happening in the market. . . . It's a process that works. Really, the pride then is how you localize it and do it better than the place you stole the idea from."

One of the keys to having effective operating mechanisms is to continuously adjust and improve them. Nardelli says he has had to tune the QMI process to suit the Home Depot environment. As a result, the calls are "becoming more crisp. They are becoming more productive. Early on, we were struggling . . . trying to get the process down and getting people comfortable enough, confident to open up on the phone. But what we've got now is the field talking to us versus us talking to the field."

In architecting any operating mechanism, working on all three phases is critical:

Phase I—Preparation: Nardelli has a couple of simple documents that he calls "flash reports" that have the data for the meeting, such as year-to-year store sales and key issues in the market. It's all on one page so it can be quickly shared.

Phase II—Face-to-face or in the QMI case, the phone call: Nardelli started with as many as fifty people on the phone call, but people told him that was too many. So he cut back the number of participants so that they could be more candid and direct. He now has about twenty to twenty-five people on the phone, and it is working well.

Phase III—Follow-up: There is a very disciplined process for following up. Nardelli makes sure on the phone call that specific people are made responsible for each action item. Then, there is a follow up e-mail to the participants with action items, and reports on the results at the next meeting.

Strategic Planning at Home Depot

The founders of Home Depot, Bernie Marcus and Arthur Blank, grew the business to 1,300 stores in 22 years, but they never really had strategic or resource planning processes. They just did things on an informal basis.

So when Nardelli came in from GE, planning was one of the first things he tackled. "I wanted to try to bring a process where we would look at a three-year mid-range rolling forecast. I wanted to bring some operational visibility and some resource planning. So we sat down and put together a program called SOAR. It stands for Strategic Operating and Resource Planning.

The process takes place around a table in a conference room. A division president and members of his team meet with Nardelli and a small team of corporate staff in a give-and-take session. Nardelli talks about where he wants the company to go; they all talk about the specifics of how to get there.

One of Nardelli's Teachable Points of View is that the company needs to become more "outside-in," getting the perspective of the customer and competitor into its decision making. In addition, he is pushing his team to look for new growth opportunities by moving more and more into services, such as installations and work with professional contractors. He uses the SOAR process both as a teaching opportunity and a chance to learn from the division presidents.

One result of examining the strategy process is the injection of a concept called "market back." This means, Nardelli explains, "looking at your marketing area and asking: What are your customer demographics? How are we doing on our own store growth? Are we really becoming neighborhood/family friendly? What do we need to do in the area in human resources? Are we really proactively thinking about the need as we go forward for new store managers, new division managers? Are we really thinking about shaping the future versus the future shaping us?"

In this case, Nardelli sees his job in this Virtuous Teaching Cycle as providing the platform for his leaders to think differently about the business, but it is their job to come in and teach him about what is going on in the market and ideas for improving performance.

Succession Planning

In the area of succession planning, which Nardelli calls resource planning, his GE heritage clearly comes through. He and Donovan have many years of experience with the GE Session C process, and like the GE process, the one they have put in place at Home Depot requires leaders to prepare with their own teams ahead of time. It also has a very disciplined follow-through.

As at GE, the leadership meetings between the CEO and the division heads are not held at headquarters, but out in the field so that the team from Atlanta can meet and interact with more people. The meetings generally last a full day and end with a town hall meeting.

"We spend a full day with each division president," says Donovan. "We start off with the division president one on one, talking about his or her direct reports. Then we bring in all of the direct reports to the president to discuss their leadership teams. Bob and I then have lunch with 40 to 60 of our high-potential associates. We each spend 45 minutes with half the group, then swap so we can spend the remaining 45 minutes with the other group." This may sound like a short time period, but it is effective. Nardelli very openly takes any question and answers it, and he keeps the energy flowing by challenging participants and asking for their ideas. This dialogue teaches Nardelli and Donovan about what is on the minds of these future leaders, gives them a sense of how good they are, and symbolically shows them that they are important and valued.

In the afternoon, Nardelli meets again with the division president and his team to talk about training and what things are necessary to support the strategic plans. He then holds a town hall meeting where he talks and takes questions from 100 to 300 associates.

Winners Build Teaching and Learning into Core Processes

Operating mechanisms are some of the most powerful tools that leaders have. They are the processes that keep the company running day after day, year in and year out. Everyone in the company is a participant and is touched by many operating mechanisms in the course of just one day.

Because they are repeated procedures, at many companies operating mechanisms become "routines" in the worst sense of the word. They become mindless rote procedures that at best bore everyone and at worst sap energy and stifle creativity. But when designed to be Virtuous Teaching Cycles, they have the power to make people throughout the company smarter and more aligned every day.

Winning leaders understand their role as social architect and consciously build teaching and learning into the daily processes through which the company goes about its business. It is this harnessing and constant increasing of the brains and energy of everyone in their companies that makes them winners.

Chapter 10
Trilogy University: Boot Camp and Knowledge Generation

■ **New-Hire Orientation Program Is a Key Operating Mechanism**
- It teaches kids how to transform the company.
- Their brains and energy become the R&D department.

■ **It's a Lever for Keeping Top Leadership on Target**
- Lesson planning requires the CEO to rethink the business model twice a year.
- The kids bring new ways of thinking right to the top.

■ **It Develops Leader Skills in Talented Rising Stars**
- Best performers spend three months learning to coach and teach new-hires.
- They work side-by-side, learning from the CEO.

Joe Liemandt recalls the day in 1997 when a team of twenty-one- and twenty-two-year-old new college hires at Trilogy Software pitched him an idea for selling cars on the Internet. At the time, the concept of e-commerce was in its early stages. eBay and Amazon were new start-ups. Liemandt told them that it was the dumbest idea he had ever heard, that they were totally naïve to think that people would spend that kind of money over the Internet, and that they did not understand the industry, franchise laws, or how dealers would prevent this from happening.

As Liemandt tells the story, his response really ticked off the kids. They had joined Trilogy because they thought that it was an exciting, cutting-edge kind of place. And now the founder and CEO of the company was turning out to be just another dinosaur. The kids perceived that as he approached his thirtieth birthday, he had fallen hopelessly out of touch with the times. He was too old and he just didn't get it. So they decided to prove him wrong. They went ahead and developed their car-selling Website, lined up failing dealers who were willing to cooperate, and started selling cars.

Today, Trilogy has a very successful auto industry business. It staked out its turf early on and has a very strong position in this important market, all because six kids told Liemandt to buzz off, that *he* was dumb, not them.

The development of CarOrder.com, which Liemandt permitted as a learning exercise for the students as part of their Trilogy University experience, transformed the company in ways far beyond simply the entry into an important new business. It changed some of Liemandt's fundamental beliefs about leadership, which in turn has directly affected how the company is organized and runs on a day-to-day basis.

In fact, he has made Trilogy University, the company's entry-level boot camp, its primary research and development lab. Since 1997, Trilogy has launched numerous new products because of the "dumb" ideas developed by new-hires, and Liemandt has reinvented the company several times over because of things he has learned from running Trilogy University.

Maximizing Talent from Day One

Leadership in the new millennium is fundamentally a knowledge–creation activity. In a business and social environment where new ideas and knowledge are appearing at warp speed, the primary task of a leader is to energize all organization members to be smarter every day. Liemandt and Trilogy Software, a young company in terms of both its own age and the twenty-six-year average age of its employees, provide a world-class example for doing that. Trilogy University and Liemandt's use of it as a lever for leading and energizing the whole company is a benchmark Teaching Organization.[1]

We have made the case throughout this book, and most people agree, that in the new "knowledge economy" the key to winning is maximizing human capital. Ideas and knowledge have replaced physical goods as the most valued commodities in the global marketplace. Consequently, brains, energy and talent—human capital—have replaced plant and equipment—physical capital—as the primary source of value creation. But while many people and organizations grasp the concept, few have figured out how to really utilize the talents and knowledge of everyone in the company, especially the younger new members of the company.

That's because they remain attached to old ways of thinking, the ones that say "experience knows best" and "you must prove yourself before we will listen to or seriously invest in you." This is a particularly costly way of thinking in times of highly mobile labor markets.

As recently as just a few years ago, conventional wisdom in the human resources business was that new-hires became profitable contributors after they had been on board for about two years. Today, in many fields, especially highly sought after technical ones, two years is the average tenure in a job. Thus, it is critical that companies get new-hires working productively as soon as possible so that if, or more likely the case when, a worker leaves in two years, the employer will have a positive return on the investment.

The new way of thinking that guides Trilogy University and allows Trilogy to begin immediately recouping its average $10,000 per person investment in recruiting is one that does not equate value with length of service. Rather, it says that "new people bring new energy, new talents, and most importantly new ideas. These are precious assets that must not be wasted." As a result, Trilogy University has among its specific missions not only tapping into the unique talents and personal knowledge of its new-hires, but also assessing their talents so that they can be slotted into positions that utilize them to the maximum extent as soon as possible.

"We don't care how old you are or how new you are. All we care about is finding out how good you are so that we can put you in a job that maximizes your abilities," says Allan Drummond, head of TU in explaining why the TU faculty deliberately stretches each student beyond the point of failure.

Boot Camp as a Leadership Lever

Multitasking and synergy are two of the keys to Trilogy University's success. TU directly addresses three issues that are critical to winning in today's marketplace—continuous transformation of the company, leadership development and product R&D—and it accomplishes each of them more effectively for working them in combination with the others. Further, in each of these critical areas, the learning and the teaching flow in both directions along a two-way street.

As in the case of CarOrder.com described above, the newly hired "students" are as often the leader/teachers as they are the follower/learners. The result is that everyone at Trilogy is energizing, teaching, learning and contributing from the moment they walk in the door, and the injection of a new class of TU-ers every six months keeps everyone in the company in a constant learning, teaching and thinking mode.

The essential elements of the Trilogy University formula are:

Transformation: Trilogy University and the TU-ers are Liemandt's primary lever for injecting both new ideas and new energy into the company. Liemandt founded TU in 1994 for the specific purpose of transforming the old Trilogy. Although Trilogy was only four years old at the time, Liemandt realized that it had a culture that was aimed primarily for short-term success in the IPO market.

He wanted to build a big company that would be, as the company motto now puts it, "The next great software company." So he hired 150 new people, mostly kids, isolated them from the 700 old-timers, and set about creating a powerful team of change agents who would re-create the company with the new build-for-excellence ethos that he wanted.

In the early days of TU, Liemandt was TU's hands-on director and primary teacher. Since 1999 others have taken over the official positions in TU, but Liemandt's presence and participation remain critical elements of TU. This intimate involvement of Liemandt and other Trilogy stars has led to another benefit that was at first unexpected but that is now a crucial piece of TU's contribution to Trilogy's success. It is that twice a year Liemandt and other Trilogy leaders must decide what they want to teach and how they want to focus the new class of TU change agents.

For any leader, regardless of whether he or she is ever in a class-room setting, having an up-to-date Teachable Point of View is crucial. A leader must have a clear TPOV about where the company/organization/team needs to go, a general understanding about how it is going to get there, and the ability to explain it in a way that is exciting and inspiring to others. But while leaders' TPOVs must be firm and clear, they must also be constantly evolving. As conditions change, they have to be changed to take account of the new conditions. What TU does for Liemandt and other Trilogy leaders is enforce the requirement that they update their TPOVs at least twice a year. As a result, Trilogy's goals are more recent and its focus on them more targeted than might, or probably would be, the case without the impetus from TU.

Personal and leadership development: Introducing new-hires to the company and polishing their technical skills are pretty usual stuff at entry-level boot camps, and Trilogy University has both on its agenda. But the skills part is pretty low on the list. ("They are very smart, so we figure they can pick up what they need when they need it," says Drummond.) And the introduction to the company couldn't be further from the standard fare.

Rather than teaching people how to fit in, TU, quite to the contrary, focuses on helping the new-hires build the personal attributes, networks and judgment that will allow them to change Trilogy for the better. The lessons are reinforced by the fact that they are personally taught by Liemandt and other fast-track star performers.

The development of the TU-ers, however, is only half the equation. TU is also the proving ground for developing the next generation of senior leadership at Trilogy. Each TU class is divided into sections of fifteen people—sort of like homerooms in high school—and each section is assigned a section lead. These leaders assist the head of TU and deliver some of the core curriculum to the entire class, but their primary job is to make sure that the people in their sections learn what they need to learn. Their role, basically, is to lead the students who are their charges to success. This involves engaging, energizing, judging, coaching and giving feedback.

In the hothouse of TU, and under the direct eye of Liemandt, the section leads are learning and testing out the essential skills that they will need to be the leaders of the company in the future. Further, during their three months at TU, they are not only exposed to Liemandt's latest ideas about the direction of the company, but they are engaged as partners with him in developing and implementing those ideas. They are thus transformed from being members of the "old Trilogy" into top-flight change agents and cutting-edge participants in the next round of transformation.

R&D lab: In an unusual up-ending of normal business procedures, Trilogy University is the company's primary lab for developing new businesses and products. When he set up TU in 1994, Liemandt decided that he would teach the students about business by having them try to start their own. He would be the venture capitalist, and they would have to come up with ideas, pitch them to him, and for the ones that sounded promising, he would even provide a bit of funding.

The original idea was that the projects would simply be a learning vehicle. And today, the projects still serve that function. But as he listened to the pitches, Liemandt realized that the students were coming up with some really good ideas that the folks already employed by Trilogy weren't. Further, as with CarOrder.com, some of them were really good ideas that Liemandt and the other "older" Trilogians weren't even able to recognize as good ideas.

The TU-ers represented a unique resource: A pool of some of the brightest young computer wizards in the world, eager for work and unconstrained by experience or conventional thinking. In earlier times, experience may have been an unqualified asset, but in a world where the environment and the rules change every day, experience can be a detriment. The TU-ers aren't tainted by yesterday's beliefs when thinking about tomorrow.

Since 1997, TU has been the primary R&D lab for Trilogy, and the ideas and businesses it has spawned are just a part of its contribution to Trilogy. Equally important is the impact it has had in changing the mind-sets of everyone in the company. The surprises delivered every six months by the TU-ers serve as a constant reminder that the world continues to move at warp speed, and today's winners will be tomorrow's also-rans.

Liemandt doesn't give the kids free rein. He doesn't bet the farm on untested twenty-two-year-olds. Part of the exercise is to teach them business acumen, about setting priorities, evaluating probabilities and measuring results. But giving the youngest and newest hires a central role in plotting the company's future course not only keeps Trilogy supplied with ideas out at the cutting-edge, but also creates an organization in which letting go of the past and reaching out for a new future is the expected norm.

Intense, boot-camp style orientation programs for new-hires are not new. In the mid-1980s at General Electric, I helped develop the Corporate Entry Leadership Conference, a three-day program at GE's Crotonville leadership development institute where new-hires learned about the GE strategy, its culture and a bit about themselves.[2,3]

At least since the mid-1990s, boot camps have been commonplace for new-hires at consulting firms and service companies. Many old-line industrials have also set them up, as they have realized that energizing new-hires and engaging them in the culture is just as critical as making sure that they have the technical skills to do their specific jobs. And at young high-tech firms, immersion-style boot camps are almost ubiquitous, although it is sometimes hard to distinguish the boot camp's hectic 24/7 schedules from the hectic 24/7 environment of the whole company.

Trilogy University is similar to other boot camps in that it immerses new-hires in the company culture, teaches them about Trilogy's products and customers, and polishes their technical skills so they can perform in their eventual jobs. But unlike traditional new-hire orientation programs that teach the newcomers to perform within the existing organization, Trilogy University taps into the energy and talents of the fresh hires to shape and revitalize the company.

"With each TU class, we have the opportunity to create in the minds of 60 or 160 new people the vision of Trilogy not as it is, but as we would like for it to be," says Drummond. "We make sure that they bond into a strong trust network among themselves and the leaders who mentor them at TU, which gives them confidence, and then we send them out into the company where they have the critical mass to have a real impact."

Overview of the Three-Month TU Process

Trilogy University is run twice a year. In the summer, it includes between 150 and 170 off-campus hires. In the winter it has about 60. It includes a sprinkling of freshly minted masters and Ph.D.'s, but most are from the undergraduate computer science programs at top schools such as Stanford, MIT, Carnegie Mellon and Michigan. The program generally lasts about twelve weeks. After the students have finished their TU projects (formerly called Joe Projects because Liemandt plays the role of venture capitalist), graduations are on a rolling basis as students find sponsors out in the company who are willing to take them on. "We want everyone here to be a star. So we won't graduate TU-ers until they have found positions that they want and where the new manager will take responsibility for helping them become a star," explains Danielle Rios, former head of TU.

Month No. 1

During the first month, the format of TU is a combination of "big talks," sections and tracks. Many of the big talks, which are delivered in a Socratic style to the entire TU class, are given by Liemandt. Others are by Drummond and the Trilogy stars who have been taken out of their line positions to serve for three months as TU staffers. At the end of the three months, most of them will not go back to their old jobs, but will move on to new leadership positions in Trilogy.

The big talks are about key pieces of philosophy and culture. In TU 99.5, the winter section between the classes of 1999 and 2000, Drummond's first big talk was called "Let's Think About Thinking," in which he talked about mappers vs. packers. "Your packer takes the input and a process and produces an output. A mapper sort of does the reverse. You give them an input and you say this is the output we want and they can come up with the process," says Drummond. "I tell them that this is an incredibly powerful mode of thought for us because we're trying to solve problems for which we have no process. So the first talk basically says 'Be a mapper, not packer.'" Other talks are about such things as risk-taking and having a bias for action.

A perennial favorite is a slide show of twenty-five slides called "How to Be a Trilogy Star." Examples:

Slide #1

What is this presentation?

Lots of thoughts from old-timers about how you can better ensure your success at Trilogy. Many of these recommendations seem similar. They are actually subtle variations on important themes that will make more sense over time.

Several of these recommendations seem conflicting. They are all important, so your job is to balance them.

Slide #3

Be Approachable

(a.k.a. Don't be an Asshole)

During the first month, each TU-er is assigned to a section and a track. In their track, they work on functional skills: Java, XML, how to write a project plan, how to do a customer e-mail, how to do a presentation, etc. Tracks start out with a bone-breaking assignment in the first week and then pile on increasingly difficult ones each week for the first month.

Tracks end after the first month, but sections, in a sense, continue for life. Sections are where social networks are formed and the new-hires develop friendships that will support them throughout their careers. It's also where they have long debates and wrestle with the ideas and values presented in the big talks.

Drummond describes sections as the "skills training on what kind of company we are building. Why do we do what we do. It's where we get them to challenge the fabric and the framework of the company so that you get the real engagement."

In the early weeks, "we are rebooting their brains and creating the image of the company that we want them to go out and build," says Drummond. "If people don't learn Java in TU, I don't care. They are very bright. They can pick up what they need. If they don't develop nearly unbreakable bonds with fellow TU-ers, if they don't learn to prioritize and make smart decisions and all the kinds of things the sections do, if they don't leave charged up, TU is a failure."

The first month is also a time when a lot of measuring and evaluating is done. A database tracks each student. The five weekly track assignments are graded, and the section leads and the head of TU enter comments and grades on such things as technical skills, quality of interaction and, in some cases, skills in making presentations to clients. Section leads, who are officially charged with making sure that each of their TU-ers succeeds, use this information to coach them and direct them toward areas of the company where their particular strengths are most useful.

Month No. 2

Month number 2 is TU Project Month. It is when the TU-ers, mostly twenty-two years old and employees of the company for one month, take on the assignment of reinventing the company. "We tell them that old Trilogy is irretrievably broken. There is no amount of incrementalism that can fix it. The legacy folks who are already here have done the best that they can. So in order for the company to survive, they [the TU-ers] have to come up with a frame-breaking great new business idea for the company," says Liemandt. "And it works, because I really believe it."

It is here that Liemandt takes the role of venture capitalist. In 1998, the students rebelled when he rejected some of their ideas, telling him that he was trying to have it both ways, when he told them to "go for the fence" and then dismissed their ideas. "It was hard for me to let go, but I realized that they were right," he says. So he instituted the "no veto rule." Any student who is really committed to an idea is allowed to pursue it. In order to get funding, however, they still have to sell the idea to Liemandt.

Only about 15% of the projects survive beyond the month that is allocated to them in TU, but Liemandt figures that nearly all of them are good investments. The students have to come up with the ideas, create the business models, build the products, develop the marketing, and then try to persuade Liemandt that it is worth investing in.

The experience the kids get is worth the price, he says. It shows up in both their skills and the attitudes they take away. The ones who see ideas fail that they thought were brilliant have a new humility and appreciation for what it takes to create a winner. "They have gotten something out of their system, and now they are ready to let go of it, move on and learn what they need to learn to make the next one a success," says Drummond.

At the same time, the seriousness with which Liemandt and all the rest of Trilogy take the projects builds confidence. "We encourage them to go for the fence with their ideas, and while we don't reward failure around here, we don't punish them for it either," says Liemandt. "So when people leave TU, most of them are thinking, 'I know I can make a difference and I am not afraid to try,' which is exactly what we want them to think."

Month No. 3

In the third month, a few students continue with their TU projects, but most move on to graduation projects, which generally are assignments within the various Trilogy business units. The TU-ers' entry into the company is carefully orchestrated. In the first few weeks of TU, they are very isolated from the rest of the company.

"We are trying to build in their minds an image of the company as we want it to be, not necessarily as it is, so we carefully control who gets to talk to them," explains Drummond.

As the weeks go by, the amount of contact increases. By the third month, they are ready to venture out into the company while retaining their home base and their support network back in TU.

"It's not like we just eject them into the organization and say, 'Oh welcome. Go do it right,'" says Drummond. "We need them to stay grounded in TU while they are first experiencing the rest of the organization" so they won't lose their energy for being change agents.

"Any time you discover that the world is not what you think it is, there are two responses. One is: 'I was wrong. I got the wrong data.' Basically, I was lied to. The other response is: 'This doesn't seem right.' Next you decide either to let it ride even though you know that it's wrong, or you can say 'I'm going to go fix that.' As they graduate after three or four months, they aren't actually capable of individually implementing some sort of huge structural change. But the net input of 50, 100, 150 people into the organization is like 10% of the company, so the statistical change is fabulous. You just layer TU classes on to the company and every one of them is living inside the new Trilogy and you get that big organizational sort of reinventing."

The graduation projects offer TU-ers the opportunity to make contacts and bone up on skills or knowledge that will help them find jobs out in the company. In order to graduate, a TU-er must have a manager who is willing to accept and sponsor him or her. The TU faculty sometimes helps persuade managers who are reluctant to take a risk, but a TU-er who ultimately can't find a sponsor is out of the company.

The graduation process is a meeting between the manager, the TU-er and the section lead. Before the meeting, each has been asked to evaluate the TU-er on various abilities. At the meeting, the three of them discuss the evaluation to resolve disagreements. "We don't just want understanding, we want agreement," says Drummond. "On all of the rankings where there is a disparity, they have to reach an agreement."

The TU-ers have also written lists of things they want to accomplish and their thoughts on how they want their careers to unfold. The manager responds to these with a list of specific goals that the TU-er must agree to. Typically, the manager will set three to five goals with a personal development component, a main-line execution component, and an organizational development goal. A typical example is to execute a list of projects, to develop a specific set of skills, and organizationally to teach others and help with a change process.

The graduation meetings also serve as another change lever in the organization. That's because in order for managers to get TU graduates—a desirable resource—into their units, they must attend the graduation meetings and set goals that the TU-er and the section lead buy into. This provides an opportunity for the section lead "to deliver some messages to the managers so they understand what the new Trilogy vision is," explains Drummond. "It allows us to build a relationship with the manager."

A VTC: Senior Execs and New-Hires

With its multitasked mission and a 360 degree teaching and learning environment, Trilogy University is truly a Virtuous Teaching Cycle in which the company's best performers personally teach its youngest and greenest new-hires about business, while the new-hires point the leaders to new ideas and in new directions that they might not have thought of. The result is an amazing leveraging of energy and talent.

"I and most of Trilogy don't think of TU as a training program. It is a transformational experience," says Drummond. It transforms the TU-ers, Liemandt and other Trilogy leaders, and ultimately, the company.

"TU is the place in Trilogy where we have been able to create more excitement, grander scope and scale, more compelling stories, around the kind of company we're building than in any other place in the company. It's an incredibly valuable asset just from the business side of being able to keep us focused on what should the standard be for the company we want to build? What does it mean?" He adds: "We can hold up GE from a revenue and profit side—or Microsoft from the profit side—saying, 'Those are the companies we want to build,' but for sheer enthusiasm, vision, capability, talent, excitement, etc., we don't have to look at outside companies. We can look inside at TU and say, 'We've got it. How can we keep it going? How can we expand it? How can we make it better?' If the whole vision is that Trilogy is going to be GE for the new economy, TU will be Crotonville for the new economy."

Lessons for Others

Sophisticated benchmarking is not meant to copy, it is meant to uncover the underlying ideas that can be translated across different contexts. There are very few software companies with a thousand twenty-something employees. However, there are thousands of companies across a broad spectrum of industries. TU should challenge our conventional thinking, whether in the auto, telecommunications, retail or packaged goods industries. Across all of these, the fundamental challenges for winning are the same:

1. The need for continuous transformation of the company to stay competitive.
2. The need for the rapid development of capable leaders at all levels of the organization.
3. The need to innovate, develop new products and services.

The mega idea, which is the sophisticated use of Virtuous Teaching Cycles, can be applicable in any organization. It requires a leadership that is truly committed to teaching and continuous learning and sees this as a two-way street no matter what level of the organization.

The mind-set is that of generating knowledge for everyone, the CEO as well as the new-hires. Thus, hierarchy is not a blocker of mutual learning and teaching. The CEO learns as much as he teaches in working with the new off-campus hires. This should be true for McDonald's Hamburger U as it is for Motorola University. Both of these world-renowned institutions could be better if they made knowledge-generation their top priority and learning a two-way street. After all, who knows more about what kids are looking for in a fast-food outlet? An eighteen year old or a forty-five year old?

Step 1: The top must embrace the concept of a Virtuous Teaching Cycle. There must be a radical shift for most in thinking about human capital. It is enhanced by a teaching and learning process. The top must truly believe that they are responsible for creating the context for this to happen and that the top is going to fully engage in enhancing their own knowledge.

Step 2: Sufficient resources must be made available. TU is a huge financial investment for Trilogy. More importantly, it requires the investment of the company's scarcest resource, the time of the senior leaders as well as the rising leaders who serve the section leads.

Step 3: Compressed action learning—work in a real pressure cooker environment. This is more like Top Gun or Navy SEALs training than traditional corporate education.

Real risks are taken, people are pushed to their limits, and people drop out, because either they realize this is not for them or are asked to leave. Compressed action learning means compressing as much life experience in as short a period of time as possible. For TU-ers it includes being pushed to transform Trilogy, grow personally, come up with new R&D ideas and translate them into marketable products.

Elements of compressed action learning have been in place on a large scale at GE's Crotonville center since the mid-1980s. When I ran Crotonville in the 1980s, a team of us introduced it so that thousands of GE managers could go through programs where they tackled real GE problems. Jack Welch and his senior team participated and learned as much as they taught.

Mary Tolan at Accenture is using it in a leadership development program with five teams working on real strategic projects sponsored by her and her management team. The participants are young high-potential manager/consultants about to become partners. This is both a huge developmental lever for enhancing them as leaders for the future as well as an intense Virtuous Teaching Cycle for Tolan to generate new knowledge and answers to the strategic challenges.

The methodology is not new, but what is new is carrying it down to the entry-level the way TU does.

Step 4: Multiple levels of leadership development—the section lead position takes advantage of TU for developing new leaders for the company. The section leads improve their teaching skills, while working side-by-side with the CEO and learning from other senior leaders who participate in TU. The process produces TU graduates who are better equipped to add value to Trilogy, and it also enhances the abilities/value of the teachers. Companies that rely on HR staff and consultants to run their leadership programs get neither of these benefits.

TU: The Challenge

Why are there no other benchmarks like the TU "boot camp." We have many good examples of more limited entry and orientation programs ranging from the Marine Corps basic training to various corporate boot camps. These are all designed to push new recruits to their limits. Each day offers some nearly insurmountable challenge and the reward for it is overcoming an even harder one the next day. They are intense and intimidating, but people emerge highly confident that they are prepared for anything. They also come away with deep bonds to their fellow recruits and to the organization.

These two goals—preparedness and bonding—are usually the whole focus of a boot camp. And achieving them is worth a great deal. That's why so many of the top performing companies put their faith in such programs.

"Old Man Watson" at IBM ran them, as did Ross Perot when he founded EDS. So does Andy Grove at Intel. It's why we launched the Corporate Entry Leadership Conference at GE in the 1980s. And for years, the commercial banks have run commercial lending boot camps for college hires.

In the past decade, firms and service organizations have dramatically increased their investments in orientation programs for new recruits. Many old-line industrials have also set them up because they realize that energizing new-hires and engaging them in the culture is just as critical as making sure they have the technical skills to do their specific jobs. What Trilogy University has that is missing in most of the others is the Virtuous Teaching Cycle. Where TU engages leaders at all levels of the company in interactive teaching and learning, the other programs are pretty much one-way teaching that says, "We will tell you what you need to know to fit into the organization."

To crack the code, top-level leadership must be on the scene and truly committed to learning as a two-way street. With the twenty-first-century knowledge economy, with big pharmaceuticals and biotech companies bringing in thousands of new scientists a year, with information technology still in its infancy, and with companies like GE investing in new technologies, the brains of these new recruits must be engaged in Virtuous Teaching Cycles. TU challenges our thinking about how to do this.

TU: An Emotional Journey

The three months at TU are an emotional roller coaster for the kids. Compressed into twelve weeks are as many life experiences as possible, ranging from the outdoor team-building ropes course to a trip to Las Vegas to have "fun" and take some risks, to being continuously evaluated on values and performance to having to develop a project that can transform Trilogy. Vince Mallet describes his journey.

"The first day Joe walks in, and, like, his very few first words are, 'You're going to be the future of Trilogy. The company is relying on you . . . and everybody's waiting on you guys.' . . . I just want to go out in the company and be able to have this impact. And if the CEO just comes in, and he really thinks that's the way it's going to be, and we are going to make things happen, then great. I am totally happy.

"The next day we were all asked to tell the most significant emotional experience of our lives. At first some people were cynical, 'Yeah we're going to tell stories about us, whatever.' " But what really happened was very impactful. It wasn't a game. People got totally into it and really listening and trying to feel it. Some people were crying. Some people were making other people cry. I think that's like whoa—it's totally unusual. It starts building the community, the human bonds."

The emotions start on a downward trend in the first month. The pressure of the amount of work and learning required is compounded by the onset of business world reality. Mallet says he began to feel that "if all I'm doing in Trilogy is building Websites and stuff like that, I don't care. That's not going to make me happy, and that's not what is going to help me move the company. Like, yuk, and so I was tired and so I was, like, deep, low down."

His section lead helped Mallet out of the low point by putting things in perspective and making him feel that the leaders at Trilogy would do their best to make him successful.

Then as the students moved into the TU project phase, Mallet says his energy level soared. "We spent, like, 120% of our time. We spent the whole time cracking on it and making it happen . . . We had such a good response from all the people . . . There's an attraction instantly just because we're from TU and we're going to change the company and we're passionate about it, and everybody at Trilogy is like 'Yeah, I'm going to help you on this.' "

Then comes the trip to Las Vegas. A Trilogy tradition is the challenge to put up $2,000 for a number on the roulette wheel. It forces all the TU-ers to face their views on risk-taking. All the numbers are covered by TU members, so someone from Trilogy wins $70,000 but all the rest lose a lot of money.

"Some of them are, like, not really ready to lose $2,000, and some are just psyched to do it. Then you all stand around. You know this is going to last for only five seconds. Then you have won, like, some crazy amount of money or you just lost some crazy amount of money . . . but all the people participating—they're your friends, you know one is going to win . . . the tension when the ball rolls is great . . . I'm so glad I did it, I'm so glad. I don't know why they were so glad to do it, but the whole group was so glad."

Whether a student plays or not, the event is a rite of passage for TU-ers. Next, it's on to graduation projects.

Figure 10
TU Overview

	Theme	What	Who leads?
Month 1	Skills, Values, Networking	Individual, graded assignments	Section leads
		Small group discussions and debates about Trilogy values	CEO and business unit leaders
		Special speakers, "Joe Talks"	Trilogy stars, top performers from around the company
		Bonding activities, from sharing significant emotional events to nights out on the town	
Month 2	Innovation, Vision	The "Idea Riot"—a trade show of new ideas and a competition to choose the best ones	The TU-ers, assisted by the section leads and Joe
		TU projects—small teams (1–4 people), three weeks of work, and a presentation to senior management	
		Trip to Las Vegas	
Month 3	Find your place	Graduation projects done under the "TU umbrella" but with actual business units	Section leads and future managers
		Successful TU projects continue	
Ongoing	Get things done	Day-to-day work	The class
		Active e-mail lists, frequent reunions	Section leads are "section leads for life"—anchor, friend and career counselor for their section

Chapter Eleven
Digitizing the Teaching Organization

■ **The Next Wave: Virtual Teaching Cycles**
- Streaming videos, feedback loops allow 24/7 interactivity.
- Polls, gauges, data sampling provide new metrics of leadership results.

■ **People at All Levels, Around the World Share Ideas and Responses**
- Everyone hears the same messages in the same format.
- Posting video TPOVs challenges everyone as a leader.

■ **Open Databases and Public Discussions Create Transparency and Alignment**
- Leaders can't duck when issues are raised in public.
- No one has an excuse for being out of the loop.

Leadership.com for the CEO

Most nights before he heads to bed, Joe Liemandt, founder and CEO of Trilogy Software, pulls up one final screen on his computer. It is an electronic dashboard similar to the ones that executives use to monitor operations and financial performance. It has graphs, gauges, lists and trendlines. But this one doesn't track order flows, economic indicators or stock prices, and it isn't just a reporting system. It is an interactive multimedia platform called

Leadership.com that allows Liemandt to stream videos and engage in dialogues with individuals and groups throughout the company. It is his leadership dashboard.

Liemandt's dashboard measures such things as how engaged and excited Trilogians are by their work, what are the hottest topics being tossed about on the Trilogy intranet, and how much progress Liemandt has made toward reaching his own personal goals.

It also enables him to view video clips of Trilogy leaders sharing their Teachable Points of View, their vision and their storyline for their part of the organization. It provides him with real-time information about what is going on in the company, how he is doing as a leader, and where he needs to pay more attention.

Most important of all, it is a teaching and learning platform for him and the whole company. It is a Web-assisted tool for expanding knowledge within Trilogy, aligning and energizing people, and creating a Teaching Organization.

One night, Liemandt is pleased to see that eight more Trilogians have put up their own leadership videos, showing how they are working toward Trilogy's vision and strategy. He is distressed to see that the company's emotional energy scale continues to trend downward. But the thing that concerns him most is a survey about "Trust at Trilogy." It shows that 30% of the people responding to an on-line survey have cited it as "a major issue." Liemandt sees this as a big warning sign.

If Trilogy is going to move as quickly as today's Web-enabled markets demand, its people must be informed, aligned and energized. They need to know what is going on in the outside world. They need to be equally up-to-date on what is going on in the company. They must have a shared vision of its goals, values and strategy. And they must have the freedom and self-confidence to act independently.

All of this requires learning and teaching new knowledge up and down and throughout the company. There must be a constant daily give and take among people everywhere in the organization, with everyone learning and sharing what they learn with others. In order for this to happen, people must respect and trust one another. Survey results are telling Liemandt that he and his top team have not been communicating clearly enough to win people's confidence. He will raise this at his senior leadership meeting tomorrow.

He also notes that more than 500 Trilogians have viewed and graded his own Teachable Point of View video about making customer success the starting point for product development. He thought he had made it clear why thinking about what customers need rather than what Trilogians think will be the next cool application that will make Trilogy more successful. From the grades and the feedback comments he has received, he sees where he has missed the mark in fitting some of the pieces of the concept together and that he hasn't been clear enough about explaining some of the others. He realizes that he must do some rethinking about the idea and sets a date for that week to redo his video to address his new learning.

He ends his session on-line by viewing the Teachable Point of View video of the head of his large consulting group to get a feel for how he is communicating. It shows both some fuzziness in the content as well as a lack of strong emotional energy. Seeing the video, Liemandt realizes that he isn't giving the consulting head the focus and direction he needs.

He goes to bed, formulating a plan as he dozes off.

Leadership.com for the New-Hire

Across town, in one of the labs of Trilogy University, a twenty-two-year-old who has been with the company for two months may also be signed on to Leadership.com via the company's intranet. She might be looking at the videos of her TU section head and of Allan Drummond, the head of TU. Trilogy University is a 24/7 boot camp that provides a business orientation and skills polishing to all of Trilogy's new off-campus hires. TU lasts about three months depending on how quickly a student completes the required work and finds a place to land in the company.

One of the assignments for each TU class that must be completed before anyone graduates is to come up with a frame-breaking great new business idea for the company. In an unusual up-ending of normal business procedures, Liemandt hit on the idea when he set up TU in 1994 that he would use it to develop cutting-edge new products and businesses. Trilogy hires the top computer grads from such schools as MIT, Stanford, Michigan, Berkeley and Cornell. Each TU class contains some of the brightest young computer wizards in the world. So while he has them together in a group that is untainted by the experiences of old twenty-four- and twenty-five-year-old veterans, Liemandt picks their brains about where the company should be going next. Past TU classes have created CarOrder.com, Insurance.com and several other new Trilogy business units, including Leadership.com.

An Innovative Idea from Trilogy University

The development of Leadership.com is a perfect example of Trilogy University's Virtuous Teaching Cycle at work.[1]

In looking around for a project that had the potential to transform the company, a team of Trilogy University students in the winter of 1999 decided that the vision and energy they were getting from Trilogy's star players in TU wasn't getting out into the rest of the company. It was great to have Joe Liemandt giving his Teachable Point of View to the newest hires. But wouldn't the impact be greater if the whole organization could be hearing it, too?

With that in mind, they developed an Internet platform for Liemandt to post his TPOV and get feedback. That quickly expanded into Leadership.com.

The students learned from Liemandt about Teachable Points of View and the importance of spreading them quickly and gaining alignment in an organization. Then they taught Liemandt how to use technology to do a much better job of that.

The process of coming up with, evaluating, getting funding and implementing the new business ideas is a hands-on action learning exercise for building the skills and knowledge that the students will need to be successful employees of Trilogy.

Like all TU-ers (pronounced T-U-ers—It's what the students are called. The rest of the company are called Trilogians.) this new-hire is eager to come up with a winning idea. But she is having trouble. She has some ideas that she likes, but she hasn't been able to sell them to her section lead and Drummond. So at the end of a long day, she is signed on to Leadership.com to see if she can figure out why.

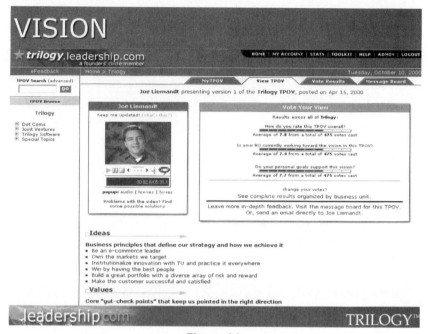

Figure 11

The videos she pulls up are five-minute clips of each of them sharing their Teachable Points of View about where they believe Trilogy needs to go and what they are doing to get it there. She sees both of them almost daily, and Liemandt spends a lot of time teaching and hanging out around TU as well. So she thought she was aligned with all of them. But her failure to sell her ideas has sent her searching for more data. What she discovers when she watches the videos is that Drummond and her section lead aren't as clear in their ideas, or at least in their presentations of them, as she had thought. And, further, they don't seem to be completely aligned with each other or with Liemandt.

So even though she had logged on to get input to help her, she might as well respond and send feedback. So she clicks on a dial and gives Drummond an overall rating of 7 (out of 10) for the presentation and sends him a couple of comments explaining why. She grades her section lead and sends along comments to him as well. Then she sends both of them a note saying that she wants to talk to them tomorrow to help her get on track better.

She shuts down her computer, stops by the well-stocked TU kitchen to pick up an ice-cream bar, and heads home.

A Word about Technology

The use of Leadership.com does not by itself create a Teaching Organization. The fundamental concept of the Teaching Organization is not about technology. It is about people and human networks. It is about people learning new things, developing new ideas, and sharing what they know with others. It is about creating a Virtuous Teaching Cycle in which teachers and learners teach and learn from each other and everyone gets smarter as a result. The principles and dynamics are real and valid irrespective of technology.

It is important to note, however, that the use of the Web and other new technologies is integral to creating such an organization. In fact, some valuable pieces of the Virtuous Teaching Cycle infrastructure may seem like pie in the sky, great ideas but impossible to execute, without the use of Web technology, which allows people to interact across time and distance.

In recent years, the Internet has been used for frame-breaking B2B (business-to-business) applications, B2C (business-to-customer) interactions, and P2P (data exchanges between individuals). To date, however, it has not been used very effectively at all inside of companies and has had little impact on how they are run. E-mail abounds, but it is a very crude tool that has become mostly a nuisance for people seriously interested in getting work done. Leadership.com represents an early stage of a new class of applications, L2L, leader to leader.

Leadership.com uses Web technology to help people within organizations interact and share information. The real breakthroughs in L2L will come with new advances in broadband capability that will enable digital-quality video interactivity with multiple sites. This tremendous collaborative capacity will open up myriad possibilities for organizations to teach, align and energize large numbers of people in far-flung locations around the world. In just a few years, Leadership.com will look like a very primitive tool. In the meantime, however, it points to where companies will have to go in the future.

In addition to making large-scale Teaching Organizations possible, new technologies make building them more imperative. As access to information becomes easier and cheaper, it increases pressure on organizations to move even more quickly and to use the available information productively.

Further, as the technologies become available and more and more companies begin using sophisticated L2L applications, everyone who wants to compete against them will have to use them, too. In the recent past, many big industrial companies have lost out to little entrepreneurial upstarts because the little guys figured out how to use the net to pick up on customer needs and satisfy them more quickly.

In the near future, the companies that don't figure out how to integrate the Web into their management practices are going to be similarly outpaced by those that do. It is no longer dot-com start-ups vs. old companies—it is digitized vs. non-digitized—everyone, old or new, will only succeed if they are using digital technology to run every facet of the business.

In the interest of full disclosure, I have to say that Leadership.com is a joint project between Trilogy Software and me. I am highlighting it, however, not as a sales pitch, but because in a microcosm it addresses many of the issues that leaders will face in building companies to compete in the twenty-first century. Whether you use Leadership.com or some other platform, the issues remain the same.

Leadership Backdrop

Speed and constant motion are the hallmark characteristics of life in the twenty-first century. The driving/enabling force behind them is the technology that allows almost instant access to information, and with each advance in technology the concept of "fast" is only going to get faster.

This access comes not only in the form of the ability to move data around the world in a nanosecond, but also in the ability to sift through it and manipulate it. Patterns and trends that were impossible to see in the days when information was housed in mainframe computers that required IT professionals to access, are now readily visible to anyone with a PC and a hookup who cares to apply a few screens.

Moreover, as technology shrinks the cycle time between an action, a reaction and a re-reaction, it becomes possible for people who might otherwise never be in direct contact to engage in a nearly constant flow of dialogue. The result is not only that technicians in Bangalore, India, and Waukesha, Wisconsin, can seamlessly work on the same project, passing it off as the day ends in one hemisphere and begins in the other, but also that a newly hired consultant at EDS can have a meaningful dialogue via videos and e-mail with CEO Dick Brown about what he sees in his territory.

Meanwhile, markets for goods and services and the capital markets change directions with astounding speed. Consumer trends are in a state of constant flux as a flood of new products appears every day to supplant older ones that often have been around only a few months themselves.

Market expansions morph into contractions seemingly overnight. It isn't that the cycles are getting closer together. The economic expansion of the 1990s was one of the longest in U.S. history. Rather, it is the momentum when they turn that has accelerated. On March 13, 2000, the NASDAQ composite stock index peaked at 5132. By April 14, it had slumped to 3265, a loss of nearly 40% in one month. In such a volatile environment, the ability to grow, shrink and redeploy assets quickly and intelligently is a critical competence for survival.

What has happened so far is just a preview. We have only scratched the surface in using the capabilities of the current technology, not to mention the new technologies and capabilities that are coming on stream every day.

The earliest uses of most new technologies are aimed at making old processes work better. Once computers came out of the science labs, their first mainstream uses were for such things as automating accounting and inventory controls. These applications were valuable in that they got the bills out faster and let a company make better purchasing and scheduling decisions. But once you consider the activities required for entry and retrieval, some weren't much more effective in terms of cost or time consumption than doing things the old way.[2]

Using New Technology to Do New Things

The real kick from a new technology comes when it is used for new applications. Web-enabling the sales process eliminated a few jobs and a few errors, but it didn't fundamentally change the process or create new value. The breakthrough use was e-commerce. When Amazon.com founder Jeff Bezos decided to use the new technology to build individual relationships with millions of book buyers and turn those buyers into a community that builds networks and attracts other buyers, he revolutionized retailing.

It is impossible to predict exactly where new technologies will take us, but when you look at the companies that are succeeding, you'll see that they are not just using the new technologies to do the same old things better. They are using the new technologies to do things that were impossible to do before the new technology came along. Leaders, therefore, must build organizations that can thrive in a shifting environment where the *what gets done* changes along with the *how it gets done.*

Like other new applications, the new L2L (leader-to-leader) applications will be both the result and the cause of changes. In the future when people talk about e-leadership, as I am convinced they will, they will use the term in much the same way as we talked about e-business a few years ago, before all business became e-business. The concept will include the technology and the type of results that the technology delivers, but it will also refer in a broader, metaphorical sense to the world created and inhabited by the use of the technology.

In the case of e-leadership, the environment is boundarylessness, but a souped up millennial version that makes the 1990s prototype seem as walled in as Alcatraz. "Boundarylessness" is a term that was coined by Jack Welch at GE in the early 1990s and spread by his many emulators. Welch came up with it to explain what he was seeking as he revised, reorganized and rebuilt GE.

His idea, he explained, was that by getting rid of unnecessary hierarchical layers, tearing down functional walls, and eliminating boundaries with suppliers and customers, he would get speed. Faster communication with less distortion, and faster decision making with fewer turf battles would allow GE to deliver more products, faster, using fewer assets. Experience has proven that Welch was right. GE has been voted by the stock market as the most valuable company in the world for most of the past decade.

What Leadership.com does is take the concept of boundarylessness to new levels. It tears down walls and opens up dialogue among levels and in corners of a company that would not be possible without its ability to deliver 24/7, on-demand interactivity. And the energy, the sharing of knowledge, and the alignment of purpose that result are the critical differentiators that will determine who wins and who loses in the knowledge economy.[3]

Providing the Compelling Teachable Point of View

The most fundamental thing that a leader must do is to craft a compelling and winning vision for the organization. This means wrestling through the key elements of business strategy and then translating them into an energizing vision that motivates the organization to action. This requires the tough intellectual work of looking at the market, and then figuring out a business idea and a business model that will succeed in that environment. Further, it requires the crafting of a message to articulate them, so that people will not only understand the business idea and model, but find them compelling.

No tool, regardless of its technology, can deliver creative, intuitive breakthroughs. Leadership.com, however, does encourage leaders to focus on the necessary intellectual work by having at its core video presentations that require clear and concise statements of their business ideas and models.

Trilogy's Leadership.com site, for example, contains streaming videos of people within Trilogy giving their own explanations of the vision, values and goals of the company, their business unit, their department, or just of themselves. The first of these TPOVs to go up on the site were by the top leaders of the company and the business unit heads, but successive rounds of development have added about 80% of the company. The goal is 100% with updates twice a year or more. TU-ers must post versions explaining what they think the company is all about and how they are going to help it succeed before they can graduate.

Once the leader has his or her Teachable Point of View and has figured out how to articulate it, then the task is to get it communicated in an exciting and compelling fashion. This is where Leadership.com uses technology to make a huge difference. For directness, clarity and energizing eye-to-eye contact, video is a close second to face-to-face. The video is streamed onto the Leadership.com platform, which allows anyone in the company to view it anytime. Further, it provides various types of feedback, including ratings for content, clarity and presentation, discussion forums, and of course an e-mail link directly to the leader. It creates a large-scale platform with the capability for 24/7 interactivity.

Good leaders lead through stories, ones that enlist others to join in a journey, a quest for some larger inspiring vision. Video provides a technological medium for conveying the story and sharing emotional energy, both verbally and nonverbally, with a richness that has a far greater impact than simply the written word or even oral messages. When this is coupled with the feedback potential among members of the organization, it is possible to turbocharge the mutual learning and create a Virtuous Teaching Cycle of people from all over the organization.

Increasing the Collective Intelligence

The second major challenge for leaders is to become effective teachers and to teach others to be leader/teachers.

The time-tested best way to do this is through coaching and role modeling. Jack Welch is a dedicated teacher and coach. He personally went to GE's Crotonville leadership development institute at least twice a month to meet with leaders at all levels and teach. These sessions allowed him not only to spread his vision in a compelling manner, but also to serve as a role model in teaching. The sessions put him in personal contact with thousands of his leaders each year.[4]

Also, he ran nearly all of his management meetings as coaching clinics, guiding and giving feedback to participants to help them perform better. This is, I believe, one of the key reasons that he is such a great leader. His close interactions with the people of GE as a mentor and teacher was a critical ingredient in his transformation of the company from a slow, stodgy, industrial behemoth to an agile, Web-enabled e-world competitor.

Nothing can replace face-to-face teaching, but elements of the Leadership.com platform facilitate the coaching and the interaction. The first of these is the requirement that people at all levels of the company create their own TPOV videos. Developing and articulating a vision and a plan for fulfilling that vision are essential to leadership skills.

As with the top leaders, for everyone at all levels of the organization, the very effort involved in creating the videos is valuable. It helps them to synthesize and articulate their thoughts. The video format, however, leverages the effort by making the presentations available 24/7 to a wide audience.

For Joe Liemandt to have observed the consulting head's energy problem without Leadership.com, the two would have had to have been in the same place at the same time. With on-demand video, the consulting head made the video when he was ready and Liemandt watched it when he wanted. This freedom from synchronicity means that Liemandt has the opportunity to teach many more people and the consulting head has the opportunity to get coaching and feedback from many more people.

The feedback loop, however, is as helpful in teaching top leaders as it is in coaching those in the ranks. When Liemandt puts out his videos, he also wants and expects feedback. Strong pushback from the troops or feedback that misses the essential message give him guidance about ideas he needs to clarify or issues he needs to consider. The comments also, either directly or indirectly, provide him with leadership coaching. The measure of his leadership is how well he succeeds in getting the followers where he wants them to go. Whether the commenters critique his video or simply don't buy into his message, he knows that he has work to do.

Creating/Tracking Positive Emotional Energy

Creating positive emotional energy is the third key task for leaders. Engaged and energetic workers are always faster—to learn, to change, to get off their butts and help the customer—than apathetic and uninspired ones. Everyone knows this, and good leaders have always paid attention to building morale and emotional energy. But building emotional energy has often been a tacit effort, rather than an explicit one. And, as such, has generally not received the recognition or focused attention that it merits.

Leadership.com not only works to inspire and energize workers by asking for their feedback, but it also signals the importance that the organization's top leaders place on maintaining energy levels by explicitly asking employees to click on a scale that records how they are feeling emotionally about the company.

The gauge on Liemandt's dashboard is a company summary. It is available not only to Liemandt, but to everyone in the company, as is the underlying database. The platform offers everyone the ability to track trends and read people's comments. The ensuing electronic forums and discussion strings give top leadership an even better understanding of how people are feeling and opportunities to impact that. It is a large-scale, Web-enabled alignment tool.

How Leadership.com Alters Leadership Behavior

Web enablement is the next frontier in leadership. Scott McNealy, John Chambers and Michael Dell will not be the only ones modeling the way. Expect Bob Nardelli at Home Depot and Jeff Immelt at GE to be up with the fastest Web enablers.

The reason that Leadership.com is so valuable is that it works on multiple fronts to encourage teaching and learning. By offering 24/7 broadband capability, the technology makes it possible for a large number of people to interact. It also leverages the reach of leaders across the organization. More importantly, it creates boundaryless behavior and takes layers out of the connections between people.

In addition, there are also a number of other powerful factors that we haven't mentioned so far. These could be clustered under the headings of fostering leadership behaviors and creating an environment that nurtures the sharing of knowledge and the growth of leaders. When these behaviors are collectively harnessed in an organization, the intelligence and energy that is created is exponentially greater than what can occur without the technology.

In addition to all the ways listed above, Leadership.com enhances Trilogy's teaching and leadership growth by:

Putting the people on the spot: By making each person's video presentations and goal objectives visible to everyone else, Leadership.com increases the pressure to do one's homework and perform well. The TPOV videos require that each person must have clear ideas and values and be able to articulate and communicate them in ways that make them understandable and usable by others. These are fundamental leadership skills.

Making leaders vulnerable role models: People who won't admit to mistakes or ignorance never learn. To create an environment where people are constantly learning and improving, leaders must set an example. They must open themselves to public scrutiny and learn from feedback. Leadership.com both puts them under the microscope and encourages the feedback.

Creating multiple Virtuous Teaching Cycles: Leadership.com creates Virtuous Teaching Cycles that can involve people who don't know and never see one another.

Setting up a cycle of continuous improvement: Leadership.com's public feedback loop demands public responses to critiques, which sets up a cycle of continuous improvement.

Creating transparency in the organization: The videos, discussions and responses by top leaders make visible their thinking and decision-making processes. This not only makes the decisions more understandable, but also role-models decision making.

Reducing process loss: Process loss is what happens when you pour a liquid from one container into another. A bit of it sticks to the sides. The loss in each transfer may be tiny, but if you do it often enough, eventually the liquid is all gone. In organizations, process loss means that leaders' ideas and messages get diluted and distorted as they filter out through the organization. Even without deliberate misrepresentations, they lose their clarity and force. Leadership.com puts everyone only one degree of separation from the leader.

Providing consistency of message   Even without the distortions of others, people tend to vary their messages as time goes by and they talk to different audiences. This can lead to misunderstandings and lack of alignment among the different audiences. Leadership.com allows everyone to hear the same message, in the same words and the same context.

Focusing everyone on critical corporate goals: Preparing and reviewing the videos keeps people thinking about key issues.

Developing interactive alignment: Alignment throughout an organization is needed for quick, smart, frictionless action. But usually there's the risk that the push for alignment will result in a shutting down of creativity or some form of corporate brainwashing. Leadership.com allows the process to be interactive, with the result being more of a consensus than a command.

Leveraging the return on leaders' time: By putting some of the basics on video, leaders can use their face-to-face meetings for more meaningful interactions.

Providing timely insights and information: Transparency created by chat rooms, message boards and non-private feedback loops allows leaders to detect weaknesses and fix them before they cause too much damage.

Leadership.com leverages the effectiveness of a Teaching Organization by using technology. It does this by embodying and engendering the key elements of effective Virtuous Teaching Cycles. In the future, technology will increasingly be an essential element of organizational processes and structures. The organizations that figure out how to use new technologies, not just in products for customers, but in their internal management processes, will be at a great competitive advantage over those that don't.

Chapter Twelve
Global Citizenship: A World of Opportunities

■ **Business Leaders Must Engage as Citizens**
  - Businesses operate in a global community and have global obligations.
  - Giving money isn't enough. Active participation in the community is essential.

■ **VTCs in the Community Benefit the Company, Individuals, Community**
  - Volunteer activities hone leadership skills, offer opportunities for learning.
  - They energize workers, build bonds.

■ **It's a Matter of Stewardship**
  - Leaders must have a TPOV on citizenship.
  - Approached as a learning/teaching activity, the investment pays big rewards.

Now more than ever before, people want to win, but they want to do it with heart, and both things are important in a twenty-first-century company. You have got to find a way to attract people who know how to give back to the environment, and give back to the community, and give back to the workplace.

Jeff Immelt, CEO of GE

■ ■ ■

In all of the executive development programs I run, I include at least a half day of community service as an integral component. Over the past fifteen years, I have put MBAs and executives from around the world to work as volunteers in homeless shelters and drug rehabilitation centers, or as mentors to middle school children. I have sent them to build houses with Habitat For Humanity and to deliver food to the elderly poor.

My Teachable Point of View on the subject is simple: Successful business leaders at all levels must be engaged as good citizens. I frame the issues as follows:

The GDP of the developed world—the United States, European Community and Japan with a total population of about 750 million—is more than $23 trillion. The rest of the world, including China with 1.2 billion people and India with about 1 billion people, lives on less than $3 trillion in GDP. Take the world's five largest companies, GE, Exxon/Mobil, Microsoft, Pfizer and Wal-Mart—their market capitalization is bigger than the GDP of India.

In the twenty-first century, we live in a world where the global corporations must play a role in dealing with corporate citizenship issues. These include the environmental issues of toxic pollution, global warming, depletion of nonrenewable resources and loss of biodiversity, as well as the human issues of distribution of wealth, nutrition, health, housing and education.[1]

I am in full agreement with Peter Drucker, who says that "citizenship in and through the social sector is not a panacea for the ills of post-capitalist society and post-capitalist polity, but it may be a prerequisite for tackling these ills. It restores the civic responsibility that is the mark of citizenship, and the civic pride that is the mark of community."[2]

I also agree when he goes on to say that "individuals, and especially knowledge workers, need an additional sphere of life, of personal relationships, and of contribution outside and beyond the job, outside and beyond the organization, indeed, outside and beyond their own specialized knowledge area."

As a result of my long commitment to citizenship activities, I have come across and dealt with the whole range of resisters and naysayers on the topic of public service. Some hard-line free-enterprise types say that the purpose of business is to make money by producing goods and services and not to do "social work." At the other end of the spectrum are the anti-business social activists who see any corporate effort as paternalistic and trivial. In the middle are the country club "do gooders" who proudly claim that they have a role to play, and then think they have fulfilled it by writing a check to the Red Cross or the United Way.

My response to all of these is the same: When a leader gets involved and invests his or her time and personal energy in community service, it is good for the company, good for the individual, and good for the community. The fact that the efforts of corporations and the individuals in them may not solve any of the major problems of the world is irrelevant. The point is that the effort and the interaction among people who might otherwise never meet produces real benefits for everyone.

Myth and Reality

In the past dozen years, I have engaged 5,000 MBAs and more than 3,000 executives in University of Michigan programs in corporate citizenship activities. I have also been involved in company-wide community service activities that involved well more than 150,000 employees globally at Royal Dutch/Shell, Ford, Genentech, Ameritech, HarperCollins and other companies.

Here are some common myths about corporate citizenship and the realities that I have discovered.

Myth   MBA students will be turned off by corporate citizenship volunteer work required in orientation. "They aren't coming to the Michigan Business School to do social work."

Reality   After a decade, it is one of the pillars of the business school culture. It helps build teamwork and engages students in dealing with diversity issues. Over 70% stay involved in community service activities after orientation with two students clubs, Global Corporate Citizenship and Global Network, existing not only at Michigan but in chapters at more than fifty business schools.

Myth   Short visits to inner-city sites and offering help like painting or career coaching is exploitive and hurtful.

Reality   When done right it adds value, such as getting a homeless shelter or halfway house painted and cleaned up by fifty executives in a half day, or career advice given to rehabilitating addicts. The key is clarity of expectations with the agency and integrity in the interactions with a respect for the dignity of all those involved.

Myth   This volunteer stuff is too American—it won't be accepted globally.

Reality   Royal Dutch/Shell engaged thousands throughout Europe. The University of Michigan's very successful Global Leadership Program had executives from Japan, the United States and Europe spend 20% of their time on global citizenship issues in China, India, Russia and Brazil.

It is amazing to me that so few leaders understand the value of community service. And when social or political pressure impels them to do it, they do it so badly. Reaching out into the community, solving problems and helping others ought to be an energizing endeavor for everyone in the company. It ought to make people feel good. But more often, especially in large corporations, the effect is just the opposite.

The use of coercive pressure to get 100% participation in United Way campaigns and the grand ballyhooing of financial contributions made solely for the purpose of publicity, not only fail to create positive energy among workers, but they actively cause the opposite. At best, they drain energy and create cynicism. At worst, the coercion and hypocrisy breed open hostility. What should be a value-producing and energizing experience for employees turns out to be yet one more source of alienation.

Perhaps even worse from the standpoint of stewardship of assets is that leaders who take this approach fail to get anywhere near the return that they could get on their expenditures. They may spend large sums of money on donations, but because they don't get their workers actively involved, they miss opportunities to broaden the experiences of their people and teach them new things. Done properly, community service can yield enormous direct rewards for a company.

Leadership Development Opportunities

In addition to producing the benefits of actually helping out and of allowing a company to be seen as a good corporate citizen, volunteer activities also offer prime opportunities to develop leaders for the organization. The teaching and learning skills that workers learn in community service activities help them become better leader/teachers on the job. This factor alone should be reason enough for leaders to encourage their employees to go out and work in the community.

"Volunteering in the community is an incredibly powerful teaching/learning experience for the organization," says Len Schlesinger, COO of Limited Brands. "We are working to make sure that people understand their volunteer leadership roles are in fact leadership roles."

What it really comes down to are the principles that underlie Teaching Organizations. It is through teaching and learning that people grow. People who leave the comfort zones of their familiar environments and go out into the world learn more and become smarter than the people who don't. So it isn't just about writing checks and making donations. Those are important things to do. But people don't learn, don't get excited, and don't develop strong commitments to check-writing. What really makes a difference, definitely for the donors and I would argue for the recipients as well, is the face-to-face interaction.

Even for the recipients of the aid, the learning and the growth are primary benefits. In emergency situations, the need to provide immediate food, shelter, health care and support services may take precedence over meaningful personal interchanges. But solving problems over the longer-term, so that crises are less likely to occur, depends on people with resources working with the people most affected by the problems to come up with solutions. This requires spending time together and a mutual openness to teaching and learning. In the long run, it is the most effective form of social activism because it draws on the diverse talents of a wider spectrum of society.

Many people assume that the people with the resources will also be the people with the best ideas, but that is often not the case. In many instances, the people who are suffering from and most familiar with a problem can see the better solutions, but they have no means of implementing them. Most often, however, it is the combining of the brains and experiences of the two groups that comes up with the best solution to the underlying causes. It's the old story: Give a hungry man a fish and you feed him for a day. Help him learn to fish, and he's fed for life.

The processes and best practices that go into building Virtuous

Teaching Cycles within companies and with customers, partners and suppliers are equally valuable when it comes to reaching out into the broader community. And they produce the same results—making everyone involved smarter, more energized to get things done, and more aligned about what needs to be done and how to do it.

Leaders Must Have TPOV on Citizenship

Every business leader at the beginning of the twenty-first century needs to have a Teachable Point of View about corporate citizenship and community service. This isn't a point of view about whether the company should take a role and encourage its employees to be involved in community service. As far as I am concerned, there is no question about that.

My Teachable Point of View is that every successful business leader and institution in the twenty-first century will also be highly visible as a dedicated global citizen. The stakes in maintaining the stability of both the social and physical environment and the benefits of community engagement are too great to be overlooked. Companies that ignore them will fall behind those that don't.

Rather, each leader must develop a Teachable Point of View about how they will be personally engaged and how they will get the corporation as an institution and the people within it engaged.

Les Wexner of Limited Brands, for example, has started a program to get every kindergartner/first grader in Ohio together with a tutor. The single best predictor for who will graduate from high school, he says, is who masters reading in the first grade. So he is enlisting volunteers across the state starting with employees of Limited Brands.

"Les has always been actively engaged on a personal level, but until recently, he was reluctant to push others in the company," says COO Schlesinger. But now he has a Teachable Point of View that says "Being good citizens is what makes this company different. We are over being uncomfortable and are being clear that community service is an expectation."

The communities, the abilities that reside in a company, and the interests of its people will differ. The job of the leader, however, is to develop a plan and an action agenda around community service and to make sure that it is taken seriously within the company.

I believe that business leaders must engage with their communities in a much more creative and profound way than ever before. Partnerships with government cannot be lobbying efforts for self-interests. Global issues cannot be put off as "beggar thy neighbor" problems. We are all interconnected. Those in the developed world can control their own destinies only by engaging in long-term global citizenship issues. The stakeholders go well beyond Wall Street and the customer. They include the context of the free enterprise system and the societies in which businesses operate throughout the planet.

Building VTCs In the Community

The exciting news about all of this is that my experience over the last twenty years clearly indicates that business leaders and employees generally get multiple benefits of engaging in Virtuous Teaching Cycles with the community, not the least of which is adding to the esprit de corps of the company. Giving back through volunteering turbocharges the workforce. When people feel good about themselves and their companies for supporting such activities, they are generally energized to work harder for the company as well.

I have seen it over and over again, where working in inner-city homeless shelters, or food programs, or mentoring programs gives people a renewed perspective on their own lives and the blessings that they have in life. This carries over into the workplace, putting some of the day-to-day problems and frictions of worklife in a new perspective. It is also a place to learn about leadership, stewardship and the effective use of resources.

When I take business executives to work at Focus: HOPE in Detroit, they are regularly blown away with how much can be done with so few resources, and how mission/value driven organizations can mobilize thousands of people with no financial compensation. On a budget of less than $70 million, it feeds 50,000 people a month, trains machinists and engineers, runs a fast-track high school program as well as a children's center and several for-profit machine tool businesses.

Lloyd Reuss was so impressed with it that after he retired as president of GM, he became the executive dean of Focus: HOPE's Center for Advanced Technologies. Chief Operating Officer Tim Duperron took early retirement as a Ford executive to work there. I am so impressed with Focus: HOPE and its leaders that I have brought more than 40,000 business leaders to do volunteer work there over the decades. These have included groups from companies such as Ameritech, Ford, HP and Shell. In addition, I run MBA orientation sessions on leadership development at Focus: HOPE, and I personally spend as much as 20% of my time doing pro bono leadership development work with Eleanor Josaitas and her Focus: HOPE team.

But not all social service agencies are Focus: HOPE. Lacking the discipline of the marketplace, many nonprofits are notoriously ineffective and wasteful. The experience of being in one of these is often an eye-opener that leads executives to rethink how their own operations run. The shortcomings in the volunteer agencies that are so obvious to them as outsiders are sometimes not all that far from the shortcomings that they have been unable or unwilling to see in their own organizations.

While there have been some highly publicized examples of self-dealing, greed and downright dishonesty in major nonprofits, most often the inefficiencies just reflect a lack of business acumen on the part of poorly trained staff and volunteers. In these situations, the corporate leaders often have expertise that would be helpful. But delivering this expertise requires a big commitment of time, as well as some finely honed leadership skills.

That's because in the dynamic of most nonprofits, the professional staff is expected to take the lead, while the volunteers drop in to be the followers. So it is a very tricky proposition when a volunteer has more expertise than the agency's staff. In order to teach and transmit that knowledge effectively, the volunteer first has to establish credibility, then he or she has to communicate in a way that doesn't threaten the staffers and make them shut down.

These are essential leadership skills. Putting them to work this way in volunteer activities helps both the volunteer and the agency. But this kind of interaction is never going to happen if the potential volunteer remains in the office, writing checks and never becoming a volunteer.

A Framework for Service

While ongoing, long-term relationships such as those between Hewlett-Packard and the East Palo Alto's OICW and Cisco's support of thousands of inner city school programs to teach "Cisco Networking" skills are certainly the most productive, even brief half-day encounters can be valuable if they are well thought out.

Over the years, I have probably put 200,000 students and executives to work in various community service projects. These ranged from a one-day cleanup of a park, to painting a halfway house in London, to ongoing tutoring programs in Chicago, New York and Detroit, to Habitat for Humanity projects. Even though many were one-time community service events, a significant number, about 20%, evolved into ongoing programs that continued over multiple years. These include a Focus: HOPE volunteer program that has hundreds of Ford employees delivering food monthly to seniors, Saturday morning reading programs in Chicago by Ameritech managers, and annual Habitat for Humanity money raising and volunteering by the Michigan MBAs.

Doug Hoover, a senior executive at EDS, went back from a service event and has mobilized hundreds of his colleagues to work in the community. He personally gives a lot of time to Focus: HOPE. An executive from Otsuka Pharmacy in Japan who visited an AIDS clinic in Washington, D.C., went back to Japan and altered some of the company's research and development to increase its focus on AIDS drugs. It was the result of the Virtuous Teaching Cycle created when he actually sat down with a dying AIDS patient that made the difference. He worked on R&D for the company but he had never actually met anyone with the disease.

The key thing is to structure the projects so that they do deliver real results. On very brief projects, the results are going to be limited, but they need to be concrete and in line with the expectations.

Whenever I take business leaders into the community, I use a three-step framework that creates an interactive teaching and learning environment from the very beginning.

Step 1: Shared diagnosis of the problems in the community. The visiting students or executives sit down with people from the community or the agency we are visiting and develop a systems map of the forces at play, i.e., drugs, poverty, health issues, educational issues, housing, political corruption, racism, etc. This opens the dialogue.

Step 2: Analysis of why the community agency we are visiting works. What are the key elements of success? Often these are things like clear vision, strong values, passionate leadership, partnerships across many constituencies, courage to take risks, and persistence in the face of adversity.

Step 3: Reflection on learnings from the community that are relevant to the business leaders, in terms of their own organizations, the role of business in society, and their own personal roles as community leaders.

One example of how this can work in even a very short time-frame is a visit I made with senior executives in our Michigan Global Leadership Program to Clean and Sober Streets in Washington, D.C. The Michigan Global Leadership Program was a five-week action-learning experience that brought together teams of Japanese, American and European leaders from major corporations. The primary action-learning vehicle was country assessments in China, India, Russia and Brazil, based on extended interviewing and reporting in those countries. The program began with team building at the Outward Bound School on Hurricane Island, Maine, then moved for a day in Washington, D.C.

The purpose of the day in Washington was to hone the students' skills at diagnosing community issues such as poverty, racism, drugs, health care, etc., and to get them to begin wrestling with some tough leadership questions. These included how they would shape their own leadership agendas when they returned to their companies.

Clean and Sober Streets is a residential drug rehabilitation center in Washington D.C., attached to the Mitch Snyder Homeless Shelter, one of the largest in the country. The clients of Clean and Sober Streets are some of the hardest core addicts in the city. In order to be admitted to the program, a person must have been on drugs for many years.

We began by having our thirty executives arrive at 6:00 A.M. to help prepare breakfast with the residents. Then they had breakfast with the residents. Everyone sat at round cafeteria tables, three of our executives and three of the residents. Our group included VPs from Sony, Honda, Merck, IBM, Exxon and Nokia, among others.

The format was for each table to discuss a series of questions. It started with each person telling his or her life story and how they came to be seated at the table. Then they moved on to talking about their aspirations, and finally, each executive had to offer each resident at the table a piece of concrete advice.

When I describe it, it sounds superficial, but the one-to-one human connections really did make a difference to both the executives and the residents. The executives were pulled way out of their comfort zones and were forced to see a side of life that was totally foreign to them. And the residents, even though the visit was short, had the benefit of having the complete and focused attention of people with brains and resources whom they would otherwise never meet.

Nobody was under any illusion that the residents were going to get it together to save money and go to college. All of them were addicts, many had felony records, and 60% were HIV-positive. So the executives had to learn a whole new way of thinking—as someone trying to get into the system from the bottom instead of as a member of the elite for whom doors and paths easily open.

The advice they came up with wasn't exactly startling. It included such things as how to get rid of street talk, what to wear and why, how to deal with a felony past, and what skills were worth developing at Clean and Sober Streets. But the comments carried extra weight for being directed at the specific individual resident. It wasn't just a generic platitude. It was a personal message, and therefore, it had to be taken more seriously.

By the end of the several hour breakfast, everyone was chattering like old friends—which is important in itself. Eleanor Josaitis of Focus: HOPE has a policy of having her students line up to shake hands with visiting executives. The reason for doing this, she says, "Has nothing to do with the executives. It has to do with my students' pride and dignity, their self-esteem, and claiming their place in society."

The session at Clean and Sober Streets was short, and I do not pretend that we made a world-shattering difference for the residents. But for these executives who have, or someday may have, stewardship over significant resources, it was an important step in their education. I am firmly convinced that the residents of Clean and Sober Streets did get a direct benefit from their participation. But even if they didn't, they themselves were making an important contribution to social improvement by serving as teachers and helping focus these future leaders on the reality of some significant social problems.

MBA Citizenship Program

Starting in 1990, all of the incoming MBAs at Michigan have spent two days in corporate citizenship activities with companies in the community. We started the program as the result of a Virtuous Teaching Cycle that we got going with the first class of the Global Leadership Program.

In that program, the faculty challenged each of the executives to go back to his or her organization and do something with global citizenship. We challenged them each to develop a personal leadership agenda and action plan in this area. Then they turned to us on the faculty and said: "What are you doing at the Business School? You have a chance to shape the next generation of leaders. What are you doing with your MBA students?"

So, Michael Brimm from INSEAD in France started a program to engage INSEAD MBAs in global citizenship, and I began the citizenship program as part of the orientation for each incoming MBA student at Michigan.

One group always goes to Focus: HOPE. Another section of seventy students goes up to Benton Harbor to work with Whirlpool in community development in an inner-city type environment outside of their headquarters area. When we gather back on campus, we then open up a conversation to challenge the students to think about what citizenship means for them personally, what it means for business, and whether they will stay involved.

When I proposed the program, my colleagues at the business school were reluctant, saying that community service would potentially turn off our incoming MBAs who were, after all, money-focused capitalists, not social workers. The reality has been 180 degrees different. They love it, and a full 70% stay involved doing community volunteer work during their MBA experience. Global corporate citizenship is now a core part of the Michigan MBA leadership development experience.

It's Everyone's Responsibility

We ran the Global Leadership Program for ten years, through 1998. During that time, we engaged more than 250 executives from around the world in citizenship activities. We asked them to make a commitment to citizenship when they returned to their companies, but we knew that even with the best of intentions many of them would not follow through.

When we followed up, however, we were happy to discover that 50% actually kept the commitments. The projects we found included such things as engaging all of their reports in inner-city tutoring to taking their teams to work at Habitat for Humanity, to running workshops on global citizenship. In speaking to alumni years later, they often talk about this element of the program as the most impactful.

It got me to realize that I needed to integrate community service as an element of leadership development in every institution, every organization and every client that I work with. The results have been gratifying. Since 1990, all of my leadership development experiences have involved at least half a day to a day of community service as part of both team building and leadership development.

When we cascade leadership development throughout a company, we require executives and leaders at all levels to run three-day workshops. For half a day of this, we have them take their teams out to the community both to engage in the community and to learn from it. At Ameritech, we took 30,000 people out for half-day community service projects and thousands of them became volunteers afterward.

In the mid-1990s, Ford required the top 2,000 leaders to take more than 100,000 people on half-day citizenship projects. The result of the activities around the world from Beijing to Cologne to Dearborn, led Bill Ford and Jacques Nasser to allocate two days for paid community service for all salaried employees at Ford Motor Company—140,000 of them. The caveat is the projects have to be team activities in which a group picks a project and goes out as a team. This was because they saw corporate citizenship as a team development activity as well as doing good.

Royal Dutch/Shell has likewise involved 50% of its 100,000 employees worldwide in community service activities as part of its leadership development programs. US West, which is now a part of Qwest, as well as a number of Silicon Valley high-tech firms, have implemented similar programs.

My point here is that it never fails. Given the right leadership and the right opportunities, companies and the people within them benefit from engaging in the community. The key is to approach it as a Virtuous Teaching Cycle. Its purpose isn't to hand out charity, but to create an opportunity for mutual teaching and learning.

In 1993, the first time we took a group of Ameritech senior executives into the community, we went to Cabrini Green, a high-rise environment that's one of the toughest in inner-city Chicago. Gangs control Cabrini Green at night. There are metal detectors when you enter the buildings. Three weeks before we arrived, a kindergartner had been shot accidentally during a gang fight in the neighborhood.

Our project was to go in teams, pair up with a family in an apartment, and take an afternoon to paint the whole apartment.

There was obviously a lot of advance planning and setting up of equipment so that it could all get done in one day. But for several hours the executives and the families worked together scraping, preparing the walls and painting.

Most of the executives had never even been near Cabrini Green, and given its reputation for crime, many weren't eager to go there. So on the trip from their comfortable hotel, we reminded them that the people of Cabrini Green were their customers. These people had phones. And they also had lives and aspirations. The objective goal of the afternoon was to get the apartments painted, but more importantly, we needed to understand and spend time with them. So it wasn't enough to just go in there and paint, they had to talk, teach and learn.

We ended the session with a debriefing in which the executives talked about what they had learned and what they were going to do with the learning. As a result of these visits, there's still a reading program in Cabrini Green every Saturday morning with Ameritech (now owned by SBC) executives as volunteers. Ameritech has also built a playground and created internships for some of the kids.

Focus: HOPE, A Best Practice Model

Focus: HOPE is a civil rights organization in inner-city Detroit that provides food for people, and helps them acquire the education and skills to enter the economic mainstream. It's an organization with a 34-year mission to look for intelligent and practical solutions to racism and poverty.

Because its primary mission is social activism, I am not holding it up as a role model for corporations and business executives to copy. But I want to describe it here as an example of how Virtuous Teaching Cycles can cross all kinds of boundaries, and to show just how effective community service activities can be.

It is a model of how partnerships with the community, government, business, universities and foundations can create meaningful change for both individuals and the community. It should serve as a challenge for our imaginations as to what is possible, and a catalyst for creative thinking.

Focus: HOPE grew out of the 1967 Detroit race riots. At the time,

Father William Cunningham was a young Roman Catholic priest teaching English at Sacred Heart Seminary. As Army Airborne units invaded the city, he looked around and saw the poverty, rage and despair that permeated the inner city's black neighborhoods and decided:

"I can't keep teaching Beowulf and Shakespeare and English composition . . . with the choppers coming and the half-tracks and the 50-caliber machine guns turned on the side of buildings, and the encampment of Central High School . . . [I felt] we had to do something." So, he and Eleanor Josaitis, a suburban housewife at whose parish he had been a weekend pastor, founded Focus: HOPE.

They started out only with the determination to make a difference. They went into the community to do their research and find out how. Their first conclusion was that there were a lot of hungry babies growing up in inner-city Detroit. Malnourishment in infancy was costing children 20% of their brain power, which was never to be returned. They were growing up angry and lacking the ability to compete in the marketplace for jobs.

So the first thing that Cunningham and Josaitis did was design a food program where they focused on trying to give nutrition and health care to babies. The program they designed included prenatal and postnatal care, as well as food and nutritional education. It ended up being a model for a national supplemental food program run by the U.S. government. To this day, Focus: HOPE distributes food to 43,000 people each month.

But that was just the beginning. Each program they created took them deeper into the community. And as each program got up and running, Cunningham and Josaitis would look around to see what they could do better and what needs were going unfulfilled.

The success of the feeding program, for example, was a red flag. There were way too many hungry babies in Detroit. So they looked around for a way to reduce the need for food giveaways. They quickly saw that the children were hungry because their parents didn't have jobs. So they decided, if they really wanted to have a long-term impact, they needed to help the adults acquire the skills to find work. And they didn't want it to be just entry-level work. They wanted to offer people the opportunity to have careers with upward mobility.

Since the biggest employer in Detroit was the auto industry, and some of the best paying and most stable jobs were as machinists, Cunningham and Josaitis decided that they would teach inner-city workers not only to be machinists, but to be some of the best machinists in the world. Focus: HOPE graduates would get and keep jobs not because socially conscious employers pitied them, but because they would be solid, reliable workers with skills that the employers needed. In the year 2001, entry-level pay for machinists was an average $11 an hour. Upward mobility is very possible.

Once they started the machinist training program, they realized that people needed help with more basic skills. Even people who had graduated from Detroit public schools often didn't have the tenth grade math and reading skills needed to succeed in the machinists program. So they put together a Fast Track program, to take people through several grade levels of math and English in seven weeks so they could apply for the machinist program, or go out into the market to look for other jobs.

Then, when they found that a lot of eager people weren't even ready for Fast Track, they started an even more basic program.

Another big challenge facing applicants to the program was childcare. The parents wanted to come to school, but they often had no one to take care of their children. So next Focus: HOPE started a child care center and a Montessori school.

A very strong Teachable Point of View at Focus: HOPE is that you must never lower standards. If people are to succeed in the mainstream economy, they must be able to meet all of the demands. So to reinforce this, they set up a for-profit machine shop as part of the Focus: HOPE program. Its products are some of the highest-precision items required by such customers as Detroit Diesel Products, General Motors, Ford and Chrysler. The test for the students is whether they can please the customers and keep them coming back.

In 1993, with the support of the government, corporations, banks and foundations, they opened the Center for Advanced Technologies (CAT), a 220,000-square-foot manufacturing and education facility on Oakman Boulevard in Detroit, Michigan. The former industrial engine plant—renovated at a cost of $22 million—now houses some of the most modern manufacturing equipment available. A coalition of five major manufacturing companies and five leading engineering universities was formed with Focus: HOPE to develop a world-class curriculum to educate "renaissance engineers." Three of those universities—Lawrence Technological University, Wayne State University and the University of Detroit Mercy—award associate and bachelor level degrees to graduates of the CAT program in manufacturing engineering technology.

The Focus: HOPE Center for Advanced Technologies includes both academic study and hands-on experience in a real-world manufacturing environment. It produces engineers whose starting salaries are $4,000 to $5,000 above MIT grads. In large part, this is because of their hands-on experience in actual production and fulfillment of major industry contracts. More importantly, they have a strong work ethic and have Focus: HOPE's values about working with and developing others.

Focus: HOPE is truly a Teaching Organization. Everyone is responsible, no matter how long they've been there, for teaching the people who are coming along behind them. It now totals about 600 people. It has a forty-acre campus and a budget of nearly $70 million a year. Father Cunningham died in 1997, but Eleanor Josaitis remains as the head teacher. At seventy years old, she walks the manufacturing and educational facilities every morning starting around six. She interviews every single candidate who applies to work there to screen for values and emotional energy. And she lets them know what the values of Focus: HOPE are.

Why Focus: HOPE Works

Focus: HOPE is so successful because it incorporates a number of critical elements. These include:

Grass roots   The organization is based on the local community. Its leaders live in the community and are involved in the life of the community, so it is closely attuned to what the real needs of the community are.

Value-based mission   The mission of Focus: HOPE is intelligent and practical solutions to racism and poverty.

Human dignity   Every person is valued whether they have been unemployed for forty years and are food program recipients, or have graduated with a bachelors degree and are starting a $45,000-a-year job. Everyone walks the walk on respecting the dignity of every human being.

An enlightened capitalism model   Focus: HOPE is built on a firm belief in capitalism. The goal is to give people opportunities to gain the mainstream economic values of living in a capitalist society. On the other hand, they will not refuse food to anyone in need. There's a belief that taking care of people's true needs as well as holding them to high standards to perform in a capitalistic society are not inconsistent.

Leadership at all levels   Everyone is expected to lead, whether they've been there for one week or for twenty-five years. This is not a hierarchical organization, but rather a group of colleagues, each leading to the best of their limits.

Virtuous teaching cycles at all levels   Everybody tries to make everyone else smarter. Teaching/coaching occurs at all levels. Because of the values system and the approach of Focus: HOPE, there are illustrations of Virtuous Teaching Cycles all over the organization.

Boundaryless behavior   There are minimal hierarchical boundaries at Focus: HOPE, and there is a great deal of movement across functional boundaries and program boundaries. People communicate, share best practices and engage in community activities across the whole institution.

Knowledge generation   Focus: HOPE is continuously trying to make itself smarter, as well as every one of its colleagues. In its partnerships with universities and the business community, it is always looking for information and best practices. For example, it surveys 300-plus machine-tool companies to learn what they want in the way of people. It gets feedback and follows up on graduates, and it has mentors in the industry for its students.

It's all about human transformation   Focus: HOPE is about transforming lives. Engineers are taught not only technical skills but work ethic, values and leadership skills. They are not just trained, they are fundamentally transformed as a result of the Focus: HOPE experience.

Focus: HOPE is an incredible organization. It develops leaders at all levels, and it incorporates Virtuous Teaching Cycles everywhere. Every one of the more than 50,000 volunteers a year, as well as the universities, private foundations, governments, local agencies, national agencies and corporations who partner with them, comes away having learned something. The most valuable learnings are about getting people aligned, energized and working productively.

The good news is that it works. The bad news is there's only one Focus: HOPE, and it's been around for more than three decades. Many people have seen it and talked about replicating it, but they haven't done it. I've had MBA teams take a summer and study ways of trying to replicate Focus: HOPE in South Africa, funded by Ford. I had another MBA team go to Northern Ireland to see if a Focus: HOPE would be a partial solution there. I've had an MBA team in East Palo Alto working with HP, Oracle and Covad executives to build a Focus: HOPE. In fact many elements of Focus: HOPE have been replicated there, but the world needs thousands of Focus: HOPEs.

Learning from the Community: Eleanor's Punch in the Nose

Focus: HOPE was built on the philosophy of the Virtuous Teaching Cycle. After the Detroit riots of 1967, Father William Cunningham and Eleanor Josaitis moved into inner-city Detroit, right where the riots occurred, with a commitment to make a difference. They brought their own Teachable Point of View captured in their mission statement, the essence of which was "intelligent and practical action to overcome racism, poverty and injustice."

They learned first that there were many malnourished babies and children in the community. They also learned that these babies grew up angry and would lose 20% of their brain power. So they launched Focus: HOPE with a food program for children and pregnant women. Then, one day, Josaitis had an eye-opening conversation with a seventy-five-year-old woman.

As Josaitis tells the story, the woman, who was clearly distressed, had called up to ask about the food program. And Josaitis began telling her enthusiastically about the great elements of the program and how it was helping pregnant mothers and children. But, "I hadn't really listened to how she asked the question. So I finished telling her all about the great things we were doing, and the next thing I know, she is yelling into the phone, 'Do you mean that I have to get pregnant in order to get food?'

"I was stunned. I had missed the fear in her voice when she called. I hadn't heard the panic about being able to survive." Josaitis thought she was interacting and teaching this woman about her great food program, but she was really just preaching. She hadn't opened herself up to learning from her. "It was a lucky thing that the woman got so angry and starting yelling. It got my attention. I realized that there was a huge need that we were ignoring."

That "aha" changed Josaitis's Teachable Point of View so that she said, "We need to take care of the elderly population." They were afraid and dying of malnutrition. She and Father Cunningham started what turned out to be several years of battle in Congress to get funding for some new food programs. It took Josaitis more than twenty-two trips to Washington with multiple hearings in both the House and Senate.

She finally succeeded in making some headway when she staged a teaching event for twenty-five congressional staffers. She borrowed a corporate jet from one of the auto companies and took them on a field trip to Detroit. She led them into the inner city and drove them around in a bus, taking them into the elderly homes and having them physically experience what she was trying to sell Congress. They went back and convinced their Congressional leaders to enact legislation to support new feeding programs for the elderly. Today, Focus: HOPE provides food to 28,000 senior citizens every month.

This is one of many Focus: HOPE examples where a Virtuous Teaching Cycle of listening, learning and teaching led to new programs and initiatives.

The Future of Global Citizenship

I want to end this chapter with some personal reflections on global corporate citizenship and what I see for the future. The challenges for all of us, especially those in senior leadership roles in business, have gone up exponentially. The events of 9/11 and the ongoing war on terrorism have created a new world playing field. It is one that, I believe, makes it a business imperative to lead in new ways. A way must be found to turn the uncertainty and chaos of the world—the multiple ethnic wars, the global terrorism—into a sustainable, just, and growing global economy.

As if the challenge of building Teaching Organizations within institutions the size of General Electric, 3M, Home Depot, or Yum! Brands weren't enough, the leaders within institutions now need to reach out and engage the larger communities within which these institutions operate in Virtuous Teaching Cycles.

The long-term well-being of the world requires a global war on poverty, one aimed at creating new opportunities for more and more of the planet's more than 6 billion inhabitants. At the most fundamental level, this means making food, health care and education available for an ever expanding proportion of the world's population. If we don't do this, we risk that the vicious cycle of poverty will result in misery, ethnic strife and terrorism. As Peter Drucker points out, this century is the one that will—or should—finally bring enlightenment and opportunity to the majority of humankind.

I endorse Drucker's belief that a business leader's obligation is not just to the direct stakeholders in his or her organization—i.e., investors, employees, customers, suppliers, the immediate community—but also to the wider community at large. After all, this is enlightened self-interest.

On a cosmic scale, the global environment, the global economy, and the physical and financial well-being of people affect a company's performance—people need disposable incomes to buy the things that most companies are selling. If they don't have that, and if they are rioting in the streets or becoming terrorists because they feel disenfranchised, this is very bad for business. Likewise, if we kill off the planet, business is not going to do well, either.

But this is a ridiculously broad argument, and further, it isn't realistic to think that any company is going to save the world. Nonetheless, companies need to be good corporate citizens. They must not only "do no harm," they must actively do their part toward improving and maintaining the health of the global community.

It is the obligation of leaders to have a TPOV on how to engage their corporations as entities and to encourage the people who work in them to be good citizens. The specific steps that a leader or a company takes may seem small or like tokens, but no matter how limited the impact, they do make a contribution. And small initial steps can lead people to significant lifelong commitments.

Virtuous Teaching Cycles are a great vehicle for citizenship activities. They allow people from very disparate worlds to engage with one another in teaching and learning—which is how things are going to get better.

GE Pioneering the Future of Global Citizenship

Jeff Immelt was dealt a hand that not only included the world's most valuable enterprise and the world's most respected company, but he also was given a foundation of corporate citizenship dating back to 1928. That was the year that CEO Gerald Swope founded the Elfun Society to foster "loyalty, fellowship, cooperation, innovations and resourcefulness among GE's managers." It was set up to achieve these goals internally and to make a difference in local communities. It has been in operation ever since.

During the Welch era, the Elfun Society grew to about 40,000. About half are retirees, and the rest professional and managerial level personnel. Welch encouraged them to be active and to rededicate themselves, "rallying Elfun around the concept of volunteerism and taking advantage of the tremendous GE retirement team which can truly make a difference in each community where we live and work."

In 1992 the Elfuns began expanding globally, forming new chapters in Japan, Singapore, Malaysia, Mexico, Brazil, the United Kingdom, the Netherlands and Hungary, which joined the previously established chapters in Puerto Rico and Canada. The society anticipates further expansion, as GE businesses increase their operations and staffing around the world. The aim throughout the 1990s was to expand the partnerships with public schools and other community service organizations.

Jeff Immelt and his senior team at GE who inherited this platform are strong believers in Elfun. But even though he believes that it has made a difference, as he looks to the future, he says that GE must do more, a lot more, to promote healthy societies.

I talked with him as he was preparing for his first officers' meeting in the fall of 2001. While I was in his office, the news came that an NBC employee had tested positive for Anthrax. We were sitting at Welch's old round table when he said to me:

"In the past, it's been that as long as our stock was good, we were the most admired company. But I think the world demands more today. I'd given this a lot of thought before 9/11, but now it takes on a new meaning.

"Fundamentally, GE's my life. This company is all I think about. It's who I am. Twenty years ago, here's what Jack saw. Here's what he did, and, you know what? We got a better place. Today, here's what I see, and it's not enough. GE's great, but not great enough . . . We have to be a more important company. We have to be a more vocal company on causes. We have to stand for something more than the value of the stock price.

"I'm trying to do this in a very respectful way, but also set a new trajectory . . . We are the best and we've proven that, and Jack handed us the best company. That's the hand I was dealt. But in tomorrow's world, that is not enough. It can't be paternalistic. It has nothing to do with paternalism . . .

"The first thing is this has got to be a place where people are put first, people are treated with respect. Start with people. You know, it's going to be people, including the community . . . I've been a little bit hesitant to really go all the way here, but now that 9/11 has happened, I am absolutely certain."

I was delighted by this conversation. Jeff Immelt is right in saying that GE needs to do more. And Peter Drucker is right in saying that the world depends on companies like GE doing their part. In legal terms, corporations have many of the same rights and privileges as individuals. They also have many of the same obligations, including the duty to be good citizens.

Conclusion . . .
The Virtuous Teaching
Cycle Challenge

It starts with a commitment to continuously improve yourself and others around you. Eleanor Josaitis never misses an opportunity both to learn from others and to teach others. It can be as seemingly insignificant an act as picking up gum wrappers on the sidewalk, which she routinely does during her morning tour of Focus: HOPE. She does this because she knows that this symbolic behavior teaches others about standards, responsibility and pride in the Focus: HOPE environment . She believes what Wayne Downing says: "If you walk by a problem, no matter how little it is, you as a leader have set a new standard." No detail is too tiny for either Eleanor or Wayne to attend to, because they realize that they are always teaching. This is not about micro-managing, it is about how they are always in their role as leader/teachers. They live the Virtuous Teaching Cycle.

The Mirror Test: I am hoping that this book has been a mirror test for you: that you have taken an honest look at your performance as a leader. And, as a result, I am hoping that you have decided to raise the bar on your performance. It may have been one of the stories or benchmarks that got you to thinking that you could do more as a teacher. Or, maybe it was one of the concepts or frameworks that made you realize you need to re-think your Teachable Point of View.

No matter what the triggers were, or where it is that you have decided to begin, it is now up to you to look inside yourself and set the standard. The book has given you the examples and tools. Now you have to do the work to build a Teaching Organization and become a better leader/teacher yourself.

Get in the Learning Zone: In order to learn and grow you have to keep pushing the boundaries. People don't learn by comfortably doing the same old routines. This means that as a leader, you must continuously reach out to see and hear new things. You need to consciously create opportunities for your own learning.

At times, this will definitely take you outside your comfort zone. But once you have risked doing it a few times and realized the amazing results of new insights and experiences, you will relish the experience. For myself, I have taken to thinking of the area just beyond my comfort zone as my learning zone.

Think about your own learning zone. What can you do to stay in it as much as possible? Start with designing every day with learning in mind. Run meetings that get you into Virtuous Teaching Cycles. Schedule regular benchmarking visits to other companies especially outside of your industry, and then come back and teach what you learned to others. Run Work-Out sessions to engage your organization in getting rid of unnecessary bureaucracy. Engage customers in teaching and learning dialogues. Run workshops with your suppliers. Hold regular town hall meetings with your employees at all levels, and most impactful of all, engage personally with teams in the community.

Keep Revising Your Teachable Point of View: Take a page from Jack Welch and keep re-writing and revising your Teachable Point of View. And I mean that literally. Write it down, and do it yourself. When you have a Teachable Point of View that you feel passionate about, you will be excited to teach it and keep revising it.

The mind-set of a leader/teacher is that the real joy and satisfaction comes with teaching and learning. All too often, I have to counsel senior leaders to get out of the PowerPoint presentation mode, because it is a one-way vehicle that focuses the leader on teaching but not on learning.

Create Virtuous Teaching Cycles: You need to be very deliberate about this. A leader with a total commitment and a leader/teacher mind-set will be able to see a tremendous number of opportunities to create the conditions for Virtuous Teaching Cycles. A VTC can be something as simple as a one-on-one interaction with your staff.

At first, you need to be self-conscious about creating teaching and learning interchanges. Think about: Do you end each interaction having learned something? Do the people you interact with leave having learned something? What could you have done to allow each of you to get more out of it? After a while, you won't have to self-consciously create VTCs, because it will become second nature for you to set them up in everything you do.

Use Your Power to Build Teams: Surprisingly, team building is very rarely a consensus activity. A leader almost always has to use power and edge to get people to work together on developing a shared Teachable Point of View. The reason for this is that there is always resistance. Developing a shared TPOV pushes people out of their comfort zones and often threatens the power bases of senior executives. So, good teachers know that they must use their power to manage the process and demand participation.

The paradox of working with your team is that you need to use "command and control" to get them there and to follow the process, but then you want to minimize hierarchy and create an open collaborative teaching/learning environment.

The bottom line is that it takes time. You must find quality time measured in days, not hours, to work with your team, and you must have the courage to require it.

Organizational Teaching Infrastructure: No matter how big or small your organization, you have to build a variety of teaching infrastructures. The list ranges from "boot camps" for new hires like Trilogy University and large-scale operations like GE's Crotonville leadership institute, to total company programs like Six Sigma and the learning communities that Mary Tolan has created at Accenture.

The Operating Systems: The operating mechanisms are critical. Because they are recurring activities that keep the organization running, they offer enormous opportunities for teaching and learning. But very few companies have figured that out. Thus, they miss out on the enormous leverage they could get by making them Virtuous Teaching Cycles. Strategy, budgeting and succession-planning operating mechanisms are all too often bureaucratic or political rain dances where knowledge actually gets destroyed and people become misaligned rather than aligned.

The starting point here is to conduct an audit of what the current state of these operating mechanisms is. How much positive energy, teaching, and learning occur at each phase: the preparation phase, the face-to-face phase and the follow-up phase? To fix these requires a leader to take on the role of social architect, deciding on who gets together, how often, for what purpose, and in what setting.

The key to building Virtuous Teaching Cycles into the operating system is constant attention, research, and development. As we discuss in the book, Jack Welch was always experimenting and tinkering with the operating mechanisms to make sure they were teaching/learning vehicles.

Global Citizenship: The real high bar is for all of us to make our contribution to creating a world of Virtuous Teaching Cycles. The major problems of the world are rooted in educational deficits. People who are illiterate are locked out of the world economy, so some of the challenge is very basic and rudimentary.

The long-term sustainability of the planet must be built on continuous improvement in the education level of as many humans as possible. It will require an increasing effort on the part of businesses and business leaders around the globe with both environmental and human capital issues.

Jeff Immelt challenges us all with his call for leadership at GE with more "heart," who will give back more to the environment and to the communities in which they operate.

Think Big: For all of your Virtuous Teaching Cycles, think big, think creatively, and think how to sustain them over time. Here is one final Virtuous Teaching Cycle benchmark to stimulate your imagination:

UPS sends out 40 to 50 high-potential middle managers a year to live for a while in rural or urban poverty areas. Their assignment is to work side by side with community members to solve problems. The managers, who are among UPS's best, share the experiences they bring from living outside the community, along with their knowledge about business, how to get things done, and possible new ways to get and use resources. In return, they learn about the communities in which they operate, they often learn a whole new set of management and coping skills from people who are masters at making a little go a long way, and they usually return turbocharged with a whole new perspective on life. Going out of their comfort zones and being left to live there day-to-day is a high-impact leadership development experience.

The managers win. The community wins. UPS wins. We all win.

Now, it's your turn.

The Cycle of Leadership Handbook

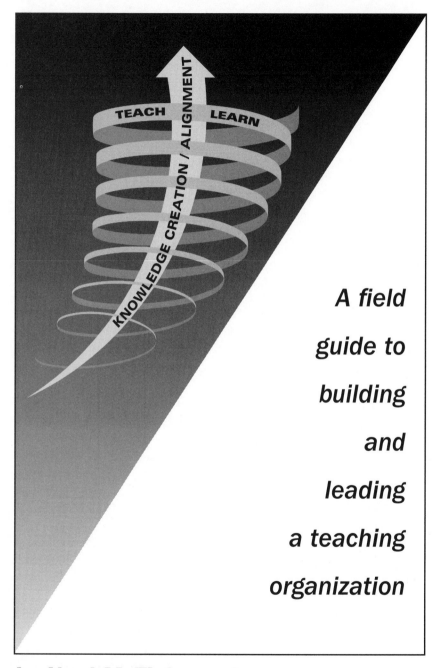

A field

guide to

building

and

leading

a teaching

organization

by Noel M. Tichy and Chris DeRose

Introduction
Creating Aligned Brains and Leadership at All Levels

The leadership job of the twenty-first century is to enhance the brainpower of an organization by having leaders at all levels engaged in Virtuous Teaching Cycles. The case has been made that we now live in a knowledge era where the value of intellectual capital has supplanted physical assets. In this world, leaders must make everyone smarter while simultaneously aligning the energy and commitment of the people in their organizations. This Handbook provides a "how to" for doing this.

Thomas Stewart, a *Fortune* editor and a leading thinker in the field, outlined the foundations for the knowledge economy with powerful simplicity in his most recent book, *The Wealth of Knowledge:*

> The knowledge economy stands on three pillars. The first: Knowledge has become what we buy, sell, and do. It is the most important factor of production. The second pillar is a mate, a corollary to the first: Knowledge assets—that is, intellectual capital—have become more important to companies than financial and physical assets. The third pillar is this: To prosper in this new economy and exploit these newly vital assets, we need new vocabularies, new management techniques, new technologies, and new strategies. On these three pillars rest all the new economy's laws and its profits.

In a May 2001 *Fortune* article, Stewart made an attempt, with the help of financial consultants, to assess which companies were best at understanding these new management approaches. His list of the companies that have created the greatest intellectual capital is:

285

Figure 1: *Fortune* Knowledge Capital Rankings

Rank	Name	Knowledge capital (in millions)	Knowledge earnings (in millions)	Market value/ book value	Market value/ comprehensive value
1	General Electric	254,381	12,435	8.1	1.34
2	Pfizer	219,202	7,686	15.1	1.03
3	Microsoft	204,515	8,735	6.9	1.16
4	Philip Morris	188,538	10,226	7.0	0.52
5	Exxon Mobil	176,409	10,050	4.1	1.17
6	Intel	173,964	7,339	5.1	0.91
7	SBC Communications	155,402	7,897	4.8	0.78
8	International Business Machines	148,679	7,534	8.1	0.99
9	Verizon Communications	141,471	7,494	3.8	0.74
10	Merck	139,494	7,497	11.5	1.11
11	Wal-Mart Stores	99,973	5,018	6.9	1.63
12	Johnson & Johnson	94,769	4,976	6.9	1.14
13	Bristol Myers Squibb	85,837	4,709	12.5	1.21
14	Coca-Cola	73,976	3,906	12.7	1.42
15	Dell Computer	72,985	2,499	11.4	

Stewart's ranking reflects a massive movement underway to actually measure intellectual capital. Getting the metrics right is still more art than science. Attempts are in their infancy and will take years to perfect. Nevertheless the concept is correct and we put Stewart's work right at the front of this handbook to reinforce the importance for companies to continue defining, measuring and improving ways of generating new intellectual capital.

Plan for This Handbook

This handbook will help you determine ways for maximizing the intellectual capital you already have and develop ways to generate new knowledge. You cannot be an effective leader or build a Teaching Organization by simply copying what someone else has done. The case studies throughout this handbook are instrumental: they demonstrate basic principles that should stimulate your thinking and serve as guides for planning your actions. This handbook offers some practical exercises and tools—many that we have used successfully with thousands of executives as they struggle to come up with answers for their own organizations. As you work through the following pages, remember that you are on a journey that will take time, commitment, experimentation, and frequent self-reflection.

Sections I through IX will help you assess the current state of yourself as a leader and your organization's ability to create Leader/Teachers at all levels. They will also challenge you to define concrete actions that you, as a leader, can take to create a Teaching Organization. Section X concludes by helping you think about your first step.

Section I: The Teaching Organization
- Understand why Teaching Organizations win.
- Assess your teaching capability.

Section II: The Hand You Have Been Dealt
- Rate your organization versus world-class Teaching Organizations.
- Identify ways to better leverage your company's scale, speed, and know-how.

Section III: Building Your Teachable Point of View
- Benchmark your company's growth and efficiency versus the best.
- Define operational values and how you will energize your team.

Section IV: Pulling it All Together
- Convert your Teachable Point of View into a compelling story that will energize your organization.
- Develop stories that excite people about you, your team, and your vision.

Section V: Building a Team Teachable Point of View
- Use leadership and power to successfully engage your team in defining a collective Teachable Point of View.
- Design a Virtuous Teaching Cycle event for your team.

Section VI: Architecting the Leadership Pipeline
- Gauge how good your organization's leadership pipeline is today.
- Build a Leader/Teacher pipeline.

Section VII: Scaling the Teaching Organization
- Create Virtuous Teaching Cycles throughout your entire company.
- Apply best-in-class approaches for teaching effectively with speed and scale.

Section VIII: Building Teaching into the DNA
- Develop operating mechanisms that develop leaders and drive business results.
- Build an operating system that stimulates knowledge creation and drives alignment.

Section IX: Global Citizenship
- Understand how to leverage citizenship to develop leaders.
- Design your global citizenship event.

Section X: Start the Journey
- Turn your plans into action.

Section One
The Teaching Organization

TEACH
LEARN
KNOWLEDGE CREATION / ALIGNMENT

Winning Organizations Are Teaching Organizations
- *Everybody teaches. Everybody learns.*
- *Practices, processes, values all promote teaching.*

They Are Built Around Virtuous Teaching Cycles
- *The teaching isn't one-way. It's interactive.*
- *Interaction generates knowledge, makes everyone smarter.*

They Create Attributes Needed in the Knowledge Economy
- *Maximum use of everyone's skills and talent.*
- *All-level alignment needed for smart, speedy action.*

In this section you will

■ Define the characteristics of successful leaders who are teachers.

■ Identify a time that you experienced a Virtuous Teaching Cycle.

Section One
The Teaching Organization

In the preceding pages, this book has described what it takes for a company to build a Virtuous Teaching Cycle and the benefits of a Teaching Organization. In today's fast-paced, hypercompetitive environment, winning organizations will have smarter, more aligned leaders. Teaching Organizations, in which leaders at all levels actively contribute to the collective knowledge pool, enable employees to act faster and more effectively. This is because they have cultures where everyone is expected to teach others, to learn and to contribute new ideas. These institutions have fundamental building blocks that are required to succeed in the new era of knowledge:

Figure 2: Building Blocks for a Teaching Organization

- Creating knowledge that is applicable in the marketplace is a primary organizational objective.
- There are leaders at all levels who have a Teachable Point of View.
- People are energized to work at the company.
- The senior leadership team is united around its Teachable Point of View but constantly seeking new input.
- There are formal and informal operating mechanisms for reinforcing and refining the Teachable Point of View.
- There are mechanisms for involving the entire organization swiftly.
- Technology and digitization play a complementary role.
- There is a carefully crafted architecture for succession planning and leadership development.

In a Teaching Organization, learners at all levels are teachers. This creates a Virtuous Teaching Cycle, or self-reinforcing pattern that keeps everyone engaged in a teaching and learning process, which improves the organization's effectiveness. This ability to break down traditional hierarchical and functional walls that compartmentalize knowledge generation differentiates Teaching Organizations. It is achieved because the views of leaders at all levels are valued, and mechanisms exist for putting them into action.

At the opposite end of the spectrum from Teaching Organizations are those that deplete their intellectual capital and actually become less smart, less aligned and less energized every day. People in these vicious non-teaching organizations rarely understand the business plan and are expected to check their brain at the door. These organizations, typified by the command-and-control structures imposed by autocrats, alienate workers and undermine self-confidence. Obviously no one organization fits the normative case for a perfect Virtuous Teaching Cycle and there are probably no pure vicious non-teaching organizations. Figure 3 contrasts the knowledge creation of Virtuous Teaching Cycles with the knowledge destruction of vicious non-teaching cycles.

Here are a few examples of organizations that have created Virtuous Teaching Cycles:

United States Special Operations Forces: Individual SOF personnel in the field had the authority to make combat and targeting judgments literally from horseback in Afghanistan. Given only the broadest mission parameters, they were able to use tactical knowledge available only from their ground position to make real-time decisions outside the traditional command-and-control structure. They were responsible for teaching central command and others in the field so that everyone was fully informed about the battle landscape.

General Electric Six Sigma Black Belts: Over 12,000 high-potential middle managers have been highly trained in the statistical principles and tools of Six Sigma quality. They are responsible for disseminating these to all GE employees through hands-on application. Their projects use data to directly challenge faulty assumptions or decisions, often made by managers several hierarchical layers above them.

Yum! Brands Customer Award: Front-line employees at Yum! Brands are entrusted to solve problems of up to $25 without seeking manager approval. Considering Yum! Brands directly or indirectly employs more than 700,000 people through its company-owned and franchise-operated stores, this could create tremendous potential financial exposure. However, the front-line operators are trusted and taught to take care of customer issues. More important, the feedback

Figure 3: Virtuous Teaching Cycles vs. Vicious Non-Teaching Cycles

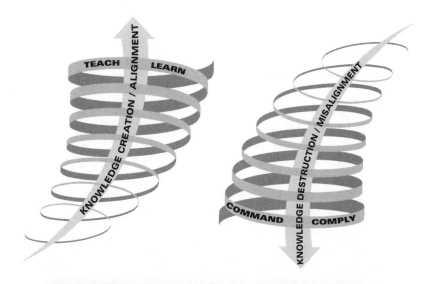

VIRTUOUS TEACHING CYCLE	VICIOUS NON-TEACHING CYCLE
Leadership at all levels	Leadership top down
Teach and interact	Command and control
Open communication	Defensive communication
Teamwork	Passive-aggressive behavior
Grows self-confidence	Reduces self-confidence
TPOVs at all levels	Rigid top down TPOV
Collective knowledge at all levels	All intelligence assumed to be at the top
Everyone's brain counts	Brains of the masses checked at the door when work starts
Organizational knowledge grows	Organizational knowledge is depleted
Positive emotional energy grows	Emotional energy sucked out of the organization
Boundaryless	Boundary-ful and turf oriented
Mutual respect	Fear of boss
Diversity valued	Homogeneity of thought

the front-line employees provide when explaining why a store credit was issued offers Yum! Brands tremendous insight into how its policies and practices adversely impact customers.

The Evolution of the Teaching Organization

Teaching Organizations are the needed response to today's emphasis on knowledge creation. Today, intellectual assets trump physical assets in nearly every industry.

Figure 4 shows four critical factors for Teaching Organizations:

1. Reliance on Alignment Through Dialogue, not Authority

Teaching Organizations challenge traditional ideas of authority. Old hierarchical structures assumed that managers were more intelligent and knew more than those at layers below them. Teaching Organizations expect great insights to come from all levels of the organization. Leaders at the top guide the organization by pulling together a coherent firm-wide Teachable Point of View and energizing everyone to win.

2. Commitment and Contribution by All Employees

Since everyone in the organization is heard and, more important, expected to teach others, they have direct input into the organization's overall direction. Ultimately, the senior management team must set direction and choose to act on some ideas while ignoring others. However, everyone freely contributes by teaching others.

3. Level of Knowledge Creation

The competitive edge of Teaching Organizations is that they generate more knowledge and intellectual capital. They not only value everyone's input, they demand that people put ideas into practice by working with others.

4. Sharing Best Practices and Knowledge Across All Boundaries

People who create fiefdoms or insulate themselves from new ideas are the bane of Teaching Organizations. Leaders within Teaching Organizations respect the fact that good ideas can come from anywhere. By definition, this means that leaders are simultaneously learning while teaching others.

Figure 4: Evolution of a Teaching Organization

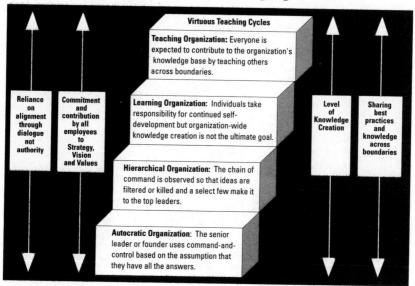

Yourself as a Leader/Teacher

Leaders who believe that teaching and learning are the foundations for marketplace success create Teaching Organizations and invest the time to develop their own Teachable Point of View. If you are old enough to read this book, you have a point of view on what it takes to be a good teacher. By the time children are in fifth grade they have been exposed to a number of good and bad role models: parents, school teachers, church instructors, Boy or Girl Scout leaders, athletic coaches, etc. In order to develop your own teaching style, consider the qualities of a good teacher based on your own experiences:

_____

_____

_____

_____

Figure 5: Characteristics of World-Class Leader/Teachers

Here are just some of the characteristics we have heard from thousands of executives:

- **Good listener**
- **Passionate about the subject**
- **Knows the subject well**
- **Tells stories and uses practical examples**
- **Provides context for why the subject is relevant to the learner**
- **Makes a personal connection to the topic**
- **Takes time to understand learner's capabilities**
- **Open to learning from the student**
- **Makes teaching and learning interactive — Virtuous Teaching Cycle**
- **Can use visual, audible, and physical teaching tools effectively**
- **Sincerely cares about whether the learner understands**
- **Never gives up, gets frustrated, or gets bored**

Opening Up to Learning

Leader/teachers do not care where good ideas come from. They eagerly listen to new ideas with an open mind, fully expecting that the best insights may come from people outside their industry or below their hierarchical level. They do not let their egos prevent them from absorbing new learning. Regardless of where it comes from, Leader/Teachers will listen and learn.

Jack Welch's punch in the nose: After pursuing the strategy to be No. 1 or No. 2 in any industry where GE operated, Welch was told by a group of middle managers that executives were gaming industry definitions to meet Welch's criteria. He described it as a "punch in the nose" but one that ultimately led him to call for every GE business to redefine itself so that it had less than 10% of total market share. This ultimately created billions of dollars of top-line growth for GE.

David Novak's multi-branding effort: Several years ago, Yum! Brands, which operates KFC, Pizza Hut and Taco Bell, was vigorously trying to bundle its multiple brands under a single restaurant roof. While Yum! Brands CEO David Novak was preaching about the benefits of this approach, he learned from a franchisee that Yum! Brands's policies and systems directly contradicted these types of integration efforts. As a result, he simplified back room systems, put a centralized coordination team in place, and created unified operating procedures. This has led to the successful roll-out of multi-branded locations, which may now be extended to Yum! Brands's recent acquisitions of A&W and Long John Silver's.

The leaders cited above started by teaching others their point of view. But as they listened, they discovered they had as much to learn. Their strategies and behaviors changed as a direct result of what they heard. This type of two-way learning and teaching is the basis for a Virtuous Teaching Cycle.

Consider a time when you were a teacher but had your point of view significantly changed by the person you were teaching:

_____

_____

_____

_____

If you could not remember a time, reflect on how open you are to learning and how good you are at listening while you teach.

Section Two
The Hand You Have Been Dealt

Teaching and Learning Are Key Competitive Factors
- *Leaders build time for teaching and reflection into their calendars.*
- *Routine processes are built on teaching/learning rather than command/control.*

The Knowledge Revolution
- *Intangibles/brains replace physical goods/equipment as main sources of value.*
- *Winners must figure out how to be big, fast and smart — and do it quickly.*

In this section you will

▮ Audit your organization's teaching mindset and capabilities.

▮ Generate ideas for better leveraging scale, increasing speed to market, and breaking down organizational boundaries.

Section Two
The Hand You Have Been Dealt

Building an organization with the DNA of Virtuous Teaching Cycles at all levels is a never-ending aspiration. The process of creating a Teaching Organization with Virtuous Teaching Cycles starts with an honest assessment of which building blocks your company has in place, how well it is using them, and which need to be created from scratch.

There is no single model or paint-by-the-numbers formula for building a Teaching Organization. Each will reflect the ideas, values and personalities of the people within them. At the heart of each, however, are certain characteristics:

1. *The teaching organization mind-set:* There is a deeply entrenched mind-set that teaching is a top priority for everyone and the best means of generating knowledge throughout the organization.
2. *The leader learning mind-set:* Great teachers are also great learners. They see every interaction as a potential learning opportunity. They encourage informal idea sharing and do not compartmentalize learning by hierarchy, function or business.
3. *Teaching is built into everyday operations:* Systems, processes, operating mechanisms and cultural values that guide daily action all reinforce teaching and building knowledge.
4. *There is a strong teaching and development infrastructure:* Teaching is built into systematic development opportunities, such as new-hire orientation, town hall exchanges, development programs, Six Sigma training, company recruiting, etc.

The Teaching Organization Audit

Use the audit below to see where you stand on the Teaching Organization scale:

Teaching Organization Audit

Building Blocks

Your Organization

	Not at All				Very Strong
1. **Senior Leadership**—Our CEO and senior leaders are passionately committed to teaching.	1	2	3	4	5
2. **Teaching Infrastructure**—There are organization-wide mechanisms and development programs architected to drive teaching throughout our company.	1	2	3	4	5
3. **Operating System**—Our operating mechanisms (strategic planning process, budgeting and succession planning) are more focused on creating Virtuous Teaching Cycles than meeting internal bureaucratic needs.	1	2	3	4	5

Your Leadership

4. **TPOV**—I have a clear Teachable Point of View that I actively use to teach and learn from others.	1	2	3	4	5
5. **Engaging Storyline**—My TPOV is crafted into a compelling, motivating storyline that I use to engage internal and external stakeholders.	1	2	3	4	5
6. **Priorities**—I define my leadership role as teaching, and I spend a significant portion of my time (i.e., 30% or more) teaching and developing others.	1	2	3	4	5

Your Team

7. **Power**—I handle the paradox of power well—requiring people to teach and participate in events to develop our collective TPOV.

1	2	3	4	5

8. **Local VTCs**—As a team, we engage our people in Virtuous Teaching Cycles that force us to change our thinking and behavior.

1	2	3	4	5

9. **Teaching Environment**—We foster informality and actively help our people build self-confidence so they can engage and teach us.

1	2	3	4	5

Your World

10. **Citizenship**—We have large-scale involvement in the wider community that engages our organizational members in corporate citizenship activities.

1	2	3	4	5

Score Yourself

45–50: The essential building blocks are in place—Use them!

35–44: Pick some key areas for change.

25–34: Great change is needed—start by getting commitment at the top and commit yourself to this change.

10–24: Dramatic transformation is required—this is old-way, command-and-control.

Implications of This Audit

	Specific Actions Required	By When
Your Organization		
Your Leadership		
Your Team		
Your World		

The Winning Path

Despite the boom and bust of the recent dot-bomb era, there is no question that we are in the early stages of an era in which technology and biotechnology will have inescapable consequences for how businesses are run and organized. The practices, systems, policies and mind-sets that prevailed in the old industrial economy will not do the job. The foregone conclusion of the late 1990s that the old industrial behemoths would be displaced by agile start-ups is equally wrong for the times.

Rather, we now know that the winners of the future will adapt and innovate to exploit emerging technological and social changes. They will be big, fast and smart. The winners will create value by having a workforce that is more aligned, energized and smarter than their competitors. They will leverage size and act with speed across internal and external organizational boundaries.

Leveraging Scale

In today's global, networked economy, big can be beautiful. Many managers think of largeness as a liability, fearing that they will never be able to effectively control an organization as it grows. This is true. Leading by command-and-control doesn't work at scale. However, Teaching Organizations harness the collective intelligence of hundreds of thousands of people by engaging them and using large-scale processes to drive alignment. Teaching enables companies to leverage the resources and reach associated with big organizations because leaders are directly engaged with their people. They are not trying to broadcast messages from the top floor of world headquarters, or hoping that bland, bureaucratic rules will direct people to success.

Getting to scale can be achieved through internal growth, external partnerships or a combination of both. The key is to have enough marketplace mass that you can help define the competitive rules of your industry.

Consider Dell Computer. In 1995 Dell was a mid-tier player in the computer industry. It had not even fully established its direct business model, as it didn't have a direct sales Website until the following year. Once the power of the Dell business model was understood and its advantages versus traditional retail outlets became apparent, Dell expanded its product and geographic footprint. Between 1997 and 2000, Dell revenues more than quadrupled, with more than half of its revenue coming from new product categories and geographies. Dell built size and critical mass in the market that could not be ignored. Indeed, the Hewlett-Packard/Compaq merger and Gateway's business model change were direct responses to Dell's competitive threat.

Dell achieved its success by teaching the entire organization about one of the fundamental elements of its business model—Return on Invested Capital (ROIC). In a process led by then CFO Tom Meredith and orchestrated through its treasury department, Dell employees learned what they could do to ensure that the company not only grew, but grew profitably.

Take a moment to think about how well your organization is managing its size:

Meeting Customer Needs

Lack products, services, geographic reach or integrated solutions to meet customer needs.　　1　2　3　4　5　　Provide fully integrated solutions to customers' toughest problems.

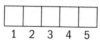

Market and Industry Impact

Our action has no or little impact on our competitors and industry dynamics.　　1　2　3　4　5　　We can define the competitive rules of the game.

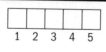

Leverage from Resources

We have insufficient resources to meet customer demand, or we get bogged down in bureaucracy.　　1　2　3　4　5　　We strategically leverage our deep pockets and take measured risks that smaller competitors cannot.

Speed to Market

In a world of increasing commoditization, speed is the sustainable competitive differentiator. Companies need to be the fastest to understand dynamic customer needs, create new technologies or products, and constantly adapt. Teaching Organizations are fast because knowledge is disseminated broadly, not hoarded in functional silos. People are expected to share information about customers and the market in an effort to continuously change. Similarly, new people brought into the organization are expected to make contributions early in their careers. They are not discounted as rookies; their views are heard and incorporated.

Trilogy Software, the Austin-based company that has dominated the high-end configuration software market since its founding by Stanford dropouts, demonstrates just how quickly new people can make meaningful contributions with its Trilogy University. New recruits are immersed in several months of technical, sales and leadership training. As part of the experience, they take on projects that can fundamentally redefine product offerings and often engage customer CEOs.

Consider how fast your company truly is:

Gathering Data and Communicating

We respond to market or customer changes after our competitors move first.

1 2 3 4 5

We translate real-time information into action that gives us a competitive advantage.

Developing New Technologies, Products and Services

Our development cycle lags the competition—we generate "me too" offerings.

1 2 3 4 5

Our development cycle time and pipeline is the industry best and benchmarked as world-class.

Developing Human Assets

We require many months or years before employees can make meaningful contributions.

1 2 3 4 5

We generate a higher return from each employee in a shorter time frame than our competitors.

Transformation

We fail to respond to market changes until damage has already been done.

1 2 3 4 5

We adapt to emerging trends and market changes as quickly as possible.

Breaking Down the Walls

In the knowledge era, it is brains and motivation that make the difference. As we all know, beating one's head against bureaucratic walls is both stupid and frustrating. One of the challenges for Teaching Organizations, therefore, is to create an environment of free-flowing knowledge so that people can teach and energize one another. Internal fiefdoms, bureaucratic red tape, constraining company processes and not-invented-here attitudes can destroy an organization's ability to stay ahead.

Teaching Organizations are deliberate in their efforts to break down horizontal walls between divisions, functions and departments. They also minimize the importance of vertical boundaries created through the organizational hierarchy by encouraging anyone to talk to anyone else, regardless of level. They encourage best-practice sharing across geographic boundaries. Finally, they actively share and leverage strategic relationships with customers, suppliers and partners so that information permeates the organization.

Jack Welch captured this idea in a single word: boundaryless. Welch likened GE to a house that had been built over many years and constructed countless vertical and horizontal walls as the house continued to grow. Welch compared his task at GE to a massive demolition project in which the company would be rebuilt with an open floorplan so that people could quickly see, hear and teach one another.

Consider how good your organization is at crossing boundaries:

Boundaryless Audit

Vertical Boundaries		
Decisions must escalate to the highest hierarchical level so that they can be passed back down to those on the front line—the process can take weeks or months.	1 2 3 4 5	Decisions are made by those who are closest to the work and the customer—approvals take hours or occasionally days.

Horizontal Boundaries		
Divisions and functions hoard knowledge and resources in a zero-sum game of internal competition.	1 2 3 4 5	Best practices and ideas flow across all parts of the company and are readily adopted.

Geographic Boundaries

Countries and regions are expected to fend for themselves—differences in local cultures and business practices are emphasized.

1	2	3	4	5

People actively seek to help, teach and learn from colleagues in different regions.

Outside-In Boundaries

People inside the company are shielded from ideas and interaction with customers, suppliers and partners.

1	2	3	4	5

External relationships provide key strategic information and are the basis for innovation by those inside your company.

Implications

	Specific Actions Required	By When
Leveraging Scale • Meeting Customer Needs • Market and Industry Impact • Leverage from Resources		
Speed to Market • Gathering Data and Communicating • Developing New Technologies, Products, and Services • Developing Human Assets • Transformation		
Breaking Down the Walls • Vertical Boundaries • Horizontal Boundaries • Geographic Boundaries • Outside-In Boundaries		

Section Three
Building Your Teachable Point of View

TEACH   LEARN

KNOWLEDGE CREATION / ALIGNMENT

A Teachable Point of View:
Making Your Knowledge Available to Others
- *Step 1:*   *Sorting through ideas and beliefs to figure out what you know.*
- *Step 2:*   *Developing ways to communicate it clearly to others.*

The Elements of a Teachable Point of View:
Ideas and Values
- *The ideas are about a plan for success.*
- *The values are ones that support achieving it.*

The Elements of a Teachable Point of View:
Emotional Energy and Edge
- *Leaders must generate excitement about the ideas and values.*
- *Making tough decisions and teaching others to do so is essential.*

In this section you will

▎ Consider business ideas to generate more revenue and better efficiency.

▎ Define the operational values that fit with your business ideas.

▎ Develop ways of energizing your team.

▎ Exercise edge as you evaluate your portfolio and people.

Section Three
Building Your Teachable
Point of View

The opening pages of this book make the case that the essence of leading is not commanding but teaching. Through teaching, leaders are able to open people's eyes and minds and to motivate them to achieve collective goals. In order to teach, however, a leader must have a Teachable Point of View.

A Teachable Point of View is a cohesive set of ideas, values and ways of energizing people that can be articulated and put into action. Part of the application is making tough decisions or exercising what we call edge. The following metaphor usually helps people see just how simple this is.

Imagine that you were the high school tennis coach for fifty kids. When the kids show up on the first day, what would you teach them? First, you need to have a set of clear ideas about how tennis is played. This would include the rules of the game and the fundamentals such as stance, holding the racket, serving, forehand and backhand. You would also need a set of values regarding sportsmanship, fairness and integrity that would be translated into court etiquette. You would need to have some teaching methods that energize the kids and keep them excited about tennis. Finally, if someone broke the rules, you would need to exercise edge and possibly remove them from the tennis team if the infraction were severe.

Home Depot provides a great benchmark for a Teachable Point of View. The central idea that guided founders Bernie Marcus and Arthur Blank was low-price, high-volume superstores that eliminated middlemen in purchasing. Underlying its wide selection and competitive prices, Marcus and Blank built a culture of customer service that would give do-it-yourselfers the information and confi-

Figure 6: Elements of a Teachable Point of View

The same elements are needed to make your organization successful:	
• Ideas:	How does your business make money and win in the marketplace?
• Values:	What behaviors are required to put your business ideas into practice?
• Emotional Energy:	How do you keep people motivated and working with high energy?
• Edge:	Which difficult decisions must be made?

dence they needed to feel comfortable working on their own homes. Cultivating repeat customers among the DIY market was essential, so customer service became the primary corporate value. One of the ways that store associates were energized to help customers and improve the company was by building a spirit of entrepreneurship. Stock options were distributed broadly to Home Depot associates so that helping customers and working to improve the share price was in their direct interest. Finally, the company built edge at the front lines by giving store associates the power to recommend what was in the customer's best interest, not what created the highest Home Depot profit. Arthur Blank recounted with pride the story of an associate who sold a $1.50 part for a faucet repair to a customer who was fully prepared to spend $200 replacing his faucet.

The Teachable Point of View is a starting point. It provides a basis for dialogue and debate to ensure that people are aligned and that the best, most recent information is being acted upon. Although the company's Teachable Point of View must ultimately come from the top, everyone has input. If each person has a Teachable Point of View regarding their part of the business, they are explicitly aware of the connections and disconnections between their daily experience and the organization's stated goals and purpose. This enables the company Teachable Point of View to continuously evolve to meet changing market needs. Home Depot, now under the leadership of Bob Nardelli, is actively reshaping some elements of its Teachable Point of View while still retaining some of the fundamentals that have made the company so successful.

Figure 7: Home Depot's Teachable Point of View

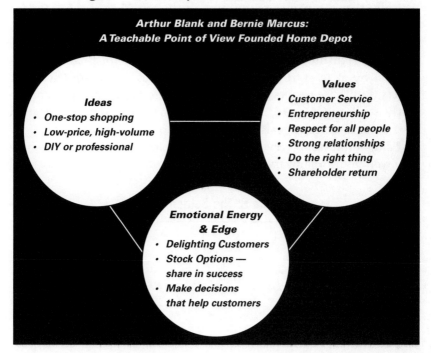

Developing Your Ideas: How We Make Money

All businesses are built around ideas. A leader's central idea lays out his or her concept for organizational success in terms of products, services, distribution channels, customer segments and the like. A century ago, Theodore Vail organized AT&T around the idea of "universal service." The purpose of the company, and the cultural legacy that lived well into the 1990s for AT&T and its progeny, was to provide every home in the United States with basic telephone service. Likewise, Sam Walton built Wal-Mart around the central idea of bringing big-company purchasing economies to customers in rural areas. Dell's idea, mentioned above, was to sell direct to consumers and bypass retail outlets.

Leaders must provide ideas that become the intellectual catalyst for action in the company. The ideas must provide sustainable competitive advantage and solid financial returns. For publicly traded companies, the test of adding value is simple: The capital markets reflect value-added in the companies' changing stock price.

Larry Selden, a professor at Columbia University, has shown statistically that companies performing in the top 25% of the Standard & Poor's 500 have two things in common. First, they produce annual revenue growth of at least 12%. Second, they improve their annual operating return on assets (or equity, in the case of financial institutions) by at least 16%. For most companies, these are Olympian targets. But these results are exactly what the capital markets consistently seek and reward. Finding ideas that help the organization meet these ambitious goals is a leader's responsibility.

Using Professor Larry Selden's grid below, place a dot to show how well your organization is performing:

Figure 8: The Selden Grid

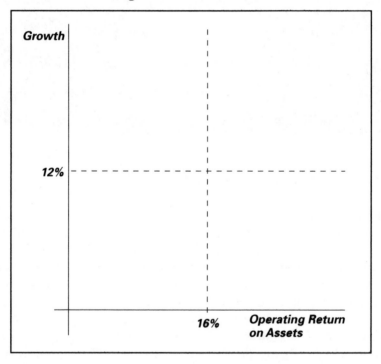

Even the companies that are in the upper-right quadrant know they need new ideas to continue their success.

Consider the questions on the facing page to see what opportunities may exist to improve your organization's performance:

Revenue Growth

▌Can we do a better job of serving our customers?

_____

_____

▌Are there potential customers who we aren't serving?

_____

_____

▌Are there new products or services that we could offer?

_____

_____

Return on Assets

▌Do we have problems maintaining an appropriate level of working capital?

_____

_____

▌Do we have assets that are underutilized or that sit idle?

_____

_____

▌Do we exceed desired inventory levels or do we assume the need for high inventory rates?

_____

_____

▮ Are our work processes maximally efficient and focused?

_____

_____

▮ Do our competitors or benchmarks complete the same work but consume fewer resources?

_____

_____

Developing Your Values

Every organization has values. Some start-ups have an implicit set that can be observed, but are rarely articulated. Conversely, some dinosaur organizations have values printed on pocket cards or mounted on plaques, but that have little to do with how people actually behave. In extreme cases, hypocrisy around values can lead to a company's undoing. Former Enron executives who were directly embroiled in the company's improprieties were once waxing about integrity and honesty.

The values of an organization must be explicit and they must support achievement of the business ideas. Leaders create, shape and reshape their cultures by consciously developing desired values. These values must be manifested in behaviors that help the company succeed. There are three types of values.

Societal—This includes immutable values like honesty or integrity that are underpinnings for how any society operates. Figure 9 shows an example of how integrity has been applied at GE.

Subjective—This includes politicized or normative statements about which values are "correct" in the moral or religious sense. Such value sets, family values or libertarian values are examples, are highly subjective and often divisive. Unless the organization has the advancement of such values as its core purpose, leaders rarely take a stand on such values.

Operational—This includes values that directly link to fulfillment of an organization's business theory, such as customer service, entrepreneurship or boundarylessness.

Figure 9: Defining Integrity at GE

INTEGRITY

In Jack Welch's last annual report letter he articulated it as follows:

It's the first and most important of our values. Integrity means always abiding by the law, both the letter and the spirit. But it's not just about laws; it is at the core of every relationship we have.

Inside the Company, integrity establishes the trust that is so critical to the human relationships that make our values work. With trust, employees can take risks and believe us when we say a "miss" doesn't mean career damage. With trust, employees can stretch performance goals and can believe us when we promise that falling short is not a punishable offense. Integrity and trust are at the heart of the informality we cherish. There are not witnesses needed to conversations nor the need to "put it in writing." None of that—our word is enough.

In our external dealings, with our unions and governments, we are free to represent our positions vigorously, in a constructive fashion, to agree or disagree on the issues, knowing that our integrity itself is never an issue.

A period of transition is a period of change, and some of our values will be modified to adapt to what the future brings. One will not: our commitment to integrity, which beyond doing everything right, means always doing the right thing.

Societal values are often givens within an organization. They should be discussed and reinforced, but teaching and changing them isn't much of an issue. Operational values, on the other hand, must be carefully defined, explained and taught throughout the organization, since they form the basis for the company winning in the market. Operational values help to define the daily behaviors of everyone within an organization. They should encompass behaviors related to:

- Co-workers
- Customers
- Suppliers
- Partners
- Competitors
- Shareholders
- Community

A first step in defining your organization's values is thinking
about those required to match your business ideas. Take a few minutes and build on the work you did to articulate a set of ideas. Think
about how the values system of your company can reinforce that. In
the next exercise, you'll work on articulating the connection between the ideas and values.

Step 1: Write your ideas in the bubble on the left.
Step 2: Write your values in the bubble on the right.

Figure 10: Connecting Ideas and Values

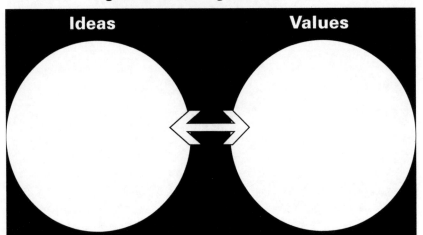

An equally important part of establishing and teaching values for
your organization is recognizing that you may need to deal with
legacy values. You must start by looking at the reality of what the
present values are, stated and unstated. Then you must decide which
of the values are helpful and should be retained, which are detrimental and must be eliminated, and which entirely new values are
needed.

People often have difficulty articulating their organization's actual values. However, it is much easier for them to describe the behaviors they want to keep and those they want to kill. Start by
thinking about the existing behaviors that will undermine your organization's ability to execute your business ideas:

Figure 11: Existing Undesired Behaviors

Existing undesired behavior/value	Why people do this today	Why it will be detrimental in the future	How I will eliminate or modify it
1.			
2.			
3.			
4.			
5.			

For each of the values that you want to keep or add, you must teach these so that every person in your organization can articulate and live them.

Developing Energy

The best articulated ideas and values are meaningless unless people are motivated to put them into action. Leaders must therefore take deliberate actions that generate emotional energy and channel it to productive uses. Emotional energy can be generated by both positive and negative stimulus, and it is highly dependent on the people and personalities involved. Leaders use a repertoire of activities, events and interactions to generate energy. They also do so in a style that is uniquely their own.

David Novak at Yum! Brands is an avid believer in positive energy. The customers that Yum! Brands relies on interact only with relatively low-paid, high-turnover counter personnel. Keeping the counter staff energized and aligned with customer needs is essential to the business' success. Although Yum! Brands uses a number of ways to energize people, there are two that stood out in discussions with Novak. This is because they both spring from his style and personality. While some might think they are hokey, they work because of his sincerity and intensity.

When Novak became CEO of Yum! Brands, he immediately instituted a best practice that had worked for him while president of KFC. At KFC, whenever someone did something outstanding, they would be immediately recognized. Novak believes recognition is essential for keeping people energized. However, instead of giving out what he refers to as "boring, old, CEO prizes," like watches or plaques, Novak would give the star performer a floppy chicken that had a hand-written note of personal thanks on it. He would also give them a $100 check since, as Novak puts it, "You can't eat a floppy chicken." The floppy chickens not only achieved their purpose—recognizing a job well done—they also engendered an attitude of fun and playful celebration. Now, as CEO of Yum! Brands, Novak gives out a pair of novelty chattering teeth with legs. He calls this the "walking the talk" award.

The second thing that Novak did was simple, yet highly symbolic. Whenever he catches someone doing something right, he has a picture taken with the person. His office walls—and soon the ceiling—are lined with pictures. Novak jokes that the pictures are cheaper than artwork, but they serve a very serious purpose: They are a highly public symbol of Novak's spirit of teamwork and his pride in the capability of his team members.

Novak's approach will not work for everyone. He has a gregarious, casual and humorous style that fits with these gestures. However, each leader has the same challenge: you must implement a variety of ways, formal and informal, that energize individuals and the entire organization that is consistent with your own style. While there are no prescriptions, there are five conditions that can help leaders generate energy.

1. A sense of urgent need that is clear and palpable to everyone in the organization.
2. A mission that is inspiring and clearly worth achieving.
3. Goals that stretch people's abilities.
4. A spirit of teamwork.
5. Self-confidence and the realistic expectation that team members can meet the goals.

As you try to energize people to change and grow, you must be familiar with the psychodynamics around change. A very simple formula from the late MIT professor Dick Beckhard, one of the fathers of organizational psychology, captures this:

$$Change = [D + V + FS] > I$$

In short, a person's Dissatisfaction with the status quo, combined with an appealing Vision of the future, plus some clear First Steps toward achieving the vision, must overcome the person's Inertia to remain the same. Inertia is a natural tendency as people become comfortable with the status quo. One way to provide energy to an organization is teaching people about the components of Beckhard's formula.

Use the grid below to think about your team members and how motivated they will be to act on the new ideas and values in your Teachable Point of View. For each person on your team, first rate the extent to which they are driven to overcome inertia. Put a number in the appropriate box on a scale from 1 to 5:

Figure 12: Individual Drive to Overcome Inertia

1 To little or no extent	2	3 Somewhat	4	5 To a great extent

Once you've rated the people on your team, provide some reasons for each rating. As a final step, rate the level of inertia and resistance to change on a scale of 1 to 15, where 1 is no inertia and 15 is an overwhelming amount of resistance.

Figure 13: Current State of Team Energy

Team member	Level of positive dissatisfaction with the status quo	Degree to which the person is excited by vision of future opportunities	Degree to which the person can take clear first steps		Strength of inertia against change
1.Tom Smith *(example)*	2 — constantly questions reasons for change	4 — department and his responsibilities will grow in importance — potential for higher rewards	2 — failed to create plans for reorganizing his department	< = >	10 — has never been a change leader — power base in maintaining status quo
2.				< = >	
3.				< = >	
4.				< = >	
5.				< = >	

Action Plan for Energizing Change

Emotionally energizing people starts with an understanding of how they feel and of the things that actually motivate them. No two people are excited by exactly the same factors. Take some time to consider how you can energize your team members. List specific things you can do to help create more energy on your team.

Figure 14: Action Plan for Energizing Change

	Dissatisfaction	Creating a Compelling Vision		Helping People Take the First Step	
Team Member	Creating a sense of urgency	Providing a sense of mission and accomplish-ment	Setting stretch goals	Fostering a sense of teamwork	Generating self-confidence
1.					
2.					
3.					
4.					
5.					

Developing Edge

Demonstrating edge is the most difficult thing a leader has to do because it requires courage. A leader with edge makes clear yes/no decisions. Exercising edge means taking responsibility for a tough decision, not deferring it by hiring consultants or abdicating responsibility to a committee.

Leaders are confronted with edge decisions in two areas. The first revolves around allocating resources and investing in the business portfolio: Which businesses should the organization enter or exit, which products should be funded and which projects killed, which activities should the company pursue and which should it absolutely eliminate? The second is even tougher. It focuses on removing the people who fail to perform or live the values.

If there is a shortage of leadership at corporations today, it is almost always equated with a lack of edge. Yet when you see it, it is unmistakable and often determines the course of a team, department or entire company. Noel recalls interviewing John Chambers of Cisco before the market crash. When Chambers spoke of his time at Wang Computer before joining Cisco, he described implementing layoffs for hundreds of employees as one of the toughest moments in his life. He said his aim was never to have to do the same at Cisco. When the market turned against technology, however, Chambers did not shy away from the awful burden to once again lay off workers. He saw it as the only solution for Cisco's survival and ultimately a necessary act to protect the thousands of Cisco employees who would keep their jobs.

Leaders with edge do not make such decisions lightly. And they feel the pain and heartache that any person would if faced with a similar situation. However, they see it as their responsibility to face reality and act based on their ideas and values. They literally demonstrate the courage of their convictions.

Use the exercises below to develop your business and people edge:

Business Edge

Even if you do not exercise control over your business' portfolio, you do control how you spend your time. This is your most valuable asset, particularly if you are a knowledge worker. Leaders focus their time on the activities that generate the most value for their organizations, and they have the confidence to strip out the rest. A leader's business edge is often challenged during times of extreme cost cutting. Many managers are tempted to spread cost cutting around evenly because they believe this is most equitable. The reality is that this harms the organization by depriving those units with the most promise of needed resources while failing to clearly communicate which units are in trouble. As Welch put it to his leadership group: "Your whole reason for being is to say 'yes' to some and 'no' to others, to pour the coals to some and squeeze the others. Your kid can come in a rocking chair and say '10% across the board.' That ain't the game. The game is to differentiate around opportunities."

Every organization builds up unnecessary activities and bureaucracy over time. Leaders challenge tradition to make sure that they are devoting their brains and energy to things that will please the customer.

There is a simple tool designed by Len Schlesinger, a former Harvard professor who is now COO of Limited Brands, as part of General Electric's Work-Out process. It helps people eliminate low value-add work by asking them to look at how they spend their time on reports, getting approvals, in meetings, conducting measurements and adhering to policies or procedures. The tool, RAMMP, is an acronym:

Reports
Approvals
Meetings
Measurements
Policies

During GE's Work-Out process, thousands of managers applied this tool to identify unnecessary bureaucracy. They would spend one to three days working in teams determining all of the things that stood in the way of serving GE's customers to the best of their ability. On the last day of these workshops, the team's boss would spend a half-day reviewing their recommendations. Eighty percent of the items were expected to be "rattlesnakes," or things they could kill immediately. The other items were "pythons," which would be squeezed out of the business over the next thirty days, or the boss would clearly say no to the recommendation and explain why. In all of the Work-Out sessions there was an incredibly small percentage of No's.

When Welch pushed Work-Out into every GE business, he did so because he saw the productivity impact getting rid of bureaucracy could have. But he also had a more important motivation. Helping people kill bureaucracy was an incredible confidence builder. It built people's confidence that their boss would trust and listen to them. It also built self-confidence to challenge the system and have real edge in making recommendations.

Use the matrix on the following page to determine which of the RAMMP items you can kill:

Figure 15: RAMMP Matrix

	Under My Control	Under Team or Department Control	Under Business Control	Under Centralized Control	Under Customer Control
Reports					
Approvals					
Meetings					
Measurements					
Policies					
Others					

People Edge

General Electric's point of view on people edge became clear in its 1991 annual report, which categorized people into four groups:

1. The first is one who delivers on commitments—financial or otherwise—and shares the values of our Company. His or her future is an easy call. Onward and Upward.
2. The second type of leader is one who does not meet commitments and does not share our values. Not as pleasant a call, but equally easy.

3. The third is one who misses commitments but shares the values. He or she usually gets a second chance, preferably in a different environment.

4. Then there's the fourth type—the most difficult for many of us to deal with. That leader delivers on commitments, makes all the numbers, but doesn't share the values we must have. This is the individual who typically forces performance out of people rather than inspires it: the autocrat, the tyrant, the big shot. Too often all of us have looked the other way . . . But now these people must go.

A useful way to conceptualize *how* people are performing versus *how well* they perform is to look at the Performance/Values matrix. As Welch pointed out above, looking at performance alone is hopelessly short-sighted. Leaders embed values into an organization by behaving consistently with these beliefs on a daily basis. Those who don't measure up to the company's stated values are destructive and must be helped to improve, or leave.

Assess the people with whom you work closely on both of the dimensions on the next page. Place each person's initials in the box that most accurately reflects their performance and their ability to role model your organization's values.

Figure 16: Performance Values Matrix

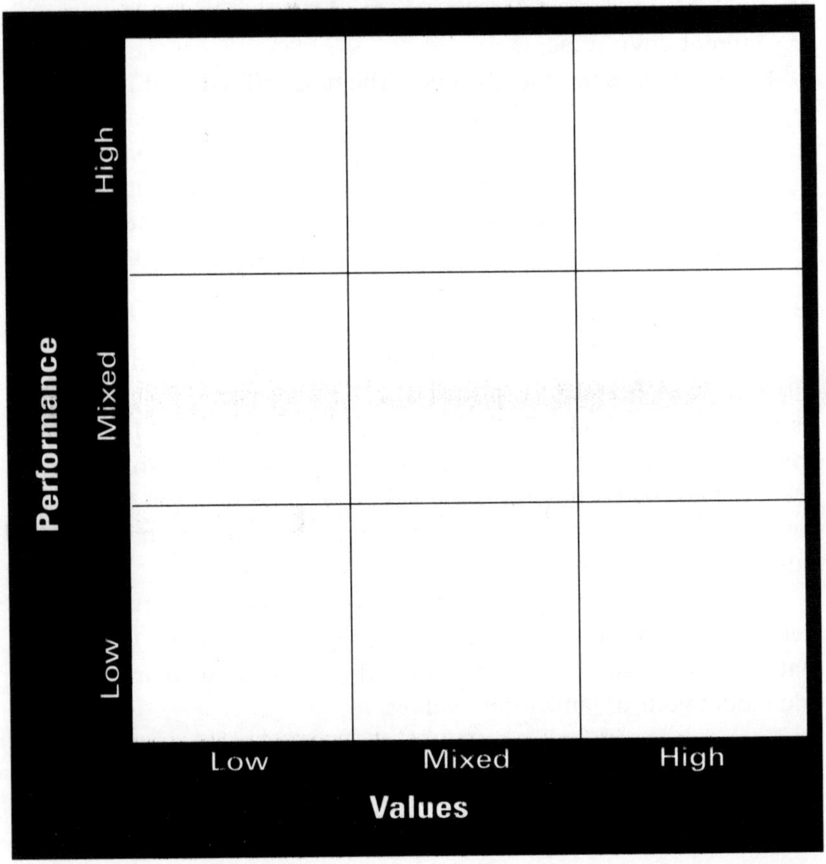

When we ask executives to do this exercise, invariably 15 to 20% categorize their entire team in the High-High box. While we wish this reflected reality, when we push them in discussion, these executives almost always either lack a good performance benchmark or have extreme difficulty being honest with themselves and others in this area.

Welch has a compelling argument—one that has been echoed by managers we have worked with from Prague to Singapore—that helps to remove some of the sting out of such assessments. Welch says that avoiding the truth when assessing people is "false kindness." He cites as evidence his challenge while downsizing GE in the mid-1980s. As Welch puts it, "We broke a lot of people's hearts . . . They said to us, 'Look at my appraisals, I've been lied to.' And they had." These were people in their forties and fifties with kids in college and mortgages to pay who had been given "above average" rat-ings for their entire careers despite their actual contribution. Welch had no choice but to cut costs when faced with competition from Asia and an increasingly global economy. Many under-performers were surprised when confronted with the reality of their perfor-mance and the loss of their jobs.

In 2000, GE had six times the revenue and 30% fewer people than when Welch joined. But the lesson has stuck with him: "Not telling people where they stand is cruelty. It's not kindness. Nothing is worse than doing that to them." As Welch learned, it is far more hu-mane to be honest with people early and consistently throughout their careers.

You have taken the time to identify the elements of your Teach-able Point of View. This is a first step. With more time and practice, you will continue to refine it. The next section will help you turn your Teachable Point of View into a compelling story that will moti-vate others on your team.

Section Four
Pulling It All Together

TEACH LEARN

KNOWLEDGE CREATION / ALIGNMENT

Developing a TPOV is an Essential Job for Leaders
- *It's an iterative process of reflection, writing, testing and amending.*
- *Feedback from others will help refine it, but the leader must craft it first.*

Then You Must Craft a Plan For the Future
- *Where do you need to get, and how will you get there?*
- *Come up with a storyline that makes it vivid and exciting.*

In this section you will

- Link the elements of your Teachable Point of View.
- Exercise the discipline of writing your story-line.

Section Four
Pulling It All Together

In the previous section you outlined the elements of your Teachable Point of View. Take some time to identify how these elements fit together and summarize them on the chart below. Writing your TPOV is a critical step. Many people, particularly those who are good public speakers, are content to wing it. We have heard many people say that they do better extemporaneously, and that writing makes them feel artificial. The sentiment may be genuine, but, as a matter of practice, it is absolute nonsense. Having watched thousands of leaders struggle to define and articulate their TPOV, it is clear that there is no substitute for time, practice and the discipline of writing. Putting thoughts to paper is a necessary step that forces clarity and reveals gaps in your thinking.

You might imagine that you have to prepare an overhead to talk to the new-hires at your company and are going to explain your Teachable Point of View. Look back at the Home Depot figure on page 313 for an example. Write the key bullet points for your Teachable Point of View in each of the circles in Figure 17 on the following page.

Figure 17: Your Teachable Point of View

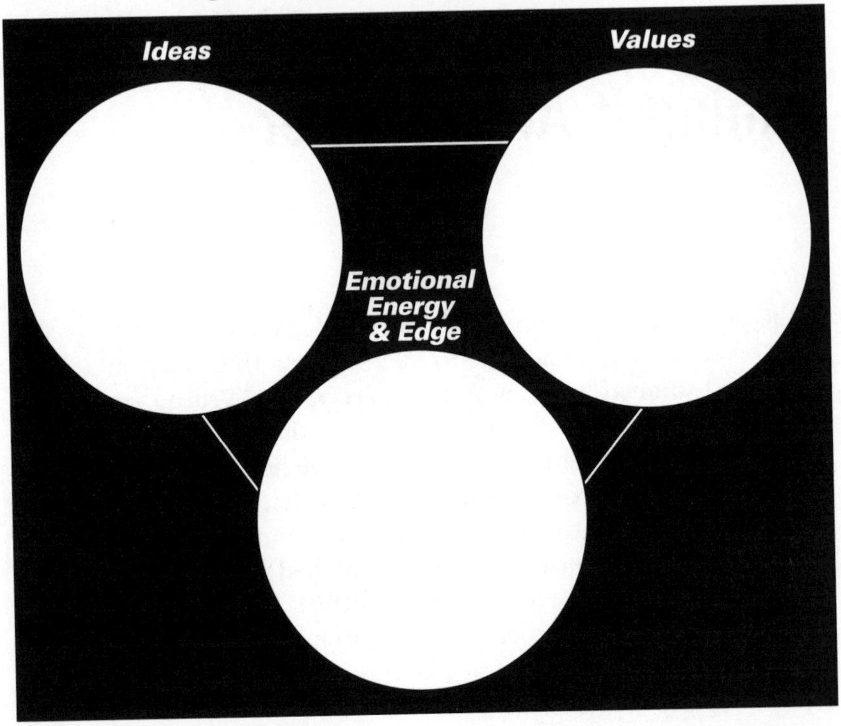

Find someone you can practice with as you try to explain this. Your Teachable Point of View must ultimately be:

Figure 18: Building a Successful Teachable Point of View

- **Clear:**   Easily understood and jargon-free
- **Compelling:**   Believable and exciting
- **Concise:**   Although you can explain it to a level of detail that would take hours, it should take only a few minutes to communicate the essential points
- **Consistent:**   The ideas, values, emotional energy and edge should be interdependent and mutually supportive

Crafting a Story

Having a Teachable Point of View is a necessary starting point for building a Teaching Organization. However, to make the elements of your point of view engaging, it cannot be a dry distillation in bullet point format. You must bring it to life.

In his book *Leading Minds,* Howard Gardner, the noted Harvard psychologist, points out that humans understand the world through dramatic stories. From early ages, children learn from fables and fairy tales because they feature individuals with whom they can identify, and they portray dramas of life that reflect the world around them. As Gardner says, even as people mature, "adults never lose their sensitivity to these basic narratives."

Gardner identifies three storylines that leaders have used successfully throughout history:

- *Who Am I:* Personal stories that explain the history and life experiences that have shaped the leader and his or her point of view.
- *Who Are We:* Stories that demonstrate the joint experiences, attitudes and beliefs of the group that form the basis for a shared point of view.
- *Where Are We Going:* Stories that capture the necessity of change and excitement about the future direction of the group.

Ultimately, leaders who are successful are able to weave the three types of stories together into a tapestry of group identity and ideals. Think of Dr. Martin Luther King, Jr. as one example:

- *Who Am I:* King's stories and letters outlined the prejudice that he had personally faced and the pain of explaining racism to his children, but were balanced by reminders of his personal faith in religion and American ideals.
- *Who Are We:* Unparalleled by his contemporaries, King's message was one of inclusiveness and unity. The "we" in King's stories did not revolve around race; they reminded everyone of their shared identity as Americans by invoking references to history, religion, geography and political symbols, such as the Constitution.
- *Where Are We Going:* King's dream changed history. His message was so compelling and vivid that it came to life for the listener. Yet King spoke of the struggle to come and the steps required to prevail in the fight against injustice.

Putting Together Your Storyline

Winning leaders use all three storylines. Start by reflecting on the life experiences that have shaped you as a leader. Consider the emotional ups and downs that have led to the development of your Teachable Point of View. For example, Myrtle Potter, COO of Genentech, recalls experiencing racism as a youth and the diagnosis of her son with pervasive development disorder as life situations that have made her resilient and fearless. From her son, who was initially expected to be so severely limited that he would be unable to place an order at McDonald's but has gone on to enter mainstream education, Myrtle realized the importance of working to develop people. Consider the personal experiences that created your leadership point of view.

Who Am I story:

_____

_____

_____

_____

_____

_____

_____

Gardner's second story asks you to define what is special about your team, group or organization. As individuals we all have a sense of belonging to the social groups of which we are a part. The strength of that bond often rests on the ability to see and value the uniqueness of the group. For example, Les Wexner, founder and CEO of Limited Brands, has always engaged in community service. He was once reluctant to bring that connection inside his company, but has since seen how people resonate with the idea of doing good in the community. It creates a special identity for employees of the company.

Who Are We story:

_____

_____

_____

_____

_____

_____

_____

Gardner's last story, however, may be the most important in try-ing to change a business organization. Leaders who are respected and engender a sense of team will still fail if they cannot create a vision of the future so compelling that people will sign up. Gardner's "Where Are We Going" story has three components:

- Case for change: Why does the team or organization need to change?
- Where are we going: What is your picture for the organiza-tion in the future?
- How will we get there: What steps will you take and will every other person in the organization have to take to achieve the vision, and why should people have confidence it can be done?

Where Are We Going story:

_____

_____

_____

_____

_____

_____

_____

_____

_____

_____

_____

_____

_____

_____

_____

_____

_____

_____

_____

_____

_____

_____

Section Five
Building a Team Teachable Point of View

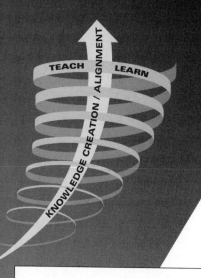

Building a Teaching Organization is a Radical Act
- *The top team must be unified and enthusiastic role models for change.*
- *The top leader must work to build that unity and enthusiasm.*

Moving Along the Power Continuum
- *Leaders must be willing to command participation while hearing others.*
- *Effective use of power requires a constant cycling through different roles.*

In this section you will

▮ Identify effective and ineffective ways to exercise power.

▮ Design a workshop for your team to develop a collective Teachable Point of View.

Section Five
Building a Team Teachable Point of View

After Noel wrote his last book, *The Leadership Engine,* he realized that he missed an essential element of Teaching Organizations. Noel knew at the time that leaders must be teachers and that a Teachable Point of View was a requirement for organizations to succeed. What he failed to recognize was the importance of interactivity in developing and constantly refining an organization's Teachable Point of View. Eckhard Pfeiffer, former CEO of Compaq, was a teacher with a point of view. Unfortunately, Pfeiffer did not listen to his people and instead set about directing them.

The Teachable Point of View, because it is a work that is never finished, must be open for constant dialogue. This does not mean that every point is negotiable. At some point the leadership team must select a course and stick to it. However, the senior leaders must always be willing to teach those who are earnestly trying to understand the rationale behind the Teachable Point of View. In doing so, they open themselves up to dialogue that can change their perspective. As Section I explained, this dialogue process created fundamental change at General Electric and Yum! Brands.

By contrast, there are some people who will argue with you not because they do not understand your Teachable Point of View, but because they do not like it. These people need to be brought aboard or removed. Part of the art of leadership is understanding when people are sincere and when they are just resisting, and how to deal with both.

This process must start with the top team getting aligned around a Teachable Point of View for the organization. What is surprising is the amount of effort it takes to get senior teams together. It is as important as it is difficult. A leader who fails to do so can never build a Teaching Organization.

Creating the right conditions for the team to come together and create a Teachable Point of View that is then reflected in the behavior and actions of the team members takes the effective use of power. This is tricky. First, the CEO or hierarchical leader may be uncomfortable using power. Second, the other team members may resent the leader's mandate to go off-site and attend a meeting. This is increasingly true the closer to the top of the hierarchy you get. By definition, the top team includes the biggest power players in the organization. These are the people who are most used to running their own show and have the most turf to protect. Some even fear that clarity around the organization's direction will entail a political loss for them personally.

It inevitably takes the direct order of the leader to get the team to focus on the Teachable Point of View. This paradoxical use of power—issuing orders so people will voluntarily open up and hold a dialogue with the group—is a necessary prerequisite for building a Virtuous Teaching Cycle. However, it must be handled with care. If the leader is too autocratic and dictates by fiat, the team members may never engage. By contrast, if the leader waits for consensus, it will never emerge. The leader must use a repertoire of means to exercise power so that the entire team is committed and excited.

In some ways, we would liken this to coalition building among countries during times of crisis. Just looking at recent U.S. wartime history, the intention to go to war in Iraq and Afghanistan was clearly stated before the coalition of allies and partners had been cemented. The United States never would have achieved consensus that war was necessary. However, once its resolve was known, the United States used a variety of tools with allies and partners to skillfully build a coalition, particularly during the Gulf War.

Business leaders obviously operate on a smaller scale with far less at stake. Nonetheless, they must not blink. And they must work at maintaining power within their team on a daily basis. The notion that a "balance" of power is ideal or can even be achieved is misleading. Power relationships are built on a fluid give-and-take that must be cultivated carefully.

Sociologist Amitai Etzioni has a helpful framework for looking at the source of a leader's power and the consequences of using that power on others. According to Etzioni, there are three fundamental sources of power:

- *Coercive:* One party demands something of another based on the direct threat of punitive action; this generates little psychological commitment from members.
- *Utilitarian:* An agreement to exchange one thing for another; this generates more commitment than coercion but does not usually change values.
- *Normative:* A common commitment to a set of internalized values binds the parties together; appeal to these values generates the desired behavior.

The ultimate exercise of power is firing someone. If the leader is not perceived to be willing to use this, he or she has lost an enormous source of power. At Home Depot, Bob Nardelli has had to change several team members. The same is true of Dick Brown at EDS and Jim McNerney at 3M. However, an autocratic bully who rests on this power base will soon send the people in the organization who are truly team oriented running for the door. Likewise, the degree to which utilitarian and normative power can be used will vary depending upon the individual and the circumstance. At various times, leaders must use all of these.

As mentioned above, using power starts with you, as the leader. People have varying comfort levels using power. Use the space below to reflect on times when you have used the different power modes successfully and unsuccessfully:

Coercive Power	
Time I used this successfully:	Time I used this unsuccessfully:
Lessons learned about using Coercive Power:	

Utilitarian Power	
Time I used this successfully:	Time I used this unsuccessfully:
Lessons learned about using Utilitarian Power:	

Normative Power	
Time I used this successfully:	Time I used this unsuccessfully:
Lessons learned about using Normative Power:	

Kick Starting the Team

As a first step, you need to design the process for developing the Teachable Point of View for your organization. You must consider who should be involved and how you will get them committed. Use the space below to identify a specific person and the actions you can take to convince him or her that this is in the best interest. Think through how you might use each of Etzioni's power types. Remember, you will need different approaches for different people and a contingency plan if one approach does not work as expected with a team member.

Getting Commitment to a Team TPOV

Team member	Potential issues or concerns	How I can use coercive power	How I can use utilitarian power	How I can use normative power
1.				
2.				
3.				
4.				
5.				

Once you have built each team member's commitment to work on a Teachable Point of View for your organization, you must carefully architect the event where this occurs. As the leader organizing the team, you must have your TPOV developed. However, you should not share this in advance or overpower the dialogue during the event. You must give the team a process for working through the elements of the Teachable Point of View. Most often, this will mean sharing your views after others have spoken and providing input to the dialogue as a team member, not the hierarchical leader. Your primary role will be to inject energy to keep the process engaging and open. At times, particularly where there are "boundary issues" that you do not want to open for discussion, you must make your point of view known and understood. Jeff Immelt, the current CEO of GE, captured this paradox best: "I make every decision. I get lots of advice, but I don't delegate. I ask, 'What do you think' from everyone. Then, boom—I decide."

Designing the Event

As you design the process, there are a number of issues to carefully consider. We recommend that the event be held off-site and include an overnight stay. Getting off-site takes people away from the day-to-day transactional business and helps ensure they are focused for the entire event. Coupling the event with an evening, ideally before the first workday, provides an opportunity for people to have dinner together and engage in some social mixing. If staged correctly, this will help create a sense of team and informality before the session begins.

Section VIII will talk about operating mechanisms, but the checklist that we use for operating mechanisms applies equally to your handling of this meeting. First, what preparation do you want to have people do before the session? Is there data collection required that will help decision making or reading that will help to stimulate thinking? Then consider how you will run the session face-to-face. Finally, the implementation occurs after the event. During the session, you must make clear how you will capture commitments and follow-up to ensure execution happens.

Figure 19: VTC Checklist

	Emotional	**Physical**
Preparation	▪ Who should be responsible for putting an issue on the agenda?	▪ Where should the preparation be conducted?
	▪ Who does what with whom during the preparation?	▪ Will people be able to communicate using an effective infrastructure?
	▪ How long should the preparation take?	▪ Will the preparation involve travel that affects the decision-making time frame?
	▪ Who should be consulted or informed during the preparation?	
	▪ Who decides when the preparation has finished and how is this decision communicated?	
Face-to-Face	▪ Who should meet to make the decision?	▪ Where should the meeting take place?
	▪ What are the bases for decision making?	▪ Does the meeting length require breaks or meals?

Figure 19: VTC Checklist (continued)

	Emotional	**Physical**
Face-to-Face *(continued)*	▪ How candid is the discussion around the decision?	▪ Who sits where to promote networking and interaction?
	▪ How is conflict handled?	
	▪ To whom and how is the decision communicated?	
Follow-Up	▪ Who defines the follow-up plan?	▪ Where does the follow-up take place?
	▪ Who is responsible for assessing the success of the decision?	▪ Is the follow-up assessment part of normal responsibilities, or an after-hours assignment?
	▪ Who does what with whom?	▪ Does the follow-up involve travel or another meeting?

As you plan the agenda for the session, we also recommend that you follow the steps provided in the checklist below:

Figure 20: Principles for VTC Team Workshop

Understanding these principles helps the leader get the input of the team and helps the team collectively reach a jointly-owned TPOV.

Step 1: Concepts
Frame the issues for the team. Give them the conceptual framework for how to think about business ideas, values, emotional energy and edge.

Step 2: Benchmark
Share benchmark examples of other leaders. Elicit benchmarks from the team as well.

Step 3: Individual written work
Have the team members think and commit their thoughts in writing before opening the dialogue. This maximizes diversity of ideas.

Step 4: Group sharing and debate
The leader runs a very open dialogue, which gets out the diverse individual written work as well as generates new thoughts.

Step 5: Final decisions on TPOV
This is where the leader exercises power to bring closure. Participation and input must result in closure. It is up to the leader to make the summary of what gets decided, hopefully with as much consensus as possible, but the call ultimately is the leader's.

Use the space below to plan the activities for your TPOV workshop:

	Day One	Day Two
Morning		
Afternoon		
Evening		

Creating the conditions necessary for the team to unite behind a Teachable Point of View is necessary to build a Virtuous Teaching Cycle. It is the leader's responsibility to make this happen.

Section Six
Architecting the Leadership Pipeline

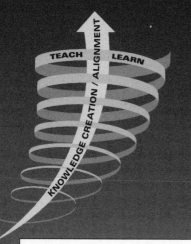

A Special Need: Grooming Leaders for the Senior Team
- *Most companies wait until it is way too late to find a CEO successor.*
- *Winners don't find successors — they create them.*

The Leadership Pipeline Should Run From the Entry Level to the CEO's Office
- *The apprentice method isn't efficient.*
- *Leaders must be systematically taught.*

Design Principles: Develop a Core Curriculum
- *Create developmental goals for every level.*
- *Use all available teaching tools — on the job, off the job, stretch assignments.*

In this section you will

■ Evaluate your organization's leadership pipeline.
■ Define the leadership capabilities required of leaders at different career stages.
■ Identify changes to your leadership pipeline so the right people are developed, the right way.

Section Six
Architecting the Leadership Pipeline

Leaders create a Teaching Organization in order to develop more leaders. They do so because they recognize that organizations that win in the market have more leaders at more levels than their competitors. These leaders and their organizations are better equipped to understand their customers' needs and fulfill them quickly and efficiently. In order to sustain their success, leaders at all levels actively teach others.

The Virtuous Teaching Cycle, by its very nature, helps to develop leaders. It creates the conditions for leaders to discuss, debate and revise their Teachable Point of View. In order to sustain leadership development, therefore, it must be built into every development opportunity. Teaching is the underpinning not only for development programs, but also for daily coaching and feedback on work assignments.

It is the CEO's responsibility to architect a leadership development pipeline for the organization. One of the biggest failings of any institution is the failure to develop leadership bench strength. Regardless of the results that any individual produces, she or he must develop someone who can sustain the organization's performance after they are gone.

Creating the leadership development pipeline takes time, discipline and foresight. Les Wexner, founder and CEO of Limited Brands, learned this the hard way. Wexner is one of the most talented entrepreneurs in recent history. From a single store in Ohio, he built a global corporation with nearly $10 billion in revenue, including premier brands such as Victoria's Secret and Bath & Body Works. But Wexner didn't fully understand the difficulty of people development until he sat down with his HR vice president one day and realized the company didn't have a list of future leaders, and no idea how to develop them. From that point on, with the help of COO Len Schlesinger, he made it a priority and built a teaching infrastructure to support it. Today, Limited Brands has been referred to as one of the most talent-rich companies in retail.

While at GE, Noel worked with Jack Welch and several colleagues to develop the leadership pipeline in the mid-1980s. In subsequent years, the content and processes have evolved, but the underlying framework continues to cover the principles required to architect a pipeline. GE's results have been impressive. It is frequently cited as an "academy" company because so many of its alumni go on to CEO or senior leadership posts at other companies. Welch had more than seven viable contenders for his job. Contrast that with the dozens of businesses that have had to hire CEOs from outside their company in recent years. GE's capability at people development was no accident. Welch started to plan for his succession virtually from the day he started, and he put the resources into creating a pipeline to develop a CEO for the future, not a mirror image of the past. He understood that architecting the pipeline was the ultimate responsibility of the CEO, not of HR or any other staff member.

The questionnaire below will help you assess how good your leadership pipeline is and how effective it is at developing Leader/Teachers:

Leadership Pipeline Audit

Leader identification

	Score				
	Not at all				Definitely
1. There are at least three viable contenders for each senior position on the team.	1	2	3	4	5
2. Our leadership pipeline screens leaders for their Teachable Point of View.	1	2	3	4	5
3. The leaders who are contenders to move up have demonstrated that they can develop other leaders behind them by creating Virtuous Teaching Cycles.	1	2	3	4	5

Pipeline architecture

4. Deliberate development opportunities are created at each career stage.	1	2	3	4	5
5. We have identified competencies and values required of future leaders, not those of the past.	1	2	3	4	5
6. There is deliberate effort to ensure that leaders have a broad base of experience to understand the business (across geography, business unit, P&L capability, etc.).	1	2	3	4	5

Even if you are not the CEO of your organization, you have a dramatic impact on the leadership development of the people who work with you. Changing the company's leadership pipeline may be beyond your control, but you can certainly influence the development of those on your team. The first step is to consider which capabilities are required of Leader/Teachers in your organization at different career stages. This process usually starts by looking at the organization of the present. For each existing career position, you can examine the competencies and capabilities that are needed. The critical step is to look where the organization is going and determine how the capabilities will change at each stage and how the career ladder itself may change.

At GE, although Welch looked at the existing organization, he asked Noel and his colleagues to take a clean sheet of paper to identify what they thought would be needed in the future. This created the basis for heated debates with Welch and other senior leaders because they were trying to predict the future bases for GE's competitiveness, what the organizational and job structure would look like, and the future capabilities that would be required of leaders at every level. They did not get the answers completely right, but the dialogue process forced everyone at GE to have a Teachable Point of View so that the company could adapt as the world changed.

Figure 21 shows the position assignments and capabilities that they thought would be relevant:

Figure 21: GE's Leader/Teacher Pipeline

	Interpersonal skills	Functional/ Product skills	Organizational skills
Individual contributor	• Build effective communication and relationship skills. • Effectively deal with personal strengths and weaknesses.	• Develop specific functional skills. • Learn roles and relationships within the functional/ product unit. • Develop work planning, programming and performance assessment skills.	• Synthesize personal values with organizational value system. • Understand how his/her function and business relates to the entire company. • Grasp role of the company in the global marketplace. • Learn about customers and suppliers.

(continued on next page)

Figure 21: GE's Leader/Teacher Pipeline (continued)

	Interpersonal skills	Functional/ Product skills	Organizational skills
New manager	<ul><li>Learn to delegate work and get things done through other people.</li><li>Learn to effectively appraise the performance of subordinates and secure their improved performance.</li><li>Acquire and effectively apply team-building skills.</li><li>Learn to share insights and values with others so that effect is multiplied.</li></ul>	<ul><li>Acquire basic managerial skills, such as budgeting or program planning.</li></ul>	<ul><li>Reconcile personal values with company's shared values.</li><li>Learn to integrate work of unit with related units.</li></ul>
Experienced manager	<ul><li>Develop negotiation skills and effectiveness in dealing with conflict situations.</li><li>Gain executive communication skills required for broad-scale communications.</li><li>Increase ability to deal with ambiguity, paradox and situations where there is not a single "right" answer.</li></ul>	<ul><li>Gain deep, well-rounded understanding of all related functional skills in area of prime assignment.</li></ul>	<ul><li>Develop strategic thinking skills and the capacity to use both inductive and deductive problem solving.</li><li>Learn how to effectively implement organizational change.</li><li>Understand the difference between what is best for the customer and what is easiest for the business.</li><li>Maximize understanding of global business dynamics and interfunctional relationships.</li></ul>
General manager	<ul><li>Gain capacity to deal concurrently with multiple issues of increasing complexity and ambiguity.</li><li>Develop a recognition that she/he cannot and should not try to solve all problems personally.</li></ul>		<ul><li>Refine broad perspective that extends to the well being of the entire organization.</li><li>Sharpen analytical and critical thinking skills for organizational problem solving.</li></ul>

Figure 21: GE's Leader/Teacher Pipeline (continued)

	Interpersonal skills	Functional/ Product skills	Organizational skills
General manager *(continued)*	▪ Build skill in framing problems for others to solve. ▪ Understand how to maximize contributions of individual, team and staff. ▪ Develop a recognition that asking for help is a sign of maturity rather than weakness. ▪ Develop the sensitivity to respond to the needs of others based on limited stimulus or cues.		▪ Play an active role in the development of the vision for his/her business.
Business leader	▪ Learn to effectively exercise power in making those decisions that only the leader can make. ▪ Develop projection and extrapolation skills to deal with situations where she/he has no first-hand knowledge. ▪ Develop sensitivity to the forces that motivate people to behave as they do.		▪ Develop multi-functional integration skills to manage a business based on profit-and-loss basis. ▪ Develop and effectively articulate the vision for the business. ▪ Develop the capacity to conceive, not just adopt, change. ▪ Develop an effective understanding of the dynamics of the industry. ▪ Develop a balanced posture between leadership of the business and integration/cooperation among the functions or other business in the company. ▪ Develop the capacity to effectively manage community relations.

As a first step, use the table below to identify the existing position assignments and capabilities in your organization:

Position Assignment	Current Capabilities Required
1.	
2.	
3.	
4.	
5.	

Next, based on your Teachable Point of View, think about how the organization will change over the next five to ten years. (Pick a time frame that suits the pace of change in your industry and the pace of needed succession in your organization.) Identify the new positions and capabilities that will be required.

New Position Assignments	New Capabilities Required
1.	
2.	
3.	
4.	
5.	

Once you have forecast future needs, you must consider how you will develop leaders with these capabilities. Remember the following design principles as you do:

- *80/20 Rule:* More than 80% of development comes from on-the-job experience.
- *Teachable Moments:* Transition periods, such as when a new employee joins or when a person moves from one job to another, offer times when people are most open to learning.
- *TPOV Development:* Specific opportunities must be created to help leaders at every level develop their Teachable Point of View. These may include work assignments, enrichment opportunities (such as work on a task force or short-term role change), perspective broadening opportunities (such as international transfers or participation in cross-functional groups), formalized and informal coaching assignments, and educational development programs offered by the company or an outside university.

Use the following table to consider the types of experiences you will create at each level to help leaders develop their Teachable Point of View and build broader leadership bench strength in your company:

Developing Leaders with a TPOV

Position assignment	Ways to develop ideas	Ways to develop values	Ways to develop emotional energy	Ways to develop edge
1.				
2.				
3.				
4.				
5.				

As mentioned above, your answers may be directionally correct but there is no way to accurately forecast the future. That is why the final step of architecture development is ensuring that you have operating mechanisms for reviewing this with others on the team at regular intervals. You must continuously assess how well the pipeline you built is developing leaders. The evaluation of your pipeline is easy. Just ask if it is producing:

- *Leaders at all levels* in both the quantitative and qualitative sense. Are there slates of candidates to fill leadership positions at all hierarchical levels? Are the leaders as good as or better than the people they will replace?
- *Leaders with a Teachable Point of View* who use it to guide how they will create value for the organization. Can people explain it clearly and persuasively? Is it linked to their daily roles? Do they see how they contribute to the organization's success on a daily basis?
- *Leaders who develop other leaders.* Is the Virtuous Teaching Cycle taking hold so that everyone sees leadership development as his or her primary role?

Take some time to consider what actions you will take to ensure that the right people are reviewing the leadership development pipeline and changing it as needed:

_____

_____

_____

_____

_____

_____

_____

Section Seven
Scaling the Teaching Organization

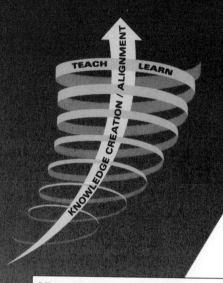

Virtuous Teaching Cycles Must Reach Throughout the Organization
- *Leadership pipelines are for the top leaders of the future.*
- *Cascades are for everyone.*

You can't have only half the team playing
- *Teaching and learning behaviors must be organizational values.*
- *You must move quickly to build energy and trust.*

In this section you will

■ Define the best approach for large-scale teaching, development and alignment.
■ Apply best practices to improve the speed, scale and effectiveness of your teaching.

Section Seven
Scaling the Teaching Organization

Architecting the leadership pipeline, as you just did, is necessary to build a Teaching Organization. However, the pipeline focuses on developing and filtering people for the narrowing stream that will ultimately fill the future CEO position. Teaching Organizations must also encourage dialogue on the Teachable Point of View throughout the entire organization on a regular and systematic basis. Building a Teaching Organization requires routinely engaging with people and finding ways to reach every single employee. In short, it takes a methodology to reach scale quickly and efficiently.

Just think about the leadership challenges that companies like Wal-Mart, Home Depot, Yum! Brands and General Electric face. They have literally hundreds of thousands of people who must act in alignment to serve customers and execute their organization's strategy. Other organizations may not have the same number of people, but they are equally challenged to drive dialogue and alignment throughout the ranks.

When we discuss this with executives, the importance is usually obvious to them. Amazingly, though, as we discuss how they approach building alignment in their companies, nearly all of them lack effective mechanisms. Most focus on pushing one-way messages down the chain of command. Worse still, the messages being pushed are usually the fad of the moment that employees know they must endure in the short-term, but can ultimately ignore as the organization's leadership turns its attention elsewhere.

Companies that are serious about building alignment do not expect to create Virtuous Teaching Cycles by launching half-hearted initiatives. They use carefully designed processes to engage tens or hundreds of thousands of people and to encourage teaching, coaching and open discussion.

Myrtle Potter, the Chief Operating Officer and head of Commercial Operations for Genentech, a twenty-six-year-old biotechnology firm, launched a process in March 2002 to help align the organization around a historical shift in strategy and business values. As a first step, Myrtle and her three-person leadership team spent two days off-site developing an integrated TPOV. Following further work and teaching preparation, Myrtle and her team spent three days personally teaching the top fifty-four leaders in their organization. In her opening remarks, Myrtle set the expectation that the fifty-four would teach everyone in Genentech's Commercial Operations, stating that "everyone needs to have a Teachable Point of View and it's our job as leaders to teach, listen and learn from the organization." Leadership from Myrtle and her team set the tone for their entire organization. More important, they spent three full days teaching, dialoguing, learning and preparing others to teach by giving them structured practice opportunities.

The first step in this process is identifying leverage points for driving teaching at scale. As leaders prepare to scale teaching throughout their organizations, there are two approaches:

1. *Vertical*. Use the chain of command to teach people at a specific organizational level and then expect them to cascade teaching through their chain of command. This can be very effective. Unfortunately, many companies think this means giving a group of executives in a huge auditorium a PowerPoint presentation to regurgitate. We once watched an executive go through forty-six slides in forty-two minutes in one such session. The audience members' eyes had glazed over within the first ten minutes and there was not a single question. This obviously is not teaching. Using the vertical approach means sharing the organizational Teachable Point of View with a select group of leaders, giving them a robust process for teaching their people, training them to teach, and expecting them to engage in dialogue and hands-on teaching. In most large organizations, teaching usually starts with the group of 50 to 100 leaders immediately beneath the senior team.

2. *Horizontal*. Use a specially trained group, much like a SWAT team, to cascade teaching throughout the organization. The difficulty we usually see with this approach is that staff people

who command little respect and do not know the business are expected to tell other people how to run their day-to-day activities. Using horizontal teaching effectively means training the SWAT team not only in technical areas but also in process skills so that they can help people throughout the business apply the Teachable Point of View to their area. Dell did this effectively when it used a group from its Treasury Operations to teach return-on-invested-capital to thousands of people. Royal Dutch/Shell created a special team, known as the Leadership and Performance group, staffed almost entirely of high-potential line leaders that helped disseminate large-scale change efforts.

Figure 22: Two Approaches to Teaching at Scale

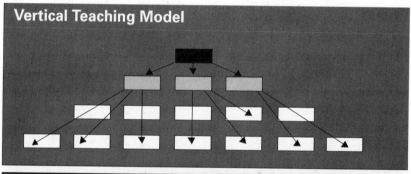

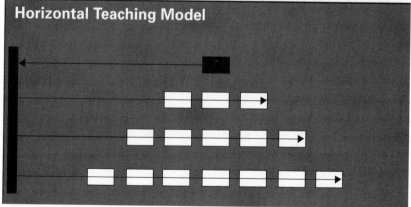

People often ask if their company really needs to reach everyone immediately, or if it is acceptable to start in one part of the organization and let the VTC grow from there. What they are really saying is that they do not have a Teaching Organization and are trying to build support for one. It is possible to create a small-scale Virtuous Teaching Cycle in one part of your business, and the results may be persuasive in convincing others to embrace teaching. However, if the CEO and senior team are ultimately not supportive, the business will never truly be a Teaching Organization.

The other question we often hear is which model is preferable, vertical or horizontal. The answer is that both are required to truly achieve scale. GE uses a number of vertical methods, starting with working through the Teachable Point of View at their annual officers' meeting in January. The officers are then expected to teach all the people in their business. GE also uses horizontal methods, such as Crotonville programs and Six Sigma black belts, who are charged with teaching everyone about the Six Sigma methodology. The starting point you choose will depend upon many factors—the CEO's commitment, alignment at the top team level, the organizational structure, the diversity of businesses, the total number of people in your company. But you must create both types of mechanisms to reach the destination of a Teaching Organization.

Answer the questions below to think about how you will achieve teaching scale in your business:

1. The total number of people in my organization: _____

2. Which vertical level in our company has the most leverage for teaching people (e.g., group below senior team, group in the middle of our organization, etc.)?

_____

_____

_____

_____

3. Which horizontal teams are well respected and capable of teaching everyone in our business?

_____

_____

_____

_____

4. If we were going to create a horizontal teaching team, who should be on the team and why?

_____

_____

_____

_____

Once you have identified the leverage points to scale teaching in your organization, you must design your teaching mechanisms. The chart below shows the core design principles for scaling teaching and some examples of how they have successfully worked at two benchmark companies, General Electric and Royal Dutch/Shell.

Figure 23: Principles for Teaching at Scale

Principle	Example	How the company applied the principle
1. Mandate speed and scale: Companies that are serious about teaching make it a priority. Left to their own devices, managers will defer teaching to focus on fire-fighting instead of building long-term capability. It takes the CEO or another leader to mandate what people must accomplish in a short, three-to-six month time frame.	▪ GE's Work-Out process: GE reached every employee, worldwide, in a process designed to eliminate low value-add work and bureaucracy.	▪ One-third of the business leaders told Welch that he was micro-managing. His response was that the business leaders had control of their strategy, pricing, organization and nearly every other lever. Driving alignment and self-confidence into the workforce was too important to be laissez-faire.
	▪ Royal Dutch/Shell Focused Results Delivery: Royal Dutch/Shell used the Teachable Point of View to align everyone throughout a country operating unit in approximately 120 days.	▪ A country or business unit employing FRD started with a kick-off workshop led by the senior team. After 100–120 days, teams would gather to discuss how they had driven the Teachable Point of View into the organization's systems, processes and daily behaviors.

(continued on next page)

Figure 23: Principles for Teaching at Scale (continued)

Principle	Example	How the company applied the principle
2. Line leaders teach and drive the process: Having an open dialogue around a company's TPOV requires the leader to be present and engaged. This cannot be delegated to consultants or staff.	▪ GE's Work-Out process: Welch mandated that each business unit leader spend twenty-four days a year in Work-Out sessions.	▪ Many of the business unit leaders initially rebelled against this level of time commitment. However, Welch tracked and enforced it and the leaders ultimately became Work-Out's biggest supporters.
	▪ Royal Dutch/Shell Focused Results Delivery: Royal Dutch/Shell committed to launch Focused Results in a country or business unit only if the leadership team agreed to an initial off-site and then full-time participation in follow-up workshops.	▪ Country leaders were used to acting autonomously in Royal Dutch/Shell and many would make half-hearted commitments. The group running FRD for Royal Dutch/Shell's chairman ultimately developed the confidence to cancel workshops when they did not see visible and enthusiastic support from the line leaders.
3. Teach and role model teaching: Companies that want line leaders to teach need to help prepare them for this.	▪ GE's Change Acceleration Process: The follow-up phase to Work-Out was the implementation of CAP. All consultants were taken out and line leaders were taught the process and facilitation skills that were part of Work-Out.	▪ CAP took the skills and tools of Work-Out and embedded them internally in GE leaders at all levels. This ensured that the mind-set and approach of Work-Out was not episodic; it became part of each leader's everyday approach.
	▪ Royal Dutch/Shell Focused Results Delivery: The initial workshop for a business unit or country leadership team helped them pull together their Teachable Point of View.	▪ The line leaders were first given a methodology to develop their Teachable Point of View and then were given active teaching roles so that they could work with their people in a follow-up workshop.

Figure 23: Principles for Teaching at Scale (continued)

Principle	Example	How the company applied the principle
4. Real business issues are coupled with soft value issues: The processes should reinforce all aspects of the Teachable Point of View. The key business issues should be tied to living the values and making edge calls. The process itself should be energizing.	• General Electric: All GE processes, from Work-Out to CAP to Six Sigma, combine real work with new ways of working. • Royal Dutch/Shell Focused Results Delivery: Teams from within the business unit or country operations identify business projects for implementation that will also help them exhibit the organization's values.	• The GE processes focus people to work in new ways: demonstrating speed, simplicity and self-confidence in the case of Work-Out or living boundary-lessness as Six Sigma black belts fix broken cross-functional processes. • The Royal Dutch/Shell values are operationalized at the country or business unit level. As teams work on the business issues required to implement their organization's business theory, they put the values into daily practice. How they perform against the values is assessed at a follow-up workshop.
5. Start with the chain of command before moving cross-functionally: Many of the biggest alignment challenges in organizations are found in cross-divisional, cross-geography or cross-functional areas. However, starting in these areas does not lead to quick wins and may encourage people to be critical of others before attending to their own issues.	• GE's progression from Work-Out to Six Sigma: GE started functionally with Work-Out and built into cross-functional efforts over time. • Royal Dutch/Shell Focused Results Delivery: The process started within the country (business unit), not at the corporate level.	• In the early days of Work-Out, attempts to tackle cross-functional issues usually led to political infighting. Once GE had spread boundaryless behavior, it was easier to address cross-function efforts through Six Sigma and CAP. • Business unit or country leaders could tackle cross-functional issues within their span of control, but were discouraged from trying to change corporate policy until they had demonstrated results within their own unit.

(continued on next page)

Figure 23: Principles for Teaching at Scale (continued)

Principle	Example	How the company applied the principle
6. Focus on building a VTC: Companies that embrace teaching do not think of it as one-way "communication." They focus on getting feedback and learning from people as they engage all parts of the business.	• GE Work-Out: The participants in the process tell their boss what is broken.	• The hierarchical boss is confronted with activities that do not add value. This forces him or her to think through the activities, teach people if there is lack of understanding, and learn how the organization is really functioning versus theory.
	• Royal Dutch/Shell Focused Results Delivery: The teams working within the business unit and country teams were responsible for proposals on everything from organizational design to process improvement.	• Everything from identification of billions of dollars worth of oil reserves in Bahrain to the organizational structure of New Zealand have been determined through recommendations from front-line teams.

Consider how to apply these principles as you design your own mechanisms for driving large-scale teaching in your organization. Use the chart below to think through each principle:

Principle	How I will apply the principle to create a Teaching Organization
1. Mandate speed and scale	
2. Line leaders teach and drive the process	
3. Teach and role-model teaching	
4. Real business issues are coupled with soft-value issues	
5. Start with the chain of command before moving cross-functionally	
6. Focus on building a VTC	

Section Eight
Building Teaching Into the DNA

TEACH LEARN

KNOWLEDGE CREATION / ALIGNMENT

Operating Mechanisms Are the Routine Processes for Running the Company
- *Because they are recurring, at many companies they become rote.*
- *Because they are recurring, they are great opportunities for teaching.*

The Big Three Are Succession, Strategy and Operations
- *Old style, they are bureaucratic and adversarial.*
- *As Virtuous Teaching Cycles, they promote collaboration and innovation.*

The Leader Must Take the Role of Social Architect
- *Who participates in each process is a critical element.*
- *Activity flow and social interaction are also key design features.*

In this section you will

▮ Understand why your organization's core processes may be killing energy and ideas.

▮ Build operating mechanisms that let everyone contribute through Virtuous Teaching Cycles.

▮ Develop an integrated operating system for running your business.

Section Eight
Building Teaching Into the DNA

Prioritizing teaching as a leader's role and a company's primary way to create knowledge starts as a philosophical commitment. Turning this into reality requires leaders to carefully architect teaching into all of their routines and processes. Every company has operating mechanisms that cover everything from getting the doors unlocked in the morning to setting corporate strategy. A leader's responsibility is to design these operating mechanisms so that they promote teaching and knowledge generation to the greatest possible extent.

By definition, operating mechanisms are repetitive. In many organizations, they become rote processes that are followed because they represent how the company has always done business. They are the social equivalent of legacy systems. Like any system, however, they must be constantly reassessed and improved in order to create a Virtuous Teaching Cycle.

Operating mechanisms create Virtuous Teaching Cycles when they reflect the organization's Teachable Point of View and provide the opportunity for interactivity. The key differences between rigid, bureaucratic processes and successful operating mechanisms are summarized on the following page.

Companies can create operating mechanisms for many purposes. Wal-Mart, for example, holds a videoconference every Saturday that involves thousands of store managers. Wal-Mart's senior management uses it as a platform to share best practices across stores and ensure that everyone understands what is selling and how the competition is trying to attack Wal-Mart. This is a process that gives the company the speed and consistency required to execute its business strategy.

Likewise, Home Depot has a heritage of store walks. Every senior manager, and even board members, is expected to walk store floors

Figure 24: World-Class Operating Mechanisms

Rigid, Bureaucratic Processes	Successful Operating Mechanisms
Processes are inherited	Leaders create processes to drive the Teachable Point of View
Processes never change	Leaders actively design and experiment
Events drive show-and-tell presentations	Teaching and interactivity are designed into processes
Emotional Energy is drained from people	Processes create new energy
Boss' job is to criticize, others passive	Everyone contributes
Most work is done outside or around processes	Processes leveraged to drive ideas and energy
Goal is to "get through it"	Changes expected and desired
No opportunity for leadership development	Processes designed to create teachable moments

and interact with customers and employees. Most don the signature Home Depot orange apron like any other sales associate. During the course of these interactions, they learn what is selling and what issues the stores are having, and they coach people to make their processes more effective.

Although companies have a diverse set of operating mechanisms, every organization needs to have at least three processes at their core. First, they must have a process for setting and driving strategy. Next, they must have a clear means for allocating resources and making budgeting decisions. Finally, they must facilitate succession planning.

Over the twenty years that Jack Welch ran GE, he re-architected the operating mechanisms to reflect GE's changing values and to scale the ideas and best practices that made GE win in the market. The essence of the GE system is the degree to which the individual operating mechanisms build upon one another. The teachings and learning in one feed into and shape the next. The diagram on the next page, taken from GE's 1999 Annual Report, shows how this system works.

This diagram essentially reflects the GE corporate calendar. Unlike most corporations, GE's processes are interwoven. The diagram's flow is best understood by starting at September. This is when the heads of all GE businesses meet to assess the results of the prior year, reformulate their TPOV, and set priorities for next year. Best practices are shared, external role models identified, and initiatives evaluated for customer impact. Based on this honest, customer-facing assessment, the officers come together again in October to begin determining operating plans and budgets for the following year. By January, when the top 600 GE leaders come together in Boca Raton, the key corporate initiatives have been defined so that they can be energized. Execution begins in the first quarter as the top 600 GE leaders teach and cascade to all 300,000 GE employees. In April, the CEO's on-line survey asks employees to assess GE's progress and provide their improvement ideas.

May is the month that GE provides performance feedback and differentiates employees by allocating rewards, promotions and removing some from the business. It is not just a mechanical process of checking boxes and filling out forms. It is designed to be an on-going Virtuous Teaching Cycle, one in which leaders of each business and the CEO intensively review the top 500 positions and the slate of candidates for each. This results in a review of several thousand people, with rigorous debate and learning.

June to September is the window for resetting strategy. Every year in July, all GE businesses look at their three-year strategy and make updates based on current economic and competitive projections. The corporate initiatives, which are few and generally long-term, such as Work-out or Globalization or Six Sigma quality, are also evaluated for customer impact so best practices can be shared. There is also a videoconference in July with the CEO, head of HR, and heads of each business to discuss implementation of succession planning decisions made during May.

In September, the business leaders meet at Crotonville to assess the results of the prior year, update their TPOV, and kick off the process again. GE's process is intense and disciplined, but it is not bureaucratic. The processes build on and reinforce GE's core values of informality, speed, simplicity and self-confidence. They also integrate and reinforce key corporate initiatives. For example, in 1998, Six Sigma was a top priority. Consequently, succession planning had

Figure 25: GE's Operating System

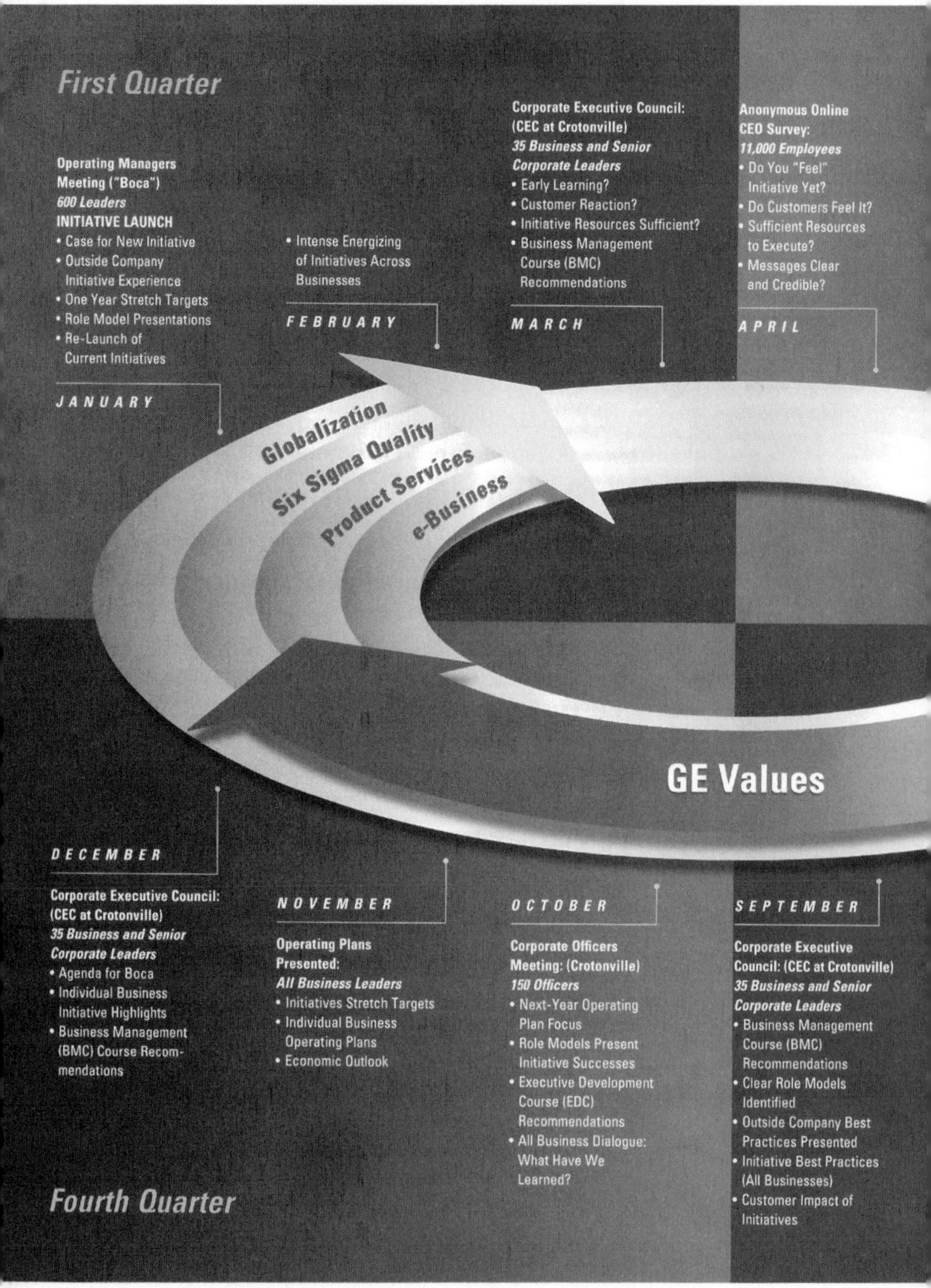

First Quarter

Operating Managers Meeting ("Boca")
600 Leaders
INITIATIVE LAUNCH
• Case for New Initiative
• Outside Company Initiative Experience
• One Year Stretch Targets
• Role Model Presentations
• Re-Launch of Current Initiatives

JANUARY

• Intense Energizing of Initiatives Across Businesses

FEBRUARY

Corporate Executive Council: (CEC at Crotonville)
35 Business and Senior Corporate Leaders
• Early Learning?
• Customer Reaction?
• Initiative Resources Sufficient?
• Business Management Course (BMC) Recommendations

MARCH

Anonymous Online CEO Survey:
11,000 Employees
• Do You "Feel" Initiative Yet?
• Do Customers Feel It?
• Sufficient Resources to Execute?
• Messages Clear and Credible?

APRIL

Globalization
Six Sigma Quality
Product Services
e-Business

GE Values

DECEMBER

Corporate Executive Council: (CEC at Crotonville)
35 Business and Senior Corporate Leaders
• Agenda for Boca
• Individual Business Initiative Highlights
• Business Management (BMC) Course Recommendations

NOVEMBER

Operating Plans Presented:
All Business Leaders
• Initiatives Stretch Targets
• Individual Business Operating Plans
• Economic Outlook

OCTOBER

Corporate Officers Meeting: (Crotonville)
150 Officers
• Next-Year Operating Plan Focus
• Role Models Present Initiative Successes
• Executive Development Course (EDC) Recommendations
• All Business Dialogue: What Have We Learned?

SEPTEMBER

Corporate Executive Council: (CEC at Crotonville)
35 Business and Senior Corporate Leaders
• Business Management Course (BMC) Recommendations
• Clear Role Models Identified
• Outside Company Best Practices Presented
• Initiative Best Practices (All Businesses)
• Customer Impact of Initiatives

Fourth Quarter

Second Quarter

Third Quarter

Leadership Performance
Reviews at Business
Locations:
All Business Staffs
• Initiative Leadership
Review
• Level of Commitment /
Quality of Talent on
Initiatives
• Differentiation
(20% / 70% / 10%)
• Promote / Reward /
Remove

MAY

Corporate Executive Council:
(CEC at Crotonville)
*35 Business and Senior
Corporate Leaders*
• Initiative Best Practices
• Review of Initiative
Leadership
• Customer Impact
• Business Management
Course (BMC)
Recommendations

JUNE

JULY

Session I: 3 Year Strategy
• Economic / Competitive
Environment
• General Earnings Outlook
• Initiatives Update /
Strategy
• Initiative Resource
Requirements

AUGUST

• Informal Idea
Exchanges at
Corporate and
Businesses

The GE Operating System

The Operating System is GE's learning culture in action—in essence, it is the operating software of the Company.

It is a year-round series of intense learning sessions in which business CEOs, role models and initiative champions from GE as well as outside companies, meet and share the intellectual capital of the world: its best ideas.

The central focus is always on raising the bar of Company performance by sharing, and putting into action, the best ideas and practices drawn from our big Company-wide initiatives.

The Operating System is driven by the soft values of the Company—trust, informality, simplicity, boundaryless behavior and the love of change. It allows GE businesses to operate at performance levels and speeds that would be unachievable were they on their own.

What may appear in the diagram to be a typical series of stand-alone business meetings is in reality an endless process of enrichment. Learning at each meeting builds on that of the previous, expanding the scope and increasing the momentum of the initiatives.

Globalization has been enriched through more than a dozen cycles. **Six Sigma** is in its fifth cycle, **Services** is in its sixth, and **e-Business** its third. The GE Operating System translates idea to action across three dozen businesses so rapidly that all the initiatives have become operational across the Company within one month of launch, and have always produced positive financial results within their first cycle.

a strong emphasis on making sure the best talent in each business was assigned to black belt Leader/Teacher roles. The strategy and budgeting processes were also built using Six Sigma tools and incorporated expectations for Six Sigma project results.

Throughout the year, the results of projects by classes at Crotonville and other operating mechanisms are also fed into the system. This provides a direct link between the learning that occurs at Crotonville and the management of the company. The leadership at GE learns from the work of the students, which is one more Virtuous Teaching Cycle.

All together, the GE Operating System creates forums in every GE business for the head of a business to interact with, learn from and teach people at multiple levels. It is also part of the glue that differentiates GE from a holding company and helps to ensure that it has a central Teachable Point of View for the entire organization.

There are many kinds of operating mechanisms, and leaders need to create mechanisms that best serve their immediate needs. Dave Baglee and John Pemberton, the plant managers for Intel's largest semi-conductor fabrication facility, did just that. Fab 11, which employs thousands of people, and turns out products that account for as much as 80% of Intel's corporate profits in some years. Baglee and Pemberton took key members of their team to a University of Michigan Business School Executive Education program that we run in Naples, Florida, every year. They used the time to craft a new TPOV for the plant that they immediately put into action when they returned. They had historically emphasized cost reduction, but had begun to see quality and yield levels plateau at their plant. The plant was also going through a major strategic shift as new facilities were coming on-line and Intel's product mix was forecasted to change. While re-crafting their TPOV, they had recognized that improving yields at Fab 11 could increase profits by millions per week when running at full capacity. This dropped directly to Intel's bottom line and had far more impact than any cost-cutting initiatives that had been previously defined. However, they lacked an effective way to teach people the importance of improving yields and to instill best practices for doing so.

One of their most important steps was creating a new operating mechanism, known as the Yield Strategy Meeting. The weekly Yield Strategy Meeting started with Baglee and Pemberton doing most of the talking. However, they were explicit with their team about the importance of using this as an opportunity to teach each other. To emphasize this, they changed their behavior in subtle but important ways: They asked more questions, they sat among the staff instead of in their traditional spots, and they openly asked the team for feedback on where they were being inconsistent. Over the course of a month, the dialogues became non-defensive and everyone started to participate. After three months, they had created the foundation for an ongoing Virtuous Teaching Cycle. Today, participants in the meetings positively challenge and coach one another, best practices are openly shared, and the Fab 11 TPOV is reinforced and improved. As you would expect, yield rates are better than ever.

The Intel experience demonstrates how designing an operating mechanism requires careful thought about the social environment. The leader must take on the role of social architect. He or she must do this by establishing several key elements:

- *People:* Who should be involved?
- *Time:* How often, for how long, and working on which issues?
- *Physical space:* Where is the meeting held?
- *Social space:* How should people interact with one another?

The leader must also consider the operating mechanisms as a series of events and interactions that take place over time. Every operating mechanism has preparation that is required. In almost every case where a major decision will be made, there is a face-to-face meeting. Finally, there must be a follow-up phase to assess results and ensure execution of the decision made at the face-to-face meeting. The leader must consider key issues at every phase of designing an operating mechanism:

Figure 26: Three Phases of Operating Mechanisms

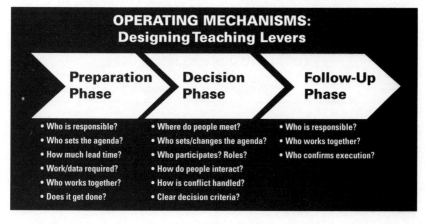

Designing an Operating Mechanism

As a leader, your job is to define the operating mechanisms for your organization, using them to align the TPOV and create positive emotional energy. If you are not the CEO, you may not have complete freedom, but you can make the most of the operating mechanisms you do have and create entirely new ones.

Before creating or changing operating mechanisms, you need a candid assessment of what you already have in place. Score your current operating mechanisms using the chart below:

1 = Highly ineffective: Contradicts the TPOV and/or creates a vicious non-teaching cycle.

3 = Somewhat effective: Moderate reinforcement of the TPOV and generates some two-way teaching.

5 = Highly effective: Consistent with the TPOV, everyone teaches and learns.

Current State of Operating Mechanisms

	Preparation	Face-to-face	Follow-up
Strategy			
Budget/Finance/ Resource allocation			
People/Succession planning			

Based on your assessment of your existing operating mechanisms, identify which changes you want to make during each phase in the future:

Vision for VTC Operating Mechanisms

	Preparation	Face-to-face	Follow-up
Strategy			
Budget/Finance/ Resource allocation			
People/Succession planning			

Building an Operating System

Once you have considered how to leverage your individual operating mechanisms to create Virtuous Teaching Cycles, you must also ensure that the pieces fit together. Each piece of the GE Operating System is both highly consistent with the GE leadership's TPOV and mutually supportive of other operating mechanisms.

Figure 27: Interwoven TPOV and Operating Mechanisms

GE operating mechanisms	How it reinforces the TPOV	How it is interwoven with other operating mechanisms
Strategy operating mechanisms: Session 1/ CEC meetings/Boca top 600	• Used to drive and reinforce key initiatives (ideas). • Emphasizes GE's values of boundaryless best practice sharing and customer focus. • Annual CEO survey creates direct teaching dialogue for improvement.	• Backdrop for budgeting process. • Key initiatives often define capabilities and values for assessment and coaching of all employees.
Resource allocation operating mechanism: Session 2	• Focus on teamwork among all businesses—if one GE business comes up short, others are expected to cover the gap. • Promotes transfer of ideas, resources and people across businesses. • During dialogues in each business, everyone participates, coaches and teaches to ensure best possible resource allocation.	• Once strategy discussion is finalized, it is not reopened during resource allocation dialogue. • Budgeting is based on honest assessment of capabilities required to execute strategy— what skills do people have, what do they need, where does the business require new people?
Succession planning operating mechanisms: Session C/Crotonville	• Focus on differentiation (edge) and rewarding the best. • Reinforces fact that GE's primary capability is growing and developing people.	• Developmental learning from Crotonville programs used as input to CEC strategy dialogues. • People assessed on ability to execute a budget and make stretch financial targets.

Use the blank calendar on the next two pages to plot your operating mechanisms so that they create a self-reinforcing operating system:

Figure 28:
Architecting a
Virtuous Teaching
Operating System

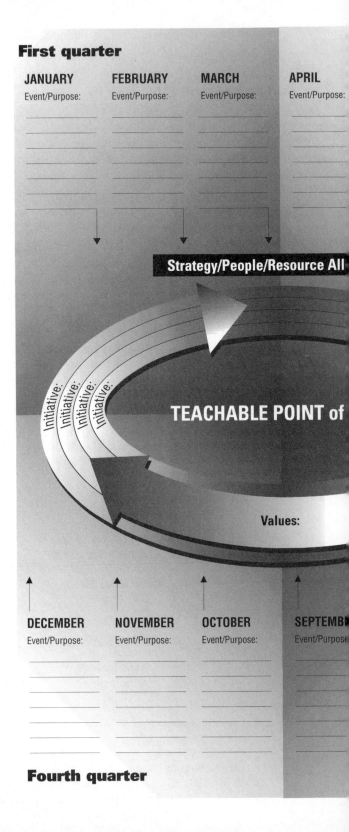

First quarter

JANUARY
Event/Purpose:

FEBRUARY
Event/Purpose:

MARCH
Event/Purpose:

APRIL
Event/Purpose:

Strategy/People/Resource All

Initiative:
Initiative:
Initiative:
Initiative:

TEACHABLE POINT of

Values:

DECEMBER
Event/Purpose:

NOVEMBER
Event/Purpose:

OCTOBER
Event/Purpose:

SEPTEMB
Event/Purpose

Fourth quarter

Second quarter

MAY
Event/Purpose:

_____
_____
_____
_____
_____

JUNE
Event/Purpose:

_____
_____
_____
_____
_____

:ion

EW

AUGUST
Event/Purpose:

_____
_____
_____
_____
_____

JULY
Event/Purpose:

_____
_____
_____
_____
_____

Third quarter

Architecting a Virtuous Teaching Operating System

Use this framework to design a series of inter-connected operating mechanisms. These should help you decide how strategy will be formulated, how annual operating plans assembled, and how succession planning is conducted. You may also want to include other operating mechanisms that help you create more Virtuous Teaching Cycles in your business.

The operating system is built on the foundation of the Teachable Point of View for your organization. The core operating mechanisms and key initiatives should improve your business' ideas for how to succeed in the market. The behaviors of people as they work through the operating system must align with your company's values. People must feel productive energy as they participate in all aspects of the operating system. And, finally, the operating system must lead to decisions with edge that clearly communicate what the organization will and will not do.

Follow the steps below to create your own operating system:

STEP 1: VALUES
Write your values in the outer circle. These should be reflected in everyone's behavior as they work together at every stage of the operating system. As the leader, you must create group processes that reinforce these values.

STEP 2: INITIATIVES
Use your ideas to guide the key initiatives that you are trying to drive in your business. These should be consistent with your company's Teachable Point of View, and link to actions required for success in the market.

STEP 3: LAY OUT THE OVERALL CALENDAR
Develop a macro-view of how your business will run during the year. Identify when each of the core operating mechanisms (strategy, operations, succession planning) will take place. There should be reinforcing teaching/feedback loops for each of the operating mechanisms throughout the year to create Virtuous Teaching Cycles. Remember, each operating mechanism should have the following components:

> **Preparation**: what is prepared, who is involved, over what period of time, what are the deliverables

> **Face-to-Face**: who is involved, who makes decisions, how is the meeting run

> **Follow-Up**: what is done, who is responsible for ensuring commitments are delivered

STEP 4: LINK YOUR OPERATING MECHANISMS
Identify areas of overlap and interdependence between the operating mechanisms that help to create Virtuous Teaching Cycles. Consider how the output of one operating mechanism impacts the others.

Section Nine
Global Citizenship

TEACH LEARN

KNOWLEDGE CREATION / ALIGNMENT

Business Leaders Must Engage as Citizens
- *Businesses operate in a global community and have global obligations.*
- *Leaders must have a TPOV on citizenship.*

VTCs in the Community Benefit the Company, Individuals, the Community
- *Volunteer activities hone leadership skills, offer opportunities for learning.*
- *They energize workers, build bonds.*
- *Approached as a learning/teaching activity, the investment pays big rewards.*

In this section you will

❚ Generate ideas for how you can create VTCs in the community that will benefit your business.

❚ Design a community event for your team.

Section Nine
Global Citizenship

There is a societal shift occurring that coincides with the rise of knowledge workers. Peter Drucker captured this best when he said, "Individuals, and especially knowledge workers, need an additional sphere of life, of personal relationships, and of contribution outside and beyond the job, outside and beyond the organization, indeed, outside and beyond their own specialized knowledge area."

It is a desire to be part of something larger than oneself, to contribute value at a societal and local level. This sentiment was the positive side of the dot-com companies. The twenty-somethings we spoke with at the height of the Silicon Valley craze didn't just talk about money; they talked about making a difference by being part of a technological revolution that would improve people's lives. We can look back at it now and say they were naïve, but they reflected a values shift that is becoming more prevalent and widespread, and one that companies ignore at their peril. GE's Jeff Immelt summed this up when he said during a recent interview:

> Now, more than ever before, people want to win, but they want to do it with heart, and both things are important in a twenty-first-century company. You have got to find a way to attract people that know how to give back to the environment and give back to the community and give back to the workplace.

Ironically, just as this new societal awareness arose, anti-globalization has grown, labeling many of the multinational corporations as greedy destroyers of local business and culture. Nearly simultaneously, the Enron debacle and other corporate scandals have created all-time low levels of trust in corporate leaders on the domestic front. If ever the conditions existed for corporations to utilize the

385

skills of their knowledge workers to better their local and global communities, surely now is the time.

The case for corporate citizenship can be made in utilitarian terms (i.e., it enhances an organization's reputation leading to economic benefits) or moral terms (i.e., it is the right thing to do). Although we can argue it on both grounds, ultimately a leader in today's society must have his or her own point of view on the matter. We argue for corporate citizenship here, however, based on the premise of this book: When executed properly, it leads to the creation of Virtuous Teaching Cycles and develops teaching capabilities.

Noel has made corporate citizenship a part of his work for more than twenty-five years. Together, we have led thousands of leaders in

Figure 29: Teaching and Winning Through Citizenship

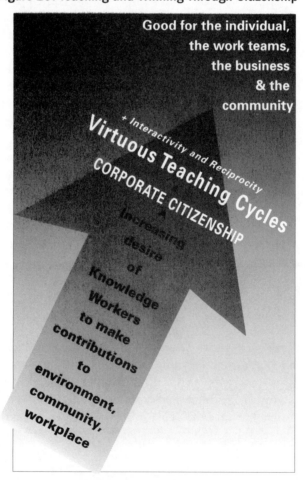

community activities. Watching leaders engage in these efforts has made it obvious how much development occurs when leaders invest time and personal energy in community service. It is good for the individual, good for work teams, good for businesses and good for the community.

> *Personal development:* Individuals are taken into new situations and gain new understanding of what it means to "walk in someone else's shoes." Dialogue and reflection forces individuals to develop their own point of view on their corporation's role in the community. Explaining what they do and what value their business produces also helps individuals express their TPOV more simply and clearly.

> *Team development:* Having teams work together on citizenship projects reinforces a sense of shared group identity, provides an opportunity for social interaction in a non-work setting, and offers a chance for team members to work together in ways that generate positive emotional energy.

> *Business development:* When many businesses bring people into the community, they are engaging their customers or potential customers. Dialogue with people helps business leaders understand how their company is perceived and how it treats people. Getting into the community also reveals issues that are affecting the potential future workforce. Some corporations, such as Microsoft and Cisco, have put community development programs together that explicitly address shortfalls in the education system.

The fact that the efforts of corporations and the individuals in them may not solve any of the major problems of the world is irrelevant. The point is that the effort and the interaction among people who might otherwise never meet produces real benefits for everyone.

Virtuous Teaching Cycles Are the Key

Many people equate corporate citizenship with writing a check to the United Way Fund or two hours in a soup kitchen around the holiday season. While such actions have merit, they do not create opportunities for the deep development noted above. The precondition for leadership and team development in the community is interactivity. This is ideally achieved on a 1-to-1 basis between community members and organizational leaders.

The Virtuous Teaching Cycle is necessary because it engages two people, usually from different backgrounds and with different socio-economic standing, to meet as human beings. Having an executive exchange life stories with a drug addict, homeless person or fifth grader from a low-income district strips away the veneer of corporate authority. It forces business leaders to listen and to try to understand the myriad forces impacting the other person that they are routinely shielded from. In the process, leaders often gain a new perspective on leadership. They recognize how small their water cooler issues are in comparison and see true resilience in action. Some non-profit organizations and a Detroit-based organization called Focus: HOPE, particularly, are world-class Teaching Organizations that executives can benchmark and learn from as well.

The other precondition for successful corporate citizenship activities is reciprocity. Over the years, some people we have taken into the community have remarked that they feel their efforts are the proverbial drop in the ocean. They feel their contribution is so insignificant that it could not have made a difference, while at the same time they have received tremendous personal growth. This often stems from an awakening to community needs and an overwhelming desire to give more. In truth, executives who interact and offer coaching to community members and those who complete small projects side-by-side with community members are providing a great service. Many people engaged in self-improvement through community agencies do not have the opportunity for completely candid dialogue with an experienced business person. Thirty minutes of coaching on interview dress and protocol with people attempting to re-enter the workforce, or career counseling to a sixth grader, can have a profound impact on the person's life.

Preparing for Your Community Experience

To make your experience successful, we suggest a minimum of three hours working at an agency with a ratio of no more than two executives for every agency member. Some nonprofit organizations cannot support interactivity or do not have enough infrastructure to handle volunteers. The first step in creating a community experience for yourself and your team is preparation. The only way to ensure that you have selected a qualified agency is to speak directly to the agency director and conduct a site visit.

Figure 30: Criteria for Selecting a Suitable Agency

- The agency addresses a significant social issue, preferably one that has a direct relationship to your business.

- The agency can support your timing and interactivity.

- There is a well-defined agency leader who will take charge of organizing your visit.

- There is a win-win opportunity for your team to learn and to add value to the agency (e.g., coaching, project work, working an event).

- There are no health or safety precautions.

Designing the Experience

When designing your agenda, it is important that you start with a clear discussion of why you and your team are working in the community. It is important to recognize that work in the community touches on people's personal values and will simultaneously make many people uncomfortable. You may experience hesitation, even outright resistance from some team members. This is an opportunity to share your TPOV and work with your team members on their own.

A typical community experience that we design has the following elements:

- *Introductions*—Start with a person-to-person introduction, then share a brief overview of the organizations involved.
- *Tour*—A short tour of the facilities, led by members of the agency in small groups or 1-to-1, helps people get an understanding of how the agency works. It is critical to have people diagnose what makes the agency work and what barriers it must overcome, not simply go on a sight-seeing tour.
- *Experience*—A 60- to 120-minute project that engages people in side-by-side work. Examples include mentoring students, painting, fixing equipment, building a playground, or cleaning up a neighborhood.

- *Diagnosis*—A dialogue between your team and community agency members on what makes the agency successful and what your organization can learn.
- *Emotional debriefing*—An honest dialogue about emotional reactions to the experience and what personal, team or business learning can be applied.

Design your event below:

Time	Activity/Teaching notes

Section Ten
Start the Journey

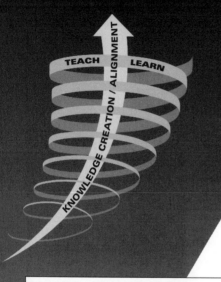

You Can Always Improve
- *Creating a Teaching Organization is a never-ending journey.*
- *Leaders recognize they always have more to learn.*

Learning Requires Action
- *Experience and experimentation are prerequisites to improvement.*
- *It's always about better results.*

In this section you will

■ Determine what you can do immediately.

Section Ten
Start the Journey

This handbook began by asking you to honestly assess your organization and yourself as a leader. You may not like what you saw or you may be well along the way. Regardless, every leader and every organization still has work to do.

At the heart of every Teaching Organization is a relentless striving to be better. The benchmarks in this book all have it. Their leaders know that they can always learn more, that another breakthrough can be achieved, and that a new standard of excellence can be set. It is the creation of Virtuous Teaching Cycles that enables these leaders to continue learning and business results to steadily improve.

If you have completed this handbook, you have the essential concepts, tools, and building blocks to create a Teaching Organization. By now, you understand the importance of developing Virtuous Teaching Cycles. You also know that improving business results happens as a result of—not at the cost of—developing future leaders.

The exercises have also asked you to approach your role as a leader/teacher from many perspectives:

- *Individual*—You developed a Teachable Point of View.
- *Team*—You identified how to engage your team and designed an initial event.
- *Organization*—You built a Leader/Teacher Pipeline for succession planning and defined an operating system that creates Virtuous Teaching Cycles.
- *Global*—You created opportunities for your team to engage the larger community so they can both teach and learn.

This book has offered a framework. You contribute the most important ingredient—action. Wherever you are on the journey toward

393

creating a Teaching Organization, you will learn the most by doing. The best leaders we see are not afraid to experiment. They adapt new learning and practices to their own context, keeping what works and improving or eliminating the rest. Throughout this handbook you have defined many actions you will take. Make a commitment to yourself right now. What is the most important first step you can take—starting immediately—to put your learning into practice?

Figure 31: Virtuous Teaching Cycle

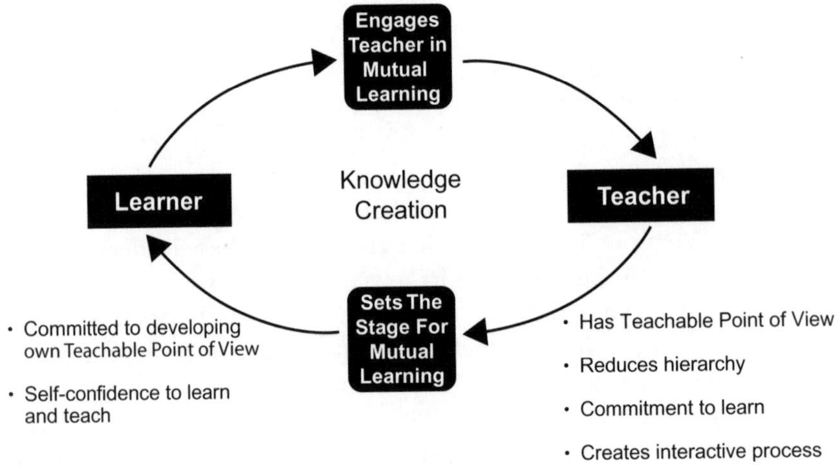

Engages Teacher in Mutual Learning

Knowledge Creation

Learner

Teacher

Sets The Stage For Mutual Learning

- Committed to developing own Teachable Point of View

- Self-confidence to learn and teach

- Has Teachable Point of View

- Reduces hierarchy

- Commitment to learn

- Creates interactive process

What I Will Do:

By When:

Notes

Chapter 1: The New DNA of Winning

1. GE 2000 Annual Report

   Jack Welch describes this in more detail in his book *JACK: Straight from the Gut* (New York: TimeWarner, 2001, 202–204). Included on page 203 are the handwritten notes he prepared for his challenge to the team of GE's top 500 Boca meeting, where he had challenged them all to come to the strategy session with a plan for how they would define their business at less than 10% market share in order to unleash new growth.

2. Eli Cohen and Noel Tichy, "Operation—Leadership," *Fast Company,* September 1999. This article describes how the Special Operations Forces create high-stress simulations and then engage in a Virtuous Teaching Cycle to debrief, called the After Action Review.

3. Michael Harry and Richard Schroeder, *Six Sigma, The Breakthrough Management Strategy Revolutionizing the World's Top Corporations* (New York: Currency, 1999). For a good description of the origins of Six Sigma at Motorola and its application at Honeywell and GE.

4. For a detailed description of how Crotonville was transformed into an action-learning platform for Welch, see "GE's Crotonville: A staging ground for corporate revolution," *Academy of Management Executive,* May 1989.

5. In the January 2001 issue of the Japanese edition of the *Harvard Business Review,* Noel Tichy laid out the story of how Welch built the world's largest teaching infrastructure.

6. For an in-depth framing of the issues in a knowledge-based economy, see Lester Thurow's book, *Building Wealth* (New York: HarperCollins, 1999). He has a concept called the Wealth Pyramid, which is a multidimensional framework for understanding the drivers of wealth creation: natural resources, tools, skills, creating knowledge, entrepreneurship to social organization.

7. The Roger Enrico program is discussed in detail in a *Fortune* article, by Noel Tichy and Christopher DeRose, November 27, 1995.

8. For a conceptual framework to understand organizational networks, see Noel Tichy, Chapter 11, "Networks in Organizations," in *Handbook of Organizational Design,* by Paul Nystrom and William Starbuck. (London: Oxford Press, 1981.)

9. Andy Grove laid out his Teachable Point of View for how to be a good leader and how he wanted leaders at Intel to behave in his book, *High Output Management.* (New York: Random House, 1983.)

10. John Huey and Geoffrey Colvin, editors at *Fortune,* conducted a video interview with then CEO of Southwest Airlines Herb Kelleher and then CEO of GE Jack Welch where they discussed their Teachable Points of View on how to successfully run big companies. One of the issues Welch talked about was informality and how he infused learning and teaching throughout the company. "3rd World Wide Lessons in Leadership Series," 1998.

Interview Sources

Dedrick, Greg, Yum! Brands. Interview by Noel Tichy, December 2001.

Immelt, Jeffrey, GE. Interview by Noel Tichy, October 2001.

Nardelli, Robert, Home Depot. Interview by Noel Tichy, October 2001.

Novak, David, Yum! Brands. Interview by Noel Tichy, December 2001.

Welch, Jack, GE. Interview by Noel Tichy, November 2001.

Chapter 2: Two Roads to Winning

1. Thurow, Lester. *Building Wealth*. New York: HarperCollins, 1999.

2. Drucker, Peter. *Management Challenges of the 21st Century*. New York: HarperCollins, 2001.

3. In the book *Digital Capital* (Boston: Harvard Business School Press, 2000.), Don Tapscott, David Ticoll and Alex Lowy provide a road map and travel log of how many of the digital companies developed in the latter half of the 1990s. They clearly warned and foreshadowed the failure of the ones that did not have real competitive strategies.

4. In *Future Wealth,* Stanley Davis and Christopher Meyer provide another viewpoint on the knowledge economy. (Boston: Harvard Business School Press, 2000.)
5. Thomas Stewart's book on knowledge and intellectual property is a classic. *The Wealth of Knowledge: Intellectual Capital and the Twenty-First Century Organization.* (New York: Currency, 2001.)
6. George Von Krogh, Kazuo Ichijo, and Ikujiro Nonaka provide compelling case examples and a how-to guide to unlocking tacit knowledge and turning it into innovation in the marketplace. The book is *Enabling Knowledge Creation.* (London: Oxford, 2000.)
7. For a description of boundarylessness and how it was implemented at GE, see *Control Your Destiny or Someone Else Will* (2nd ed.), by Noel Tichy and Stratford Sherman. (New York: Harper-Business, 2001; 635–645.)
8. The three-act drama framework was first laid out by Noel Tichy and Mary Anne Devanna in *The Transformational Leader.* (New York: Wiley, 1986.)

Interview Sources

Chambers, John, Cisco. Interview by Noel Tichy, April 2000.

Saylor, Michael, MicroStrategy. Interview by Noel Tichy and Nancy Cardwell, February 2000.

Welch, Jack, GE. Interview by Noel Tichy, September 1999, November 1999, March 2000, October 2000, March 2001.

Chapter 3: Building the Teaching Organization

1. The Enrico program and its impact are described in detail in "The Pepsi Challenge," *Training & Development,* May 1996, 58.
2. For a tragic tail of hubris, Elizabeth Wasserman wrote a chronology of the rise and fall of Michael Saylor, founder and CEO of MicroStrategy, in *Industry Standard,* January 22–29, 2001; 58–61.
3. Social psychologist from Yale, Irving Janis, has a concept called "group think," which explains much of the tragedy of the *Challenger* disaster. He produced a training video that has actors reconstructing the tragic events. (*Groupthink,* CRM Learning, 1996.)
4. Michael Dell lays out his Teachable Point of View on leadership and how to run Dell in *Direct From Dell,* by Dell and Catherine Fredman (New York: HarperBusiness, 1999.)

5. The growth concepts are developed in depth in the book *Every Business Is a Growth Business* by Ram Charan and Noel Tichy. (New York: Times Books, 1997.)
6. *Fortune*. "The Odd Couple." May 1, 2000.
7. This article, which was an example of the output of a personal Virtuous Teaching Cycle, appeared in *Administrative Science Quarterly*, Vol. 18, 1973; 194–208, titled "An analysis of clique formation and structure in organizations."

Interview Sources

Dell, Michael, Dell. Presentation and dialogue with Michael Dell at Ford Motor Company, conducted by Noel Tichy, January 1999.

Downing, Wayne, Special Operations Command. Interview by Eli Cohen, June 1996, August 1999, March 2000.

Enrico, Roger, PepsiCo. Interview by Noel Tichy, Febuary 1995.

McNerney, James, 3M. Interview by Noel Tichy and Nancy Cardwell, September 2001.

Novak, David, Yum! Brands. Interview by Noel Tichy, December 2001.

Saylor, Michael, MicroStrategy. Interview by Noel Tichy and Nancy Cardwell, February 1999.

Chapter 4: You Must Start With a Teachable Point of View

1. Michael Dell and Catherine Fredman are very clear on Michael Dell's Teachable Point of View regarding who and how to hire new employees, as he spells it out in *Direct From Dell: Strategies that Revolutionized an Industry*. (New York: HarperCollins, 2000.)
2. Bernie Marcus and Arthur Blank with Bob Andelman, *Built From Scratch*. New York: Times Business, 1999.
3. Kevin and Jackie Freiberg. *Nuts!* New York: Broadway Books, 1998.
4. Andrew Grove. *Only the Paranoid Survive: How To Exploit Crisis Points that Challenge Every Company and Career*. New York: Currency, 1996.
5. GE 1991 Annual Report Letter.
6. John Byrne. *Chainsaw: The Notorious Career of Al Dunlap in the Era of Profit-At-Any-Price*. New York: HarperBusiness, 2002.

Interview Sources

Dell, Michael, Dell. Presentation and dialogue with Noel Tichy at Ford Motor Company, January 1999.

Nardelli, Robert, Home Depot. Interview by Noel Tichy and Nancy Cardwell, October 2001.

Novak, David, Yum! Brands. Interview by Noel Tichy, March 2001, August 2001.

Welch, John F., GE. Series of interviews by Noel Tichy, 1988–1995.

Chapter 5: How to Develop a Teachable Point of View

1. Tichy, Noel and Stratford Sherman. *Control Your Destiny or Someone Else Will* (2nd ed.). New York: HarperBusiness, 2001, appendix—Jack Welch's letters to shareholders 1991–2000.
2. Ibid., Chapter 11. It describes how Crotonville played a key role in the development and dissemination of the GE shared values. In addition, the *Handbook for Revolutionaries* at the end of the book provides specific guidelines for others developing shared values for their own companies.
3. Immelt, Jeffrey, GE. Presentation at Stanford Business School, March 2002.
4. Drucker, Peter. "Business Theory." *The Wall Street Journal,* February 2, 1993. Peter Drucker. "Theory of the Business." *Managing in a Time of Great Change.* New York: Dutton, Truman Talley Books, 1995.
5. Howard Gardner. *Leading Minds: An Anatomy of Leadership.* New York: Basic Books, 1996.

Interview Sources

Chambers, John, Cisco. Interview by Noel Tichy, February 2000.

Donovan, Dennis, Home Depot. Interview by Noel Tichy and Nancy Cardwell, October 2001.

Immelt, Jeffrey, GE. Interview by Noel Tichy, October 2001.

Nardelli, Robert, Home Depot. Interview by Noel Tichy and Dennis Donovan, October 2001.

Novak, David, Yum! Brands. Interview by Noel Tichy, August 2001.

Potter, Myrtle, Genentech. Interview by Noel Tichy, March 2001.

Welch, John F., GE. Series of interviews by Noel Tichy, 1985–1993.

Chapter 6: The Paradox of Power

1. Noel Tichy. *Managing Strategic Change.* New York: Wiley, 1984. This book has a framework for analyzing resistance to change—technical, political and cultural.
2. Noel Tichy. "Simultaneous CEO Succession and Transformation." *Organizational Dynamics* (Summer 1996).
3. Morton Deutsch and R. Krauss. *Theories in Social Psychology.* New York: Basic Books, 1965.
4. Amatai Etzioni. *A Comparative Analysis of Complex Organizations.* New York: Free Press, 1961.

Interview Sources

Herkstroter, Cor, Royal Dutch/Shell. Series of interviews and discussions by Noel Tichy, 1993–1998.

McNerney, James, 3M. Interview by Noel Tichy and Nancy Cardwell, October 2001.

Novak, David, Yum! Brands. Interview by Noel Tichy, March 2001.

Pfeiffer, Eckhard, Compaq. Interview by Noel Tichy and Eli Cohen, March 1996.

Saylor, Michael, MicroStrategy. Interview by Noel Tichy and Nancy Cardwell, February 2000.

Weiss, William, Ameritech. Series of interviews by Noel Tichy, 1991–1996.

Welch, John F., GE. Series of interviews by Noel Tichy, 1993–1998.

Wendt, Gary, GE Capital. Series of interviews by Noel Tichy, 1995–1997.

Chapter 7: Building the Leader/Teacher Pipeline

1. Noel Tichy with Eli Cohen. *The Leadership Engine.* New York: HarperBusiness, 1997. For a set of practical guidelines see the Handbook.
2. Donald Kane, Noel Tichy, and Eugene Andrews. "A Leadership

Development Framework," *GE Executive Management Staff,* November 1987. OEN-6.

3. V. Pucik, Noel Tichy, and Nancy C. Barnett. *Globalizing Management: Creating and Leading the Competitive Organization.* New York: John Wiley & Sons, Inc. 1992. For a historical view of how action learning was developed and incorporated into GE and Crotonville, Chapter 11 provides this framing.

Interview Sources

Immelt, Jeffrey, GE. Interview by Noel Tichy, October 2001.

McNerney, James, 3M. Interview by Noel Tichy, October 2001.

Nardelli, Robert, Home Depot. Interview by Noel Tichy, October 2001.

Schlesinger, Leonard, Limited Brands. Interview by Noel Tichy, October 2001.

Welch, John F., GE. Series of interviews by Noel Tichy, 1991–2001.

Wexner, Les, Limited Brands. Interview by Noel Tichy, October 2001.

Chapter 8: Scaling the Teaching Organization

1. John Huey and Geoffrey Colvin, editors at *Fortune,* conducted a video interview with then CEO of Southwest Airlines Herb Kelleher and then CEO of GE Jack Welch ("3rd World Wide Lessons in Leadership Series," 1998).
2. Noel Tichy and Stratford Sherman. *Control Your Destiny or Someone Else Will* (2nd ed.). New York: HarperBusiness, 2001.
3. Ibid. See the "Handbook for Revolutionaries."
4. GE Annual Report letter by John F. Welch, 1998.
5. Janet Guyon, "Why is the world's most profitable company turning itself inside out?" *Fortune,* August 4, 1997.
6. Shell Business Framework—internal pamphlet, 1996.
7. Noel Tichy and Christopher DeRose. "Death of Rebirth of Organizational Development." *Organization 21C.* Prentice Hall, 2002.

Interview Sources

Herkstroter, Cor, Royal Dutch/Shell. Series of interviews and discussins by Noel Tichy, 1993–1998.

Steele, Gary, LEAP Group, Shell. Interview by Noel Tichy, February 2002.

Welch, John F., GE. Series of interviews by Noel Tichy, 1991–2001.

Chapter 9: Creating Virtuous Teaching Cycles

1. John F. Welch with John Byrne. *Jack: Straight From the Gut*. New York: Time Warner, 2001. Welch describes the Wal-Mart process and how it influenced the development of Quick Market Intelligence at GE.
2. Noel Tichy and Stratford Sherman. *Control Your Destiny or Someone Else Will* (second edition). New York: HarperBusiness, 2001.
3. Ibid. See the "Handbook for Revolutionaries."
4. *Harvard Business School Case Study*, "General Electric Company: Background Note On Management Systems," 1981. 181–211.
5. Charles Fombrun, Noel Tichy, and Stewart Freeman. "GE Succession Planning Process." *Strategic Human Resource Management*. New York: John Wiley & Sons, Inc., 1984.
6. GE Annual Report 2001.
7. Noel Tichy and Stratford Sherman. *Control Your Destiny or Someone Else Will* (second edition). New York: HarperBusiness, 2001. See the GE Timeline.

Interview Sources

Brown, Richard, EDS. Interview by Noel Tichy, April 2002.

McNerney, James, 3M. Interview by Noel Tichy and Nancy Cardwell, October 2001.

Nardelli, Robert, Home Depot. Interview by Noel Tichy, October 2001.

Tolan, Mary, Accenture. Interview by Noel Tichy, November 2001.

Welch, John F., GE. Series of interviews by Noel Tichy, 1991–2001.

Chapter 10: Trilogy University

1. Noel Tichy. "No Ordinary Bootcamp." *Harvard Business Review*. February 2001.

2. Noel Tichy and Stratford Sherman. *Control Your Destiny or Some-one Else Will* (second edition). New York: Harper Business, 2001.
3. Noel Tichy. "GE's Crotonville: A Staging Ground for Corporate Revolution." *The Academy of Management Executive.* 1989, Vol. 2.

Interview Sources

Drummand, Allan, Trilogy University. Interview by Noel Tichy, December 2000, January 2001.

Liemandt, Joe, Trilogy. Interview by Noel Tichy and Nancy Tanner, December 2000, January 2001, February 2001, March 2001.

Chapter 11: Digitizing the Teaching Organization

1. Noel Tichy. "No Ordinary Bootcamp." *Harvard Business Review.* February 2001.
2. In the book *Digital Capital* (Boston: Harvard Business School Press, 2000.), Don Tapscott, David Ticoll, and Alex Lowy provide a road map and travel log of how many of the digital companies developed in the latter half of the 1990s. They clearly warned and foreshadowed the failure of the ones that did not have real competitive strategies.
3. Tom Stewart. *The Wealth of Knowledge: Intellectual Capital and the Twenty-First Century Organization.* New York: Currency, 2001.
4. John F. Welch with John Byrne. *Jack: Straight From the Gut.* New York: Time Warner, 2001.

Interview Sources

Drummand, Allan, Trilogy University. Interview by Noel Tichy, December 2000, January 2001.

Liemandt, Joe, Trilogy. Interview by Noel Tichy and Nancy Cardwell, December 2000, January 2001, February 2001, March 2001.

Roraty, Dan, Trilogy. Interview by Noel Tichy, September 2000, December 2000, January 2001, February 2001, March 2001.

Chapter 12: Global Citizenship

1. Noel Tichy with Andrew McGill and Lynda St. Clair. *Global Corporate Citizenship.* San Francisco: Jossey-Bass, 1997.

2. Peter Drucker. *Managing in a Time of Great Change.* New York: Dutton, Truman Talley Books, 1995.

Interview Sources

Immelt, Jeffrey, GE. Interview by Noel Tichy, October 2001.

Josaitis, Eleanor, Focus: HOPE. Series of interviews by Noel Tichy, 1998–2001.

Knowling, Robert, Simbion Technologies. Interview by Noel Tichy, June 2001, December 2001, January 2002, June 2002.

Potter, Myrtle. Genentech. Interview by Noel Tichy, March 2001.

Sources

Annual Reports

Accenture, 1999 Annual Report.
Accenture, 2000 Annual Report.
Accenture, 2001 Annual Report.
Cisco Systems, 1999 Annual Report.
Cisco Systems, 2000 Annual Report.
Cisco Systems, 2001 Annual Report.
Dell Computer, 1999 Annual Report.
Dell Computer, 2000 Annual Report.
Dell Computer, 2001 Annual Report.
EDS, 1999 Annual Report.
EDS, 2000 Annual Report.
EDS, 2001 Annual Report.
Genentech, 1999 Annual Report.
Genentech, 2000 Annual Report.
Genentech, 2001 Annual Report.
General Electric, 1991 Annual Report.
General Electric, 1998 Annual Report.
General Electric, 1999 Annual Report.
General Electric, 2000 Annual Report.
General Electric, 2001 Annual Report.
Focus: HOPE, 1999 Annual Report.
Focus: HOPE, 2000 Annual Report.
Focus: HOPE, 2001 Annual Report.
The Limited, 1999 Annual Report.
The Limited, 2000 Annual Report.
The Limited, 2001 Annual Report.
3M, 1999 Annual Report.
3M, 2000 Annual Report.
3M, 2001 Annual Report.
The Home Depot, 1999 Annual Report.
The Home Depot, 2000 Annual Report.
The Home Depot, 2001 Annual Report.

Nokia, 1999 Annual Report.
Nokia, 2000 Annual Report.
Nokia, 2001 Annual Report.
Royal Dutch/Shell, 1999 Annual Report.
Royal Dutch/Shell, 2000 Annual Report.
Royal Dutch/Shell, 2001 Annual Report.
Southwest Airlines, 1999 Annual Report.
Southwest Airlines, 2000 Annual Report.
Tricon Global Restaurants, 1999 Annual Report.
Tricon Global Restaurants, 2000 Annual Report.
Tricon Global Restaurants, 2001 Annual Report.
Trilogy, 1999 Annual Report.
Trilogy, 2000 Annual Report.
Trilogy, 2001 Annual Report.

Articles

Aley, James and Lenore Schiff. "The Theory that Made Microsoft." *Fortune,* 29 April 1996.

Bennis, Warren. "Learning to Lead." *Executive Excellence,* 1 January 1996.

Berenson, Alex. "Rapid Growth Makes Cisco a New Leader." *The New York Times,* 13 June 2000.

Birchard, Bill. "Hire Great People Fast." *Fast Company,* August 1997.

Browning, E. S. "Tech Lovers Begin to Fret About 'V' Word: Valuation." *The Wall Street Journal,* 23 March 2000.

Buckman, Rebecca. "Microsoft Takes Lessons from an Old Economy Stalwart." *The Wall Street Journal,* 6 October 2000.

Byrne, John. "The 21st Century Corporation: The Great Transformation." *Business Week,* 28 August 2000.

Byrne, John, Andy Reinhardt, and Robert Hof. "The Internet Age—The Search for the Young and Gifted." *BusinessWeek,* 4 October 1999.

Byrne, John and Debra Sparks. "What's an Old-Line CEO to Do? Net-crazed investors sneer, no matter how sturdy the performance." *BusinessWeek,* 27 March 2000.

Charan, Ram and Geoffrey Colvin. "Making A Clean Handoff." *Fortune,* 17 September 2001.

Cohen, Eli and Noel Tichy. "Operation–Leadership." *Fast Company,* September 1999.

Collins, James C. and Jerry I. Porras. "Building a Visionary Company." *Waters Information Service,* 1 January 1995.

Colvin, Geoffrey. "America's Most Admired Companies." *Fortune,* 21 February 2000.

———. "Managing in the Info Era." *Fortune,* 6 March 2000.

Corcoran, Elizabeth. "The E Gang." *Forbes,* 24 July 2000.

Cringely, Robert X. "The Top 50." *Worth Magazine,* May 2000.

Deutsch, Claudia H. "A Do-it-Yourselfer Takes on Home Depot." *The New York Times,* 29 July 2001.

———. "New Economy, Old-School Rigor; G.E.'s Management Methods Are Put to Work on the Web." *The New York Times,* 12 June 2000.

Drucker, Peter. "Business Theory." *The Wall Street Journal,* 2 February 1993.

Dunham, Kembra J. " 'Hire me, hire my friends,' tech recruits are saying." *Star Tribune,* 27 June 1999.

Economist. "The Case for Globalization." 23 September 2000.

———. "Saturday Morning Fever." 8 December 2001.

———. "A Survey of Business and the Internet." 26 June 1999.

————. "A Survey of the New Economy." 23 September 2000.

————. "What the Internet Cannot Do." 19 August 2000.

————. "When Companies Connect." 26 June 1999.

Eisenberg, Daniel with Julie Rawe. "Jack Who?" *Time,* 10 September 2001.

Financial Times Limited. "New Dynamics of Strategy in the Knowledge Economy." 11 October 1999.

Fisher, Daniel. "Pulled in a New Direction." *Forbes,* 10 June 2002.

Fox, Justine. "Nokia's Secret Code." *Fortune,* 1 May 2000.

Fraim, John. "Imperfect Information." *The Industry Standard,* 17 April 2000.

Frantz, Douglas. "To Put G.E. Online Meant Putting a Dozen Industries Online." *The New York Times,* 29 March 2000.

Gerstner, Louis V, Jr. "Blinded by Dot-Com Alchemy." *BusinessWeek,* 27 March 2000.

Grove, Andrew S. "How (and Why) to Run a Meeting." *Fortune,* 11 July 1983.

Guyon, Janet. "Why is the World's Most Profitable Company Turning Itself Inside Out?" *Fortune,* 4 August 1997.

Hamel, Gary. "Edison's Curse; Electricity created dynamic productivity gains—and shrank margins." *Fortune,* 5 March 2001.

————. "Take It Higher; The Net changes more than just your operating speed." *Fortune,* 5 February 2001.

Hammonds, Keith H. "Grassroots Leadership: U.S. Military Academy." *Fast Company,* June 2001.

Hansen, Morten T., Nitin Nohria, and Thomas Tierney. "What's Your Strategy for Managing Knowledge?" *Harvard Business Review,* March–April 1999.

Hawkins, Lori. "Austin Software Company Focuses on Recruiting." *Associated Press Newswires,* 17 September 1997.

Hostetler, Michele. "Cisco Systems' John Chambers." *Investor's Business Daily,* 2 June 1999.

Jaffe, Harry. "The Seven Billion Dollar Man." *Washington Magazine,* March 2000.

Johnson, Carrie. "For the Jobless, It's More Than a Waiting Game." *The Washington Post,* 1 April 2001.

Kirsner, Scott. "Faster Company." *Fast Company,* May 2000.

Kurtzman, Joel. "Thought Leader: Howard Gardner." *Strategy & Business,* First Quarter 1999.

Leibovich, Mark. "Baiting the Hook for Tech Talent." *The Washington Post,* 3 August 1998.

Lewis, Michael. "The Search Engine." *The New York Times,* 10 October 1999.

Lieber, Ron. "First Jobs Aren't Child's Play." *Fast Company,* June 1999.

Loomis, Carol J. "Dinosaurs?" *Fortune,* 22 February 1993.

Lublin, Joann S. "An E-Company CEO Is Also the Recruiter-in-Chief." *The Wall Street Journal,* 9 November 1999.

Macfarquhar, Larissa. "Caesar.com; A Beltway Billionaire and His Big Ideas." *New Yorker,* 3 April 2000.

Morris, Betsy. "Can Michael Dell Escape the Box?" *Fortune,* 16 October 2000.

Mullaney, Timothy J. "How to Take the Hype Out of IPOs." *BusinessWeek,* 27 March 2000.

Ramstad, Evan. "High Rollers: How Trilogy Software Trains Its Raw Recruits To Be Risk Takers." *The Wall Street Journal,* 21 September 1998.

Reinhardt, Andy. "Meet Mr. Internet." *BusinessWeek,* 13 September 1999.

Roberti, Mark. "General Electric's Spin Machine." *The Industry Standard,* 22 January 2001.

Salter, Chuck. "Insanity Inc.: Trilogy Software Inc. is one of the fastest-growing software companies around." *Fast Company,* January 1999.

Schafer, Sarah and Amy Joyce. "Managers Making Their Move." *The Washington Post,* 1 May 2000.

Schlender, Brent. "The Odd Couple." *Fortune,* 1 May 2000.

Schlesinger, Jacob M. "Double Take—Puzzled Investors Ask: Will the real economy please step forward?" *The Wall Street Journal,* 22 March 2000.

Serwer, Andy. "There's Something About Cisco." *Fortune,* 15 May 2000.

Stipp, David. "Blessings from the Book of Life." *Fortune,* 6 March 2000.

Swoboda, Frank. "Wired Economy; A Late Realization Draws General Electric Into the Net." *The Washington Post,* 5 April 2000.

Tapscott, Don. "Virtual Webs Will Revolutionize Business." *The Wall Street Journal,* 24 April 2000.

Taylor, William. "Who's Writing the Book on Web Business?" *Fast Company,* October 1996.

Thomas, Evan. "Caesar and Edison and . . . Saylor?" *Newsweek,* 1 January 2000.

Thurm, Scott. "At Fast-Moving Cisco, CEO Says: Put customers first, view rivals as 'good guys'." *The Wall Street Journal,* 1 June 2000.

————. "Joining the Fold: Under Cisco's system, mergers usually work." *The Wall Street Journal,* 1 March 2000.

Tichy, Noel M. and Ram Charan. "How Creativity Can Take Wing at Edge of Chaos." *The Wall Street Journal,* 19 October 1996.

Tichy, Noel and Christopher DeRose. "Roger Enrico's Master Class." *Fortune,* 27 November 1995.

Tichy, Noel M. and Stratford Sherman. "A Master Class in Radical Change." *Fortune,* 13 December 1993.

USA Today. "Chainsaw's Self-Portrait." 30 August 1996.

Useem, Jerry and Noshua Watson. "It's All Yours, Jeff. Now What?" *Fortune,* 17 September 2001.

Von Hippel, Eric, Stefan Thomke, and Mary Sonnack. "Creating Breakthroughs at 3M." *Harvard Business Review,* September– October 1999.

Walsh, Mary Williams. "Where G.E. Falls Short: Diversity at the top." *The New York Times,* 3 September 2000.

Warner, Melanie and Daniel Roth. "Ten Companies that Get It." *Fortune,* 8 November 1999.

Wasserman, Elizabeth. "A Search for Redemption." *The Industry Standard Magazine,* 22 January 2001.

Welch, Jack, Rik Kirkland, and Geoffrey Colvin. "Jack: The Exit Interview." *Fortune,* 17 September 2001.

Welch, Jack, Scott McNealy, John Huey, and Brent Schlender. "The Odd Couple." *Economist,* 1 May 2000.

Wingfield, Nick and Paul Beckett. "MicroStrategy, Results Restated Is MacroLoser." *The Wall Street Journal,* 21 March 2000.

Wysocki Jr., Bernard. "Team Effort: Yet another hazard of the new economy." *The Wall Street Journal,* 30 March 2000.

Yang, Catherine. "MicroStrategy's Saylor: "We Have Been Caught in That Gray Zone." *BusinessWeek Online,* March 1999.

Books and Academic Journal Articles

Bennis, Warren. "Learning to Lead." *Executive Excellence,* January 1996.

Bridges, William. *Jobshift*. Reading, Mass.: Addison-Wesley, 1994.

Burns, James MacGregor. *Leadership*. New York: Harper & Row, Torchbooks, 1978.

Byrne, John. *Chainsaw: the notorious career of Al Dunlop in the era of profit-at-any-price*. New York: HarperBusiness, 2002.

Clayton, Ed and Patrick MacDonald (editor) and David Hodges (illustrator). *Martin Luther King, Jr.: The Peaceful Warrior*. New York: Pocket Books, 1992.

Cohen, Eli D., Lynda St. Clair, and Noel M. Tichy. "Leadership Development as a Strategic Initiative," *Handbook for Business Strategy 1996*. New York: Faulkner & Gray, 1997.

Cohen, Eli and Noel M. Tichy. "How Leaders Develop Leaders." *Training and Development,* 1 March 1997.

Collins, James C. and Jerry I. Porras. *Built to Last*. New York: HarperCollins, 1995.

Conger, Jay A. "Leaders: Born or Bred?" *Frontiers of Leadership: An Essential Reader*. Oxford: Blackwell Publishers, 1992.

Davis, Stanley and Christopher Meyer. *Blur.* Reading, Mass.: Addison-Wesley, 1998.

————. *Future Wealth.* Boston: Harvard Business School Press, 2000.

Dell, Michael with Catherine Fredman. *Direct from Dell.* New York: HarperBusiness, 1999.

Deutsch, Morton and R. Krauss. *Theories in Social Psychology.* New York: Basic Books, 1965.

Drucker, Peter F. *Management Challenges for the 21st Century.* New York: HarperBusiness, 1999.

————. *Managing in a Time of Great Change.* New York: Dutton, Truman Talley Books, 1995.

Enrico, Roger and Jesse Kornbluth. *The Other Guy Blinked: How Pepsi Won the Cola Wars.* New York: Bantam Books, 1996.

Etzioni, Amitai. *A Comparative Analysis of Complex Organizations.* New York: Free Press, 1961.

Fombrun, Charles, Noel Tichy, and Stewart Freeman. *Strategic Human Resource Management.* New York: John Wiley & Sons, Inc., 1984.

Freiberg, Kevin and Jackie Freiberg. *Nuts!* New York: Broadway Books, 1998.

Gardner, Howard. *Leading Minds: An Anatomy of Leadership.* New York: Basic Books, 1996.

Gardner, John William. *On Leadership.* New York: Free Press, 1990.

Gates, Bill. *Business @ The Speed of Thought.* New York: Warner Books, 1999.

Greiner, Larry E. "Evolution and revolution as organizations grow." *Harvard Business Review,* May–June 1998.

Grove, Andrew. *Only the Paranoid Survive: How to exploit crisis points that challenge every company and career.* New York: Currency, 1996.

Grove, Andrew S. *High Output Management.* New York: Random House, 1983.

Harry, Michael and Richard Schroeder. *Six Sigma, The Breakthrough Management Strategy Revolutionizing the World's Top Corporations.* New York: Currency, 1999.

Hornstein, Harvey. *Managerial Courage: Revitalizing Your Company Without Sacrificing Your Job.* New York: Wiley, 1986.

Kenyon, Henry S. "Dell University—Breaking paradigms and leveraging the future at the world's fastest-growing PC manufacturer." *Corporate University Review,* July–August 1998.

Komisar, Randy with Kent Lineback. *The Monk and the Riddle.* Boston: Harvard Business School Press, 2000.

Marcus, Bernie and Arthur Blank with Bob Andelman. *Built From Scratch.* New York: Times Business, 1999.

Mills, Daniel Quinn. *Broken Promises.* Boston: Harvard Business School Press, 1996.

Nystrom, Paul and William Starbuck. *Handbook of Organizational Design.* London: Oxford Press, 1981.

Peters, Tom. "Get Innovative or Get Dead." *California Management Review,* winter 1991.

Peters, Tom and Robert Waterman. *In Search of Excellence.* New York: Harper & Row, 1982.

Pottruck, David S. and Terry Pearce. *Clicks and Mortar.* San Francisco: Jossey-Bass, 2000.

Pucik, V., Noel Tichy, and Nancy C. Barnett. *Globalizing Management: Creating and Leading the Competitive Organization.* New York: John Wiley & Sons, Inc., 1992.

Quinn, Robert E. *Beyond Rational Management: Mastering the Paradoxes and Competing Demands of High Performance.* San Francisco: Jossey-Bass, 1988.

Quinn, Robert E., et al. *Becoming a Master Manager: A Competency Framework.* New York: Wiley, 1990.

Schein, Edgar H. *Organizational Culture and Leadership.* San Francisco: Jossey-Bass, 1992.

———. "Organizational Learning as Cognitive Redefinition: Coercive persuasion revisited." Unpublished Paper, MIT Sloan School of Management, 1997.

Smart, Bradford D. *Topgrading.* Paramus, N.J.: Prentice Hall Press, 1999.

Stewart, Thomas. *The Wealth of Knowledge: Intellectual Capital and the Twenty-First Century Organization.* New York: Currency, 2001.

Tapscott, Don, and Alex Lowy, and David Ticoll. *Digital Capital.* Boston: Harvard Business School Press, 2000.

Thurow, Lester. *Building Wealth: The new rules for individuals, companies, and nations in a knowledge-based economy.* New York: HarperCollins, 1999.

Tichy, Noel. "An Analysis of Clique Formation and Structure in Organizations." *Administrative Science Quarterly,* Vol. 18, 1973.

———. "GE's Crotonville: A staging ground for corporate revolution." *The Academy of Management Executive,* Vol. 3, No. 2, 1989.

———. "Jack Welch's GE Leadership Engine." *Harvard Business Review: Japanese Edition,* January 2001.

———. *Managing Strategic Change.* New York: Wiley, 1984.

———. "No Ordinary Bootcamp." *Harvard Business Review,* February 2001.

————. "Simultaneous Transformation and CEO Succession." *Organizational Dynamics,* Summer 1996.

Tichy, Noel and Ram Charan. *Every Business Is a Growth Business.* New York: Times Books, 1997.

Tichy, Noel M. and Ram Charan. "The CEO as Coach: An Interview with AlliedSignal's Lawrence A. Bossidy." *Harvard Business Review,* March/April 1995.

Tichy, Noel and Christopher DeRose. "Death of Rebirth of Organizational Development." *Organization 21 C.* Prentice Hall, 2002.

Tichy, Noel and Andrew McGill. *Global Corporate Citizenship.* San Francisco: Jossey-Bass, 1997.

Tichy, Noel M. and Christopher DeRose. "The Pepsi Challenge." *Training & Development,* May 1996: 58.

Tichy, Noel M. and Mary Anne Devanna. *The Transformational Leader.* New York: Wiley, 1986.

Tichy, Noel M. and Stratford Sherman. *Control Your Destiny or Someone Else Will.* New York: Doubleday, Currency, 1993.

Tichy Noel M. with Eli Cohen. *The Leadership Engine.* New York: HarperBusiness, 1997.

Tichy, Noel and Eli Cohen. "The Teaching Organization." *Training & Development,* July 1998.

Von Krogh, George, Kazuo Ichijo, and Ikujiro Nonaka. *Enabling Knowledge Creation.* London: Oxford, 2000.

Walton, Sam with John Huey. *Made in America.* New York: Bantam Books, 1993.

Welch, John with John Byrne. *JACK: Straight From the Gut.* New York: Time Warner, 2001.

Harvard Business School Cases

"Trilogy (A)." 9-699-034. 1998 (revised 2001).

"General Electric Company: background note on management systems." 181–211. 1981.

Internal Documents

Kane, Donald, Noel Tichy, and Eugene Andrews. "A Leadership Development Framework." *GE Executive Management Staff,* November 1987. OEN-6.

Shell, "Shell Business Framework." 1996.

Interviews

Abrahamson, Colonel David, United States Special Operations Command. Two interviews by Eli Cohen, April 1996.

———. Interview by Eli Cohen, February 1997.

Abroscotto, Stephanie, Ameritech. Interview by Eli Cohen, February 1996.

Alpuche, Charles, PepsiCo. Interview by Noel Tichy and Eli Cohen, April 1996.

Baglee, David, Intel Corporation. Interview by Noel Tichy and Chris DeRose, May 2002.

Bossidy, Lawrence A., AlliedSignal. Interview by Noel Tichy and Ram Charan, November 1994.

Brown, Richard, EDS. Interview by Noel Tichy, February 2002.

Cantu, Carlos, ServiceMaster Inc. Interview by Noel Tichy and Eli Cohen, January 1996.

Dammerman, Dennis, GE Corporate. Interview by Noel Tichy and Eli Cohen, February 1996.

Dedrick, Gregg, Yum! Brands. Interview by Noel Tichy, December 2001.

Denny, Specialist Jason C., 1st Battalion 75th Ranger Regiment United States Army. Interview by Eli Cohen, February 1997.

Derickson, Sandra, GE Capital. Two interviews by Eli Cohen, April 1996.

Downing, General Wayne, United States Special Operations Command (Retired). Interview by Eli Cohen, July 1996.

Enrico, Roger, PepsiCo. Interview by Noel Tichy, February 1995.

Immelt, Jeff, General Electric. Interview by Noel Tichy, October 2001.

Kelleher, Herb, Southwest Airlines. Interview by John Huey and Geoffrey Colvin ("3rd World Wide Lessons in Leadership Series"), 1998.

Ligacki, Kathleen, Ford Motor Company. Interview by Noel Tichy, June 2001.

McNerney, James W., 3M. Interview by Noel Tichy and Nancy Cardwell, September 2001.

Nardelli, Bob, Home Depot. Interview by Noel Tichy and Nancy Cardwell, October 2001.

Novak, David, Yum! Brands. Series of interviews by Noel Tichy, February–December 2001.

Ollila, Jorma, Nokia Corporation. Interview by Noel Tichy, January 2002 tk.

Pemberton, John, Intel Corporation. Interview by Noel Tichy and Chris DeRose, May 2002.

Pfeiffer, Eckhard, Compaq Computer. Interview by Noel Tichy and Eli Cohen, March 1996.

Platt, Lewis, Hewlett-Packard. Interview by Noel Tichy, June 1996.

Potter, Myrtle, Genentech. Interview by Noel Tichy, February 2002.

Schlesinger, Leonard, Limited Brands. Interview by Noel Tichy, October 2001.

Schroder, Sergeant Brian, 1st Battalion 75th Ranger Regiment United States Army. Interview by Eli Cohen, February 1997.

Stimac, Gary, Compaq Computer. Interview by Noel Tichy and Eli Cohen, March 1996.

Tolan, Mary, Accenture. Interview by Noel Tichy, November 2001.

Welch, John, General Electric. Interview by Noel Tichy and Ram Charan, March 1996.

Welch, John, General Electric. Interview by John Huey and Geoffrey Colvin ("3rd World Wide Lessons in Leadership Series"), 1998.

Speeches/Presentations

Dammerman, Dennis D. "Changing GE: Lessons Learned From Along the Way." Remarks to Cornell University Durland Memorial Lecture, Ithaca, New York, April 1, 1998.

Immelt, Jeffrey. "GE." Remarks at Stanford Business School, March 2002.

Videos

Janis, Irving. "Groupthink." CRM Learning, 1996.

Web Sites

Glasner, Joanna. *Caste System of the Digital Age* [Online]. Available: *http://www.wired.com/news/print/0,1294,20710,00.html* [1999, July 19].

Khirallah, Diane Rezendes. *The ABCs Of E-Business* [Online]. Available: *http://www.informationweek.com/778/train.htm* [2000, March 20].

McDougall, Paul. *Flat Earnings Lead Dell to Seek New Markets* [Online]. Available: *http://www.informationweek.com/773/dell.htm* [2000, February 14].

McGee, Marianne Kolbasuk. *E-Business Makes General Electric A Different Company* [Online]. Available: *http://www.information-week.com/771/ebiz.htm* [2000, January 31].

Violino, Bob. *E-Business 100; The Leaders of E-Business* [Online]. Available: *http://www.informationweek.com/765/leaders.htm* [1999, December 13].

Wilder, Clinton and Marianne Kolbasuk McGee. *Putting The "E" Back In E-Business* [Online]. Available: *http://www.information-week.com/771/ebiz.htm* [2000, January 31].

Company Web Sites

Accenture, *http://www.accenture.com*

Cisco, *http://www.cisco.com*

Dell, *http://www.dell.com*

EDS, *http://www.eds.com*

Focus: HOPE, *http://www.focushope.edu*

Genentech, *http://www.genentech.com*

General Electric, *http://www.ge.com*

The Home Depot, *http://www.homedepot.com*

Limited Brands, *http://www.limitedbrands.com*

3M, *http://www.3M.com*

Nokia, *http://www.nokia.com*

Royal Dutch/Shell, *http://www.shell.com*

Southwest Airlines, *http://www.southwest.com*

Trilogy, *http://www.trilogy.com*

Yum! Brands, *http://www.yum.com*

Index